A·N·N·U·A·L E

MW01717370

Economics

05/06

Thirty-third Edition

EDITOR

Don Cole

Drew University

Don Cole, Professor of Economics at Drew University, received his Ph.D. from Ohio State University. He has served as a consultant to a variety of public and private organizations, and is co-founder of the Drew University Semester on the European Union in Brussels, Belgium. An innovator in the use of computer-assisted instruction in economics, Dr. Cole is the author of articles on various subjects, including economic policy, monetary theory, and economic education. He is also the editor of over thirty McGraw-Hill/Dushkin publications, including *The Encyclopedic Dictionary of Economics* and two other *Annual Editions* anthologies, *Microeconomics* and *Macroeconomics.*

McGraw-Hill/Dushkin

2460 Kerper Blvd., Dubuque, IA 52001

Visit us on the Internet

http://www.dushkin.com

Credits

1. **Introduction**
   Unit photo—© CORBIS/Royalty-Free
2. **Microeconomics**
   Unit photo—© Getty Images/Geostock
3. **Income Distribution and Economic Justice**
   Unit photo—© Getty Images/Ryan McVay
4. **Macroeconomics**
   Unit photo—© CORBIS/Royalty-Free
5. **The Changing Global Economy**
   Unit photo—© Getty Images/PhotoLink

Copyright

Cataloging in Publication Data
Main entry under title: Annual Editions: Economics. 2005/2006.
1. Economics—Periodicals. I. Cole, Don, *comp.* II. Title: Economics.
ISBN 0–07–291731–8 658'.05 ISSN 1092–776X

Thirty-third Edition

Cover image © Keith Brofsky/Getty Images and Corbis/Royalty Free
Printed in the United States of America 1234567890QPDQPD987654 Printed on Recycled Paper

Editors/Advisory Board

Members of the Advisory Board are instrumental in the final selection of articles for each edition of ANNUAL EDITIONS. Their review of articles for content, level, currentness, and appropriateness provides critical direction to the editor and staff. We think that you will find their careful consideration well reflected in this volume.

Staff

Preface

In publishing ANNUAL EDITIONS we recognize the enormous role played by the magazines, newspapers, and journals of the public press in providing current, first-rate educational information in a broad spectrum of interest areas. Many of these articles are appropriate for students, researchers, and professionals seeking accurate, current material to help bridge the gap between principles and theories and the real world. These articles, however, become more useful for study when those of lasting value are carefully collected, organized, and reproduced in a low-cost format, which provides easy and permanent access when the material is needed. That is the role played by ANNUAL EDITIONS.

This thirty-third edition of *Annual Editions: Economics* has been largely revised since previous editions and continues the tradition of providing the most up-to-date readings on contemporary economic issues. In view of the recent explosion of interest in the subject of economics, it is important that students are given opportunities to observe how economic science can help them to understand events in the real world. This anthology is designed to meet such a need.

The volume is divided into five major units. Unit 1 introduces several general concepts involving economic analysis. At the heart of economics is the notion of "opportunity cost," the idea that in choosing one economic alternative, we must forgo other choices. What, for example, is the opportunity cost of a human life? How might a knowledge of economic reasoning assist us in making daily decisions?

Unit 2 presents articles that treat economic issues from a microeconomic perspective. Microeconomics studies the way in which market values are established through the interaction of consumers (households) and producers (firms). For instance, what role does the Internet play in the choices consumers make and the size of business enterprises? How do mergers affect the business climate? How does government regulation of industry affect market competition?

Issues involving work and income distribution are examined in unit 3. You will find that this is an area of intense controversy, particularly as it relates to government programs that attempt to alter the distribution of income and wealth. Questions raised include: What are the causes of growing income disparities in America? What role do unions play in the U.S. economy? Should the federal government attempt to eradicate poverty and, if so, how? Is federal welfare reform working? Should Social Security be privatized?

Broader economic issues are the focus of the next two units, which involve macroeconomics (unit 4) and the global economy (unit 5). The economy-wide perspective of macroeconomics leads us to consider ways of gauging an economy's health, vis-á-vis levels of employment, the degree of price stability, and the rate of economic growth over time. Readings selected for this unit raise questions of great consequence to the United States. For example, what is the current outlook for the U.S. economy? How do tax cuts and changes in the money supply affect the economy? Should we be concerned about the growing federal deficit?

Finally, unit 5 examines recent changes in the world economy. In the last decade we have witnessed a series of unforeseen events: the globalization of the world economy; the aftershocks of the 9/11 terrorist attacks; the rush by many former communist states to embrace the market system; and the impoverishment of many developing countries burdened by staggering international obligations. How did such developments come about, and what do they portend as the global economy enters a new century?

In this edition of *Annual Editions: Economics 05/06* there are *World Wide Web* sites that can be used to further explore the topics.

Whether you are currently pursuing studies in economics or are just a casual reader eager to learn more about some of the major economic issues of the day, you will find *Annual Editions: Economics 05/06* to be one of the most useful and up-to-date anthologies available. Your input can be valuable for the next edition. Please offer your opinions by filling out and returning to us the postage-paid *article rating form* on the last page of this book.

Don Cole

Don Cole
Editor

Contents

UNIT 1
Introduction

UNIT 2
Microeconomics

The concepts in bold italics are developed in the article. For further expansion, please refer to the Topic Guide.

UNIT 3
The Economics of Work and Income

The concepts in bold italics are developed in the article. For further expansion, please refer to the Topic Guide.

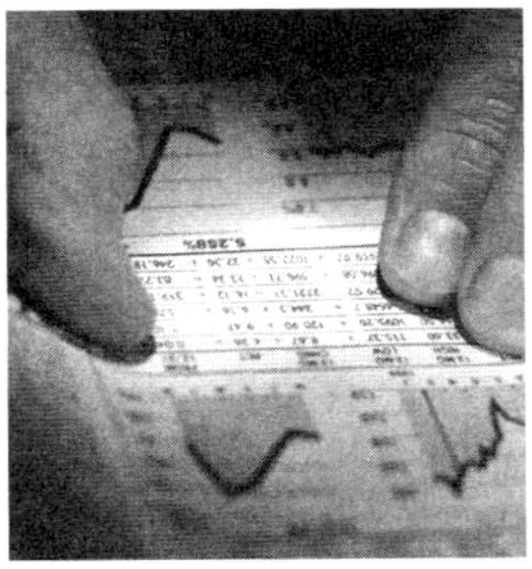

UNIT 4
Macroeconomics

The concepts in bold italics are developed in the article. For further expansion, please refer to the Topic Guide.

The concepts in bold italics are developed in the article. For further expansion, please refer to the Topic Guide.

UNIT 5
The Changing Global Economy

The concepts in bold italics are developed in the article. For further expansion, please refer to the Topic Guide.

The concepts in bold italics are developed in the article. For further expansion, please refer to the Topic Guide.

The concepts in bold italics are developed in the article. For further expansion, please refer to the Topic Guide.

Topic Guide

This topic guide suggests how the selections in this book relate to the subjects covered in your course. You may want to use the topics listed on these pages to search the Web more easily.

On the following pages a number of Web sites have been gathered specifically for this book. They are arranged to reflect the units of this *Annual Edition*. You can link to these sites by going to the DUSHKIN ONLINE support site at *http://www.dushkin.com/online/*.

ALL THE ARTICLES THAT RELATE TO EACH TOPIC ARE LISTED BELOW THE BOLD-FACED TERM.

World Wide Web Sites

The following World Wide Web sites have been carefully researched and selected to support the articles found in this reader. The easiest way to access these selected sites is to go to our DUSHKIN ONLINE support site at *http://www.dushkin.com/online/*.

AE: Economics 05/06

The following sites were available at the time of publication. Visit our Web site—we update DUSHKIN ONLINE regularly to reflect any changes.

General Sources

AmosWEB

http://www.amosweb.com

This site seeks to be the premier Internet site for instructional economic information. Main features include a glossary of over 500 economic terms and concepts, a reading room, and an interactive question-and-answer resource.

The Dismal Scientist

http://www.dismal.com

Often referred to as the "best free lunch on the Web," this is an excellent site with many interactive features. It provides access to economic data, briefings on the current state of the economy, and original articles on economic issues.

UNIT 1: Introduction

Economics: Complete Guide to Economic Resources on the Web

http://economics.miningco.com

This frequently updated resource "mines the Net" for information on economic subjects. It includes a large number of links and online articles from economics magazines and journals.

Litigation Analytics: How Much for a Human Life?

http://www.humanlifevalue.com/index.html

"How much is a human life worth?" This site provides an interesting interactive excercise involving this question.

Resources for Economists on the Internet

http://econwpa.wustl.edu/EconFAQ.html

Sponsored by the American Economic Association, this Web site is an excellent starting place for any research in economics by academic and practicing economists.

UNIT 2: Microeconomics

Antitrust Policy

http://www.antitrust.org

Sponsored by the Owen Graduate School of Management at Vanderbilt University, this site provides detailed information on such topics as case studies in price fixing, merger simulations, and the evolution of U.S. antitrust policy.

CEO Express—Business and Financial News

http://www.ceoexpress.com

A comprehensive source of news on business, finance, and technology, this site provides users with extensive tools for researching companies through direct links to the home pages of *Fortune* 500 and many other firms.

Corporate Watch

http://www.corpwatch.org

Corporate Watch is an online magazine and resource center designed to provide an array of tools for investigating and analyzing the activities of transnational corporations.

Internet Public Library: Business and Economics Reference

http://ipl.org/ref/RR/static/bus0000.html

This comprehensive reference library on the production, distribution, and consumption of goods and services includes many subtopics about consumer issues, employment, business and industry, and labor and the workplace.

New York Times Business Connections

http://www.nytimes.com/library/cyber/reference/busconn.html

This page of links to business and economics sites on the Web was prepared for use by journalists of the *New York Times* for their own research purposes. It includes links to such categories as Markets, Companies, Business News, Banking and Finance, and Government.

Small Business Administration

http://www.sbaonline.sba.gov

The U.S. Small Business Administration provides financial, technical, and management assistance to 23 million small businesses.

UNIT 3: The Economics of Work and Income

Center on Budget and Policy Priorities

http://www.cbpp.org

This nonpartisan research organization and policy institute conducts research and analysis on a range of government policies and programs, with an emphasis on those affecting low- and moderate-income people.

Joint Center for Poverty Research

http://www.jcpr.org

This site examines what it means to be poor and to live in America. Issues considered include changing labor markets, the causes of inequality, family functioning, the impact of concentrated urban poverty, and implications for public policy.

Today's Unions
http://www.aflcio.org

The AFL-CIO Web page provides access to a large number of topics concerning ways in which labor unions might improve the lives of working families.

The Urban Institute
http://www.urban.org

The Urban Institute investigates national social and economic problems and analyzes solutions.

U.S. Department of Health and Human Services
http://www.hhs.gov

The Department of Health and Human Services is the U.S. government's principal agency for protecting the health of all Americans and providing essential human services, especially for those who are least able to help themselves.

U.S. Department of Labor
http://www.dol.gov

This Department of Labor Web site includes information about the department and its agencies, labor laws and trends, press releases, and texts of regulations.

U.S. Immigration and Naturalization Service (INS)
http://www.ins.usdoj.gov

The INS is responsible for enforcing laws regulating the admission of foreign-born persons to the United States and for administering various immigration benefits.

Welfare-to-Work
http://wtw.doleta.gov

A federal government Web site that examines the transition from welfare-to-work from the perspective of individuals, employers, and communities is found here.

WorkIndex
http://workindex.com

This index is an annotated guide to Internet resources in human resources, labor relations, benefits, training, technology, staffing, recruiting, leadership, motivation, insurance, relocation, legal issues and more.

UNIT 4: Macroeconomics

Bureau of Economic Analysis (BEA)
http://www.bea.doc.gov

The BEA is the nation's accountant. It issues the Survey of Current Business and is a good source for data on industrial and regional development.

Citizens for Tax Justice
http://www.ctj.org

Citizens for Tax Justice is a research and advocacy organization that "seeks to give ordinary people a greater voice in the development of tax laws."

Congressional Budget Office
http://www.cbo.gov

The Congressional Budget Office seeks to provide "objective, timely, nonpartisan analyses needed for economic and budget decisions and with the information and estimates required for the Congressional budget process."

Federal Reserve Board
http://www.federalreserve.gov

The Web site of the Federal Reserve Board (the Fed) links to all the Federal Reserve Banks and other federal agencies. It provides access to the Fed's "Beige Book," a report published eight times each year on current economic conditions by the Federal Reserve district.

History of Money
http://www.ex.ac.uk/~RDavies/arian/llyfr.html

An award-winning site that provides a comprehensive chronology of money from ancient times to the present day, this page includes articles on the Origins of Banking, Money in North American History, Britain and the European Monetary Union, and Third World Debt in the 20th Century.

The Public Debt
http://www.publicdebt.treas.gov/opd/opd.htm

Features of this site include estimates of "daily amounts to the penny of the debt," interest costs of the outstanding public debt, and long-term trends.

UNIT 5: The Changing Global Economy

The European Union in the U.S.
http://www.eurunion.org

Here is a comprehensive Web site for those interested in the nature and origin of the European Union. Topics include EU policies and legislation, information on member states, and EU–U.S. relations.

Institute for International Economics
http://www.iie.com

Since its founding in 1981, the Institute for International Economics has provided objective analysis of key international economic problems and has proposed concrete solutions.

Inter-American Development Bank (IDB)
http://www.iadb.org

The Inter-American Development Bank was established in 1959 to help accelerate economic and social development in Latin America and the Caribbean. This site offers access to IDB reports and information on member countries.

North American Free Trade Association (NAFTA)
http://www.nafta-sec-alena.org

NAFTA's objective is "to provide accurate and timely information to U.S. exporters experiencing market access barriers in Canada or Mexico."

Organization for Economic Co-operation and Development (OECD)
http://www.oecd.org

The Web site of the OECD page provides information on OECD activities, news, and documentation. One interesting feature is links to the Center for Co-operation with Non-members.

Sustainable Development.Org
http://www.sustainabledevelopment.org

Extensive links at this site lead to such sustainable development categories as agriculture, energy, environment, finance, health, microenterprise, public policy, and technologies.

United Nations Development Programme (UNDP)
http://www.undp.org
The UNDP helps people in 174 countries to help themselves by focusing on poverty elimination, environmental regeneration, job creation, and the advancement of women.

World Resources Institute
http://www.wri.org
The World Resources Institute provides information and practical proposals for policy and institutional change that will foster environmentally sound, socially equitable development.

We highly recommend that you review our Web site for expanded information and our other product lines. We are continually updating and adding links to our Web site in order to offer you the most usable and useful information that will support and expand the value of your Annual Editions. You can reach us at: *http://www.dushkin.com/annualeditions/*.

UNIT 1

Introduction

Unit Selections

1. **How Much for a Life? Try $3 Million to $5 Million**, Peter Passell
2. **Things That Every Economist Takes for Granted Could Help a Lot of Other People Avoid Some Costly Mistakes**, Virginia Postrel
3. **U.S. Is Far More Efficient Than in '70s—But Also More Determined to Consume**, Kris Axtman
4. **Counter-Terrorism: The Private Cost of More Security**, Peter Navarro

Key Points to Consider

- Is life priceless? Explain your answer in terms of the opportunity cost principle.
- How might economic reasoning be applied to decisions encountered in every-day life? In what sense is the U.S. more efficient today than it was three decades ago?
- What are the economic implications of the 9/11 attacks?

DUSHKIN ONLINE **Links: www.dushkin.com/online/**
These sites are annotated in the World Wide Web pages.

Economics: Complete Guide to Economic Resources on the Web
http://economics.miningco.com

Litigation Analytics: How Much for a Human Life?
http://www.humanlifevalue.com/index.html

Resources for Economists on the Internet
http://econwpa.wustl.edu/EconFAQ.html

Economics concerns the decisions we face in meeting our material needs. Examples of such decisions can be found everywhere: college students confront rising tuition costs; a local business firm announces that it will lay off workers; a newspaper editorial comments on the merits of minimum-wage legislation; the U.S. Congress debates proposals to reform the Social Security system. Like a view on a very clear day, a list of all possible economic problems appears to have no end.

Beginning students of economics often wonder why this is so. Why are the 6 billion citizens of the planet not able to find a way to meet their needs for material existence? More than a half century ago, the British economist Lionel Robbins provided an interesting answer to this question. He suggested that we are unable to do all the things we may wish to do for the simple reason that our economic resources—human talents, the natural endowment, and the stock of capital—are finite. Robbins defined "the economic problem" as one of scarcity: Our resources are scarce because the number of possible uses to which they might be put in meeting our material needs is unlimited. Economics, therefore, ultimately concerns the hard choices we must make, both private and public, about ways to employ these resources. Because such choices always carry a price (or "opportunity cost") in terms of alternatives forgone, economics leads us to consider the costs and benefits of things we choose to do.

This unit offers different perspectives on the subject of resource limits and opportunity costs. First, Peter Passell raises an age-old question: What is the value of a human life? People sometimes chide economists for knowing "the cost of everything and the value of nothing." Yet, as Passell demonstrates, economic reasoning has great usefulness in understanding why people do the things they do, even—indeed, especially—when those things involve risky behaviors. When smokers light up, for example, they are making economic decisions (however subconsciously) about the value of the risks they incur. In effect, they are placing a value on their own lives. One of the tasks economists have is to remind us of is that no behavior is without cost and that at times these costs can be substantial.

In the next essay, Virginia Postrel maintains that things that economists take for granted could help a lot of other people avoid some costly mistakes. While most people think of economics as a field that studies the stock market and government policy, Postrel demonstrates how much richer and more insightful the subject is.

Then, Kris Axtman discusses a key economic concept: efficiency in the use of scarce resources. She focuses on the subject of automobiles and energy use. She maintains that the U.S. is far more efficient today than three decades ago, but also more determined to consume.

Finally, the unit concludes with an article in which Peter Navarro examines the possible costs of providing more security, in view of the tragedy of the 9/11 attacks on the World Trade Center. He argues that the greatest danger that terrorism poses to America may be purely economic, in the form of "productivity shocks."

How Much For A Life? Try $3 Million to $5 Million

Even so, risk experts say some safety laws just aren't worth it.

Peter Passell

You've watched in horror a dozen times: Scenes of barely recognizable aircraft parts strewn across smoldering moonscapes, with the occasional shoe or child's toy the only reminders of lives snuffed out in unimaginable terror. And no doubt you've wondered when it would be your turn, a thought quickly shrugged away but never truly forgotten.

Flying, everyone knows, is a risky business. Any expense that makes it safer thus seems an expense worth making. And the only question most people ask after a crash is how to get the regulators to get off their duffs before the next one.

But the truth comes in shades of gray, not black and white. Americans' obsession with the tiny probability of dying in an airline accident is, at best, a distraction from the reality that commercial aviation is one of the great blessings of the age. At worst, it is an invitation to expensive and even self-defeating fixes, a symptom of our inability to cope sensibly with risk. But Republican conservatives in Congress are now pressing for a more sharp-penciled analysis of the cost of government health and safety regulations.

Just how safe is flying in America? Based on the experience of the last two decades, Arnold Barnett, a management professor at the Massachusetts Institute of Technology, sets the probability of dying from unnatural causes on your next commercial jet flight at about one in seven million. A flier who boards a jet each day can thus expect to meet the grim reaper every 19,000 years.

The propeller planes linking hundreds of small cities to big airports are three or four times as dangerous. But that only brings the odds of ending up a grim statistic to one in two million. The chance of suffering a heart attack while waiting for the conveyor belt to mangle your luggage is much greater.

The yawning gap between the actual and imagined risk of flying no longer surprises specialists in risk analysis, who make careers of explaining why people who brush aside the dangers of driving on icy highways or gorging on cookie dough ice cream are so ready to believe that portable phones cause brain cancer. But a comparison of the way risk analysts think about safety with the way Government balances risk against potential gain is sobering.

Probabilities alone don't offer much insight into which chances are worth taking. That question, suggests the brave new science of risk analysis, can be answered only by weighing the cost of avoiding a statistical death against the subjective value of life.

Try that one again. Assume for the sake of argument that it would cost $500 per car to put anti-skid brakes in each of the 10 million cars sold this year—a total of $5 billion. Assume that installing the gadgets on this year's fleet would ultimately save 5,000 lives, or $1 million per life. Assume that, on average, people value their lives at up to $5 million. Since the $1 million cost of saving a life is less than the $5 million value of life, the safety feature must be worth buying.

How Much is a Saved Life Worth?

Safety regulations are rarely free of cost. If seat belts cost, say $50 per car, and equipping a million cars with seat belts will save 1,000 lives, the regulators must be assuming that lives are worth at least $50,000 a piece.

Here are estimates of the minimum value of a life that are built into a sampling of Government regulations. Figures take into account the medical and hospital costs avoided because lives were saved, but they ignore other benefits of the regulations, like prevention of property damage and injuries that do not result in death.

Automobiles	Reduce lead content of gasoline from 1.1 to 0.1 grams per gallon	No net cost
	Child restraints in cars	$1.3 million
	Dual master cylinders for car brakes	$7.8 million
Ejection systems for the B-58 bomber		$22 million
Flashing lights at **railroad crossings**		$730,000
Sea walls to protect against 100-year storm surges		$96 million
Asbestos	Banned in brake linings	$230,000
	... in automatic transmission parts	$1.2 billion
Radiation	Safety standards for X-ray equipment	$400,000
	... for uranium mine tailings	$190 million

Sounds O.K., at least until the part about the value of life being $5 million. Who is to say that a life is worth $5 million rather than $500 million?

One answer is Americans couldn't afford to spend $500 million. Kip Viscusi, an economist at Duke University, estimates that if the entire gross national product were devoted to making life safer, there would only be $55 million available to prevent each accidental death. So, at least in this limited sense, life must be worth less than $55 million.

More to the point, people voluntarily accept the risk of death in return for money all the time. Dozens of studies have imputed a value to life from data on the extra wages required to lure workers to perform dangerous jobs. If, for example, it takes an extra $100,000 in lifetime earnings to persuade miners to cope with one extra chance in a hundred of premature death underground, miners must implicitly value their lives at no more than 100 times $100,000 or $10 million.

Dozens of other studies have focused on the cost of safety devices that are voluntarily purchased in order to assay how much people are willing to spend to reduce the probability of accidental death. If smoke detectors cost $20 and are widely seen as reducing the risk of a fiery death by one chance in 10,000, buyers must value their lives at least 20 times 10,000, or $200,000.

These studies hardly produce uniform answers—nor do risk analysts expect them to. After all, people have very different "tastes" for risk. But researchers are still willing to generalize. Most middle-income Americans, they say, usually act as if their lives are worth $3 million to $5 million based on what they demand in extra pay for dangerous jobs and what they spend for safety devices.

A few Federal agencies, notably the Department of Transportation, evaluate new health and safety regulations by comparing an estimate of the cost per life that would probably be saved against a benchmark figure. But most are too savvy to be caught putting a value on life. And in some cases, the law actually bars consideration of cost in deciding how safe is safe enough.

The result is a hodgepodge of cost-effective regulations mixed with inconceivably expensive ones. At one extreme are rules that actually save money as well as lives. Mandatory childhood immunization programs, for example, cost less than treating the diseases. At the other extreme are rules that probably save only a statistical fraction of a life, and at enormous cost. Strict controls on benzene emissions by the tire makers run to an estimated $340 billion per life spared.

The most wasteful rules, however, are the ones that do save dozens of lives but at farcical cost. Draconian controls on toxic wastes from a variety of manufacturing plants, as well as cleanup standards for abandoned uranium mines and chemical waste sites, fit the category. Indeed, with cleanup obligations on the books that would cost government and industry several hundred billion dollars to meet over the next decade, risk researchers argue that the net impact of the programs on life expectancy may actually be perverse.

How so? The affluent live longer than the poor, at least in part because they have the will and the means to lead more secure lives. Not only are they more likely to visit a doctor before a cough turns into pneumonia, they can afford fresh vegetables, health clubs and bicycle helmets for their kids.

Hence the life-lengthening effects of requiring auto makers to install anti-skid brakes or preventing trace chemicals from ending up in drinking water must be weighed against the life-shortening effects of reducing living standards in order to pay the bill.

Mr. Viscusi estimates that the break-even point in what specialists have dubbed "risk-risk" calculations is around $10 million. Thus by his reckoning, regulations that reduce private spending by more than $10 million per statistical life saved are probably self-defeating.

Where does airline safety fit in this picture? When pressed to mandate life-preserving technology for commercial aircraft, the Federal Aviation Agency has generally acted with one eye on the economics. According to a 1984 study, smoke detectors required in airplane lavatories save lives for about a half-million dollars each. Emergency floor lighting runs to approximately $1 million per life saved—well under the $3 million to $5 million benchmark for the value of life. Still, some of the most hotly debated proposals suggest just how seductive bad ideas can be.

Infants can't use ordinary seat belts, so they are more vulnerable than adults in survivable airplane accidents unless they are strapped into special child seats. But there is a big catch here: Airlines insist that parents buy tickets for children if kids are to be assured seats of their own. So if Washington had demanded child restraints in response to petitions from safety groups in the 1980's, an estimated one-fifth of the infants who now fly in relative safety would be priced out of the air and end up traveling at greater risk in autos. On balance, more lives would be lost in cars than saved in planes.

A parallel question—one hardly ever asked—is whether aircraft manufacturers voluntarily spend too much on safety. If free markets worked according to Hoyle, one might expect Boeing and Airbus to sell less-safe planes, were it profitable to do so. But since aircraft makers and airlines—not to mention product liability lawyers—are deeply reluctant to acknowledge that there is any acceptable trade-off between cost and safety, such calculations are apparently never made in any systematic way.

What is apparent, though, is that commercial aviation is now so safe and the system that keeps it safe is so complex that the rare fatal accident offers little insight into how flying could be made safer at reasonable cost. Take the case of USAir and its subsidiaries, which suffered seven deadly accidents in seven years—a frequency of mishaps that Mr. Barnett of M.I.T. calculates had only a 2 percent probability of being purely coincidental. Add the fact that USAir was apparently guilty of an embarrassing number of safety and training miscues, including the failure to refuel a plane before take-off, and it is understandable why many travelers are looking for other ways to get to Pittsburgh.

But like the clusters of rare cancers that occasionally make headlines, clusters of airline accidents are harder to interpret than it might at first seem. Much depends on how the universe of possible coincidences is defined. For while the probability that chance alone generated USAirs unenviable safety record was just 1 in 50, there was a probability of 1 in 8 that some major airline that was no more dangerous than its competitors would crack up seven planes in seven years. One in 8 is still daunting odds, but not quite a smoking gun.

Even if one concedes that USAir must have been doing something disastrously wrong, it is hard to pinpoint what it was doing disastrously wrong. While it is gratifying to see that USAir pilots are now on notice to double-check fuel gauges before take-off, it is far from clear that the carrier's safety lapses were more serious than those of competitors with spotless accident records.

Safe air travel is worth some money and trouble, of course. And, no doubt, the tens of thousands of people who earn their paychecks keeping it safe will come up with some affordable ideas on how to make it safer. But the fact that many Americans who can't spot the difference between a wart and a melanoma know all about aircraft de-icing techniques and Doppler radar says more about their fears than about their knowledge of risk.

Things That Every Economist Takes for Granted Could Help a Lot of Other People Avoid Some Costly Mistakes

By Virginia Postrel

THE American Economic Association begins its annual meetings tomorrow in Atlanta. While most people seem to think of economics as a field that studies the stock market and government policy, the three-day agenda demonstrates a much wider range of scholarly questions.

The research to be presented includes "The Economics of Copyright Piracy," "Bleak Expectations: The Role of Pessimism in Addiction," "Counterfeit Goods and Income Inequality" and "Is Teen Motherhood Rational?" One panel will examine how and why different sorts of contracts govern different business structures, from owner-operator trucks in the United States to maritime trade in 14th-century Venetian Crete. Economic historians will explore the "economic performance of civilizations," from East Asia to the Middle East. And those are just some of the sessions scheduled for 8 on the first morning.

Clearly, there is more to economics than interest rates and tax policy, a point this column often tries to illustrate.

But many of the field's most useful insights won't make it onto the association's panels. The conference, after all, is devoted to new scholarly research: tricky empirical questions and unsolved theoretical puzzles. Economists don't get together to tell one another what they already know.

"The economic way of thinking," as the late Paul Heyne titled his popular introductory textbook, includes the analytical tools that economists take for granted among themselves and try to teach their students. Knowing these basic concepts could keep a lot of people from making economic mistakes.

Consider a recent statement by Stephen Rubin, publisher of the Doubleday Broadway group at the Random House division of Bertelsmann. Interviewed for an article about whether book prices are too high, he told a reporter for *The New York Times:* "I am just convinced that there is no difference between $22 and $23. Let's face it, if you want a book in translation from a Czech writer, you are going to buy the book—price is not a factor if it is a book that you really want."

In economic terms, Mr. Rubin was saying that he believes that the demand for books is "highly inelastic," maybe even zero. In plain English, that means that people won't respond to price cuts. "Price is not a factor." Publishers will sell the same number of books, regardless of the price.

Experience suggests this claim isn't true. Books, like most products, do sell better at lower prices.

The reason is a familiar one to economic thinking. Although each particular title is unique, there are a lot of substitutes—another basic economic concept—for books. Instead of buying a book, a customer might go to a movie, buy magazines, converse with friends, attend lectures, watch television or go hiking. Or, deterred by the high price, the potential book buyer might borrow a copy from the library or from a friend. The more substitutes there are for a good, the more price-sensitive customers are likely to be.

Of course, Mr. Rubin is undoubtedly right about some customers. My parents are going to buy my next book, whether it's priced at $25 or $30. They'd probably pay $50 or $100. But if the price is too high, even proud parents are going to cut back on the number of books they buy as gifts. And the number of such devoted fans is rather limited.

People who love their products tend to underestimate how many tepid or wavering customers there are at a given price. They lose sales by thinking everyone will be as enthusiastic about the product as they are themselves and that potential customers will therefore be oblivious to a high price.

Hence the value of another economic concept: thinking on the margin. The question isn't how much the most enthusiastic customer is willing to pay. To that person, the difference between $22 and $23 may not matter at all.

But there are other people who would buy a book at $22 who wouldn't pay $23, or who would pay $19 but not $20. Whatever the price, there will always be incremental customers who would buy at that price but not a penny higher. That's why deciding how much to charge is the same as deciding how many units to sell. (These calculations are, of course, best estimates, subject to uncertainty about exactly how the market will respond.)

Getting the revenue side of the equation right is tricky enough, but many business executives also have trouble weighing costs. In economic terms, every cost must be calculated relative to a particular decision.

Consider the cost of printing an additional copy of a book. Managers often fall prey to the mistake of adding up every expense associated with the book, including overhead like rent and editors' salaries, and then dividing by the number of copies. (This mistake is by no means unique to publishing.)

But the rent will be the same, regardless of whether the copy is printed. So will the editor's salary. So will the costs of proofreading and typesetting, which have already been incurred.

These costs are important if the publisher is deciding whether to stay in business or perhaps whether to publish a certain title or how many titles to publish. But they have no bearing on the question of whether printing another copy of a given, already created book is a profitable thing to do.

The only costs that matter to this decision are those that wouldn't be incurred unless the publisher added another copy to the press run—the costs of printing and distribution. This is what economists mean by "marginal cost."

If those marginal costs are less than the revenue the publisher can expect to get from that last copy, then increasing the run makes sense.

Including overhead costs in the decision guarantees that too few copies will be printed.

That not only lowers profits. It annoys notoriously cranky authors. So let's make a New Year's resolution to start thinking like economists—at least on the margin. http://www.nytimes.com

US Is Far More Efficient Than in '70s—But Also More Determined to Consume.

By Kris Axtman

HOUSTON—Reminiscent of the 1970s, the line of cars stretched down the street at a west side gas station last week. Customers were waiting for 10 free gallons, compliments of a local radio station.

Because the promotion would go to the first 200 cars only, people began queuing up at 9 the night before. One woman burned up an entire tank of gas waiting for a free half tank. "People are confused about why prices are rising so rapidly," says Tim Sutherland of KHMX 96.5, the Houston station giving away 2,000 gallons of gas. "They say it's absurd to be paying $2 a gallon for regular. But nobody wants to stop driving."

While there are signs that today's record high gasoline prices are causing some consumers to reevaluate their energy use (witness the slowdown in SUV sales), for the most part people continue to burn fuel at the same rate they did last year.

In fact, AAA, the nation's largest organization for motorists, predicts drivers will hit the road in record numbers this summer. After more than a decade of prosperity, it seems the concept of energy conservation has vanished from the nation's consciousness—Jimmy Carter donning a sweater instead of turning up the thermostat a distant, almost amusing, memory.

"The same urgency that was given to fuel conservation in the '70s is not apparent in our society anymore, even with these high prices," says Geoff Sundstrom, AAA spokesman. "Some of the drastic steps taken 30 years ago are not even being discussed right now."

Lowering the national speed limit to 55 miles per hour and tightening the fuel-economy standards are two examples of laws enacted after gas shortages shocked the nation. Some believe steps like these will occur only if gas shortages return.

Indeed, many economists contend that gasoline as a percentage of household expenditure is less today than it was 25 years ago, and people simply haven't been inconvenienced to the same degree.

But others say the nation has continued to make progress on energy conservation, primarily on the technology side. While gains were faster in the 1970s and '80s, spurred on by persistently high energy prices, everything from automobiles to light bulbs is more efficient today than they were even 10 years ago, says Christopher Flavin, president of the Worldwatch Institute in Washington.

By 1990, for instance, the average American car got 40 percent more miles per gallon than it did in 1973. In the past decade, the country has saved $50 billion from the dozen or more products that have been subject to stricter federal standards. "In the 1970s, there was a limited number of choices when it came to energy efficiency," says Bill Prindle of the American Council for an Energy-Efficient Economy in Washington. "We were so accustomed to cheap energy, there was no need to find alternatives. Now there are a lot more choices."

But efficiency by itself may not be enough. Research shows that if the cost of driving or running an air conditioner is cheap enough, people will simply use more energy. The size of homes has doubled in the past century, commutes have quadrupled, and electronic gadgets have proliferated. "The general ethic of consumption has increased over the last 30 years," says Mr. Prindle. But that does not mean consumers do not want to conserve energy, he adds. They simply expect manufacturers to give them the best and most efficient product.

It also does not mean that consumers aren't willing to cut back when it's necessary. The most recent example was the 2000 California energy crisis when residents lowered their electricity use by almost 10 percent in one year.

"When push comes to shove, people show they can conserve and get into that conservation mind-set," says Jeff Deyette, an energy analyst with the Union of Concerned Scientists in Cambridge, Mass. "But it's got to really hit them in the wallet before they're willing to make some lifestyle changes."

Prices may be reaching the point where consumers are starting to make at least some adjustments. A new USA Today/CNN/Gallup Poll found that 59 percent of Americans said the high pump prices will cause them to drive less this summer than they normally would.

One reason consumers don't conserve more, some suggest, is that they don't have enough choices. American car manufacturers tell consumers that they must choose between fuel efficiency and size—when the technology allows for both, says David Friedman, research director for the clean-vehicles program at the Union of Concerned Scientists. "You can't blame the consumer until the consumer really has a role to play," says Mr. Friedman. He adds that the current energy bill does nothing to cut the country's oil dependency and to improve fuel economy.

Experts speculate that part of the skepticism about energy conservation has to do with the constant barrage of gloom-and-doom news about the environment in the 1970s.

"Back then, the newspapers and academic press were full of accounts that the world was running out of oil and that we couldn't count on this energy source for much longer," says Mr. Sundstrom with AAA. "Well, that didn't happen and many of the older population are somewhat skeptical about anybody ringing alarm bells today."

Others go even further. "I don't think the culture has ever really embraced the true conservation ethic promoted in the 1970s," says Michael Marsden, a professor of American studies at St. Norbert College in Wisconsin. "Sure, a lot of us learned to recycle, but we won't go out and buy a smaller hybrid car. We're not that committed."

While short-term attitudes may have changed in the 1970s, it often takes much longer for cultural shifts. "It takes about a century to see real change," says Dr. Marsden. "We've still got a ways to go.

COUNTER-TERRORISM: The Private Cost of More Security

By PETER NAVARRO

The greatest danger that terrorism poses to America may be purely economic, the threat of weapons of mass destruction notwithstanding. The danger lies in a severe "productivity shock" that could lead to a gross domestic product trillions of dollars below what it otherwise should be.

The most obvious source of this shock lies in a deficit-producing shift from butter to guns in the federal budget as we wage war against terrorism. Cuts in education and infrastructure spending will directly lower productivity even as deficit-driven higher interest rates indirectly cut productivity by crowding out investment in the private sector.

But the more subtle, potentially more serious productivity shock may come from a federally mandated substitution of "protective" for "productive" capital in the private sector. That is, money spent for more fences, guards and surveillance equipment at the expense of new machinery, technology and software. Over the next several years, this capital substitution will probably accelerate as a security-conscious White House and Congress impose a new layer of regulations the likes of which we haven't seen since the 1970s.

Since Sept. 11, some corporations have voluntarily put capital into protection. But the levels of counter-terrorism spending have been far below what one might have expected, particularly in light of the legal liabilities that corporations may face for failing to protect their employees and customers. Moreover, with the exception of a few sectors like petroleum, which have adopted plans to safeguard facilities from terrorist attacks, there has been little coordinated action by corporate leadership.

This relative inaction in the private sector poses an ideological problem for the Bush administration, one that has provoked considerable differences of opinion across federal bureaucracies. To understand why President Bush finds himself between a conservative rock and a pragmatic hard place, it's important to know why the private sector has failed to shoulder its fair share of the counter-terrorism burden.

First, corporate executives have been reluctant to invest in new plant machinery, let alone in protective devices, during these recessionary times. Corporations that have significantly boosted counter-terrorism spending, like Boeing, can either afford to or have no other option because of their risk exposure.

Second, some industry stakeholders have simply let others carry the burden. Bush's initial response to this "free rider" problem was classically conservative. Rather than jam new regulations down industry's throat, government should form "patriotic" partnerships with business to develop voluntary counter-terrorism obligations. But after months of corporate foot-dragging, Bush now understands that free riders will continue to shirk their duty absent federal mandates.

The recent skirmish between Bush and Congress over the chemical industry's failure to regulate itself illustrates the underlying policy conflict. The industry was initially asked to devise plans to prevent a terrorist attack on chemical plants from sending waves of toxic fumes into a major urban area. But free riders run rampant in this industry.

Of the nation's 15,000 chemical companies, only about 10% even participate in the industry's trade association. Moreover, the sector's profit margins are very low. Finally, the industry has been in almost constant regulatory warfare with the government. As a result of the chemical sector's go-slow approach to managing the terrorist threat, the Bush administration had to cancel a much ballyhooed June rollout of the president's voluntary partnerships.

Democratic Sens. Jon Corzine of New Jersey and Harry Reid of Nevada quickly used the opportunity to push legislation that would achieve what volunteerism hadn't. Outflanked, Bush tacked. Amazingly, he is moving forward on using the Environmental Protection Agency, a favorite target during his 2000 presidential campaign, to crack down on the chemical industry.

The skirmish raises a broader policy question: How best to proceed with the design, implementation and enforcement of a complex and costly layer of new counter-terrorism regulations? Unfortunately, the answer so far has many unsettling parallels with the mistakes of the regulation-heavy 1970s.

During that decade, the federal government churned out new, strict regulations on everything from clean air to water purity to occupational health and safety. We now know that their poor initial design and implementation were a major cause of a decade of lost productivity and painfully slow economic growth.

A basic problem was that overzealous bureaucrats and politicians adopted a broad range of "command and control" standards that left little maneuvering room for industry. For example, the EPA required new power plants to use expensive "best available control technology" whether or not the new plants could meet new emission standards by simply burning lower-sulfur coal.

We eventually learned that it was cheaper to use market mechanisms to bring about the desired regulatory effects. Tools like pollution and emissions credits and "smog markets" have allowed industry to meet standards in a less costly manner and not succumb to the free-rider problem.

Despite this 1970s lesson, Congress and the White House appear to be moving toward costly command-and-control mandates to get the counter-terrorism protection they deem necessary. The irony is that a corporate leadership seemingly as devoid of a cooperative spirit, patriotism and vision as it is of ethics is driving the movement.

The stakes are high. If productivity levels drop to 1970s levels again, our GDP will be at least $2 trillion lower than it otherwise would be in 10 years. Yes, this estimate is wildly at odds with the Bush administration's, which doesn't anticipate a major productivity shock. There are, however, no glasses rose-colored enough to produce honestly the administration's assessment. It's not just the disparate fiscal, monetary, regulatory and military forces that Sept. 11 has set in motion. It is also the almost breathtaking scope of the regulatory counter-terrorist checklist.

This list ranges from strengthened background checks, vulnerability assessments, bolstered plant security and tighter enforcement of immigration laws to stockpiling vaccines, establishing readiness plans in case of another terrorist attack and running a national health surveillance network. Also included are tasks like retrofitting nuclear power plants to survive a terrorist air assault, installing air filters in major buildings to combat bioterrorism and possibly equipping hazardous waste trucks with automatic braking systems to thwart sabotage and suicide bombers.

If there is any reassuring news in all this, it is this: If we allow our creativity to blossom, as we did during the space race, and if we practice our 1970s regulatory lessons, we can prosecute the war on terrorism cost-effectively while developing and deploying the new technologies necessary to outrun terror. The space program is an instructive precedent: Every dollar spent yielded seven tax dollars reaped from commercial spinoffs. If we could ensure that our counter-terrorist research and development cut in both military and civilian ways, we may be able to overcome any productivity losses resulting from our war against terrorism.

Peter Navarro teaches macroeconomics at the Graduate School of Management at UC Irvine.

UNIT 2

Microeconomics

Unit Selections

Key Points to Consider

- Why is the concept of demand elasticity important, and how might it be used? How do firms practice price discrimination?
- What is the "real" price of gasoline?
- What is "eco-economics," and how might policies be developed to aid both the environment and the economy?

DUSHKIN ONLINE **Links: www.dushkin.com/online/**
These sites are annotated in the World Wide Web pages.

Antitrust Policy
http://www.antitrust.org

CEO Express—Business and Financial News
http://www.ceoexpress.com

Corporate Watch
http://www.corpwatch.org

Internet Public Library: Business and Economics Reference
http://ipl.org/ref/RR/static/bus0000.html

New York Times Business Connections
http://www.nytimes.com/library/cyber/reference/busconn.html

Small Business Administration
http://www.sbaonline.sba.gov

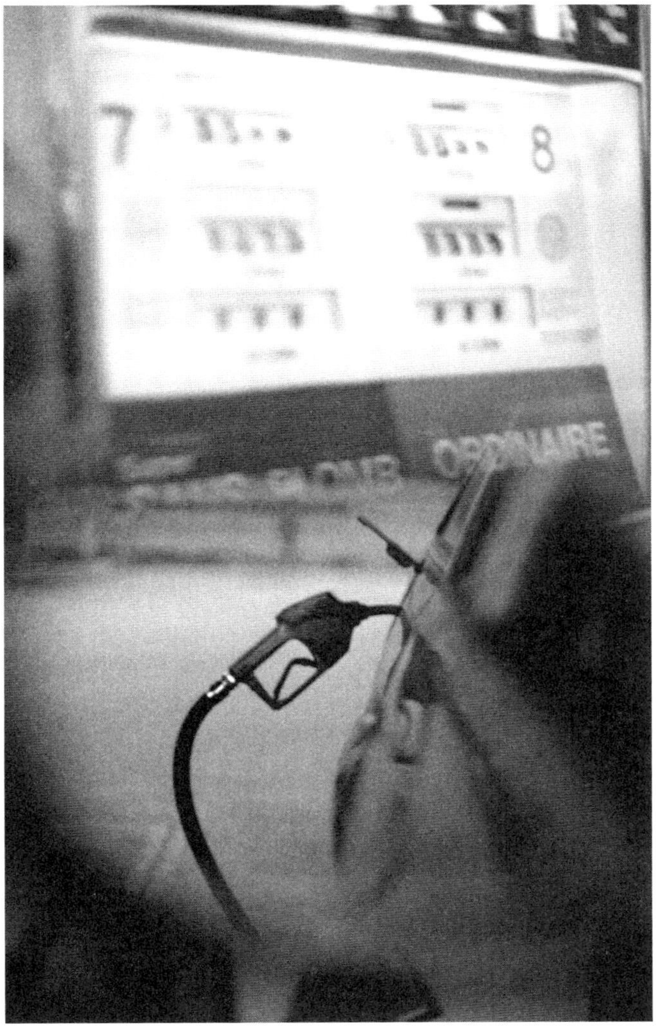

While there are many ways to subdivide the science of economics, the most common one distinguishes between macroeconomics and microeconomics. Macroeconomics is the study of the economy "in the large"; it concerns such broad issues as how gross domestic product (GDP), unemployment, inflation, and economic growth are determined. Microeconomics—the subject of this unit—involves the study of the economy "in the small"; it investigates the economy in terms of its separate components and focuses on the individual decision-making processes of consumers and producers in a market setting.

The primary roots of modern microeconomics can be traced to Adam Smith's *An Inquiry into the Nature and Causes of the Wealth of Nations*, published in 1776. In this work, Smith shows how individuals, acting in their own self-interest, serve the best interests of a market economy. Smith's argument (which is generally accepted by most economists today) provides the basis for a laissez-faire political philosophy—the belief that noninterference by government in the workings of a market system promotes the greatest good for the greatest number of people.

With the intensification of both domestic and global competition in recent years, companies are compelled to adopt new strategies (never foreseen in the days of Adam Smith), which include consideration of the size of the targeted market, superior access to resources and customers, and restrictions on competitors' options. The ability of a single firm to pursue such strategies depends, of course, on the nature of its market environment. Microeconomic analysis shows that this can range from a perfectly competitive environment (of numerous small, price-taking firms) to a monopolized one (containing a single, price-making seller).

Smoke Signals

Doubling of Cigarette Tax Sends Some Smokers Across State Lines, but Many Into Abstinence

TRENTON

Smokers in New Jersey took such a shellacking at the cash register last year that they stopped buying cigarettes in numbers never seen before. How many stopped smoking is a separate question.

Since the state cigarette tax doubled last Jan. 1, sales have declined about 12 percent, Treasury Department data show. While some sales have been chased across state borders, public health experts estimate that at least two-thirds of the decline reflects a decrease in smoking.

"Wow, that's a whole lot more than we predicted," said Larry Downs, director of New Jersey Breathes, a coalition of antismoking organizations. Before the increase, Mr. Downs said, consumption had been dropping by 2 to 4 percent a year. "Something's going on," he continued. "I'll give you 4 percent for people buying cigarettes elsewhere and I'll take the 8 percent drop."

Mr. Downs said the tax increase had set up "a real-life public health experiment": While New Jersey's tax rose to 80 cents a pack from 40 cents, neighboring states maintained their rates—Pennsylvania at 31 cents a pack, New York at 56 cents and Delaware at 24 cents. Len Fishman, the state Commissioner of Health and Senior Services, said the initial wallop was meant to drive down sales, even though most of the new revenue finances health care.

"We were hoping a dramatic increase would decrease consumption," Mr. Fishman said. "We did predict that there would be a reduction in the number of people who smoke." He said that in his travels around the state, "a lot of people have told me that they quit, and a lot told me that this was the straw that broke the camel's back."

The tax increase placed New Jersey behind only Alaska and Hawaii, at $1 a pack, and Washington State, at 82.5 cents. (On Jan. 1, California's tax rose to 87 cents a pack.) The sticker shock was compounded last month by a price increase, 45 cents a pack at wholesale and about 60 cents at the counter, from tobacco manufacturers.

The two hits raised prices by about 50 percent. At Wawa convenience stores, for example, premium brands cost $3.32 a pack, up from $2.22 before the tax increase.

Revenue from tax stamps from Jan. 1 through June 30, the end of the 1998 fiscal year, were about 13 percent below what they would have been had sales remained at their 1997 levels; when the effect of volume discounts was taken into account, the decline in cigarette sales was about 12 percent, Treasury Department officials said.

Preliminary figures for the current fiscal year show similar decreases. When the tax took effect, cigarette revenue was already falling; in the fiscal year 1997 revenue dropped 2 percent. Had that dropoff continued, 1998 revenue through November would have been about $433.3 million, or 54.2 million cartons. Instead, revenue was $379.4 million, or 47.4 million cartons. The gap, then, represents about 6.8 million cartons, and there is no way to know how many were bought in other states.

In New York, cigarette tax revenue from January to November 1998 was 0.3 percent below collections for the same period in 1997. Pennsylvania reported a 1.4 percent increase in 1998. In Delaware, where revenue was already increasing at a rate of 3 percent a year, the first half of 1998 saw a 10 percent increase over the first half of 1997. Pennsylvania's additional revenue through November represents about 1.2 million more cartons than were sold from January to November 1997, but sales were declining—by 1.8 percent in the 1997 fiscal year—and if that decline had continued, the extra tax collections would represent about 2.9 million more cartons.

Delaware's extra sales through November, assuming a continued 3 percent increase, exceeded 500,000 cartons. While researchers have consistently found dropoffs in smoking after price increases, they cannot know exactly what role prices have played. There have been few large, one-time price increases, and no precedent for a tax increase as large as New Jersey's.

Mr. Fishman cites the example of Massachusetts, which raised its tax 25 cents a pack in 1992 and registered a 12.5 percent decline in sales the next year.

"Talking about price increases can be tricky," Mr. Fishman said. "If you have gradual increases, you lose some of the impact. A state with a high tax may have had less of an increase over the years."

It is especially hard to measure the effects of cigarette prices on underage buyers. Many studies have concluded that price has a greater effect on children and teenagers than on adults. But a recent analysis by economists at Cornell University, using data on students who were eighth graders in 1988, found that price increases had very little effect on whether they took up smoking.

And while the smoking rate among adults has been inching down—to 23.2 percent of adults nationwide and 21.5 percent in New Jersey, according to the Federal Centers for Disease Control and Prevention—it has sharply risen among teenagers and children. In its most recent published survey of high school seniors, taken in 1997, the University of Michigan's Institute for Social Research found that 24.6 percent were daily smokers, a figure that has steadily climbed from a low point of 18.1 percent in 1988.

In New Jersey, the centers' 1997 survey of 9th to 12th graders found that 38 percent had smoked a cigarette in the previous month and 19 percent were daily smokers.

Mr. Fishman said his department had predicted a decline of 10 to 12 percent in smoking among children and teenagers as a result of the tax increase and that its effects would become clearer this spring, when the state surveys middle-school students.

It will be longer yet before the manufacturers' price increase, which took effect only in late November, shows measurable results. But Rich Herbeck, co-owner of Irwin Tobacco and Candy, a distributor in Trenton, said that even though the increase was nationwide, it was sending New Jerseyans across the bridges just as the tax hit had done last January.

"People were so shocked by it that they're looking for any method to save money," Mr. Herbeck said.

The CORE of the PROBLEM: Three hard years push West Michigan apple growers out of the business

By Kathleen Longcore

BELDING—It's been perfect apple-growing weather in West Michigan, but it's too late for Tom and Kathy Hall.

The Belding couple are among 20 area apple growers who have thrown in the towel in recent years, victims of bad weather, overproduction and rock-bottom prices from foreign competition.

While recent forecasts for this season's harvest have given local growers cause for hope, the Halls are not among them.

"This is our first season without apples, and we've been trying to laugh it off, but it's really awful," said Kathy Hall, 48, as she looks out at cornfields where their apple trees used to be.

"This is history; it's gone. You just can't afford to farm anymore," said Tom Hall, 50, gesturing toward fallen apple trees in rows that have grown up to weeds.

Working hard in their orchards and farm market on Belding Road, just east of the Kent County line, was a good life for the Halls and their four children, now grown.

But three bad years for apple growers did them in.

"We were hit hard by hail two years in a row, which started us on a downward spin, so it wasn't just pricing. But then last year's prices were awful," Kathy Hall said.

"There was just too much money lost in one year to stay in apples, so after harvest last year, Tom bulldozed out the trees."

The Halls aren't alone, said Phil Schwallier, a fruit specialist with the Michigan State University cooperative extension service.

"I lost 10 growers each year over the last two years," he said. About half cut down or abandoned their orchards while the other half turned them over to other growers, he said.

Schwallier said Michigan growers pulled 3,000 acres of apples out of production last year, including 700 along The Ridge in Kent, Ottawa and Muskegon counties. This year hundreds more acres have been taken out of production.

It's a troubling trend in a time when an orchard's value for development—about $4,000 an acre—is double what it will fetch for fruit growing, he said.

A recent state apple harvest estimate has growers hopeful a smaller crop this year will boost prices.

The crop is expected to be down 33 percent over last year's 30-million bushels. The culprit: Spring freeze damage in northwestern Michigan and damage from a disease called fire blight in southwestern Michigan.

The Grand Rapids region, however, was spared those problems and enjoyed almost perfect weather, Schwallier said. An early spring and plentiful summer rain has given apples good size. Sunny days with cool nights have colored the fruit.

"We've got a good crop," said Jim Jagger, an employee of Kropf Orchards in Lowell. "We've got good size, good color, good quality and plenty of 'em."

The past several years have been tough, but the worst is probably over, said Roger Kropf, 59, president of Kropf Fruit Co., the marketing arm of his 2,000-acre operation.

Michigan growers now compete with the world, because retailers can buy high-quality fresh fruit all year long, he said.

To survive, growers are taking out trees with older apple varieties and planting what's selling. But it takes seven years to get new trees in production, he said.

"We were caught in a shift in the international market and we couldn't adjust in time," Kropf said.

"We decided we had to take out 100 acres a year for five years. We've already dropped 200 acres, and we're going to keep doing that until our return line goes above our break even line," he said.

In the meantime, Kropf Orchards is exporting about 20 percent of its crop—Red Delicious and Galas to the Caribbean, Central American and Brazil; Empires and

Galas to England; and Red Delicious and Empires to Israel.

"It keeps some of the pressure off the domestic market," Kropf said.

Also, Michigan growers are pushing the U.S. Department of Agriculture to buy more applesauce, juice and pie apple slices to use in school lunches and other federal food programs.

Growers blame the past three years of depressed prices on cheap apple juice concentrate from China.

In 1990, China and the United States were about equal in apple production. But in seven years China quadrupled its production and started selling juice concentrate in the U.S. below what it costs to produce it. Between 1995 and 1998, the amount of Chinese concentrate imported by U.S. processors increased more than 1,200 percent, federal statistics show.

Growers got some relief this year when the U.S. International Trade Commission ruled the Chinese juice was unfairly harming the U.S. apple industry. The commission slapped a tax of about 52 percent on U.S. juice makers using Chinese concentrate.

Better prices are coming too late for the Halls, however.

Kathy Hall is selling real estate, and Tom Hall works second shift at Rapistan in Grand Rapids. The couple's three sons are all working for Rapistan too, and their daughter has become a travel agent.

"Companies like Rapistan are tickled to death to get my husband and my boys because they're awesome workers," Hall said.

"But when we go out (of business), it's not just us," she said. "People need to realize there's a domino effect. There's the guy we bought fuel from and parts for our equipment and all the other suppliers."

Sour Times for Cranberry Growers

In Wisconsin, many farmers are 'trying to hang on'

Tim Jones

After nearly 40 years of riding the Wall Street roller coaster as a stockbroker, John Sager planted his retirement roots in the shallow depths of cranberry marshes because he always wanted to be a farmer.

"Not the get-up-at-4-a.m.-and-milk-the-cows type, but farming with some reasonable hours," said Sager, who developed 76 acres of marshes in central Wisconsin, the heart of the nation's largest and most productive cranberry region.

Sager's experience with the small red berries has been far from reasonable and has drawn painful comparisons to the volatile business he left a decade ago. Cranberries became the boom-and-bust high-tech stock of agribusiness, and as growers harvest their crop this month, they still are struggling to pull themselves out of the muck of overproduction.

The plight of growers has been a boon to consumers, who have reaped the benefits of low prices for cranberry juice and the Thanksgiving staple of cranberry relish.

After soaring to a peak of $80 per 100-pound barrel in 1997 and then plummeting to $11 two years later, cranberry prices have regained some of their lost ground. This year, growers are expected to receive about $19 to $23 per barrel, roughly half the price before speculation triggered Wall Street-like chaos in a business whose signature is small farms run by several generations of families.

A Slow Recovery

For most, the price will not be enough to cover the cost of production, which ranges from $25 to $35 per barrel, depending on the condition of the marsh. The recovery is slow.

"A lot of them are just trying to hang on," said John Swendrowski of Northland Cranberries Inc. in Wisconsin Rapids. "At the current price, far more growers will lose money than will book a profit."

Hard knocks in agriculture are nothing new. Drought conditions this year inflicted heavy damage on major cash crops, and Congress stepped in with emergency assistance.

But cranberries, which occupy an obscure nook in agriculture dominated by farmers in Wisconsin and Massachusetts, are off the big-farm radar screen. They are not covered by federal farm subsidies, as are such crops as corn, wheat and soybeans.

Nationwide, there are only 1,200 cranberry growers, with the overwhelming majority in Wisconsin. The average size of a cranberry farm in Massachusetts is less than 20 acres.

"They're kind of a crop apart," said Neil Harl, an agricultural economist at Iowa State University. "Unless you live in those states you don't pay that much attention to them."

The cranberry business has thrived mostly in isolation for more than a century and has, in terms of growing and harvesting, changed relatively little. At Wetherby Cranberry Co. in Warrens, the harvested berries from 32 marshes ride a conveyor belt to the top of the old wooden mill and bounce through the different layers.

The berries are inspected by hand before making their way into plastic bags and cardboard boxes for sale or for juicemakers such as Ocean Spray or Northland.

"We learned how to grow them too well a few years ago," said Nodji VanWychen. She and her family are independent growers in Warrens and the third generation to tend the marshes.

"We're coming back gradually, but it's awfully slow," VanWychen said.

When Harvard Medical School reported in 1994 that cranberry juice helped protect against bladder infections, consumption jumped. Companies like Ocean Spray Cranberries encouraged more growers to enter the business.

Speculation in cranberries sent the price, normally about $35 to $40 a barrel, soaring in the mid-1990s. That encouraged an unprecedented expansion in the industry. In Wisconsin, the acreage devoted to cranberry marshes soared by 50 percent during the decade, from 12,000 to 18,000, according to the Wisconsin State Cranberry Growers Association. More cranberry farms cropped up in British Columbia and Quebec, adding to the supply.

Sager, drawing on his stock market experience, watched warily as the price shot to $80 a barrel.

"Everybody and their cousin got into it and they thought they could make a phenomenal living. It was the worst thing that could happen," Sager said.

Cranberry Industry in the Can

After peaking in 1997, cranberry prices have plummeted during the last few years.

PRICE PER BARREL (100 pounds)
Annual U.S. average

1992	$51.60
1993	$50.20
1994	$49.30
1995	$53.40
1996	$65.90
1997	$63.70
1998	$36.60
1999	$17.20
2000	$17.60
2001	$22.90

Five states account for all of the 570 million pounds produced in the U.S. each year.

Wisconsin:	52%
Massachusetts:	30%
New Jersey:	8%
Oregon:	6%
Washington:	3%

Source: Wisconsin State Cranberry Growers Association, U.S. Department of Agriculture

Harvest Restrictions

The U.S. Department of Agriculture ordered growers to restrict harvests in 2000 and 2001 to reduce the bloated inventory. That has led to a gradual price recovery. Tom Lochner, executive director of the Wisconsin growers association, said this year still will be "a tough one" despite the improved conditions, because most growers will not get the price they need to cover their costs. Some people will get out of the business this year, he said.

Despite the low prices, there is little incentive for many cranberry farmers to get out unless they face financial collapse. Marshes—or bogs, as they are called in Massachusetts—are not easily adaptable to other forms of growing, said Harl. The soil in central Wisconsin is sandy, and the surrounding wetlands rule out switching to other crops, he said.

Jeff LaFleur of the Cape Cod Cranberry Growers Association said the price "is not where it needs to be to sustain the growers long term."

Chris Phillips, a spokesman for Ocean Spray in Lakeville, Mass., said demand for cranberries is growing. Strong early sales of white cranberry juice underscore the importance of offering something new to the consumer, Phillips said.

The berries' price, though, will determine whether Nodji VanWychen will see her children remain in the business.

"We're going to have to weather the storm," she said. "But I don't know if we're ever going to see the price get back to $35."

Is Wal-Mart **Too** Powerful?

Low prices are great. But Wal-Mart's dominance creates problems—for suppliers, workers, communities, and even American culture

By Anthony Bianco and Wendy Zellner

IN BUSINESS, THERE IS BIG, AND THERE is Wal-Mart. With $245 billion in revenues in 2002, Wal-Mart Stores Inc. is the world's largest company. It is three times the size of the No. 2 retailer, France's Carrefour. Every week, 138 million shoppers visit Wal-Mart's 4,750 stores; last year, 82% of American households made at least one purchase at Wal-Mart. "There's nothing like Wal-Mart," says Ira Kalish, global director of Deloitte Research. "They are so much bigger than any retailer has ever been that it's not possible to compare."

At Wal-Mart, "everyday low prices" is more than a slogan; it is the fundamental tenet of a cult masquerading as a company. Over the years, Wal-Mart has relentlessly wrung tens of billions of dollars in cost efficiencies out of the retail supply chain, passing the larger part of the savings along to shoppers as bargain prices. New England Consulting estimates that Wal-Mart saved its U.S. customers $20 billion last year alone. Factor in the price cuts other retailers must make to compete, and the total annual savings approach $100 billion. It's no wonder that economists refer to a broad "Wal-Mart effect" that has suppressed inflation and rippled productivity gains through the economy year after year.

However, Wal-Mart's seemingly simple and virtuous business model is fraught with complications and perverse consequences. To cite a particularly noteworthy one, this staunchly anti-union company, America's largest private employer, is widely blamed for the sorry state of retail wages in America. On average, Wal-Mart sales clerks—"associates" in company parlance—pulled in $8.23 an hour, or $13,861 a year, in 2001, according to documents filed in a lawsuit pending against the company. At the time, the federal poverty line for a family of three was $14,630. Wal-Mart insists that it pays competitively, citing a privately commissioned survey that found that it "meets or exceeds" the total remuneration paid by rival retailers in 50 U.S. markets. "This is a good place to work," says Coleman H. Peterson, executive vice-president for personnel, citing an employee turnover rate that has fallen below 45% from 70% in 1999.

Critics counter that this is evidence not of improving morale but of a lack of employment alternatives in a slow-growth economy. "It's a ticking time bomb," says an executive at one big Wal-Mart supplier. "At some point, do the people stand up and revolt?" Indeed, the company now faces a revolt of sorts in the form of nearly 40 lawsuits charging it with forcing employees to work overtime without pay and a sex-discrimination case that could rank as the largest civil rights class action ever. On Sept. 24, a federal judge in California began considering a plaintiff's petition to include all women who have worked at Wal-Mart since late 1998—1.6 million all told—in a suit alleging that Wal-Mart systematically denies women equal pay and opportunities for promotion. Wal-Mart is vigorously contesting all of these suits.

Wal-Mart might well be both America's most admired and most hated company. "The world has never known a company with such ambition, capability, and momentum," marvels a Boston Consulting Group report. On Wall Street, Wal-Mart trades at a premium to most every other retailer. But the more size and power that "the Beast of Bentonville" amasses, the greater the backlash it is stirring among competing retailers, vendors, organized labor, community activists, and cultural and political progressives. America has a long history of controversial retailers, notes James E. Hoopes, a history professor at Babson College. "What's new about Wal-Mart is the flak it's drawn from outside the world of its competition," he says. "It's become a social phenomenon that people resent and fear."

Wal-Mart's marketplace clout is hard to overstate. In household staples such as toothpaste, shampoo, and paper towels, the company commands about 30% of the U.S. market, and analysts predict that its share of many such goods could hit 50% before decade's end. Wal-Mart also is Hollywood's biggest outlet, accounting for 15% to 20% of all sales of CDs, videos, and DVDs. The mega-retailer did not add magazines to its mix until the mid-1990s, but it now makes 15% of all single-copy sales in the U.S. In books, too, Wal-Mart has quickly become a force. "They pile up best-sellers like toothpaste," says Stephen Riggio, chief executive of Barnes & Noble Inc., the world's largest bookseller.

Wal-Mart controls a large and rapidly increasing share of the business done by most every major U.S. consumer-products company: 28% of Dial total sales, 24% of Del Monte Foods', 23% of Clorox', 23% of Revlon's, and on down the list. Suppliers' growing dependence on Wal-Mart is "a huge issue" not only for manufacturers but also for the U.S. economy, says Tom Rubel, CEO of consultant Retail Forward Inc. "If [Wal-Mart] ever stumbles, we've got a potential national security problem on our hands. They touch almost everything. . . . If they ever really went into a tailspin, the dislocation would be significant and traumatic."

Even so, Wal-Mart appears to be in no imminent danger of running afoul of federal antitrust statutes. The Robinson-Patman Act of 1936 was passed in large part to protect mom-and-pop grocers from the Great Atlantic & Pacific Tea Co., the Wal-Mart of its day. But contemporary antitrust interpretations eschew such David-and-Goliath populism. Giants like Wal-Mart have wide latitude to do as they wish to rivals and suppliers so long as they deliver lower prices to consumers. "When Wal-Mart comes in and people desert downtown because they like the selection and the low prices, it's hard for people in the antitrust community to say we should not let them do that," says New York University law professor Harry First.

CEO H. Lee Scott Jr. and other Wal-Mart executives are aware of the rising hostility the company faces and are trying to smooth its rough edges in dealing with the outside world. But they have no intention of tampering with its shopper-centric business model. "We don't turn a deaf ear to any criticism. We're most sensitive to what the customer has to say, though," says Vice-Chairman Thomas M. Coughlin. "Your customers will tell you when you're wrong."

Wal-Mart cites customer preferences as the reason it does not stock CDs or DVDs with parental warning stickers and why it occasionally yanks items from its shelves. In May, it removed the racy "lad" magazines *Maxim, Stuff*, and FHM. A month later, it began obscuring the covers of *Glamour, Redbook, Marie Claire*, and *Cosmopolitan* with binders. Why did Wal-Mart censor these publications and not *Rolling Stone*, which has featured a nearly naked Britney Spears and Christina Aguilera on two of its recent covers? "There's a lot of subjectivity," concedes Gary Severson, a Wal-Mart general merchandise manager. "There's a line between provocative and pornographic. I don't know exactly where it is."

Wal-Mart was the only one of the top 10 drug chains to refuse to stock Preven when Gynetics Inc. introduced the morning-after contraceptive in 1999. Roderick L. Mackenzie, Gynetics' founder and nonexecutive chairman, says senior Wal-Mart executives told his employees that they did not want their pharmacists grappling with the "moral dilemma" of abortion. Mackenzie was incensed but tried to hide it. "When you speak to God in Bentonville, you speak in hushed tones," says Mackenzie, who explained, to no avail, that Preven did not induce abortion but rather prevented pregnancy. Wal-Mart spokesman Jay Allen says "a number of factors were considered" in making the Preven decision, but he denies that opposition to abortion was one of them. "If anybody of any belief reads any moral decision [into] that, that's not right," he says.

CULTURAL GATEKEEPER

There is no question that the company has the legal right to sell only what it chooses to sell, even in the case of First Amendment-protected material such as magazines. By most accounts, though, Wal-Mart's cultural gatekeeping has served to narrow the mainstream for entertainment offerings while imparting to it a rightward tilt. The big music companies have stopped grousing about Wal-Mart and are eagerly supplying the chain with the same sanitized versions of explicit CDs that they provide to radio stations. "You can't have 100% impact when you are taking an artist to a mainstream audience if you don't have the biggest player, Wal-Mart," says EMI Music North America Executive Vice-President Phil Quartararo.

This year alone, Wal-Mart hopes to open as many as 335 new stores in the U.S.: 55 discount stores, 210 supercenters, 45 Sam's Clubs, and 25 Neighborhood markets. An additional 130 new stores are on the boards for foreign markets. Wal-Mart currently operates 1,309 stores in 10 countries, ranking as the largest retailer in Mexico and Canada. If the company can maintain its current 15% growth rate, it will double its revenues over the next five years and top $600 billion in 2011.

That's a very big if—even for Wal-Mart. Vice-Chairman Coughlin's biggest worry is finding enough warm bodies to staff all those new stores. By Wal-Mart's own estimate, about 44% of its 1.4 million employees will leave in 2003, meaning the company will need to hire 616,000 workers just to stay even. In addition, from 2004 to 2008, the company wants to add 800,000 new positions, including 47,000 management slots. "That's what causes me the most sleepless nights," Coughlin says.

At the same time, Wal-Mart will have to cope with intensifying grassroots opposition. The company's hugely ambitious expansion plans hinge on continuing its move out of its stronghold in the rural South and Midwest into urban America. This year, the company opened what it describes as "one of its first truly urban stores" in Los Angeles, not far from Watts. Everyday low prices no doubt appeal to city dwellers no less than to their country cousins. But Wal-Mart's sense of itself as definitively American ("Wal-Mart is America," boasts one top executive) is likely to be severely tested by the metropolis' high land costs, restrictive zoning codes, and combative labor unions—not to mention its greater economic and cultural diversity.

A ZERO-SUM GAME?

Certainly, Wal-Mart will be hard pressed to continue censoring its product lines using the justification of customer preference. The market for profanity-laced hip-hop may be tiny in Bentonville, Ark., but it is big in Los Angeles. Overseas, the company does not presume to impose a small-town, Bible Belt moral agenda on shoppers. "We adopt local standards," says John B. Menzer, CEO of Wal-Mart's international division. Why, then, should Los Angeles be any different?

The fact is, Wal-Mart doesn't know for certain how the majority of its customers feel about *Maxim*, or any other magazine, for that matter. It appears that the company makes no scientific

King Kong in Diapers

WAL-MART dominates sales in a number of categories:

Disposable diapers	Hair Care	Toothpaste	Pet food	Home textiles
32%	30%	26%	20%	13%

U.S. market share based on 2002 data; excludes Sam's Clubs
Data: A.C. Nielsen, Retail Forward, *Home Textiles Today*

attempt to survey shoppers about entertainment content but responds in ad hoc fashion to complaints lodged by a relative handful of customers and by outside groups, which are usually but not always of the conservative persuasion.

On the other hand, the company seldom submits to community groups that oppose its plans to build new stores. The number of such challenges has increased steadily and is now running at about 100 a year. Wal-Mart's "biggest barrier to growth is. . . . opposition at the local level," says Carl Steidtmann, Deloitte Research's retail economist. The Stop Wal-Mart movement has been bolstered of late by a series of academic studies that have debunked the notion that a new big-box store boosts employment and sales and property-tax receipts. "The net increases are minimal as the new big-box stores merely capture sales from existing business in the area," concludes a new study of Wal-Mart's impact in Mississippi. "I see it pretty much as a zero-sum game," says co-author Kenneth E. Stone, an economics professor at Iowa State University.

The most hotly contested battleground at the moment is Contra Costa County, near San Francisco. In June, county supervisors enacted an ordinance that prohibits any retail outlet larger than 90,000 square feet from devoting more than 5% of its floor space to food or other nontaxable goods. Wal-Mart promptly gathered enough signatures to force a referendum, scheduled for March. Complains County Supervisor John Gioia: "Local planning should be done by our locally elected board and not by a corporate office in Bentonville, Arkansas." Robert S. McAdam, Wal-Mart's vice-president for government relations, says corporate-sponsored referenda, which Wal-Mart has promoted elsewhere in California, are "a perfectly legitimate part of the process."

SUPERCENTER NATION

Meanwhile, the United Food & Commercial Workers union is stepping up its long-standing attempts to organize Wal-Mart stores, with current campaigns in 45 locations. For UFCW locals that represent grocery workers, the issue is nothing less than survival. The Wal-Mart supercenter—the principal vehicle of the company's expansion—is a nonunion dagger aimed at the heart of the traditional American supermarket, nearly 13,000 of which have closed since 1992.

Patterned after the European hypermarket, the supercenter is a combination supermarket and general merchandise discounter built to colossal scale. Wal-Mart didn't introduce the supercenter to America, but it has amassed a 79% share of the category since it moved into food and drug retailing by opening its first such store in 1988. Today, Wal-Mart operates 1,386 supercenters and is the nation's largest grocer, with a 19% market share, and its third-largest pharmacy, with 16%.

Wal-Mart plans to open 1,000 more supercenters in the U.S. alone over the next five years. Retail Forward estimates that this supercenter blitzkrieg will boost Wal-Mart's grocery and related revenues to $162 billion from the current $82 billion, giving it control over 35% of U.S. food sales and 25% of drugstore sales. Market-share gains of such magnitude in a slow-growth business necessarily will come at the expense of established competitors—especially the unionized ones, which pay their workers 30% more on average than Wal-Mart does, according to the UFCW. Retail Forward predicts that for every new supercenter that Wal-Mart opens, two supermarkets will close, or 2,000 all told.

To the low-price, low-cost operator go the spoils. Isn't that how capitalism is supposed to work? Certainly, the supercentering of America can be expected to result in huge savings at the cash register. On average, a Wal-Mart supercenter offers prices 14% below its rivals', according to a 2002 study by UBS Warburg.

However, those everyday low prices come at a cost. As the number of supermarkets shrinks, more shoppers will have to travel farther from home and will find their buying increasingly restricted to merchandise that Wal-Mart chooses to sell—a growing percentage of which may be the retailer's private-label goods, which now account for nearly 20% of sales. Meanwhile, the failure of hundreds of stores will cost their owners dearly and put thousands out of work, only some of whom will find jobs at Wal-Mart, most likely at lower pay. "It will be a sad day in this country if we wake up one morning and all we find is a Wal-Mart on every corner," says Gary E. Hawkins, CEO of Green Hills, a family-owned supermarket in Syracuse, N.Y.

For suppliers, too, Wal-Mart's relentless pricing pressure is a mixed blessing. "If you are good with data, are sophisticated, and have scale, Wal-Mart should be one of your most profitable customers," says a retired consumer-products executive. Unlike many retailers, the company does not charge "slotting fees" for access to its shelves and is unusually generous in sharing sales data with manufacturers. In return, though, Wal-Mart not only dictates delivery schedules and inventory levels but also heavily influences product specifications. In the end, many suppliers have to choose between designing goods their way or the Wal-Mart way. "Wal-Mart really is about driving the cost of a product down," says James A. Wier, CEO of Simplicity Manufacturing, a lawn-mower maker that decided to stop selling to Wal-Mart last fall. "When you drive the cost of a product down, you really can't deliver the high-quality product like we have."

Critics also argue that Wal-Mart's intensifying global pursuit of low-cost goods is partly to blame for the accelerating loss of U.S. manufacturing jobs to China and other low-wage nations. "It's hard to tease out, but Wal-Mart is definitely part of the dynamic, and given its market share and power, probably a significant part," says Jared Bernstein, a labor economist at the liberal

Wal-Mart by the Numbers

The world's largest company generates some amazing statistics

Supermarkets closed since Wal-Mart **saturated** Oklahoma City	**Turnover rate** for Wal-Mart's hourly workers per year	Number of Wal-Marts in Vermont, the **fewest of any state**	How much **lower** average grocery prices are where Wal-Mart competes	Percentage of **U.S. households** that made a Wal-Mart purchase last year	**Price drop** for George jeans at Britain's Asda since Wal-Mart bought it in '99
30	**44%**	**4**	**14%**	**82%**	**71%**
Data: Retail Forward, Inc.	Data: Wal-Mart Stores, Inc.	Data: Wal-Mart Stores, Inc.	Data: UBS Warburg	Data: Retail Forward, Inc.	Data: Wal-Mart Stores, Inc.

Economic Policy Institute. The $12 billion worth of Chinese goods Wal-Mart bought in 2002 represented 10% of all U.S. imports from China.

For obvious reasons, Wal-Mart has de-emphasized the "Made in America" campaign that founder Sam Walton started in the mid-1980s to great promotional effect. "Where we have the option to source domestically we do," says Ken Eaton, Wal-Mart's senior vice-president for global procurement. However, he adds, "there are certain businesses, particularly in the U.S., where you just can't buy domestically anymore to the scale and value we need." In recent years, Wal-Mart increasingly has sought additional cost advantages by bypassing middlemen and buying finished goods and raw materials from foreign manufacturers. By contracting directly with a handful of denim manufacturers in Southeast Asia, the company has driven down the retail price of the George brand jeans it sells in Britain and Germany to $7.85 from $26.67. Says Eaton: "The mind-set around here is, we're agents for our customers."

"THE WAL-MART PHENOMENON"

Wal-Mart's philosophy doesn't cut any ice with Wilbur L. Ross Jr., a financier and steel tycoon who soon will close on the purchase of beleaguered textile manufacturer Burlington Industries Inc. Ross contends that Wal-Mart is costing Americans jobs "not only as a business strategy, but as a lobbying strategy"—that is, by using its influence in Washington to oppose import tariffs and quotas and promote free-trade pacts with Third World countries, including the Southeast Asian countries that supply Wal-Mart with denim. "Everybody is now scurrying around trying to find the lowest price points," Ross complains. "It's the Wal-Mart phenomenon."

High on a wall inside Wal-Mart headquarters is a paper banner with a provocative question in big block letters: "Who's taking your customers?" Beneath it, "Wanted" poster style, hang photos of the CEOs of two dozen of America's largest retailers—Target, Kroger, Winn-Dixie Stores, Walgreen, and so on. None looks very happy, perhaps because they know that the only way to get off the wall is to fail utterly. Although Kmart is reorganizing under the federal bankruptcy code, a photo of its CEO continues to hang in Wal-Mart's rogues' gallery and no doubt will remain there for as long as Kmart operates even a single store.

Growth will only add to the clout that the Bentonville colossus now wields. There might well come a time, though, when Wal-Mart's size poses as much of a threat to the company itself as it does to outsiders. "Their biggest danger is just managing size," observes a longtime supplier. Adds Babson College's Hoopes: "The history of the last 150 years in retailing would say that if you don't like Wal-Mart, be patient. There will be new models eventually that will do Wal-Mart in, and Wal-Mart won't see it coming." Right now, though, Wal-Mart's day of reckoning seems a very long way off.

Deregulation harms public, group claims

MARILYN GEEWAX

Washington—The government's deregulation of five major industries—airlines, telecommunications, cable television, banking and electricity—has harmed customers far more than helped them, Consumers Union said Monday.

"The promises of deregulation have not been kept," said James Guest, president of the nonprofit consumer organization, which originally supported airline deregulation as a way to lower prices.

Instead of promoting vigorous competition, deregulation legislation has been written in ways that leave consumers at the mercy of "a Wild West marketplace," he said.

Guest said Consumers Union conducted a comprehensive study to determine how deregulation has affected prices, consumer satisfaction, safety, choice and innovation.

The study, published in the July issue of Consumer Reports magazine, concludes that deregulation has caused a sharp deterioration in service and dramatic increases in hidden fees and loopholes.

The results help explain why Consumers Union's mailbags are "overflowing, stuffed with complaints" from fed-up Americans, he said.

Airline passengers are among the most aggrieved, he said. Since the government deregulated airfares, schedules and routes in 1978, passengers have had to contend with more connections, flight delays, cramped seats and limited service in smaller markets, he said.

Deregulation supporters boast that fares have been falling for the past two decades. But Guest said the study shows fares fell just as rapidly in the two decades before deregulation. Moreover, before 1978, most fares were unrestricted, allowing passengers far more freedom.

Guest said the study shows Congress should make a "midcourse correction" by increasing regulation of cable TV and local telephone service and imposing a moratorium on residential electricity deregulation.

Consumers Union also wants bank regulators to crack down on predatory lending and hidden fees. It also wants antitrust enforcers to end the near-monopoly some airlines have at the "hub" airports.

Consumers Union's conclusion was rejected by Fred L. Smith Jr., president of the Competitive Enterprise Institute, a Washington-based group opposed to heavy regulation.

Smith said that without deregulation, airline travel would still be "restricted to the upper class," televisions would get just three stations, phones would come only in black and "on Friday, you'd be frantic at 3 p.m. because you forgot to get to the bank in time to cash a check."

Today's consumer problems stem from a failure to more fully deregulate, Smith said.

"Deregulation was a process," he said, "but we froze the process halfway along" so, for example, consumers are hurt by having airlines set fares, while allowing government to control airports and traffic control systems that limit capacity.

"When you free up only one part of the system, you end up with some real problems," he said.

The Consumers Union report said deregulation had hurt consumers in industries besides aviation.

In the banking industry, loans now cost more than before government deregulated savings rates and lending standards in the early 1980s, the study found. In addition, fees have increased and bank failure rates are high, it said.

In cable TV, monthly rates have risen much faster than the overall inflation rate, and consumer satisfaction is "bottom of the barrel," Guest said. About 95 percent of households have access to only one cable company, and many households cannot take advantage of competition from satellite TV, he said.

Customer satisfaction varies in electricity markets, because in some states, choices are abundant, the study found. But in others, such as California, higher prices and blackouts have resulted.

Today's telecom industry provides customers with more choices in phone equipment and long-distance service, but few alternatives for local service, according to the study.

While natural gas deregulation was not a part of the study, Georgia's 1997 experi-

DEREGULATION HISTORY THROUGH THE YEARS

ELECTRIC UTILITIES

Deregulated 1992
Average revenue per 100 kilowatt hours
- Price change in nine years before deregulation: minus 18.5 percent
- Price change in nine years after deregulation: minus 14.9 percent

LONG-DISTANCE TELEPHONE

Partially deregulated 1984
AT&T rate for a 10-minute, 200-mile daytime call
- Change in 15 years before deregulation: minus 34.3 percent
- Change in 15 years after deregulation: minus 60.4 percent

LOCAL TELEPHONE

Average monthly base rate for a residential access line
- Change in four years before deregulation: minus 7.7 percent
- Change in four years after deregulation: minus 3.5 percent

AIRLINES

Deregulated 1978
Average fare per 100 passenger miles
- Price change in 22 years before deregulation: minus 38.0 percent
- Price change in 22 years after deregulation: minus 38.3 percent

CABLE TV

Deregulated 1984; re-regulated 1992
Average monthly revenue per subscriber
- Price change in eight years before deregulation: minus 23.7 percent
- Price change in eight years after deregulation: plus 57.4 percent

Deregulated again 1996
Bureau of Labor Statistics Cable TV price index
- Change in 40 months before deregulation: plus 10.4 percent
- Change in 40 months after deregulation: plus 23.1 percent

Source: Consumers Union

ence with deregulating natural gas has, by most accounts, failed to deliver hoped-for lower prices and improved customer service.

Billing problems and marketer bankruptcies marred the transition as all customers were shifted from longtime monopoly Atlanta Gas Light Co. to unregulated marketers. Then the deregulated system was widely blamed for failing to contain natural gas prices in the winter of 2000-01.

The Legislature this year enacted a law designed to fix the most serious flaws.

The Slippery Scope of Antitrust Law

Leslie Walker

Attempting to regulate antitrust in the age of convergence is like trying to grab jellyfish in the ocean: More and more companies are combining themselves into strange globs as they seek to compete in digital markets as murky as the sea.

That, however, hasn't stopped federal regulators from trying to get their hands around these squishy new creatures.

For the past year or so, the Justice Department has been conducting antitrust investigations into Internet joint ventures formed by market leaders in five industries—music, movies, travel, bond trading and foreign-currency trading—to make sure they aren't doing things online that would be considered anti-competitive if they took place offline.

"The Sherman Antitrust Act absolutely reaches into cyberspace. You can't have virtual smoke-filled rooms," said Mark Popofsky, a former Justice Department lawyer who represents clients in the targeted industries.

To exploit the Internet's potential to distribute goods digitally, companies in many industries have been joining forces to create new online ventures. The goals typically are to share costs and maximize their impact beyond what any single player could do alone.

But the same technology that allows for more efficient communication and selling online also makes it easier—at least theoretically—for rivals to engage in prohibited activities such as price fixing and excluding competitors from key markets.

Already, those left on the sidelines have complained to federal regulators that the leaders in their respective markets are unfairly trying to curb competition through Web sites they own jointly.

Those under investigation include Orbitz, the online travel agency formed by the five largest airlines in the United States; Pressplay and MusicNet, digital-music subscription services created by the five major record labels; Movielink, a digital-movie downloading service still under development by several Hollywood studios; FXall, an online currency-trading exchange owned by 17 of the world's largest banks; and online fixed-income investing services such as BondDesk.com, Bond Book and Market Axess, developed by groups of financial firms on Wall Street.

Gina Talamona, spokeswoman for the Justice Department, confirmed that the agency is investigating Internet joint ventures in all five industries but would not comment on specifics.

The antitrust heat has been so fierce that at least one Internet joint venture fell apart before it got off the ground: In April, News Corp.'s Fox Entertainment Group abruptly withdrew from a service it was planning with Walt Disney Co. to sell movies online, citing regulatory concerns as a key reason.

As federal lawyers issue requests for information to companies involved, Congress is starting to weigh in with its own concerns.

Rep. Cliff Stearns (R-Fla.), chairman of the House Energy and Commerce Committee's subcommittee on commerce, trade and consumer protection, said through a spokesman that he wants to hold a hearing to look into the issues involved, especially in travel and foreign-currency trading. No date has been set yet.

"I have been carefully following the development of supplier-owned online distribution networks," Stearns said earlier this month.

Companies joining forces contend that their online consortiums will benefit consumers by making their businesses more efficient and creating cost savings that can be passed on to customers. Most are pursuing individual Web sites, too, some of which compete with their own joint ventures.

Orbitz contends it and other joint ventures are part of the Internet's inevitable march toward eliminating middlemen (think travel agents) who distribute goods in the non-digital world, because the computer network for the first time makes it more practical for producers of many goods (airline tickets, movies, music) to digitize and sell them electronically to consumers.

To do so, however, requires producers to explore entirely new business models. After all, many never sold directly to consumers before and lack experience at retailing. They find it inefficient to underwrite direct selling alone and have been merging, partnering and collaborating with rivals partly to share costs and also to aggregate content in ways that big retailers typically do and shoppers have come to expect.

Regulators are struggling to get their arms around these squishy new corporate entities. They're probing their governance rules, for instance, to make sure the joint ventures don't operate under inherently anti-competitive rules.

While the Justice Department is looking at supplier-owned online marketplaces today, the Federal Trade Commission two years ago took a look at similar buyer-owned exchanges formed to achieve efficiencies in procuring supplies online.

The FTC concluded that Covisint, a jointly owned Web site where automakers buy parts, did not violate antitrust laws. It gave Covisint a yellow light to operate with caution but said regulators would continue monitoring how the procurement exchange evolved.

Still, some companies excluded from such marketplaces are crying foul. A group of competing Internet ticketing agencies, for example, has complained that Orbitz requires its member airlines to give their lowest Web fares to Orbitz, a benefit not guaranteed to other travel sites. The Interactive Travel Services Association, which represents Expedia.com, Travelocity and other travel services, contends the requirement could cripple the competition that helped build the nascent Web travel market.

"What Orbitz is doing is illegal—you have five horizontal competitors that are working together to control distribution," said Antonella Pianalto, ITSA's executive director. "We feel that is a violation of antitrust law."

At the urging of Congress, the Transportation Department recently formed a commission to probe these issues in the travel industry. William Maloney, executive vice president of the American Society of Travel Agents, told the commission last week that the airlines' Internet distribution policies are designed to induce people not to buy through travel agents.

"If the airlines succeed at their long-run goal," Maloney said in a prepared statement, "consumers will have less access to optimized comparative price and service information for air travel and will pay higher than necessary prices."

Orbitz retorts that the special Web fares are not exclusively available on Orbitz. The airlines are free, if they choose, to display them on rival Web sites as well. Orbitz Vice President Carol Jouzaitis said the requirement that member airlines display their lowest fares on Orbitz was extracted in exchange for Orbitz promising the airlines that it would steadily lower their transaction costs each year for the next decade.

Similar issues are arising elsewhere. In the online market for foreign-currency trading, federal lawyers are looking at a requirement the FXall exchange imposed on its founding banks that they not participate in rival online services. The Internet music market is more complicated because of rampant music piracy, which has made the record labels cautious about distributing their music online. Nonetheless, some independently owned Web sites have groused that the labels seem more interested in licensing music to their own sites than in offering the same or similar terms to independent Internet services.

Jonathan Potter, executive director of the Digital Media Association, said the era of digital content distribution opens up worrisome possibilities for the labels to control distribution more tightly and in ways they never could offline.

Imagine, he said, that Henry Ford had invented a steering wheel but licensed it only to manufacturers who agreed to make black cars, or ones that went only 45 mph. He fears similar scenarios might unfold as the labels enter direct music retailing through their own subscription services and negotiate licensing terms for resale of their music through other Web sites.

"If the intellectual property is broadly licensed, and the licensees compete against one another, consumers win," Potter said. "If the intellectual property is broadly licensed but the competitors are not permitted by terms of the license to compete, then consumers lose."

The Real Price of Gas

Executive Summary
This report by the International Center for Technology Assessment (CTA) identifies and quantifies the many external costs of using motor vehicles and the internal combustion engine that are not reflected in the retail price Americans pay for gasoline. These are costs that consumers pay indirectly by way of increased taxes, insurance costs, and retail prices in other sectors.

The report divides the external costs of gasoline usage into five primary areas: (1) Tax Subsidization of the Oil Industry; (2) Government Program Subsidies; (3) Protection Costs Involved in Oil Shipment and Motor Vehicle Services; (4) Environmental, Health, and Social Costs of Gasoline Usage; and (5) Other Important Externalities of Motor Vehicle Use. Together, these external costs total $558.7 billion to $1.69 trillion per year, which, when added to the retail price of gasoline, result in a per gallon price of $5.60 to $15.14.

TAX SUBSIDIES

The federal government provides the oil industry with numerous tax breaks designed to ensure that domestic companies can compete with international producers and that gasoline remains cheap for American consumers. Federal tax breaks that directly benefit oil companies include: the Percentage Depletion Allowance (a subsidy of $784 million to $1 billion per year), the Nonconventional Fuel Production Credit ($769 to $900 million), immediate expensing of exploration and development costs ($200 to $255 million), the Enhanced Oil Recovery Credit ($26.3 to $100 million), foreign tax credits ($1.11 to $3.4 billion), foreign income deferrals ($183 to $318 million), and accelerated depreciation allowances ($1.0 to $4.5 billion).

Tax subsidies do not end at the federal level. The fact that most state income taxes are based on oil firms' deflated federal tax bill results in undertaxation of $125 to $323 million per year. Many states also impose fuel taxes that are lower than regular sales taxes, amounting to a subsidy of $4.8 billion per year to gasoline retailers and users. New rules under the Taxpayer Relief Act of 1997 are likely to provide the petroleum industry with additional tax subsidies of $2.07 billion per year. In total, annual tax breaks that support gasoline production and use amount to $9.1 to $17.8 billion.

PROGRAM SUBSIDIES

Government support of US petroleum producers does not end with tax breaks. Program subsidies that support the extraction, production, and use of petroleum and petroleum fuel products total $38 to $114.6 billion each year. The largest portion of this total is federal, state, and local governments' $36 to $112 billion worth of spending on the transportation infrastructure, such as the construction, maintenance, and repair of roads and bridges. Other program subsidies include funding of research and development ($200 to $220 million), export financing subsidies ($308.5 to $311.9 million), support from the Army Corps of Engineers ($253.2 to $270 million), the Department of Interior's Oil Resources Management Programs ($97 to $227 million), and government expenditures on regulatory oversight, pollution cleanup, and liability costs ($1.1 to $1.6 billion).

PROTECTION SUBSIDIES

Beyond program subsidies, governments, and thus taxpayers, subsidize a large portion of the protection services required by petroleum producers and users. Foremost among these is the cost of military protection for oil-rich regions of the world. US Defense Department spending allocated to safeguard the world's petroleum resources total some $55 to $96.3 billion per year. The Strategic Petroleum Reserve, a federal government entity designed to supplement regular oil supplies in the event of disruptions due to military conflict or natural disaster, costs taxpayers an additional $5.7 billion per year. The Coast Guard and the Department of Transportation's Maritime Administration provide other protection services totaling $566.3 million per year. Of course, local and state governments also provide protection services for oil industry companies and gasoline users. These externalized police, fire, and emergency response expenditures add up to $27.2 to $38.2 billion annually.

ENVIRONMENTAL, HEALTH AND SOCIAL COSTS

Environmental, health, and social costs represent the largest portion of the externalized price Americans pay for their gasoline reliance. These expenses total some $231.7 to $942.9 billion every year. The internal combustion engine contributes heavily to localized air pollution. While the amount of damage that automobile fumes cause is certainly very high, the total dollar value is rather difficult to quantify. Approximately $39 billion per year is the lowest minimum estimate made by researchers in the field of transportation cost analysis, although the actual total is surely much higher and may exceed $600 billion.

Considering that researchers have conclusively linked auto pollution to increased health problems and mortality, the CTA report's estimate of $29.3 to $542.4 billion for the annual uncompensated health costs associated with auto emissions may not adequately reflect the value of lost or diminished human life. Other costs associated with localized air pollution attributable to gasoline-powered automobiles include decreased agricultural yields ($2.1 to $4.2 billion), reduced visibility ($6.1 to $44.5 billion), and damage to buildings and materials ($1.2 to $9.6 billion). Global warming ($3 to $27.5 billion), water pollution ($8.4 to $36.8 billion), noise pollution ($6 to $12 billion), and improper disposal of batteries, tires, engine fluids, and junked cars ($4.4 billion) also add to the environmental consequences wrought by automobiles.

Some of the costs associated with the real price of gasoline go beyond the effects of acquiring and burning fuel to reflect social conditions partially or wholly created by the automobile's preeminence in the culture of the United States. Chief among these conditions is the growth of urban sprawl. While monetizing the impact of sprawl may prove a challenging endeavor, several researchers have done significant work on the subject. The costs of sprawl include: additional environmental degradation (up to $58.4 billion), aesthetic degradation of cultural sites (up to $11.7 billion), social deterioration (up to $58.4 billion), additional municipal costs (up to $53.8 billion), additional transportation costs (up to $145 billion), and the barrier effect ($11.7 to $23.4 billion). Because assessment of the costs of sprawl is somewhat subjective and because study of the topic remains in a nascent stage, the CTA report follows the lead of other researchers in field of transportation cost analysis and reduces the total of the potential cost of sprawl by 25% to 50% to arrive at a total of $163.7 to $245.5 billion per year.

OTHER EXTERNAL COSTS

Finally, external costs not included in the first four categories amount to $191.4 to $474.1 billion per year. These include: travel delays due to road congestion ($46.5 to $174.6 billion), uncompensated damages caused by car accidents ($18.3 to $77.2 billion), subsidized parking ($108.7 to $199.3 billion), and insurance losses due to automobile-related climate change ($12.9 billion). The additional cost of $5.0 to $10.1 billion associated with US dependence on imported oil could rise substantially, totaling $7.0 to $36.8 billion, in the event of a sudden price increase for crude oil.

RECOMMENDATIONS

The ultimate result of the externalization of such a large portion of the real price of gasoline is that consumers have no idea how much fueling their cars actually costs them. The majority of people paying just over $1 for a gallon of gasoline at the pump has no idea that through increased taxes, excessive insurance premiums, and inflated prices in other retail sectors that that same gallon of fuel is actually costing them between $5.60 and $15.14. When the price of gasoline is so drastically underestimated in the minds of drivers, it becomes difficult if not impossible to convince them to change their driving habits, accept alternative fuel vehicles, support mass transit, or consider progressive residential and urban development strategies.

The first step toward getting the public to recognize the damage caused by the United States' gasoline dependence is getting the public to recognize how much they are paying for this damage. The best way, in turn, to accomplish this goal is to eliminate government tax subsidies, program subsidies, and protection subsidies for petroleum companies and users, and to internalize the external environmental, health, and social costs associated with gasoline use. This would mean that consumers would see the entire cost of burning gasoline reflected in the price they pay at the pump. Drivers faced with the cost of their gasoline usage up front may have a more difficult time ignoring the harmful effects that their addiction to automobiles and the internal combustion engine have on national security, the environment, their health, and their quality of life.

Patent Medicine

BY DEAN BAKER

Absurdly high prices have put lifesaving prescription drugs out of reach for millions of Americans and for hundreds of millions of people in developing countries. In large part, patent protection is to blame. The patent system is a trade-off: Consumers pay a monopoly price on a drug for 17 years to provide incentives for firms to undertake research that yields large profits. But the patent system is not the only way to support drug research. Alternatives that have a proven track record of success already exist—specifically, research supported by foundations, universities, and the government. Shortening patent terms and putting most pharmaceutical research in the public domain would cut costs for consumers as well as for government. And contrary to industry propaganda, doing so would not reduce innovation.

This idea may sound radical, but look at the numbers. The drug industry currently spends around $18 billion a year on socially useful research. If research spending grows at a real rate of 3 percent annually, expenditures would total about $240 billion over the next decade. By comparison, the prescription drug plan proposed by Al Gore would cost $250 billion. If the government just picked up the full tab for drug research and did away with patent protection, most seniors would end up paying less for drugs than if the Gore plan were put in place. The federal government would save $10 billion right off the bat, in addition to savings on drug costs incurred in Medicare or Medicaid. And the rest of the population would pay 75 percent less for prescriptions.

When the patent system for prescription drugs is challenged, or when price controls or liberalized importation rules are proposed, we're warned about the perils of stifling innovation and tampering with the market. But patents are themselves a market distortion—an explicit form of government intervention: The government grants a prize (a 17-year monopoly) to people who innovate. This monopoly in effect transfers income from consumers to pharmaceutical companies. But this is neither the only nor the most efficient way to promote innovation.

> If we believe in free trade, it makes no sense to give long-term patent protection to pharmaceutical companies.

Pricing patterns in nations without effective patent protection, and on drugs after their patent has expired, suggest that the free market price for drugs averages about one-quarter of the monopoly price. In the United States, which spent approximately $106 billion last year on prescription drugs, consumers would save $79 billion if this patent protection were dropped.

What consumers get for this $79 billion in higher drug prices is $22.5 billion in domestic research from the pharmaceutical industry (another $4 billion is conducted abroad). Consumers pay more than three and a half dollars to the drug industry for every dollar of research induced by patent protection. Another two and a half dollars goes to industry profits and marketing—and to the legal costs, campaign contributions, and political lobbying needed to protect and extend the industry's patent monopolies.

Worse, much of the research conducted by the drug companies is directed not toward breakthroughs to better our lives but toward finding ways around the lucrative patents of competitors. When a drug company scores a big hit with a drug like Viagra or Claritin, competitors patent comparable but slightly different drugs so that they can enjoy a slice of the market. In a world with patent protection, this kind of limited competition can be beneficial to consumers. After all, some competition is better than none; also, a copycat drug may incidentally benefit people who react poorly to the original drug. In a competitive market, however, pure copycat research would be dropped in favor of research funded by public sources and likely to produce real improvements. [See Merrill Goozner, "The Price Isn't Right," *TAP*, September 11, 2000.]

It is difficult to pin down how much of the industry's research spending is devoted to copycat drugs. When assessing the importance of new drugs, the Food and Drug Administration (FDA) has historically considered fewer than one-third to be qualitatively new drugs. Of course, on average, new drugs cost far more to develop than replacements for existing drugs. But even if just 20 percent of the pharmaceutical industry's research were seen as wasted in copycat efforts and therefore cut, the industry's annual research budget would drop from $22.5 billion to $18 billion a year.

Prescription drugs present a classic case of asymmetric information: The drug companies know more about their drugs than the doctors who prescribe them, and far more than the patients who take them. Monopoly profits are an enormous incentive for companies to overstate the benefits and understate the risks of the newest wonder drugs. In fact, there is evidence that published research findings may be influenced by the drug industry's support. As Philip J. Hilts pointed out in *The New York Times,* when drugs were tested by researchers who were supported by the drug's manufacturer, they were found to be significantly more effective than existing ones 89 percent of the time. In contrast, when drugs were tested by neutral researchers, they were found to be significantly more effective only 61 percent of the time.

One recent study (by O.M. Shapira and colleagues at Boston University, in the September 2000 issue of *The Annals of Thoracic Surgery*) estimated that consumers waste $6 billion a year on patented calcium channel blockers, which are no more effective than generic alternatives in treating heart problems. Many other studies have also found that widely used drugs are often no more effective than cheaper alternatives. The costs are even greater when distorted information endangers health through the use of less effective drugs or ones that have harmful side effects. Monopoly drug pricing creates room for a gray market and black market in prescription drugs. The former got considerable attention recently as the result of several highly publicized bus trips to Canada by senior citizens seeking lower drug prices. While there is probably little basis for concern about the quality of drugs in Canada, the same may not be true of drugs sold in Mexico and other developing nations. Furthermore, as backdoor channels of drug supply develop, more and more drug use is likely to occur without doctor supervision. Since the mixing of drugs is often dangerous, and since patients may react differently to the same drug, the lack of proper supervision is a recipe for disaster.

Fortunately, there is an alternative to patent monopolies, and it is not merely hypothetical. Though the pharmaceutical industry is spending $22.5 billion on drug research each year, by the industry's own estimate this is less than half of the total annual amount spent on biomedical research in the United States. The largest chunk of the rest, about $15 billion, comes from the federal government through the National Institutes of Health (NIH). Another $3 billion is provided by other federal agencies, such as the Centers for Disease Control and Prevention. Universities, private foundations, and charities together fund approximately $10 billion worth of research annually.

The research supported by government and nonprofit institutions has led to numerous medical breakthroughs over the years, including the discovery and development of penicillin and the polio vaccine. More recently, NIH-supported research played a central role in the development of AZT (azidothymidine) as an AIDS drug, and Taxol, one of the leading cancer drugs. The impressive list of accomplishments at the NIH contradicts the claim that somehow the government cannot support effective research.

Historically, the NIH has focused on basic research and early phases of drug testing, whereas the pharmaceutical industry has been primarily engaged in the later phases of testing, which include clinical trials and carrying drugs through the FDA-approval process. But this division of labor is arbitrary. The NIH has done research in all areas of drug development; in some cases, the agency has even secured FDA approval. There is no reason to believe that, given enough funding, the institutes could not oversee all phases of drug research at least as effectively as the pharmaceutical industry does at present.

It is worth noting that there is a long history of publicly minded research scientists who have worked out of a desire to save lives, not to enrich themselves. For example, Selman Waksman labored for decades at Rutgers University before he eventually discovered that streptomycin could be an effective cure for tuberculosis. Even though he did get a patent on streptomycin, he used the royalties to finance an institute devoted to the study of other infectious diseases. Jonas Salk, another socially conscious scientist, developed the polio vaccine and never sought to patent it; his research in this area was supported by the National Foundation for Infantile Paralysis. Howard Florey, who discovered a method to mass-produce doses of penicillin, also never patented his process. Because he continued his research during World War II, with support from the Department of Agriculture, penicillin was widely available by the war's end to treat wounded soldiers. Few of these scientists became multimillionaires, but all were well-compensated professionals. This subculture of research motivated by the search for scientific knowledge and the quest for drugs to provide broadly diffused benefits is now at risk. The push for industry profits is crowding out other goals and turning scientists into moguls. The elimination of patent protection would not require researchers to act strictly from humanitarian motives. With tens of billions of research dollars available, there would be ample resources to reward scientists for advancing knowledge in public health.

Under the patent system, by contrast, there is increasing pressure on our best researchers to devote their skills to figuring out how to help rich people look young forever or have tall children. Patents on designer drugs in these areas are likely to be lucrative. A quite different form of government intervention would place a higher priority on, say, research directed toward curing sickle-cell anemia or malaria. (Even without patents, the wealthy would be free to support research on drugs that will improve their lifestyle; they just wouldn't be able to count on the government to help them recover their expenses.) And with a different system, poor people throughout the world would not be denied access to medicine by a government-sanctioned monopoly even when they are prepared to pay the free market price.

If we believe in free trade, it makes no sense to give long-term patent protections to pharmaceuticals. In reality, prescription drugs are a social good. Like other medical services, we should distribute them on the basis of need; one way or another, we end up paying for their retail costs socially. It would be more efficient to pay for their research and development socially as well.

DEAN BAKER is co-director of the Center for Economic and Policy Research.

The Eco-economic Revolution

Getting the Market in Sync with Nature

If we want economic progress to continue, we must systematically restructure the global economy to make it environmentally sustainable. Here's a description of a future eco-economy, along with tips on future industries and job possibilities.

By Lester R. Brown

Today's global economy has been shaped by market forces, not by the principles of ecology. Unfortunately, by failing to reflect the full costs of goods and services, the market provides misleading information to economic decision makers at all levels. This has created a distorted economy that is out of sync with the earth's ecosystem—an economy that is destroying its natural support systems.

An economy is sustainable only if it respects the principles of ecology. These principles are as real as those of aerodynamics. If an aircraft is to fly, it has to satisfy certain principles of thrust and lift. So, too, if an economy is to sustain progress, it must satisfy the basic principles of ecology. If it does not, it will decline and eventually collapse. There is no middle ground. An economy is either sustainable or it is not.

The market does not recognize basic ecological concepts of sustainable yield, nor does it respect the balances of nature. For example, it pays no attention to the growing imbalance between carbon emissions and nature's capacity to "fix" carbon, much less to the role of burning fossil fuels in creating the imbalance. For most economists, a rise in carbon dioxide levels is of little concern. For an ecologist, such a rise—driven by the use of fossil fuels—is a signal to shift to other energy sources in order to avoid rising temperatures, melting ice, and rising sea level.

An eco-economy would be one that satisfies our needs without jeopardizing the prospects of future generations to meet their needs. Creating such an economy is not a trivial undertaking; it is nothing less than an Environmental Revolution.

Ecology Over Economics

Ecologists understand the processes that support life on Earth. They understand the fundamental role of photosynthesis, the concept of sustainable yield, the role of nutrient cycles, the hydrological cycle, the sensitive role of climate, and the intricate relationship between the plant and animal kingdoms. They know that the earth's ecosystems supply services as well as goods and that the former are often more valuable than the latter.

A sustainable economy respects the sustainable yield of the ecosystems on which it depends: fisheries, forests, rangelands, and croplands. A particular fishery can sustain a catch of a certain size, but if the demands on the fishery exceed the sustainable yield by even 2% a year, the fish stocks will begin to shrink and will eventually disappear. As long as the harvest does not exceed the sustainable yield, it can be sustained in perpetuity. The same is true for forests and rangelands.

Nature also relies on balances. These include balances between soil erosion and new soil formation, between carbon emissions and carbon fixation, and between trees dying and trees regenerating.

Nature depends on cycles to maintain life. In nature, there are no linear flow-throughs, no situations where raw materials go in one end and garbage comes out the other. In nature, one organism's waste is another's sustenance, and nutrients are continuously cycled. This system works. Our challenge is to emulate it in the design of the economy.

Ecologists appreciate the role of photosynthesis, the process by which plants convert solar energy into the biochemical energy that supports life on the earth. Anything that reduces the photosynthetic product, such as desertification, the paving of productive land, or the acidification of lakes by acid rain, reduces the productivity of the earth in the most fundamental sense.

Despite this long-standing body of ecological knowledge, national governments have expanded economic activity with little regard for sustainable yields or the fragile balances in nature. Over the last half century, the sevenfold expansion of the global economy has pushed the demand on local ecosystems beyond the sustainable yield in country after country. The fivefold growth in the world fish catch since 1950 has pushed the demand of most oceanic fisheries past their ability to produce fish sustainably. The sixfold growth in the worldwide demand for paper is shrinking the world's forests. The doubling of the world's herds of cattle and flocks of sheep and goats since 1950 is damaging rangelands, converting them to desert.

The clear-cutting of a forest may be profitable for a logging firm, but it is economically costly to society.

An ecologist not only recognizes that the services provided by ecosystems may sometimes be worth more than the goods, but that the value of services needs to be calculated and incorporated into market signals if they are to be protected. Although calculating services is not a simple matter, any reasonable estimate is far better than assuming that the costs are zero, as is now the case. For example, a forest in the upper reaches of a watershed may provide services—such as flood control and the recycling of rainfall inland—that are several times more valuable than its timber yield. Unfortunately, market signals do not reflect this, because the loggers who are cutting the trees do not bear the costs of the reduction in services. National economic policies and corporate strategies are based largely on market signals. The clear-cutting of a forest may be profitable for a logging firm, but it is economically costly to society.

Another major failure of the market to provide reliable information comes when governments subsidize the depletion of resources or environmentally destructive activities. For example, over several decades the U.S. Forest Service used taxpayer money to build roads into national forests so that logging companies could clear-cut forests. This subsidy only artificially lowered the costs of lumber and paper, and it led to flooding, soil erosion, and the silting of streams and rivers. In the Pacific Northwest, it destroyed highly productive salmon fisheries. And all this destruction was underwritten by taxpayers.

In a world where the demands of the economy are pressing against the limits of natural systems, relying on distorted market signals to guide investment decisions is a recipe for disaster. Historically, for example, when the supply of fish was inadequate, the price would rise, encouraging investment in additional fishing trawlers. When there were more fish in the sea than we could ever hope to catch, the market worked well. Today, with the fish catch often exceeding the sustainable yield, investing in more trawlers in response to higher prices will simply accelerate the collapse of these fisheries.

A similar situation exists with other natural systems, such as aquifers, forests, and rangelands. Once the climbing demand for water surpasses the sustainable yield of aquifers, the water tables begin to fall and wells go dry. The market says drill deeper wells. Farmers engage in a competitive orgy of well drilling, chasing the water table downward. On the North China Plain, where 25% of the country's grain is produced, this process is under way. In Hebei Province, data for 1999 show 36,000 wells, mostly shallower ones, being abandoned during the year as 55,000 new, much deeper wells were drilled. In Shandong Province, 31,000 were abandoned and 68,000 new wells were drilled.

In an eco-economy, drilling additional wells would be banned once a water table showed signs of falling. Instead of spending money to dig deeper wells, investments would be channeled into measures to boost water efficiency and to stabilize population in order to bring water use into balance with the sustainable supply.

Evidence is accumulating that our global economy is slowly undermining itself on several fronts. If we want economic progress to continue, we have little choice but to systematically restructure the global economy in order to make it environmentally sustainable.

Imagining the Scope of Change

Converting our economy into an eco-economy is a monumental undertaking. There is no precedent for transforming an economy shaped largely by market forces into one shaped by the principles of ecology.

The scale of projected economic growth outlines the dimensions of the challenge. The growth in world output of goods and services from $6 trillion in 1950 to $43 trillion in 2000 has caused environmental devastation on a scale that we could not easily have imagined a half century ago. If the world economy continued to expand at 3% annually, the output of goods and services would increase fourfold over the next half century, reaching $172 trillion.

Building an eco-economy in the time available requires rapid systemic change. We will not succeed with a project here and a project there. We are winning occasional battles now, but we are losing the war because we do not have a strategy for the systemic economic change that will put the world on an environmentally sustainable development path.

Although the concept of environmentally sustainable development evolved a quarter century ago, not one country has a strategy to build an eco-economy—to restore carbon balances, to stabilize population and water tables, and to conserve its forests, soils, and diversity of plant and animal life. We can find individual countries that are succeeding with one or more elements of the restructuring, but not one that is progressing satisfactorily on all fronts.

Today's Economy vs. Tomorrow's Eco-Economy

Today's Economy	Eco-Economy
Shaped by market forces.	Respects principles of ecology.
Unsustainable: Maximizes profit regardless of consequences to the ecosystem.	Sustainable: Respects carrying capacity of systems; e.g., does not exceed sustainable oceanic fish catch.
Disregards nature's services.	Recognizes ecosystems' natural services.
Consumes dwindling supply of fossil fuels.	Relies on renewable resources such as wind, solar, and geothermal energy.
Pollutes the environment and destabilizes climate.	Minimal pollution, climate-neutral.
Carbon-based auto industry dependent on oil from politically unstable Middle East.	Hydrogen-based fuel-cell auto industry not reliant on specific country source.
Contributes to noisy, congested, and polluted cities.	Will create rail-centered, bicycle-friendly cities that offer less stress and pollution, more exercise.
Likely to decline in not-too-distant future as natural supplies deteriorate.	Will create major new industries; e.g., the wind industry will bring income and jobs from manufacturing, installation, and maintenance.

Source: *Eco-Economy*

An eco-economy would be one that satisfies our needs without jeopardizing the prospects of future generations to meet their needs.

Nevertheless, glimpses of the eco-economy are clearly visible in some countries. For example, 31 countries in Europe, plus Japan, have stabilized their population size, satisfying one of the most basic conditions of an eco-economy. Europe has stabilized its population within its food-producing capacity, leaving it with an exportable surplus of grain to help fill the deficits in developing countries. China—the world's most populous country—now has lower fertility than the United States and is moving toward population stability.

Denmark is the eco-economy leader. It has stabilized its population, banned the construction of coal-fired power plants, banned the use of non-refillable beverage containers, and is now getting 15% of its electricity from wind. In addition, it has restructured its urban transport network; now 32% of all trips in Copenhagen are on bicycle. Denmark is still not close to balancing carbon emissions and fixation, but it is moving in that direction.

Other countries have also achieved specific goals. A reforestation program in South Korea, begun more than a generation ago, has blanketed the country's hills and mountains with trees. Costa Rica has a plan to shift entirely to renewable energy by 2025. Iceland, working with a consortium of corporations led by Shell and DaimlerChrysler, plans to be the world's first hydrogen-powered economy.

So we can see pieces of the eco-economy emerging, but systemic change requires a fundamental shift in market signals—signals that respect the principles of ecological sustainability. Unless we are prepared to shift taxes from income to environmentally destructive activities, such as carbon emissions and the wasteful use of water, we will not succeed in building an eco-economy.

Restoring the balances of nature in energy production depends on shifting from a carbon-based economy to a hydrogen-based one. Even the most progressive oil companies, such as BP and Royal Dutch/Shell, that are talking extensively about building a solar/hydrogen energy economy are still investing overwhelmingly in oil, with funds going into climate-benign sources accounting for a minute share of their investment.

Reducing soil erosion to the level of new soil formation will require changes in farming practices. In some situations, it will mean shifting from intense tillage to minimum tillage or no tillage. Agroforestry will loom large in an eco-economy. Restoring forests that recycle rainfall inland and control flooding means reversing decades of tree cutting and land clearing with forest restoration, an activity that will require millions of people planting billions of trees.

Building an eco-economy will affect every facet of our lives. It will alter how we light our homes, what we eat, where we live, how we use our leisure time, and how many children we have. It will give us a world where we are a part of nature, instead of estranged from it.

Restructuring the Economy

We can now see what an eco-economy looks like. Instead of running on fossil fuels, it will be powered by renewable sources of energy, such as wind and sunlight, and by geothermal energy from within the earth. It will be hydrogen-based instead of carbon-based. Cars and buses will run on fuel-cell engines powered by electricity produced with an electrochemical process using hydrogen as the fuel instead of internal combustion engines. With fuel cells powered by hydrogen, there is no climate-disrupt-

Declining Industries in an Eco-Economy

Industry	Description
Coal mining	The 7% decline in world coal burning since it peaked in 1996 will continue in the years ahead.
Oil pumping	Projections based on shrinking oil reserves indicate production will peak and start declining in the next 5-20 years. Concern about global warming could bring the decline closer.
Nuclear power	Although public concern focuses on safety issues, it is the high cost that is ensuring the industry's decline.
Clear-cut logging	The rapid spread in eco-labeling of forest products will likely force logging firms to change to sustainable harvesting or be driven out of business.
Manufacture of throwaway products	As efforts to close the materials cycle intensify, many throwaway products will either be banned or taxed out of existence.
Automobile manufacturing	As world population urbanizes, the conflict between the automobile and the city will intensify, reducing dependence of automobiles.

Source: *Eco-Economy*

ing carbon dioxide or noxious health-damaging pollutants; only water is emitted.

In the new economy, atmospheric carbon dioxide levels will be stable. In contrast to today's energy economy, where the world's reserves of oil and coal are concentrated in a handful of countries, energy sources in the eco-economy will be widely dispersed—as widely distributed as sunlight and wind. The world's heavy dependence on the Middle East for much of its energy will likely decline as the new climate-benign energy sources and fuel-cell engines take over.

The energy economy will be essentially a solar/hydrogen economy with various energy sources deriving from the sun used either directly for heating and cooling or indirectly to produce electricity. Wind-generated electricity, which is likely to be the lowest-cost source of energy, will be used to electrolyze water, producing hydrogen. This provides a means of both storing and transporting wind energy. Initially, existing natural gas pipelines will be used to distribute hydrogen. But over the longer term, both natural gas and oil pipeline networks can be adapted to carry hydrogen as the world shifts from a carbon-based to a hydrogen-based economy.

The transport systems of cities have already begun to change. Instead of the noisy, congested, polluting, auto-centered transport systems of today, cities will have rail-centered transport systems, and they will be bicycle- and pedestrian-friendly, offering more mobility, more exercise, cleaner air, and less frustration.

Urban transport systems will have the same components as they do today: automobile, rail, bus, and bicycle. The difference will be in the mix. As more city planners recognize the inherent conflict between the automobile and the city, cleaner and more efficient transport systems will develop. Urban personal mobility will increase as automobile use and traffic congestion decline.

The materials sector of the eco-economy will look far different, too, as it shifts from the linear economic model, where materials go from the mine or forest to the landfill, to the reuse/recycle model, yielding no waste and nothing for the landfills.

One of the keys to reversing the deforestation of the earth is paper recycling; the potential here has been only partly realized. A second key is developing alternative energy sources that will reduce the amount of wood used as fuel. In addition, boosting the efficiency of wood burning can measurably lighten the load on forests.

Another promising option is the use of carefully designed, ecologically managed, and highly productive tree plantations. A small area devoted to plantations may be essential to protecting forests at the global level. Plantations can yield several times as much wood per hectare as can a natural forest.

Examples of Expanding Industries in an Eco-Economy

Industry	Description
Fish farming	Although growth will slow from the double-digit rate of the last decade, rapid expansion is likely to continue.
Bicycle manufacturing	Because bicycles are affordable, nonpolluting, quiet, require little parking space, and provide much-needed exercise in exercise-deprived societies, they will become increasingly common.
Wind-farm construction	Wind-electricity generation, including off-shore wind farms, will grow rapidly over the next few decades, until wind is supplying most of the world's electricity.
Wind-turbine manufacturing	Today the number of utility-scale wind turbines is measured in the thousands, but soon it will be measured in the millions, creating an enormous manufacturing opportunity.
Hydrogen generation	As the transition from a carbon-based to a hydrogen-based energy economy progresses, hydrogen generation will become a key industry.
Fuel-cell manufacturing	As fuel cells replace internal-combustion engines in automobiles and begin generating power in buildings, a huge market will evolve.
Solar-cell manufacturing	For many of the 2 billion people living in rural Third World communities who lack electricity, solar cells will be the best bet for electrification.
Light-rail construction	As people tire of the traffic congestion and pollution associated with the automobile, cities in industrial and developing countries alike will be turning to light rail to provide mobility.
Tree planting	As efforts to reforest the earth gain momentum and as tree plantations expand, tree planting will emerge as a leading economic activity.

Source: *Eco-Economy*

In the economy of the future, the use of water will be in balance with supply. Water tables will be stable, not falling. The economic restructuring will be designed to raise water productivity in every facet of economic activity.

In this environmentally sustainable economy, harvests from oceanic fisheries, a major source of animal protein in the human diet, will be reduced to the sustainable yield. Additional demand will be satisfied by fish farming. This is, in effect, an aquatic version of the same shift that occurred during the transition from hunting and gathering to farming. The freshwater, herbivorous carp polyculture on which the Chinese rely heavily for their vast production of farmed fish offers an ecological model for the rest of the world.

A somewhat similar situation exists for rangelands. One of the keys to alleviating the excessive pressure on rangelands is to feed livestock the crop residues that are otherwise being burned for fuel or for disposal. This trend, already well under way in India and China, may hold the key to stabilizing the world's rangelands.

And finally, the new economy will have a stable population. Over the longer term, the only sustainable society is one in which couples have an average of two children.

Creating New Industries

Describing the eco-economy is obviously a somewhat speculative undertaking. In the end, however, it is not as open ended as it might seem, because the eco-economy's broad outlines are defined by the principles of ecology.

What is not so clear is how ecological principles will translate into economic design. For example, each country has a unique combination of renewable energy sources that will power its economy. Some countries may draw broadly on all their renewable energy sources, while others may concentrate heavily on one that is particularly abundant, such as wind or solar energy. A country with a wealth of geothermal energy may choose to structure its energy economy around this subterranean energy source.

Building a new economy involves phasing out old industries, restructuring existing ones, and creating new ones. World coal use is already being phased out, dropping 7% since peaking in 1996. It is being replaced by efficiency gains in some countries, by natural gas in others (such as the United Kingdom and China), and by wind power in others (such as Denmark).

The automobile industry faces a major restructuring as it changes power sources, shifting from the gasoline-powered internal combustion engine to the hydrogen-powered fuel-cell engine. This shift from the explosive energy that derives from igniting gasoline vapor to a chemical reaction that generates electricity will require both a retooling of engine plants and the retraining of automotive engineers and automobile mechanics.

The new economy will also bring major new industries, ones that either do not yet exist or that are just beginning. Wind electricity generation is one such industry. Now in its embryonic stage, it promises to become the foundation of the new energy economy. Millions of turbines soon will be converting wind into electricity, becoming part of the global landscape. In many countries, wind will supply both electricity and, through the electrolysis of water, hydrogen. Together, electricity and hydrogen can meet all the energy needs of a modern society.

In effect, there will be three new subsidiary industries associated with wind power: turbine manufacturing, installation, and maintenance. Manufacturing facilities will be found in scores of countries, industrial and developing. Installation, which is basically a construction industry, will be more local in nature. Maintenance, since it is a day-to-day activity, will be a source of ongoing local employment.

The robustness of the wind turbine industry was evident in 2000 and 2001 when high-tech stocks were in a free fall worldwide. While high-tech firms as a group were performing poorly, sales of wind turbines were climbing, pushing the earnings of turbine manufacturers to the top of the charts. Continuing growth of this sector is expected for the next few decades.

As wind power emerges as a low-cost source of electricity and a mainstream energy source, it will spawn another industry: hydrogen production. Once wind turbines are in wide use, there will be a large, unused capacity during the night when the demand for electricity drops. With this essentially free electricity, turbine owners can turn on the hydrogen generators and convert the wind power into hydrogen, ideal for fuel-cell engines. Hydrogen generators will start to replace oil refineries. The wind turbine will replace both the coal mine and the oil well. Both wind turbines and hydrogen generators will be widely dispersed as countries take advantage of local wind resources.

Changes in the world food economy will also be substantial. Some of these, such as the shift to fish farming, are already under way. The fastest-growing subsector of he world food economy during the 1990s was aquaculture, expanding at more than 11% a year. Fish farming is likely to continue to expand simply because of its efficiency in converting grain into animal protein.

Even allowing for slower future growth in aquaculture, fish farm output will likely overtake beef production before 2010. Perhaps more surprising, fish farming could eventually exceed the oceanic fish catch. Indeed, for China—the world's leading consumer of seafood—fish farming already supplies two-thirds of the seafood, while the oceanic catch accounts for the other third. With this development, new jobs will be created: aquatic ecologist, fish nutritionist, and marine veterinarian.

Another growth industry of the future is bicycle manufacturing and servicing. Because the bicycle is nonpolluting, frugal in its use of land, and provides the exercise much needed in sedentary societies, future reliance on it is expected to grow. As recently as 1965, the production of cars and bikes was essentially the same, but today more than twice as many bikes as cars are manufactured each year. Among industrial countries, the urban transport model being pioneered in the Netherlands and Denmark, where bikes are featured prominently, gives a sense of the bicycle's future role worldwide.

As bicycle use expands, interest in electrically assisted bikes is also growing. These bikes are similar to existing bicycles, except for a tiny battery-powered electric motor that can either power the bicycle entirely or assist elderly riders or those living in hilly terrain, and their soaring sales are expected to continue climbing in the years ahead.

Just as the last half century has been devoted to raising land productivity, the next half century will be focused on another growth industry: raising water productivity. Virtually all societies will be turning to the management of water at the watershed level in order to manage available supply most efficiently. Irrigation technologies will become more efficient. Urban wastewater recycling will become common. At present, water tends to flow into and out of cities, carrying waste with it. In the future, water will be used over and over, never discharged. Since water does not wear out, there is no limit to how long it can be used, as long as it is purified before reuse.

Another industry that will play a prominent role in the new economy, one that will reduce energy use, is teleconferencing. Increasingly for environmental reasons and to save time, individuals will be "attending" conferences electronically with both audio and visual connections. This industry involves developing the electronic global infrastructure, as well as the services, to make teleconferencing possible. One day there may be thousands of firms organizing electronic conferences.

New Jobs in the Eco-Economy

Restructuring the global economy will create not only new industries, but also new jobs—indeed, whole new professions and new specialties within professions. For example, as wind becomes an increasingly prominent energy source, thousands of wind meteorologists will be needed to analyze potential wind sites, monitor wind speeds, and select the best sites for wind farms. The better the data on wind resources, the more efficient the industry will become.

Wind engineers will be hired to design customized wind turbines. The appropriate turbine size and design can vary widely according to site. It will be the job of wind engineers to tailor designs to specific wind regimes in order to maximize electricity generation.

Environmental architecture is another fast-growing profession. Among the signposts of an environmentally sustainable economy are buildings that are in harmony with the environment. Environmental architects design buildings that are energy- and materials-efficient and that maximize natural heating, cooling, and lighting. In a future of water scarcity, watershed hydrologists will be in demand. It will be their responsibility to understand the hydrological cycle, including the movement of underground water, and to know the depth of aquifers and determine their sustainable yield. They will be at the center of watershed management regimes.

As the world shifts from a throwaway economy, engineers will be needed to design products that can be recycled—from cars to computers. Once products are designed to be disassembled quickly and easily into component parts and materials, comprehensive recycling is relatively easy.

Technologies used in recycling are sometimes quite different from those used in producing from virgin raw materials. Within the U.S. steel industry, for example, where nearly 60% of all steel is produced from scrap, the technologies used differ depending on the feedstock. Steel manufactured in electric arc furnaces from scrap uses far less energy than traditional open-hearth furnaces using pig iron. Recycling engineers will be responsible for closing the materials loop, converting the linear flow-through economy into a comprehensive recycling economy.

In countries with a wealth of geothermal energy, it will be up to geothermal geologists to locate the best sites either for supplying power plants or for tapping directly to heat buildings. Retraining petroleum geologists to master geothermal technologies is one way of satisfying the likely surge in demand for geothermal geologists.

If the world is to stabilize population sooner rather than later, it will need far more family-planning midwives in Third World communities. This growth sector will be concentrated largely in developing countries, where millions of women lack access to family planning. The same family-planning counselors who advise on reproductive health and contraceptive use can also play a central role in controlling the spread of HIV.

In scale, the Environmental Revolution is comparable to the Agricultural and Industrial Revolutions that preceded it.

Another pressing need, particularly in developing countries, is for sanitation-system engineers who can design sewage systems not dependent on water, a trend that is already under way in some water-scarce countries. As it becomes clear that using water to wash waste away is a reckless use of a scarce resource, a new breed of sanitation engineers will be in wide demand. Washing waste away is even less acceptable today as marine ecosystems are overwhelmed by nutrient flows. Apart from the ecological disruption of a water-based disposal method, there are also much higher priorities in the use of water, such as drinking, bathing, and irrigation.

Yet another new specialty that is likely to expand rapidly in agriculture as productive farmland becomes scarce is that of the agronomist who specializes in multiple cropping and intercropping. This position requires expertise both in the selection of crops that can fit together well in a tight rotation in various locales and in agricultural practices that facilitate multiple cropping.

Investing in the Environmental Revolution

Restructuring the global economy so that economic progress can be sustained represents the greatest investment opportunity in history. The conceptual shift is comparable to that of the Copernican Revolution in the sixteenth century. In scale, the Environmental Revolution is comparable to the Agricultural and Industrial Revolutions that preceded it.

The Agricultural Revolution involved restructuring the food economy, shifting from a nomadic lifestyle based on hunting and gathering to a settled lifestyle based on tilling the soil. Although agriculture started as a supplement to hunting and gathering, it eventually replaced these practices almost entirely. The Agricultural Revolution entailed clearing one-tenth of the earth's land surface of either grass or trees so it could be plowed. Unlike the hunter-gatherer culture that had little effect on the earth, this new farming culture literally transformed the surface of the earth.

The Industrial Revolution has been under way for two centuries, although in some countries it is still in its early stages. At its foundation was a shift in sources of energy from wood to fossil fuels, a shift that set the stage for a massive expansion in economic activity. Indeed, its distinguishing feature is the harnessing of vast amounts of fossil energy for economic purposes. While the Agricultural Revolution transformed the earth's surface, the Industrial Revolution is transforming the earth's atmosphere.

The additional productivity that the Industrial Revolution made possible unleashed enormous creative energies. It also gave birth to new lifestyles and to the most environmentally destructive era in human history, setting the world firmly on a course of eventual economic decline. The Environmental Revolution resembles the Industrial Revolution in that each is dependent on the shift to a new energy source. And like both earlier revolutions, the Environmental Revolution will affect the entire world.

There are differences in scale, timing, and origin among the three revolutions. Unlike the other two, the Environmental Revolution must be compressed into a matter of decades. And while the other revolutions were driven by new discoveries and advances in technology, this revolution is being driven more by our instinct for survival.

Expanding Professions in an Eco-Economy

Profession	Description
Wind meteorologists	Wind meteorologists will play a role in the new energy economy comparable to that of petroleum geologists in the old one.
Family-planning midwives	If world population is to stabilize soon, literally millions of family-planning midwives will be needed.
Foresters	Reforesting the earth will require professional guidance on what tree species to plant where and in what combination.
Hydrologists	As water scarcity spreads, the demand for hydrologists to advise on watershed management, water sources, and water efficiency will increase.
Recycling engineers	Designing consumer applications so they can be easily disassembled and completely recycled will become an engineering specialty.
Aquacultural veterinarians	Until now, veterinarians have typically specialized in either large animals or small animals, but with fish farming likely to overtake beef production by 2010, marine veterinarians will be in demand.
Ecological economists	As it becomes clear that the basic principles of ecology must be incorporated into economic planning and policy making, the demand for economists able to think like ecologists will grow.
Geothermal geologists	With the likelihood that large areas of the world will turn to geothermal energy both for electricity and for heating, the demands for geothermal geologists will climb.
Environmental architects	Architects are learning the principles of ecology so they can incorporate them into the buildings where we will live and work.
Bicycle mechanics	As the world turns to the bicycle for transportation and exercise, bicycle mechanics will be needed to keep the fleet running.
Wind-turbine engineers	With millions of wind turbines likely to be installed in the decades ahead, there will be strong worldwide demand for wind-turbine engineers.

Source: *Eco-Economy*

There has not been an investment situation like this before. The amount that the world spends now each year on oil, the leading source of energy, provides some insight into how much it could spend on energy in the eco-economy. In 2000, the world used nearly 28 billion barrels of oil, some 76 million barrels per day. At $27 a barrel, the total comes to $756 billion per year. How many wind turbines, solar rooftops, and geothermal wells will it take to produce this much energy?

One big difference between the investments in fossil fuels and those in wind power, solar cells, and geothermal energy is that the latter will supply energy in perpetuity. These "wells" will not run dry. If the money spent on oil in one year were invested in wind turbines, the electricity generated would be enough to meet one-fifth of the world's needs.

Investments in the infrastructure for the new energy economy, which would eventually have to be made as fossil fuels are depleted, will obviously be huge. These include the transmission lines that connect wind farms with electricity consumers and the pipelines that link hydrogen supply sources with end users. Much of the infrastructure for the existing energy economy—the transmission lines for electricity and the pipelines for natural gas—can be used in the new energy economy as well. The local pipeline distribution network in various cities for natural gas can easily be converted to hydrogen.

For developing countries, the new energy sources promise to reduce dependence on imported oil, freeing up capital for investment in domestic energy sources. Although few countries have their own oil fields, all have wind and solar energy. In terms of economic expansion and job generation, these new energy technologies are a godsend.

Investments in energy efficiency are also likely to grow rapidly simply because they are so profitable. In virtually all countries, industrial and developing, saved energy is the cheapest source of new energy. Replacing inefficient incandescent light bulbs with highly efficient compact fluorescent lamps offers a rate of return that stock markets are unlikely to match.

There are also abundant investment opportunities in the food economy. It is likely that the world demand for seafood, for example, will increase at least by half over the next 50 years, and perhaps much more. If so, fish-farming output—now 31 million tons a year—will roughly need to triple, as will investments in fish farming. Although aquaculture's growth is likely to slow from the 11% a year of the last decade, it is nonetheless likely to be robust, presenting a promising opportunity for future investment.

A similar situation exists for tree plantations. At present, tree plantations cover some 113 million hectares (280 million acres). An expansion of these by at least half, along with a continuing rise in productivity, is likely to be needed both to satisfy future demand and to eliminate one of the pressures that are shrinking forests. This, too, presents a huge opportunity for investment. No sector of the global economy will be untouched by the Environmental Revolution. In this new economy, some companies will be winners and some will be losers. Those who anticipate the emerging eco-economy and plan for it will be the winners. Those who cling to the past risk becoming part of it.

About the Author
Lester R. Brown is board chairman of the Worldwatch Institute and president of the Earth Policy Institute, 1350 Connecticut Avenue, N.W., Washington, D.C. 20036. Telephone 1-202-496-9290; email epi@earth-policy.org; Web site www.earth-policy.org.

This article draws from his book, *Eco-Economy: Building an Economy for the Earth* (W.W. Norton, 2001, paperback), which is available from the Futurist Bookstore for $15.95 ($14.50 for Society members), cat. no. B-2382.

Originally published in the March/April 2002 issue of *The Futurist,* pp. 23-32. Used with permission from the World Future Society, 7910 Woodmont Avenue, Suite 450, Bethesda, Maryland 20814. Telephone: 310/656-8274; Fax: 301/951-0394; http://www.wfs.org.

CONGESTED PARKS— A PRICING DILEMMA

Dan M. Bechter

In the last year or two, newspapers and magazines have been calling attention to the problems caused by record numbers of people crowding into some of our national parks.[1] Yellowstone and Yosemite are receiving most of the publicity, but other national recreation areas are suffering similar popularity troubles. Many state and local parks, too, are being strained to accommodate rapidly increasing attendance. It is easy to conclude that these congestion difficulties justify creating new public parks and expanding outdoor recreation facilities in existing ones. Additions to supply would seem appropriate, considering the rising demand. Yet, the apparently inadequate recreational capacities of various public parks may reflect something other than a lag in adjustment of supply to demand. Governments may be distorting the recreation market by charging too little for the recreational use of public parks. Such an improper pricing practice would be misallocating resources. Some groups would be benefiting—perhaps those that are not intended to—at the expense of others. Economic analysis helps show the nature and probable consequences of the park crowding problem. It also helps reveal the complex and indirect influences on public park fees, the choices of consumers, and the markets for all recreational goods and services.

WHEN DEMAND CROWDS SUPPLY

Overflowing visitation at a public park provides a textbook display of a shortage. Park crowding means insufficient park space—or types of park space, such as camping space, driving space, fishing space, etc.—to satisfy outdoor recreationists. They want more. Their wants, however, depend directly on what they must pay. The existence of a shortage says only that the quantity demanded exceeds the quantity supplied at the going price. Excessive park crowding, therefore, reflects a park entry or a park privilege fee that is below the one that equates the amount of park space consumers want to the amount available. Chart 1 clarifies the explanation.

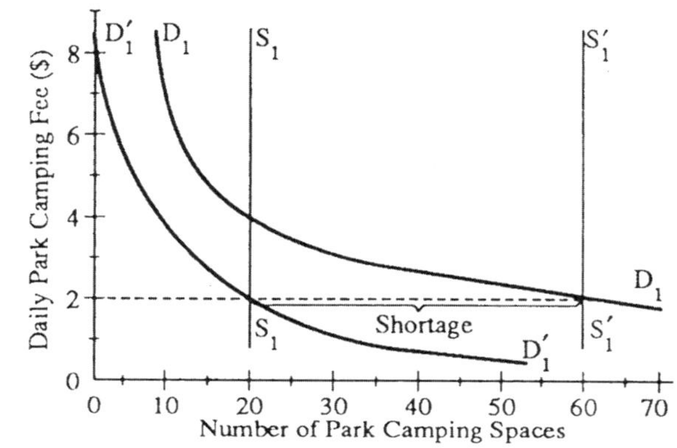

CHART 1

Chart 1 shows a set of demand and supply relationships for camping spaces in a hypothetical public park. Demand curve D_1D_1 shows that the lower the price, the larger the number of park camping spaces desired on an average summer day.[2] Vertical line S_{1S1} indicates the number of camping spaces in the park—assumed to be an invariable quantity in the very short run. Now, suppose park officials set the camping fee at $1. Clearly, quantity demanded (60 spaces) exceeds quantity supplied (20 spaces), or a shortage of 40 spaces prevails at that price.

What happens to the 40 camping families whom the park cannot accommodate? Those who can return home may disappointedly do so. Others may not show up, having heard about or previously experienced the shortage. Still others may try to squeeze and shoehorn into the camping area, or pitch their tents in unauthorized areas of the park. Some may find other public or private places to camp nearby. The remainder may stay in motels, sleep along the road, or drive all night.

As can be seen, selling a good or service below the market-clearing price—where demand equals supply, or $4, in the example simply requires other forms of rationing or adjustment, such as first come, first served, which places a premium on arrival time. Some of these adaptations, in effect, increase the cost of the outdoor recreation experience. They make the consumer spend extra time and money guaranteeing himself participation in the leisure activity. Other adjustments, such as crowding into available space, make outdoor recreation less fun.

The shortage shown in Chart 1—or any market shortage, for that matter—can be reduced by (a) increasing price, (b) increasing supply, (c) decreasing demand, or (d) a combination of the preceding. Before considering these solutions, consider a part of what is going on outside the park.

Chart 2 shows another set of supply and demand curves—those for camping spaces on private land near the hypothetical public park. Currently, entrepreneurs are making 18 such spaces available, charging the going-market price of $2.50. Note that quantity demanded equals quantity supplied at this price—no shortage here. On a day of normal demand, everyone who wants to camp in a private area can do so. Some of this demand for private camping spaces depends, of course, on overflow from the public park. Assuming that campers prefer locations within the park to those outside, it might seem strange that some are willing to pay the extra half dollar charged by private campgrounds. It must be remembered, however, that the park cannot satisfy demand at $2. Also, note that a sizable portion of the left tail of demand curve D_1D_1 (Chart 1) lies above $4, indicating that several campers are willing to pay more than this amount for places inside the park. Some of these people certainly would be willing to locate outside for less when the park is full.

Now, consider each of the solutions to the shortage of public park camping spaces. Suppose first that the park authorities raise their camping fee to $4 (Chart 1). The shortage immediately disappears. Everyone wanting a space at this price within the park finds one, because quantity demanded declines from 60 to 20 spaces. In addition, because of the increase in the park's camping fee, more people will decide in favor of the less expensive private facilities. Demand curve D_2D_2 for private camping spaces (Chart 2) will shift over to $D'_2D'_2$. For awhile, there will be a shortage of private camping spaces, and campground owners may raise their prices. Eventually they will expand, or new private campgrounds will open. This is what curve $S'_2S'_2$ shows—the number of camping spaces private landowners will supply, given the opportunity to adjust to various prices. As can be seen, the market price settles at $3 a space where quantity demanded = quantity supplied = 29 spaces.[3] ($S'_2S'_2$ slopes upward to the right, showing that costs per space increase as space is increased.) Furthermore, the market for motel rooms, and other markets, will be affected. This example only looks at the market for the most obvious substitute for public camping spaces.

Suppose that instead of increasing price, the park officials increase the number of camping spaces from 20 to 60 in Chart 1, shifting supply out to $S'_1S'_1$. Again, the shortage disappears. As a result, however, the private campgrounds may be driven out of business. (In Chart 2, D_2D_2 shifts left—not shown.) Other markets, too, are affected.

Instead of increasing the number or the price of park camping spaces, the park authorities (Federal, state, or municipal) may try to alleviate the crowding—the shortage situation—by reducing demand for these spaces. (D_1D_1 would shift left to $D'_1D'_1$ in Chart 1.) This could be done by allowing the quality of the park facilities to run down. Or, another public park could be established nearby, thereby relieving the pressure on the existing one. Subsidization of private campgrounds, to lower their costs and to encourage their expansion and improvement, offers still another means of reducing the demand for space in the hypothetical public park.

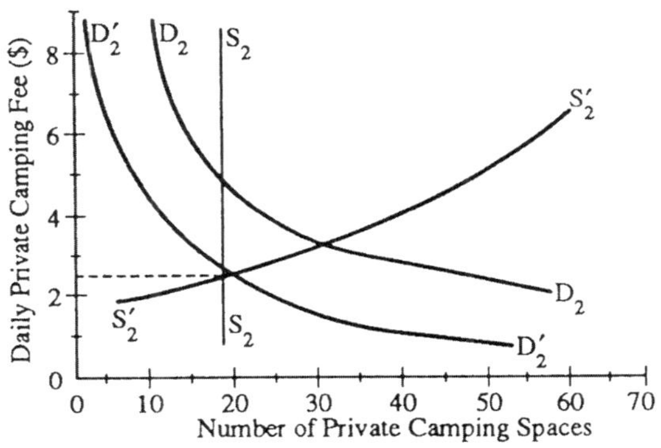

CHART 2

Each of these alternatives affects the outdoor recreation market differently. If camping conditions in the public park are allowed to deteriorate, for example, the demand for private campground space in the vicinity might rise as the desirability of these private areas increases relative to those in the park. On the other hand, the region may become less attractive as an outdoor recreation area, especially if the whole park deteriorates, and private enterprise also may suffer declines in demand. Creating more public parks or subsidizing private outdoor recreation areas in the region should, at least in the short run, decrease demand for space in individual parks. In the region as a whole, however, such measures will likely encourage more outdoor recreation by reducing its time-and-money cost to consumers.

HOW MANY PEOPLE? HOW MUCH PER PERSON?

Since undue crowding caused by an economic shortage can be so easily eliminated by increasing price, one wonders why this quick and obvious solution is not chosen. Alternatively, when "idle" space seems plentiful in the park, why not develop it for the more intensive recreational purposes that consumers want? Clearly, certain obstacles must be barring the wholesale use of these prescriptions. Indeed, several less apparent economic considerations make it difficult to determine the desirable amount of park use. Still other socioeconomic factors affect decisions of how to best allocate this use among outdoor recreationists.

Principles of Private Pricing

As a starting point, it proves helpful to think of how a public park would be managed if it were a privately owned enterprise. Microeconomic analysis proceeds from the axiom that an individual economic unit behaves in ways that it believes to be in its own self-interest. The theory of the firm treats profits as a measure of self-interest, and economists have found that the simple assumption that business enterprises act to maximize profits explains much of firm behavior. Assume that this objective—profit maximization—guides the park managers. Under such an assumption, what can one expect?

The owners may conclude that their land and water holdings would yield higher profits if used for purposes other than, or in addition to, outdoor recreation. With profit maximization as their goal, they may choose to turn the park into a farm, a strip mine, an oil field, or a residential area. Is this bad? Maybe, but the free country, free market philosophy argues that consumers, with their dollar votes, should direct the use of resources. In an idealized economic system, higher profit levels serve to stimulate production of those goods and services that society wants most. However, market imperfections and an excessive discounting of the value of resources to future generations leave our economy well shy of this idealized state. Consequently, profit signals cannot always be relied on to allocate resources in society's best interest.

In the absence of information on such shortcomings, the most profitable use of resources is presumed to be the most economically desirable. Thus, if private interests would operate resources differently from the government, the public use may have a questionable economic basis. The government should be able to defend its choice of uses by establishing the presence of considerations not fully reflected in profits and by showing that including these considerations favors using the resources in a less profitable manner. Otherwise—putting this back into context—if the government cannot show that the net economic benefits of a public park at least equal those society receives by allowing the same area of land and water to be operated for the top competing purpose, the park cannot be justified.[4]

Returning to the question of pricing, suppose that businessmen do operate the parkland as an outdoor recreation area. To keep things simple, let the rental of camping spaces be the park's sole market activity. The profit-maximizing owners will need to know (a) the demand for their camping spaces, and (b) the amount it costs them to supply varying numbers of camping spaces.

Complexities appear quickly. The relationship between price and quantity demanded is complicated by the fact that the quality of the product depends on the number of people buying it. Up to a point, the representative camper may enjoy the camping experience more as the number of other campers in the park increase. He likes their company. Eventually, however, increases in the number of campers reduce the camper's total satisfaction. He dislikes crowding.[5] Assuming the quality of camping first rises then falls with the number of campers, so does the amount the camper is willing to pay (Chart 3).

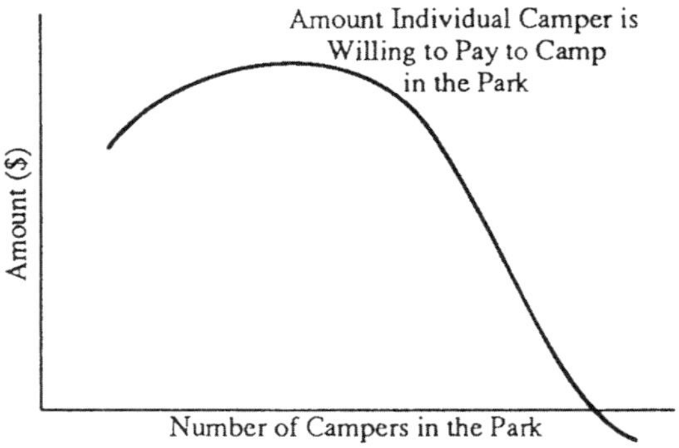

CHART 3

It is apparent that demand depends implicitly on supply. In the short run, a fixed amount of parkland cannot supply various quantities of a constant quality of camping spaces. Campers want more than just a place to sleep. They also want open, natural spaces around them. When more camping spaces are supplied, less open space remains. Because of the crowding phenomenon, quantity demanded may become unresponsive to reductions in price once certain degrees of congestion are reached. The profit-maximizing park owners would never reduce prices under such circumstances, of course.

In their cost calculations, the park owners will allow for upkeep.[6] As more camping spaces are rented, the cost of maintaining each additional one may decline as certain economies are realized. On the other hand, the least expensive ways of supplying camping spaces may be exhausted early. Also, as the number of camping spaces grows, the cost of maintaining the quality (of the decreased quantity) of open space might increase, perhaps dramatically, as certain critical levels of camping pressure are reached. For example, the park's wildlife—a prime attraction to campers—may cease to reproduce without sufficient space and seclusion.

Taking all internal cost and demand considerations into account, owners maximize profits at that price and quantity where further reductions in price would increase revenues from camping space rentals by less than the cost of supplying these additional spaces.

Principles of Public Pricing

For the economy as a whole, economic efficiency requires using resources to produce each good or service up to the point where the marginal social benefit of each good or service equals its marginal social cost. Achieving this goal is rendered impossible by insurmountable measurement problems. Rules for economic efficiency serve best to indicate when one resources use comes closer to the ideal than another. The preceding discussion argues that, because of the crowding phenomenon, the demand for camping spaces in a particular park will be downward sloping—park owners cannot rent any number of camping spaces at some competitive market price. Moreover, parks often possess unique features and are located unequal distances from the homes of their visitors. This product differentiation also implies that a downward sloping demand curve faces each park. Thus, under such monopolistically competitive conditions, if all of society's costs of park use are borne by the park owners, and if all of society's benefits of park use are received by the park visitors, it necessarily follows that the profit-maximizing price will limit park use (camping) more than is desirable. In other words, private owners will stop short of the point where the resource cost of supplying the last camping space exactly equals what society is willing to pay for it.[7]

This leads directly to the obvious but important corollary; *Under conditions of monopolistic competition where all costs and benefits of park use are internal, the socially optimal amount of park congestion exceeds that which would be permitted by unregulated private enterprise.* People may complain of crowded conditions in a public park, but that *in itself* does not justify limiting visitation. So long as the discomforts of crowding are internalized—that is, so long as they are reflected in a lower-than-otherwise price—the park visitor has no economic grounds for complaint (assuming he fully anticipates the situation).

People who do not visit a park may benefit from those who do. Juvenile delinquency, for example, may be reduced by providing city park and recreation areas. These external benefits can be regarded as negative costs, reducing marginal social costs, perhaps to the extent that a negative price—a payment to those who use the park—is called for.[8] Conceivably, therefore, society's interest could be served by subsidizing park crowds, if not more parks.

On the other hand, and much more likely to be the case for parks located outside the city, the benefits that nonvisitors receive may well be *inversely* related to the number of park visitors. The more people who drive to the park, for example, the more highway congestion and air pollution for everyone. Nonvisitors also may benefit from a park's provision of natural habitat for wildlife, its protection of rare plants and animals, and its preservation of unique natural and historical areas.[9] As already noted, greater visitor pressure can reduce park quality. To the extent that added visitation decreased the benefits that nonvisitors get from the park, park visits increase in cost to society. In the camping space example, external benefits of nonuse increase the economically appropriate price and decrease the desirable level of camping. If government officials ignore these external costs and benefits in their pricing of park services, they can end up behaving less in the public interest than would private owners.

A PRICING DILEMMA

The theory of optimal pricing is, of course, far easier than its practice. It is one thing to say that all costs and benefits should be identified and measured, another to figure out how. These difficulties are important, but not the topic of concern here. Rather, this section focuses on an obstacle that keeps park officials from charging the economically appropriate price for park use even when that price is known—public opinion.

The conditions reported at some popular public parks do not suggest an equilibrium in quantity demanded and quantity supplied. True, as shown earlier in this article, congestion is sometimes economically desirable and can be expected to cause complaints of crowding. But when people are turned away, and when overuse threatens the park's survival, something must be out of kilter. Park authorities seem to be both encouraging visitation with low fees, and discouraging visitation by not adequately expanding recreation facilities and by otherwise limiting—in nonprice fashions—the activities of the visitors.

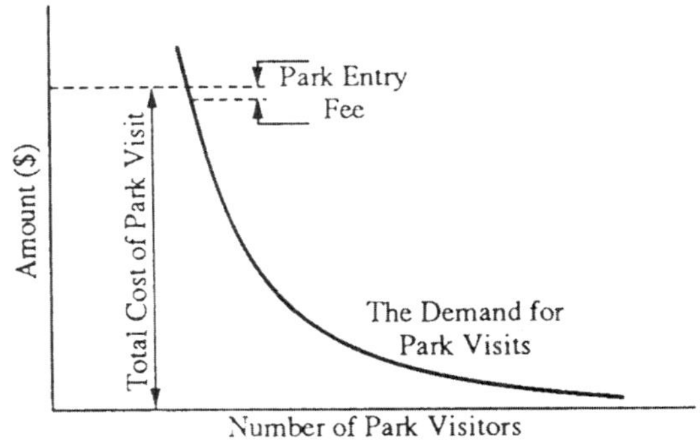

CHART 4

Public opinion forces this strange behavior. In theory, at least, economists can usually fit public opinion into the pricing system fairly easily by translating it into dollar values that society places on the activities in question.[10] In this case, however, public opinion is against the pricing system. People strongly resist public park fees and the use of these fees to allocate park use. Americans apparently feel that public parks are theirs to use free of charge (or at nominal cost) as a right of part ownership. Strangely, they do not seem to feel this way about the Nation's highways (we have gasoline taxes as well as turnpike tolls).[11]

Related to the ownership argument is the redistributive argument that entry fees would have to be raised substantially to adequately limit visitation, and that this would discriminate against the poor. It might seem unreasonable or unlikely that the demand for a one-day park visit, for sightseeing only, would be inelastic between carload entry fees of just a few dollars up to $100 or more. But this may well be the case for parks like Yellowstone, because such large increases in entry fees may amount to relatively small percentage increases in the total cost of the park visit (Chart 4). Pointing this out, however, also implies that very few poor people presently can afford to visit such parks anyway. Park-type outdoor recreation is perhaps best thought of as a luxury. Most people would agree that those who want a luxury should pay for it. Yet, the under-pricing of park-type recreation subsidizes the leisure activities of the affluent—they own the boats, the trailers, the camping equipment, and so on.[12]

Until attitudes change, government officials face great resistance to increases in public park entry and use fees. Perhaps much of this resistance would decrease if proper pricing methods were used. Accelerating park deterioration and other costs of excessive crowding certainly call for changes in the pricing of park recreation. Paradoxically, governments appear to be working in the wrong direction. New highways to parks, for example, lower the time and money cost of a visit. The golden Eagle Passport—a $10 annual permit that admits the purchaser and his passengers or his family to more than 3,000 designated Federal outdoor recreation areas—encourages more visitation.

Some groups, besides visitors, obviously benefit from park subsidies. Vested interests point to the regional activity generated by park use. Owners and employees of lodging places, restaurants, bait and tackle stores, and many other kinds of businesses and concessions, do not want to give up what is actually a subsidy to them. They logically reason that, if parks increase fees, the demand for complementary goods and services they sell will decline. Manufacturers of boats, automobiles, and other outdoor recreation equipment also benefit from the subsidization of park use.

Other groups suffer. It can be argued, for example, that the subsidization of park recreation reduces the demand for outdoor sports events, bowling, and all other activities that consumers consider substitutes. Ronald F. Lee writes, "... for most people, there is no substitute for a visit to a national park." A visit to a national park may be a unique experience, but that does not mean it has no substitutes. Most Americans already substitute other things—staying home, for example—for national park visits. And, if the price of visiting national parks is increased, even more people will substitute other leisure activities.[13]

FURTHER COMPLEXITIES AND IDEAS

Most public parks of any size supply several different types of outdoor recreation. Many of these compete with one another for available park space. One example of this has already been given—open space competes with park use. But water skiing competes with fishing, picnicking with camping, and so on. A park contains, therefore, several sub-markets, and as such it can supply any one of many, many, different types of park use mixes. Some activities use more resources than others, and these should be priced higher. In practice, it may be extremely difficult and expensive to collect for each activity engaged in by a park visitor. But it might be possible to approximate his cost by charging him on the basis of the time he spends in the park and the equipment he takes in. Perhaps simply multiplying time by total weight by a price for a standard "user unit" would do the job. This would (1) discourage long stays, (2) discourage autos, campers, boats, and other heavy equipment, and (3) permit a relatively low entry price for visitors willing to travel light within the park and willing to stay only a short period.[14]

Seasonal park congestion could also be relieved by varying visitation fees by time of year. Although used to some extent, this method of pricing is largely untapped. The advance reservation idea probably favors certain groups over others, although it does have the advantage of guaranteeing space. Unfortunately, one likely outcome of a reservation system in situations where demand exceeds supply is a black market or scalpers' market in tickets. Why not use the pricing system directly instead of driving it underground?

The cost of park-type outdoor recreation must be borne by someone. This includes not only the direct operating costs, but the opportunity costs of the resources as well. In instances where it is practical and where external costs and benefits are not significant, charging the user enough to cover these costs seems warranted. Privately owned recreation areas do this. For this reason, Professor Milton Friedman would have governments get out of the noncity park business:

> If the public wants this kind of activity enough to pay for it, private enterprises will have every incentive to provide such parks. And, of course, there are many private enterprises of this nature now in existence. I cannot myself conjure up any neighborhood effects [externalities] or important monopoly effects that would justify governmental activity in this area.[15]

But most people, it seems safe to say, simply do not trust private enterprise to preserve the natural beauty of some national and state parks. Many park resource development decisions are irreversible, and the long-run consequences of a misguided short-run profit motive could be severe. On the other hand, public ownership does not guarantee development of resources in the long-run best interest of society either.

READING QUESTIONS

1. How may government distort the public parks recreation market?
2. Discuss and evaluate various alternatives for alleviating a shortage of public park camping spaces.
3. Compare the principles of private pricing and public pricing for recreational use of parks.
4. What is the equity impact of underpricing park recreation?

Notes

1. See, for example, Paul Friggens, "Last chance for Yellowstone?" *Reader's Digest,* March 1971, pp. 190–96.
2. Assume away (as unnecessarily complicating here) the likelihood that campers prefer some of the park's campsites to others.
3. A more complete treatment of these adjustments would include probable increases in the demand for park camping spaces brought about by increases in the price of private camping spaces, and so on, back and forth, until an equilibrium is reached.
4. In choosing from alternative uses of resources, it is wrong to say that "other factors besides economics must be considered." Economics is the study of man's choices from competing alternatives. By definition, therefore, nothing else matters. The trick is to identify and appropriately include all important economic consideration, both current and future, when calculating benefits and costs. The confusion arises because many people commonly but incorrectly use the word "economics" as if it were synonymous with "profits," or "private enterprise." A few months ago on a television special about a national park, for example, it was reported that the reconsideration of plans for a new airport represented a victory for conservation over economics. Not at all. It represented a reassessment of the net benefits from building the airport. (Conservationists were responsible for bringing about this reassessment, to be sure.) For the time being, society has decided that it would be worse off—all things considered—with the airport.
5. The desire for privacy will vary among campers, and with the type of camping area. Two campers (or camping parties) in the same park may be one too many for some individuals, especially if the park is a wilderness area.
6. Private owners would allow a profitable park to run down over time only so long as, or to the extent which, the costs of doing so—losses in future profits due to lower future demand—were less than the costs of maintaining park quality. Time preference—the values owners place on future dollars versus present dollars—matters here.
7. Because owners must reduce prices on all spaces in order to rent more spaces, the additional or marginal revenue from renting one more camping space is less than the price at which it is rented. Profits decline with increased "sales" once marginal cost exceeds marginal revenue. Logically, therefore, profits are less than the maximum where price equals marginal cost.
8. It sounds strange, but why not? If, for example, it is found that children who participate in junior baseball are less likely to get sick, less likely to turn to crime, and less likely to go on welfare, might it not make sense to expand such programs even if it requires giving the participants some dollar inducement?
9. Birds that nest in a park, for example, fly, feed, and sing far outside its boundaries. (On the other side of the ledger, park wildlife can damage crops and otherwise increase the cost of farming and ranching.) Benefits are sometimes less obvious. Relatively few people have ever seen a whooping crane, but millions derive pleasure from reading and hearing about it fight for survival.
10. These values need not be expressed to the dollar. Thus we now adequately protect the bison because the gains from doing so exceed the costs by some unmeasured—but not infinite—amount. But we continue to reduce the chances of survival of the bald eagle and osprey—and other species—because the necessary costs of more protection have been judged greater than the gains.
11. On highways too, however, improper pricing results in crowded conditions. See Gabriel Roth, *Paying for Roads: The Economics of Traffic Congestion* (Baltimore: Penguin Books, 1967).
12. Two experts in outdoor recreation write: "By and large, the supply of free public parks in the United States is less adequate in crowded city areas where people are poor than it is in suburban and higher income residential areas, where the people concerned are more nearly able to pay for their own outdoor recreation. On a state or national basis, the discrepancy is even worse; the really poor people do not own the private automobiles which are necessary to get to most state parks and to all national parks and national forests, nor can they, in most cases, afford the other travel costs of such visits. The argument that free public parks help the poor is almost wholly myth." Marion Clawson and Jack L. Knetsch, *The Economics of Outdoor Recreation* (Baltimore: Resources for the Future; Johns Hopkins Press, 1966), p. 271.
13. The quote is from Mr. Lee's book, *Public Use of the National Park System,* 1872–2000 (Washington: Department of Interior, National Park Service, U.S. Government Printing Office, 1968), p. 87.
14. Some parks currently do not permit visitors to stay indefinite periods of time. This is consistent with the philosophy that it is better for society if five people spend one day in the park than if one person spends five days. If this point of view is accepted, a fee rising *progressively* with length of stay is called for.
15. *Capitalism and Freedom* (Chicago: University of Chicago Press, 1962), p. 31.

Mr. Bechter is presently the Vice President of the Federal Reserve Bank of Richmond.

Reprinted with permission from *Monthly Review* (Federal Reserve Bank of Kansas City), June 1971, pp. 80–81.

UNIT 3

The Economics of Work and Income

Unit Selections

Key Points to Consider

- In what sense are the rich getting richer and the poor poorer? Explain the major reasons for this trend.
- What is officially meant by "poverty"? Is welfare reform working? Explain your answer.
- What are the compromises which true reform of the Social Security System will require?

DUSHKIN ONLINE **Links: www.dushkin.com/online/**
These sites are annotated in the World Wide Web pages.

Center on Budget and Policy Priorities
http://www.cbpp.org

Joint Center for Poverty Research
http://www.jcpr.org

Today's Unions
http://www.aflcio.org

The Urban Institute
http://www.urban.org

U.S. Department of Health and Human Services
http://www.hhs.gov

U.S. Department of Labor
http://www.dol.gov

U.S. Immigration and Naturalization Service (INS)
http://www.ins.usdoj.gov

Welfare-to-Work
http://wtw.doleta.gov

WorkIndex
http://workindex.com

Economic justice means different things to different people. For some, the fairest way to distribute income and wealth is to "allow the market to decide," so that rewards are provided strictly on the basis of the human and property resources that individuals contribute to the economy. Others maintain that such an arrangement is inherently unfair; since people differ in their natural abilities, inheritances, age, race, sex, and luck, resources tend to be distributed in a highly unequal fashion. A market system tends to penalize those whose resources are insufficient to enable them to achieve adequate living standards.

Economists generally agree that complete equality in the distribution of income and wealth is undesirable, since then there would be no financial incentive to induce people into more difficult undertakings. However, there is widespread disagreement within the economics profession on two questions. First, if inequality is to serve as an incentive to greater efficiency in the use of resources, exactly how unequal should the distribution of income and wealth be? Secondly, what is the proper role of government in modifying the way in which a market economy distributes its rewards?

In the United States—as in all highly developed capitalist countries—there are large differences in the distribution of income and wealth. American households in the top 20 percent of the population earn about half of the total U.S. income, while those in the bottom 20 percent earn less than 4 percent of the total. Differences in the distribution of wealth are even greater. In 2004 the bottom 50 percent of the U.S. population essentially had zero net wealth, while the top fifth accounted for more than four fifths of all American wealth. While most Americans are better off today (in terms of the absolute amount of income and wealth available) than they might have been, say, 50 years ago, there are certain trends that disturb those concerned about issues of inequality. One of these is a decline (since the mid-1970s) in the purchasing power of median household earnings and a rise (since the early 1980s) in the extent of poverty.

The readings selected for this unit identify some major issues in current debates on the subject of work, income distribution, and the possible roles of government in promoting economic justice.

Looking ahead to our place in the next economy

By Matthew Budman

When we hear about manufacturing jobs moving overseas—whether in steel, cotton, textiles, or Buicks—it doesn't sting all that much anymore, unless, of course, a family member is among the pink-slipped unlucky. Somehow it seems inevitable—progress, even: *The United States is continuing its forward movement, leaving behind the remnants of the Industrial Age and bringing its diverse workforce into the Information Age, ready to lead the way.*

But news of software-programming and radiology positions being outsourced to Romania and India has a more visceral impact. Few knowledge workers—and aren't we all supposed to be knowledge workers now?—foresaw their livelihoods being jeopardized by the same free-market principles that have devastated U.S. manufacturing.

Yet technology and toppling trade barriers have left white-collar jobs as vulnerable to overseas migration as those in blue-collar industries. And U.S. workers may not even be the first choice to run call centers or manage the information that is the new economy's lifeblood: Americans are expensive, what with 401(k)s, ergonomics requirements, health care, vacation days, and life insurance, and most have little educational or training advantage over their foreign counterparts.

"I'm nervous," says the ordinarily buoyant management guru Tom Peters. "I don't think there's any job that's safe right now."

"Is the anxiety justified? Absolutely," says Dow Chemical ideation leader Andy Hines. "We're facing a real challenge."

After all, notes USC management professor Ian Mitroff, "if finance and engineering-design jobs can be moved offshore, what *can't* be moved?"

If you find the trend disquieting in principle, check out the numbers: A recent U.C. Berkeley study estimated that some 14 million U.S. white-collar jobs—11 percent of *all* jobs—are at risk of being outsourced, anytime employers want to make the move. That's significantly higher than the widely reported Forrester Research forecast of 3.3 million jobs lost over the next 15 years, not to mention the 2.5 million manufacturing jobs lost in the last three years. And who can blame U.S. companies for looking east for lower personnel costs? The Berkeley researchers, Ashok Deo Bardhan and Cynthia A. Kroll, note that Indian telephone operators earn under $1 an hour, payroll clerks just $2, paralegals $8 or less.

The baby boomers' retirement will stave off any true white-collar crisis for a few years—employers will be scrambling for warm bodies, and anyone who fits that description will probably get by. But for far-thinking organizations, the coming demographic shift is another argument for moving operations offshore even faster. In five or 10 or 20 years, will there be any work for knowledge workers—or their supervisors—to do?

Of course, few forecast a future as bleak as all that—U.S. workers have survived every previous disruption, major and minor, and they'll survive this one. It's the disruption's severity and duration that are in question—and whether top-tier workers will be able to maintain their position in the global economy.

Granted, not everything can be outsourced. Despite improvements in videoconferencing and the ubiquity of cell phones, plenty of jobs—even white-collar jobs—require face-to-face contact. We haven't—and won't—become "a nation of burger-flippers," as Lee Iacocca once feared; the service economy hasn't trumped the information age. Whatever the Internet's reach, society can't function without doctors, social workers, and police officers. The economy will continue to need trainers and researchers and economists and teachers and lawyers and editors—and executives to manage them all.

And there's the not-unimportant fact that work will always be here because here is where workers want to be. The United States remains the world's top destination spot for both well-off emigrants and destitute refugees, all seeking a dynamic, vibrant society as well as economic prosperity. Sure, the cost of living is far lower in the developing world, but America is where people want to come–and stay. It may be cheaper to start a software-development firm in Ghana or the Philippines, but how many U.S. entrepreneurs would gladly relocate their families from Ohio or Massachusetts?

So should we be worried about our prospects a decade or two down the line? What will it take to stave off downward mobility—individual and collective—and decline both economic and social? We asked some thought leaders with their eyes on the future, including a few who proudly call themselves futurists, to peer at what's ahead for American executives and knowledge workers.

Applaud the Job Exodus?

We already know what *won't* work: protectionist efforts to keep jobs here. It hasn't worked with manufacturing—the latest example, George W. Bush's clumsily enacted and globally rejected steel tariffs, ended up costing more jobs than they saved. And no program of tax-based carrots and sticks is likely to keep data-entry and accounting functions on these shores.

Anyway, creative destruction of jobs is hardly news in any industrialized nation. Each economic era has seen massive displacement of workers, of families, of entire industries. No one called it retraining, but all those cobblers and subsistence farmers and, yes, buggy-whip factories needed to transform into something else—something unforeseen.

"The loss of manufacturing jobs is just another chapter of technological progress in our economy," insists Christopher Meyer, former director of the Center for Business Innovation, who says that the ongoing white-collar volatility, like economic upheavals before it, is absolutely necessary. He sees the job exodus as "part of a long-term trend of manufacturing jobs leaving this economy—and we should applaud it." A country advances by replacing lower-level jobs: "That's how economic growth happens—the new jobs have to have higher value-added, higher productivity. It's like when automation replaced blue-collar jobs—we look at most of the jobs it displaced as brutish and short: mining coal, or having your internal organs cooked by the infrared radiation from a ladle of steel. These adjustments will allow more people to do *what* they want to do, not what they *have* to do."

> "The issue is, 'Does the United States represent the front end of the pipeline?'"

Business thinker Stan Davis, Meyer's frequent co-author, uses a pipeline metaphor to describe the pattern of job creation and motion. "I'm not concerned about U.S. job losses so long as we're feeding the front end of the pipeline with growth and innovation," he says. "As each new innovation creates new jobs and new sectors mature, those jobs migrate down the global food chain. The issue is, 'Does the United States represent the front end of the pipeline?' It's a question of how long we stay healthy and grow and innovate and create new sectors."

And no matter how many call centers and programmers head overseas, the United States has a head start in invention and innovation, according to Glen Hiemstra, founder of Futurist.com: "Our biggest competitive advantage will remain creativity and innovative thinking—as compared to routine churning out of information—because of the innovative history of the country, because of the cross-cultural mix that leads to fertility of thinking," he says.

U.S. companies and workers also benefit—though they won't do so forever—from ease and familiarity of communication, language, and organization. Futurist Watts Wacker, CEO of FirstMatter LLC, points out that no emphasis on efficiency will obviate the need for human contact—"You can't Six Sigma relationships," he says—or for unusually valuable personnel. "There will always be a premium for people who are better than others."

The question is whether U.S. workers will always be better than their foreign competitors. Meyer emphasizes that workers must stress distinctiveness over superiority: "Either U.S. income will fall to the level of those in other countries who have the same skills, or we have to have different skills," he says. "So what are those different skills going to be?"

The effort to develop those different skills must be a priority for not just individuals but entire economic sectors, says Dow Chemical's Andy Hines, who also chairs the Association of Professional Futurists. "Look at what's happened to unions," he points out. "They've had a very similar kind of challenge—in their case, with physical labor migrating overseas—and they've responded not by trying to improve what they brought to the table but by staying static and trying to hold on tight. When someone else can do the job for one-sixth the price, you're going to lose no matter how hard you fight. It's a losing game, and knowledge workers can lose too—if they stay at the same skill level as somebody in India."

Staying Ahead of the Curve

Keeping U.S. workers on the cutting edge will require efforts both individual and national. It won't just *happen*. Hines calls it a national imperative: "If we stand still, there will be up-and-coming economies that will take the things that we're doing now," he says.

Hiemstra cites "two critical things that we need to do" on a national scale. First: We must move quickly to bring a high-speed Internet connection "into every home and every business location," he says. "Other countries are moving in that direction as a matter of national policy, through a mixture of public initiative and privatization. We ought to be looking at the Korean model, and at what's happening with the telecommunications infrastructure in China and India, which are moving much faster than we are on a percentage basis. This ought to be a top national priority for us, and currently it's seen only as something that would be nice—if the telecommunications companies could make money doing it.

"Second," he continues, "to maintain our innovation lead, we need to push for more people receiving advanced math, science, and technology education. Grad schools in those areas are dominated by foreign students. We're just not generating enough people with the kind of high-level technical knowledge to do the innovation in the new technologies and in the realms of innovation that are going to be dominant in the next quarter-century."

USC's Ian Mitroff also sees education as key. "We haven't done a good job of teaching critical thinking and creative problem-solving," he says. "People find critical thinking difficult because it's a radical switch from their 20 years of education in solving well-structured problems. We've produced a nation of certainty junkies, where if you can't define a problem with precision and certainty, people go crazy. Well, welcome to the real world. The game has changed. Problems change as fast as you're working on them." Indeed, they change *because* you're working on them—or *not* working on them.

For Corporate America as a whole, if CEOs needed any more incentive to pay more attention to long-range planning and encourage entrepreneurial thinking within organizations, the offshoring trend should provide a convincing kick in the pants. "For most organizations," Mitroff says, "most of the traditional management functions get in the way of innovation. That doesn't mean that a company shouldn't have a CFO, but you have to have a different *kind* of CFO—an interdisciplinary CFO."

"You have to have a different kind of CFO–an interdisciplinary CFO."

Hines argues that companies that want to stay vital—not to mention in business—must encourage creative thinking in the workforce as well as on an organizational level. "It's not just the jobs that are going overseas—it's the corporate functions," he says. "If you're going up against a European-headquartered company, your only value-add is going to be being creative, innovative, and forward-looking."

Keeping Up on Your Own

You've seen all those articles warning knowledge workers to upgrade their skills or get left behind? Time to start photocopying them for your staff.

"Knowledge workers should be working to acquire more knowledge," Hiemstra counsels. "You've got to keep learning in new areas and improving your skills as much as you can. You've got to keep asking yourself, 'What will I be learning in the next six months?' And you need to look for opportunities to be more innovative in the settings you're in."

Both Meyer and Mitroff believe that tomorrow's successful knowledge worker will be the one who can cope with an increasingly unstable world. "Don't look for a job that's well-defined, with a lot of work rules and specifications," Meyer says. "Look for jobs where your task is to make change rather than to continually deliver the same thing—not to *do* but to *innovate*. Conceive of your job as entrepreneurial."

Mitroff insists that top workers must "be comfortable with huge amounts of uncertainty. That's part of the new skill set. They will have to learn how to solve ill-defined problems, to retool and regear, to learn inter- and trans-disciplinary education, to make connections between problems and issues. Everyone will have to learn systems thinking, what the properties are of complex systems and how that can be used as a problem-solving skill. People are going to have to learn the art of problem *formulation*. They're going to have to learn how to question assumptions—in fact, a whole *discipline* for challenging assumptions. They're going to have to grapple with complex, fuzzy issues that are often in conflict, that are contradictory. It's a totally different philosophy of inquiry."

"We have become a nation of spoiled brats! America is not about certainty."

Tom Peters echoes Mitroff's emphasis on uncertainty, in somewhat less academic language. "We have become a nation of spoiled brats!" he exclaims. "America is not about certainty. The fundamental Pilgrim-father myth may be mostly nonsense, but that myth—which has served us quite well for over 300 years—is that America is about taking chances and reinventing ourselves. We have become security junkies, and to hell with that."

For Peters, white-collar workers who can demonstrate discrete, concrete achievement are most likely to beat out their peers, domestic or foreign. Some, naturally, generate tangible results in the normal course of their work: "I give a bunch of speeches—people like 'em or don't like 'em," he says. "I write a bunch of books—people like 'em or don't like 'em. I write a bunch of articles—people like 'em or don't like 'em. Whatever. They're *stuff*." But most workers and executives are unaccustomed to thinking in those terms. "It's far more difficult if you are a purchasing manager, HR manager, or finance manager, even if you are at the $100,000-a-year level," Peters says. If asked to provide evidence of their accomplishments, "to some extent, the most that those people could say is, 'I came to work every day; I showed up; I did good work; the company is still around.'" Successful 21st-century career management—including planning for that career's next phase—demands less passivity.

"Your responsibility is to be continually upscaling," Hines says. "You need a work/life plan in which you're constantly raising your own bar. If you do that, you'll always be ahead of the outsourcing wave. It's not as though everything stands still—there's a demand for more advanced activities, and if you've been keeping yourself in professional shape, you'll go up the curve with it." He argues that, more than ever, it's crucial for workers to not leave their careers in their employers' hands. "I have a responsibility to maintain my own skill level, and I can't just get stale in one place and hope I'll be taken care of, because I won't be. I'm not sure that most people have quite that level of personal responsibility yet."

Top executives in particular, of course, face broader issues than their own careers—and are, if anything, at greater risk than front-line white-collar workers of losing their place in the next economy. If all the positions you used to supervise are 8,000 miles away, and your salary is now *thousands* of times higher than theirs, you're affordable only if you can offer something truly extraordinary.

The futurists' key advice: Expand your scope of knowledge and vision. "Put your head up," Hiemstra urges, "and start seeing what's happening. I speak frequently to groups of executives in various industries, and I ask them, 'How many know something about nanotechnology?' The typical percentage is 5 to 10 percent who've even *heard* of it, which always floors me. Then I ask how many know what's happening with global population, and even though it's become a big news item, almost no executives know about the impending decline in global population in significant parts of the world—the fact that Europe will see a population decline of 80 million people in the next 50 years. Since population and social trends are primary drivers of business, I'm always surprised that executives are barely familiar with these things."

Where Will the Jobs Come From?

As Watts Wacker puts it, the U.S. economy has evolved "from agricultural to manufacturing to social to information to mental." But the consensus is that the transition to the "mental"—a "Creative Age," in the phrase of Carnegie Mellon professor Richard Florida—remains a ways off. Hiemstra insists that "we're still in the early stages of the information age," if you date the age from the emergence of the World Wide Web.

"I think we're about two-thirds through the knowledge wave," says Andy Hines, who's excited about the prospects for the last third: "This is the part where it gets good and interesting. It takes a really long time to institutionalize and incorporate and get used to working with big innovations, like electricity and information. And now it's so routine—such a part of everyday life—that we're really figuring out how to use it."

Hiemstra looks to biotech, energy, and nanotechnology for the next boom, and Davis agrees, calling biology the "parent science" of the next economic era—one that is bottom-up and rule-based rather than top-down and law-based, as physics is.

Wacker agrees and emphasizes business process as well: "The information age has been about disintermediation; the next age will be about reintermediation," he says. "It's not that we don't need middlemen—we just need different *kinds* of middlemen, and that's where the new jobs will be."

And Hines sees the next economic wave being driven by sustainability—"the triple-bottom-line idea." In the next decade or two, "sustainability will be a driving force of what we're going to use this knowledge and innovation and creativity for." The push for increased consciousness in issues of ethics, the environment, and economic justice will come from developing countries, NGOs, and knowledge workers themselves, he predicts. "A growing number of those workers *want* to be socially responsible and environmentally responsible, and they haven't been able to express that. The demand for the triple bottom line, which used to be from the crazy NGOs and the fringe, is going to come from *us*.

"At Dow Chemical," Hines continues, "sustainability is a very important part of our company. The message has thoroughly permeated—of course, you can't measure how much everyone *believes* it, but you start to see that this is what people really want to do. It's sometimes hard in the business climate to act on what you believe, but I think we're going to see more of it: Talented workers are going to go places that let them express what they want to express."

But predictions of what the next economy will focus on, or what its "energy source" will be, or even what its unofficial name will be, don't—*can't*—point definitively to the next job sector. The tech explosion came out of nowhere and rescued the U.S. economy by boosting productivity; will the next new sector do the same? We can only guess what it will be—or what impact it may have. It's not enough to study demographics and forecast that Generation Y, in its entirety, will be staffing nursing homes for retired boomers.

Peters is fast losing faith: "I'm unnerved by this jobless recovery; I'm a lot less confident than I was 18 months ago," he says. "For 15 years, this was the pattern: We lost a manufacturing job to Mexico; we added a service job in New York—or better yet, 1.5 service jobs. I'm uncomfortable with that simplistic notion, now that we are losing high-paying jobs at an unprecedented rate—especially those damn tech jobs that we got only five years ago. It's not clear to me where the replacement jobs will come from. I think we have every right to be worried."

Silver Lining

Does overseas migration of American knowledge jobs directly benefit the United States and its workers? Definitely: As countries such as India and Ghana begin taking—and creating—high-value jobs, those countries will see an irresistible incentive to invest more in education and other human-capital expenditures, and to de-emphasize repressive policies and military escalation. And other nations will surely follow their example: *If Romania can do it, why not us*? That human-capital investment, Christopher Meyer points out, is "a prerequisite for sustained economic development."

Of course, the United States, in its current antagonistic attitude, is more concerned with security than in other nations' economic health—and the white-collar transfer aids that goal as well. "High-value jobs give countries a stake in free trade and orderly economic life, which is the best anti-terror campaign that we could devise," Meyer says, noting that in addition, exporting of opportunity tends to reduce disparities in personal income—a healthy outcome by any measure: "Within a society and across the globe, there may be no more divisive force than income inequality."

The Next Organization

It's practically a truism: The command-and-control era is dead; long live the age of empowerment and self-governed teams and decentralization and knowledge-sharing. And yet charismatic CEOs are still superstars, and plenty of old-style, top-down organizations are not only hanging tough but thriving. Top executives aren't the only ones content with the status quo: "We still have a lot of workers, a large sector of the economy, who want to spend their careers with one company, and who don't want to go anywhere—who have no intention of going anywhere," says Michele Bowman, senior VP of Global Foresight Associates and a founding member of the Association of Professional Futurists.

So will every company be *forced* to change how it does business in the next decade or two? Of course not. Some don't have to change and sure as hell don't want to. Others simply can't face that degree of disruption. Plenty will make incremental changes, and only under duress. And many of all these holdouts will get along just fine in the next economy.

But the rest of you—start thinking about new systems of thinking and organization. We mean it this time.

"For those whose business model currently is not threatened the way it is in music and telecommunications, I would not rest easy," Davis says. "I would be looking to figure out how my current model is creaky. What are the business models for the future? We don't have them yet. The dotcom bubble bursting is a perfect example of the wrong answer for the right question—the question being, 'What's your business model?' We'll figure out the models within the next decade or so, and they'll probably be bottom-up models."

Those models may come from the unlikeliest of sources. "On Sept. 11," Peters points out, "a virtual organization attacked a real organization, and at least in the short term, the virtual organization made idiots out of us."

> "What are the business models for the future? We don't have them yet."

Mitroff invokes the same unsettling example. "Al Qaeda has a 21st-century network node organization, and we're fighting them with a 19th-century bureaucracy," he says. "The war on terrorism is not just a military war—it's an organizational war. People have been educated to solve problems that say, 'Here I am—solve me,' and we don't live in that world anymore. Sept. 11 also showed that the oceans are no longer protective moats—we don't have a magic bubble around this country." The lesson applies to work as well: "The white-collar crisis represents a radical transformation of the nature of work. You now have to be able to make connections between your job—however limited it is—and an unlimited, unbounded world."

Not everyone is apprehensive about participating in an unbounded world. "Our borders keep expanding; this is really the second or third era of globalization," Bowman says. "Twenty years from now, will we have employee ideologies that reflect industry-based perspectives more than geographically based perspectives? Absolutely." She looks ahead to a world largely populated by "electronic immigrants"—workers who take jobs in other countries without actually changing residence, much less citizenship.

Hiemstra believes that spreading globalization will occasion re-examinations of corporate social responsibility. "In the next quarter-century, more and more kinds of work will be eligible to be done anywhere in the world by people who are skilled enough to do them," he says. "Companies of all kinds will be forced to ask, 'What is our obligation to, commitment to, interest in the community and our workers? What are we really here for?' I don't know what the answers will be. They may say that the only things that matter are survival of the company and shareholder value, or they'll have a more complex answer. But companies will have to sit down and decide what is really important and what that means in terms of moving the work or not moving the work."

With American workers in mind, Peters is not especially optimistic about what choices companies will make—or even about the prospects for those companies' survival. "I think we're entering a 50-, 60-, 70-, 80-year period of instability, where I can well imagine the great American economy being surpassed by the Chinese or the Indians," he says. "The certainty is gone—which suggests that workers don't have that long to screw around. You've got to figure out what you have to sell in a global economy—and then sell the hell out of it."

MATTHEW BUDMAN is managing editor of Across the Board. *He wrote "With Fresh Eyes" in the Nov/Dec 2003 issue.*

The earning power of women has really increased, right?

Take a closer look.

By Jeff Madrick

THE great defense against stagnating male wages in America over the last few decades has been the two-worker family. No doubt many women want to work to fulfill their own goals and gain financial independence. But consider the monetary advantages. The latest data show that the median income of two-worker families was nearly $71,000. If only the husband worked, the median family income was $41,000.

In the meantime, women's wages have been rising substantially over this period. Forty years ago, the Census Bureau reports, women made, on average, 59 percent of what men made. Now they make 77 percent. This is surely gratifying.

Small wonder the proportion of two-worker families has soared in America, to 62 percent of all married couples, from 39 percent in 1970.

But valuable new research by two economists, Stephen J. Rose and Heidi Hartmann, shows that such measures substantially overstate what women earn over time. A big reason, almost always overlooked, is that women work far fewer hours than men on average and often drop out of the work force for years at a time. Usually they do so for child-rearing and to tend to the family. The traditional, widely trumpeted measures of the gender wage gap track only those women who work full time for a full year—at most about half of working women in any single year.

So Mr. Rose, senior research economist at ORC Macro, a social and economic research firm, and Ms. Hartmann, president of the Institute for Women's Policy Research, decided to study actual earnings histories of men and women over 15 years. They analyzed the in-depth interviews of the University of Michigan's Panel Study of Income Dynamics, which keeps track of a representative sample of workers.

The researchers compared the earnings of men and women from 1983 to 1998 in the prime work years between ages 26 and 59.

What they found was nothing like a closing of the pay gap to 77 percent. Over that period, women on average earned only 38 percent of what men did. Adding it up, the researchers found that the average woman earned $273,592 over 15 years, compared with $722,693 for men (in 1999 dollars).

Fewer work hours account for much of the difference. It turns out that fewer than half of women earned income in all 15 years but 85 percent of men did. About 30 percent of women did not work at all for four or more years . By contrast, only one man in 27 was out of work so much.

Thus, a snapshot of the median income of two-worker families in any given year exaggerates the financial advantage to the family of the working spouse. Some combination of social mores, necessity and, arguably, parental instinct drives spouses, typically wives, to stay home and tend to the family. Married women with children usually work less than unmarried women.

But hours alone do not account for the discrepancy in pay over time. The economists' analysis turns up continuing evidence of gender segregation. A far higher proportion of females have had jobs that pay at the bottom of the income scale, and fewer of them climb to jobs of higher quality. Even when they are well educated, women predominantly take different kinds of jobs from those men do—jobs that usually pay less.

For example, Ms. Hartmann and Mr. Rose divided jobs into three categories: elite, good and less-skilled. Among the relatively elite professional jobs, women were mostly teachers, nurses and social workers. Men were mostly business executives and scientists.

The middle level for women included secretarial positions, but for men it was typically well-paid blue-collar jobs.

In each tier, the researchers find, salaries are higher for the male-dominated categories than for the female categories, even though the educational requirements are similar.

"Out of the Office"

A study by two economists, Stephen J. Rose and Heidi Hartmann, shows that from 1983-98 prolonged periods of absence from the work force were more common among women than men. Results are from a representative sample of workers age 26 to 59.

Number of years out of the labor force	WOMEN	MEN
0	48.5%	84.0%
1	10.2	7.5
2 or 3	11.8	4.8
4 or more	29.5	3.7

Ms. Hartmann and Mr. Rose argue, most disturbingly, that these tendencies are self-reinforcing. Because wives usually earn less, they are more likely to give up their jobs to do child care.

Women also often take low-paying temporary or part-time jobs that provide few benefits so they can be home for the family. This in turn creates a labor pool that business can consistently exploit, encouraging companies to orient their operations to use such low-paid workers rather than create better jobs.

And many researchers have found that there is a statistical bias against women in the work force because employers assume there is a probability that they will drop out for family reasons. This often leads to underinvestment in women's careers and a tendency to hire them for dead-end jobs.

There are encouraging trends. Women are increasingly better educated. Government policies against discrimination have had success. And a service economy reduces the advantage men once had doing heavy labor in a manufacturing economy.

Yet problems persist. They amount to a bona fide example of inherent prejudice in the labor markets, and effective public policies are called for.

First, stronger government programs to encourage paid family leave and more flexible hours will enable women to maintain long-term careers.

Second, the nation needs a serious commitment to quality day care for all as well as to the high-level personnel required for such work.

Third, Ms. Hartmann and Mr. Rose believe that there should be more federal support for discrimination oversight agencies, notably the Equal Employment Opportunity Commission and the Office for Federal Contract Compliance Programs. They argue that regular audits of large corporations for discrimination against women would be valuable.

Such policies are often seen as costs to the nation, even by traditional liberals. But they would be likely to raise the nation's productivity by fully exploiting and enhancing the talents of women, and improving family life and the development of children. There is evidence they do just that in Europe and Scandinavia.

Fourth, I believe, research is required into correcting subtle forms of prejudice in the early school years that encourage women to take jobs that pay less.

Given the self-reinforcing nature of the problem, one would think that such issues would be red meat for a presidential election year. But the presidential candidates address these matters only in passing. Perhaps we also need more research into why this is so—a place to begin might be to take note that the presidential candidates are men.

Jeff Madrick is the editor of Challenge Magazine, and he teaches at Cooper Union and New School University.
E-mail: challenge@mesharpe.com.

After 40 years, what are some results and lessons of America's war on poverty?

Alan B. Krueger

"This administration today, here and now, declares unconditional war on poverty in America." With those words, Lyndon B. Johnson began the war on poverty 40 years ago today, in his first State of the Union address.

To fight poverty, Congress started Head Start, Job Corps, Medicare and Medicaid programs, and increased the generosity of other programs, including Social Security and Aid to Families With Dependent Children. Here are some of the main results and lessons from this "40 Years War" on poverty.

Progress has been uneven, with some clear early successes followed by backsliding and then another period of progress, which has so far stalled under the Bush administration. The official poverty rate fell from 19.5 percent in 1963 to 11.1 percent in 1973. Since 1973 it has remained stubbornly stable, rising in the 1970's and 1980's and falling in the 1990's. By 2000, the poverty rate returned to 11.3 percent; last year, it inched up to 12.1 percent.

The trend is not the same for all groups. For the aged, the poverty rate fell from close to 30 percent in 1963 to 16.3 percent in 1973, then to 10.4 percent in 2002. The share of children in poverty fell from 23.1 to 14.4 percent in the first decade of the war on poverty, but increased to 16.7 percent over the next three decades. For blacks, the rate fell from more than 40 percent before the war on poverty to 31 percent in 1973, and was 24 percent in 2002, still disturbingly high but much lower than it had been.

The official definition of poverty is inadequate. It omits taxes and in-kind transfers; it pretends that the cost of living is the same in every state. Two of the most costly tools the government uses to fight poverty—the earned-income tax credit and Medicaid—are not even counted in the official statistics. Including these transfers would lower the proportion of people below the poverty threshold and hasten the decline in measured poverty in the 1990's. But the poverty line of $14,348 for a family of three is below what most Americans consider the minimum income required for a family to survive. Nonetheless, statistical adjustments are unlikely to change the perception that poverty fell rapidly in the 1960's, grew from 1973 to the early 1990's, and fell again in the 1990's.

It is still (largely) the economy, stupid. A rising tide continues to lift all boats, although the unemployment rate must fall to a lower level today—say 4 or 5 percent—than in the 1960's for poverty to decline. Still, 6 to 8 percent of the population would remain impoverished even with a booming economy because they suffer from physical disabilities or substance abuse, or are unable to work for other reasons, according to a study by the economist Richard B. Freeman of Harvard.

Demographics have a big effect. Two-parent families are much more likely than single parents to escape poverty and are more likely to be affected by economic conditions. Only 6.8 percent of married couples with children are in poverty, while a third of families headed by an unmarried woman are. The rise in one-parent families in the 1970's and 1980's, along with growing income inequality, are important reasons poverty worsened then. The decline in teenage pregnancies in the 1990's should have a positive effect on poverty in the near term.

Immigration also matters. Immigrants have a higher poverty rate, and the gap has been growing. Additionally, the rate of immigration has increased. As a consequence, the percentage of all those in poverty who are immigrants increased from 10 percent in 1979 to 20 percent in 1998.

Incentives matter. Strengthening the incentive for work in the 1990's, by expanding the earned-income tax credit and placing time limits on welfare use—in conjunction with tight labor markets—reduced poverty. The employment rate of low-skilled unmarried women with children increased from 30 to 50 percent in the 1990's after decades of stagnation, according to research by David Ellwood of Harvard. Unwed mothers saw a steep decline in poverty in the last decade.

Antipoverty policy has evolved as political winds shifted and as social science knowledge advanced. Bill Clinton ran on a platform to "make work pay" and "end welfare as we know it"—and managed to do both. Although it is tempting to conclude that the United States became less generous to the poor in the 1990's, the story is more complicated. Even as time limits restricted welfare participation, more benefits became available for those who work. Increases in the minimum wage and the earned-income tax credit, and legislation requiring states to provide Medicaid to children in poor families even if they went off public assistance, all increased the value of work. The decline in poverty in the 1990's was a result of more than a strong economy, although the boom certainly helped and its effect was probably amplified by these policy changes.

Many (including me) said the next recession would be the true test of welfare reform. Although poverty increased in the last recession and its jobless aftermath, the increase is not out of line with historical norms. This record reinforces the idea that the boom was not the only reason poverty fell in the 1990's.

David Ellwood summarizes the lessons of antipoverty policy as follows: "Cash works for those not able or expected to work, work (and work support) works for those who are expected to." Future progress will be more difficult, however, because welfare participants with the best job prospects and fewest nonwork demands on their time and energy have already joined the work force. Professor Ellwood recommends using incentives to reward responsible behaviors, like acquiring skills and providing child support. The future path of wage inequality, job growth and family structure will also critically affect the trend in poverty.

On this anniversary of the war on poverty, aides to President Bush are apparently eyeing another initiative from the early 1960's: a manned mission to the moon. Yet it is also important not to lose sight of the progress that has been made in the 40-year war on poverty, and of the work that remains closer to home.

Alan B. Krueger is the Benheim professor of economics and public affairs at Princeton University and co-editor of the Journal of the European Economic Association.
E-mail: akrueger@princeton.edu.

Election-Year Shuffle on the Minimum Wage

Louis Uchitelle

FEW proposals are more popular than raising the minimum wage. Public opinion polls are clear on this point. But what voters want rarely translates into a higher minimum, even though Congress does pay extra attention in presidential election years.

That happened in 2000, and it's happening again. The Republicans are dead set against raising the minimum wage. But in presidential election years they give the appearance of favoring an increase. And, once in a while, they even join the Democrats in approving one. They did so in the run-up to Bill Clinton's second-term victory, in 1996. As a result, the minimum wage rose to a measly $5.15 an hour, where it is still stuck.

The catalyst in this game is Senator Edward M. Kennedy, the Massachusetts Democrat. Between presidential elections, he regularly introduces minimum-wage bills that he tries to push through by attaching them as amendments to other bills. That never works. His latest proposal, introduced in the Senate on April 29 and in the House a week later, would raise the minimum to $7 an hour in three steps over 26 months.

"Only one thing stands in the way of a fairer minimum wage—one thing—and it's the Republican Party," Senator Kennedy said on the day he introduced his latest bill, listing John Kerry, the Democratic presidential candidate, as co-sponsor.

The Republicans are the obstacle; they say so themselves, although they are less outspoken in an election year. Their constituents include tens of thousands of small-business owners who pay their employees the minimum wage and don't want it to rise. Ideology also plays a role. Wages should be determined by market forces, not government mandate, Republicans argue. Mandating a higher minimum only reduces employment of the nation's least-skilled workers. Hamburger flippers are not worth more than $5.15 an hour, in this view, and the proprietors of fast-food restaurants will shrink their work forces if they are forced to raise their wages.

All these arguments seemed more plausible when Ronald Reagan took office in 1981 and halted the regular increases that for many years kept the minimum wage rising more or less in tandem with inflation. Since then, various studies have demonstrated that employers do not shed workers when the minimum rises. Twelve states have pushed up their minimums in the absence of Congressional action, and without noticeable job loss.

The most painful finding involves market forces. They indeed keep wages rising in sync with inflation most of the time for most of the work force, but not for the bottom 5 percent—the least-skilled, lowest-paid men and women. That is more than six million people. Except in a very tight labor market, like that of the late 1990's, their wages go up only when the minimum wage does.

"Raising the incomes of these people is the single most important function of the minimum wage," said Robert Pollin, a labor economist at the University of Massachusetts.

The public is sympathetic, pollsters report. In a January poll, for example, the Pew Research Center found that 94 percent of the 1,503 people questioned were in favor of an increase in the minimum wage, with 77 percent calling action by Congress either a priority or important. No wonder, then, that the Republicans in election years are loath to display their opposition to a higher minimum wage, and even offer to support an increase.

In 2000, when the Clinton administration, mostly at the insistence of Senator Kennedy, pushed for a $1 increase, to $6.15 an hour, in two annual 50-cent installments, the Republicans agreed, with provisos. The Democrats would have to accept various tax cuts as an offset, particularly cuts for small business. That compromise almost happened but failed in the final weeks of the Congressional session.

Now the Republicans are putting together a response to Senator Kennedy's latest endeavor. The response is still "a work in progress," a Republican Congressional aide said, ducking a discussion of details. Three Republican aides apparently involved in the work said they did not know enough about the proposal to describe it, although one said that a recent article in *The Hill,* a publication that reports on Congressional doings, was an accurate outline of the Republican alternative.

ACCORDING to *The Hill,* the Republicans will counterpropose an increase of $1.10 over two years, instead of Senator Kennedy's $1.85.

"We may be looking at a Republican-controlled Congress sending a minimum-wage increase to a Republican president," *The Hill* reported. "These are the election-year realities."

The sadness in these realities is the hardship. Two-thirds of minimum-wage workers are 20 years of age or older, in many cases men and women working full time and supporting children. After so many delays, even Senator Kennedy's $7 an hour would not put a breadwinner and two children above the poverty line.

Debating the minimum wage

When governments put a regulatory floor under wages, does that destroy jobs? An update on a long-running dispute

THE story so far. For many years economists took it for granted that a compulsory minimum wage, set much above the floor that emerges in an unregulated labour market, would reduce employment. Young or unskilled workers would be unable to find work at the mandatory minimum: the bottom of the demand curve would be chopped off. Of course, if the minimum were so low as to impinge on none of the wage bargains actually being struck, there would be no effect. The higher the minimum wage, once it starts to bind, the bigger the loss of jobs.

The possibility that a minimum wage would not reduce employment, and might even increase it, was acknowledged. This could happen through market failure of some kind. Suppose, for instance, employers have monopsony power as buyers of labour: they will curb their demand, to drive wages lower. A minimum wage could remedy this, raising wages and expanding employment at the same time. But in a normal, competitive labour market, this should not arise.

Then along came David Card and Alan Krueger, two of America's most distinguished labour economists. They looked at the effect of a big increase in New Jersey's minimum wage, in 1992, on employment in the local fast-food industry—and they discovered that it pushed employment up. This attracted wide attention. The claim featured prominently in their widely cited book "Myth and Measurement". It influenced the debate over raising the minimum wage in the United States; and when Britain introduced a minimum wage of its own, their findings were cited again.

Next came a paper by David Neumark and William Wascher. They went back to the New Jersey case, using different and (they argued) better data and methods. They found that the rise in the minimum wage had reduced employment, after all, much as one might have expected.

For those who follow this intriguing quarrel, there are new developments to report. In the current issue of the *American Economic Review*, after the protracted delay normally associated with that esteemed journal, both sides publish revised and polished versions of their earlier positions. They have reviewed each other's work and made adjustments. The difference has narrowed, but remains. In essence, Messrs Card and Krueger defend the validity of their earlier work; in essence, Messrs Neumark and Wascher still think it wrong. But the range of their respective estimates has shifted—enough so that they now touch, just, in the middle. Messrs Card and Krueger no longer insist that the higher minimum wage pushed employment up; they have settled for saying that (contrary to the standard model) it "probably had no effect". Messrs Neumark and Wascher have lightened the emphasis on falling employment, emphasising instead their conviction that (contrary to what Messrs Card and Krueger had first claimed) employment did not go up.

Second inning

Just as the discussion seemed about to fizzle out, two new contributions have arrived. A note by Thomas Michl suggests a different compromise: maybe both of the earlier positions were correct. After examining the data already collected, Mr Michl suggests the following possibility: that the minimum-wage increase left the overall number of workers employed roughly the same, but reduced their hours. (Not implausible, given that most workers in the fast-food business are part-timers.) Then it would be true that the wage rise reduced the demand for (hours of) labour, as the standard model says; but at the same time it could also be true, as advocates of the minimum wage say, that the incomes of the affected workers went up, thanks to the combination of fewer hours at work and the higher wage rate. In which case the policy could be judged a success, even though it had "reduced employment".

Still there? Hold on, because yet another new idea, much more hostile to minimum wages, has now been put forward. Peter Tulip, an economist at the Federal Reserve, asks a different but very interesting question: could a high minimum wage raise the equilibrium economy-wide rate of unemployment (or NAIRU)?

This directs attention away from the "affected workers" in fast-food restaurants or wherever, the focus of the earlier research, to the labour market as a whole. Suppose a high minimum wage, by pressing on the structure of pay differentials, raises wage growth and hence inflation across the economy. Higher unemployment would then be necessary to stop inflation accelerating. Employment might not fall among "affected workers", but it would have to fall in some other part of the economy. The damage would be subtler, but no less real.

Mr Tulip finds, on crunching his numbers, that this is what happens. So strong is this indirect effect, on his calculations, that the gradual fall in the relative value of America's minimum wage over the past 20 years is capable of explaining 1.5 percentage points of the fall in the country's equilibrium rate of unemployment over the same period. In Mr Tulip's view, a good part of the difference between the low equilibrium rate of unemployment in America (and Britain) and the much higher rates in continental Europe can be attributed to Europe's higher minimum wages.

That should stir things up. It will be interesting to see how other specialists respond. You will probably be able to read about it in the American Economic Review in, say, three or four years' time.

The papers referred to are: "Minimum Wages and Employment: A Case Study of the Fast-Food Industry in New Jersey and Pennsylvania: Comment", by David Neumark and William Wascher; and the "Reply" to it by David Card and Alan Krueger; AER, December 2000. "Can Rescheduling Explain the New Jersey Minimum Wage Studies?" by Thomas Michl, Eastern Economic Journal, Summer 2000. "Do Minimum Wages Raise the NAIRU?" by Peter Tulip, Federal Reserve Finance and Economics Discussion Series 2000–38 (available at www.federal reserve.gov).

Some new studies look at what to do about the troubled American health care system

By Jeff Madrick

THERE are no easy answers in reforming health care, but some economists in the field increasingly believe there may indeed be viable solutions to at least some of the nation's health problems.

The seemingly intractable issues are well known. Americans spend some 14 percent of gross domestic product on health care, while other advanced nations spend an average of 8 percent. In the United States, the proportion may rise to 18 percent by 2013.

Yet in general, judging by life span and infant mortality, most developed nations are healthier than the United States. More detailed studies find similar results. For example, a study recently published by the Commonwealth Fund measured quality of care in specific areas of medicine in five nations. It showed that America was superior in only a few. For example, this country topped the list in survival rates for breast cancer but was at the bottom for kidney transplants. It was typically in the middle in most other areas measured.

What may surprise readers, and certainly surprised this writer, is that Americans, by paying so much more, do not have many more services. In fact, according to recent research, they typically have fewer. Consider the number of doctors. In 2001, the United States had 2.7 doctors per 1,000 people, compared with a median of 3.1 in the countries in the Organization for Economic Cooperation and Development. France, accused of having a doctor shortage in last summer's heat wave, had 3.3 per 1,000.

Also, consider the number of hospital beds. The United States has only 2.9 hospital beds per 1,000 people, compared with the O.E.C.D. median of 3.9. Germany has 6.3. The United States is also behind in the actual days spent in a hospital and hospital admissions per capita. These are not necessarily bad in themselves, but the question is why we spend so much.

The reason for the high level of American spending, argue the researchers—Uwe E. Reinhardt of Princeton and Peter S. Hussey and Gerard F. Anderson of Johns Hopkins—is that American doctors and hospitals charge much more. Americans also usually pay significantly more for drugs, they say, and administration expenses are exorbitant.

The researchers argue that there is an imbalance in bargaining power between the providers of medical services, which are usually large hospitals and hospital chains, and the buyers, which are fragmented into thousands of insurance companies and health maintenance organizations. Thus, the providers can get away with unusually high prices. In some countries, insurers are sometimes allowed to bargain for better prices collectively. In others, the government itself does the bargaining.

Such research provides a stronger argument than in the past for tougher bargaining by government for services and drugs, Mr. Reinhardt said, adding that Medicare and the Veterans Administration could lead the way.

There is also renewed optimism in academia about how to improve the quality of care for every dollar spent. Economists like Joseph Newhouse of Harvard University argue that costs may be higher at American hospitals partly because they use so much high technology—not only up-to-date machinery but also the latest fancy procedures and drugs.

The question is whether high tech is worth the higher price. Despite plenty of skepticism, a growing number of economists believe that a large part of it is.

David M. Cutler, a health care economist at Harvard, summarizes what is becoming a standard conclusion among professional economists in a book, "Your Money or Your Life" (Oxford University Press, 2003). Mr. Cutler finds that new technologies and procedures in areas like heart disease and low-weight newborns have extended lives so greatly that their benefits far outweigh what America spends on them. In fact, he finds the benefits from just such procedures alone so large that they justify increased spending in all other areas.

Still, Mr. Cutler and others argue that reforms are needed because a lot of waste remains. One study concludes, for example, that Medicare spending could be cut by 20 percent without affecting care.

Also important, effective procedures are badly underused. A standout example are beta-blockers, drugs that can reduce by 25 percent the probability of a follow-up heart attack. Only half of patients who have a beta-blocker prescription now take the drug.

These economists want both the public and private sectors to adopt a market solution of sorts that calls for getting the financial incentives right. In the past, traditional fee-for-service insurance and managed care often provided reimbursement schedules that encouraged waste and ineffective care.

But recent advances in information technology are providing sophisticated ways to measure performance. These make it possible to tailor financial incentives to discourage unnecessary procedures, encourage procedures known to be useful, and reward doctors and hospitals financially for both saving lives and improving the quality of life of the unhealthy.

Several pay-for-performance programs have been adopted recently. Mr. Cutler, in particular, is optimistic about some of them. But there are also clearly obstacles. One is that paying for performance might encourage doctors and hospitals to treat only patients likely to do well.

Another is that any kind of standardization may limit doctors and hospitals too much, just as teachers complain that standardized tests limit them. "We have been paying for results in education, but we haven't been successful," Mr. Newhouse of Harvard cautions. Still, even Mr. Newhouse is in favor of experimenting with paying for performance.

To give it a chance, however, many observers, like Mr. Reinhardt, say a strong nudge from government will again be required. A group of 15 researchers, for example, recently wrote an open letter calling for Medicare reimbursements to reward performance. These health care professionals are not calling for Medicare to supersede private care, but believe the private sector will follow suit only if Medicare paves the way.

Pay for performance may not bring down costs. Any savings that result from eliminating waste will probably be offset by more intensive use of neglected procedures. But at least with pay for performance, Americans will have a better chance of getting the best care for their money. Then, the United States can decide just how much more it wants to spend, and whether further reforms are necessary.

Jeff Madrick is the editor of Challenge Magazine, and he teaches at Cooper Union and New School University.
E-mail: challenge@mesharpe.com

SOCIAL SECURITY: Note to Congress—Compromise

There are only two options: cutting benefits or committing resources.

R. KENT WEAVER

After 15 years of being largely off the national policy agenda, Social Security came back with a vengeance in 2001. President Bush established the Commission to Strengthen Social Security, giving it a clear mandate to propose a way of incorporating optional individual accounts into the system. Critics denounced the commission as a stacked body and individual accounts as the first step in a long-term plot to do away with the program. The stage was set for some difficult but important negotiations.

Then came a series of events that changed the equation. Budget surpluses that might have helped lubricate an agreement on Social Security between conservatives and liberals vanished in the aftermath of Sept. 11. The president's commission issued a report that, instead of recommending a specific plan, outlined several options for reform, thereby earning denunciations from both proponents and opponents of privatization. And the Enron scandal—or, more particularly, the retirement-savings losses of Enron employees—dimmed some of the enthusiasm for privatization. It all has made the prospects for an agreement on major substantive reform of Social Security, not especially bright before Sept. 11, seem very dim indeed in 2002.

This is a shame. If we want to avoid truly draconian policy changes in the long run, Social Security's very real long-term funding problem must be addressed quickly.

Finding a long-term solution will require both liberals and conservatives to make compromises they find unpalatable. Both sides must start by abandoning their most extreme positions. Liberals will not accept reforms that appear likely to undermine the current system of guaranteed benefits as the core of retirement-income policy by undermining its fiscal base of support over time. In particular, they will not accept the redirection of current Social Security payroll taxes to fund individual accounts. Conservatives will not accept putting any more payroll tax resources into the current Social Security program. Nor will they accept injecting significant general revenues into the current Social Security program, except perhaps for very narrow, carefully defined purposes.

Both sides also need to alter their rhetoric. Conservatives need to drop the shrill cries that we're in the midst of a severe crisis, while liberals must acknowledge there is a real long-term financing problem that must be solved. Both sides need to admit that investing in equities—either through individual accounts or collective investment of current trust fund surpluses—is not a free lunch that will solve Social Security's financing problem, but at best a healthy snack that will make it more manageable. In the long term, there are only two options: cutting benefits for retirees or devoting more resources to retirement income security.

Liberals and conservatives must accept this simple fact: The concerns raised by the other side about some of their favorite proposals are probably legitimate and need to be addressed. Specifically, liberals must agree to strong safeguards to protect against political interference in investment decisions if Social Security trust-fund money is invested in corporate equities and bond markets. Conservatives must accept limitations on administrative costs so that savings in mandatory individual accounts, especially the accounts of low-wage workers, are not eroded by high fees charged by fund managers. Eligible funds would have to be diverse in their holdings across firms and sectors of the economy to prevent a repeat, on a much larger scale, of the Enron retirement-savings debacle.

And one other thing: While we are fixing Social Security's fiscal situation, we must guard against making existing social problems worse. Despite major progress over the past 40 years, the United States still has many seniors in poverty, especially elderly widows. Many privatization proposals could make this vulnerable group even worse off.

Assuming that the two sides of the ideological divide are willing to attempt an agreement rather than trying to bash each other for fun and political profit, here are some specific ideas for bridging the Social Security divide:

- Increase the Social Security payroll tax by 2% of total earnings, split equally between employers and employees. All the new contributions would go into mandatory individual accounts. Workers would have a wide choice of privately managed funds, but all funds would have to have diverse holdings. Caps would be placed on the fees of account managers to hold down administrative costs. Funding mandatory savings accounts through payroll taxes, rather than general revenues, provides a stable income stream that is essential if mandatory savings accounts are to be a major part of seniors' retirement incomes, given that partial privatization will increase their risk in depending on market investments.
- Gradually reduce initial benefits for future cohorts of Social Security recipients as new individual accounts are phased in. Replacement rates would be set so that the combined "old" Social Security benefits and new mandatory savings accounts would roughly equal current benefits, given conservative estimates on rate of return for the mandatory savings component. Benefits would continue to be fully adjusted for inflation after retirement.
- Begin investing part of current Social Security trust-fund surpluses in equity and corporate bond markets through multiple funds. The size of individual funds would be limited to prevent any disruption of capital markets. These funds would have a strict legislative mandate to maximize return for retirees, rather than to serve social ends, and they would be privately managed. A major advantage of such an approach is the potential for increasing returns on Social Security contributions. Even more important, it would ease the cash-flow transition expected to occur around 2016 as Social Security shifts from serving as a source of financing for the federal government to being a drain on government revenues.
- Create a more generous minimum benefit for retirees, paid for out of general revenues. The current Supplemental Security Income (SSI) safety-net program for the elderly serves few people because its benefit levels are minimal and its assets tests are absurdly low. International experience suggests that it is almost impossible to eliminate poverty among the aged without increased reliance on some form of means-tested program. A new income guarantee within Social Security should have higher benefits and less stringent assets tests than the current SSI program, but not carry with it automatic eligibility for Medicaid, which would raise program costs substantially. Seniors who could meet SSI asset tests could still get Medicaid. To assuage concerns about high benefits luring immigrants, benefit guarantees should be prorated based on the years that a recipient spent in the United States as an adult—one-fortieth of the full monthly pension for every year of residency. Recertification for eligibility should occur automatically through filing an income tax return, as is done in Canada.

None of these proposals, individually or collectively, is a panacea for Social Security's problems. But they do form a balanced package that has elements appealing to both sides of the ideological divide. Seeking a middle-of-the-road solution on Social Security is not easy. But failure to reach an agreement now will pose an unacceptable burden on future generations of retirees and their children.

R. Kent Weaver is a senior fellow in the governmental studies program at the Brookings Institution and the author of the forthcoming book, "Reforming Social Security: Lessons From Abroad."

UNIT 4

Macroeconomics

Unit Selections

Key Points to Consider

- What is the current outlook for the U.S. economy? What caused the budget surpluses of the 1990s to be converted into large and growing deficits?
- What is the significance of the "underground economy"? Just how productive are U.S. workers?
- How does monetary policy affect the U.S. economy? What is meant by the term "financialization," and what does it imply about the changing nature of the economy?

DUSHKIN ONLINE **Links: www.dushkin.com/online/**
These sites are annotated in the World Wide Web pages.

Bureau of Economic Analysis (BEA)
http://www.bea.doc.gov

Citizens for Tax Justice
http://www.ctj.org

Congressional Budget Office
http://www.cbo.gov

Federal Reserve Board
http://www.federalreserve.gov

History of Money
http://www.ex.ac.uk/~RDavies/arian/llyfr.html

The Public Debt
http://www.publicdebt.treas.gov/opd/opd.htm

Macroeconomics provides an overview of the structure of an economy and the ways in which its major components—households, businesses, and governments—are related. Topics of investigation include such large, economy-wide variables as national output, the extent of joblessness, the general level of prices, and the rate of economic growth. Macroeconomics also considers ways in which government policies might be used to promote various national goals, including high levels of employment, price stability, and an adequate expansion of output over time. Since controversy abounds over the issue of the effectiveness of such policies, macroeconomics is a subject often debated by members of the economics profession.

Prior to the 1930s, most economists (known as "classicists") believed that a market economy was capable of achieving macroeconomic goals without intervention by the government. This belief was shattered by the events of the Great Depression, a period of widespread joblessness, falling incomes, bankruptcies, and political turmoil. In 1936 the British economist John Maynard Keynes attacked the classical view in his *General Theory of Employment, Interest, and Money* a book that occupies as significant a position in economic thought as Adam Smith's *Wealth of Nations*. Keynes demonstrated (on both a theoretical and a practical level) how macroeconomic goals could be reached through the management of total spending. As Keynes's ideas gained general acceptance over the next few decades, a national consensus emerged on the need for the federal government to intervene actively in the pursuit of such goals. This view was officially sanctioned in the Employment Act of 1946, which established a federal commitment to policies aimed at achieving "maximum employment, production, and purchasing power." Keynesian demand-management occurs primarily through monetary policy (controlling the supply and availability of money and credit) and fiscal policy (altering federal spending and taxes).

Although the goals mandated by the Employment Act are relatively clear-cut, actual policy-making experience since World War II demonstrates the great difficulties that America faces in implementing them. It also reflects the limitations of both economic ideology and the political system. While many of Keynes's insights still ring true, other approaches to macroeconomics (including attention to the supply side of the economy) also have value.

The unit begins with an article on the possible role which U.S. presidents play in the performance of the economy. Louis Uchitelle suggests that any president's influence over the twists and turns of the complicated American economy is inevitably less than advertised. Roberty Sidelsky then reviews Joseph Stiglitz' book "The Roaring Nineties," which chronicles the forces driving the U.S. economy to frenzy in the 1990s and collapse in 2000. Shawn Tully next examines implications of recent increases in the U.S. federal deficit, and warns of the corrosive effect this may have on American economic performance.

Elia Kacapyr examines the "underground economy," where goods and services—some legal, some not—are produced and exchanged but not reported. He contends that, among other things, the existence of this hidden economy may mean that official unemployment and poverty rates may be overestimated.

U.S. taxes are the focus of the next three articles. William Gale asks: why are taxes so complicated, and what can we do about them? Robert J. Samuelson argues that tax breaks are both more complex and less efficient than one might suppose. Then, Jonathan Weisman contends that the relationship between taxes and unemployment is far more complicated than many people (including politicians) understand.

The remaining essays focus on money, monetary policy, and the Federal Reserve system. The first article shows how Federal Reserve policy actions affect real interest rates, which in turn affect the overall economy. This is followed by an essay in which Paul Krugman is critical of Fed Chairman Alan Greenspan for having inserted himself into politics by supporting tax cuts in the early 2000s. Then, Kevin Philllips surveys important changes in the U.S. economy over the past two decades, which he identifies as the process of "financialization." He asserts that securities management, corporate reorganization, and other forms of financial packaging are steadily replacing the traditional act of making, growing, and transporting things. Finally, Kathy Chu explains why she believes that a recent wave of bank mergers has left many consumers feeling short-changed.

Beyond a President's Control

By LOUIS UCHITELLE

WE endow our presidents with mythical power, holding them responsible for the health of the economy. But any president's influence over the twists and turns of the complicated American economy is inevitably less than is advertised.

George W. Bush is not to be blamed for the recession that overtook the country two months after his inauguration. Nor is he the author of the upturn that seemed so promising in the spring. Now the economy may be weakening again, which suggests that, if he became president, John F. Kerry would preside over a downturn during his opening months in office, followed, eventually, by an upturn.

Both would be beyond his control, or any president's, although Mr. Kerry would be blamed for the downturn and praised for the rebound. Franklin D. Roosevelt exercised more influence than any modern president over the fluctuations of the economy. He did so through huge public spending, a dismantling of the gold standard and similar drastic measures. Yet even he was taken by surprise when a gradually recovering economy performed a U-turn in 1937 and plunged back into depression.

So why do voters focus so narrowly on the quarter-to-quarter health of the economy, forcing the presidential candidates into a game of musical chairs? If the economy is flourishing in the final weeks of a campaign, when the music stops, the incumbent is likely to be re-elected, assuming that other issues—like the Iraq war, in Mr. Bush's case—don't get in the way. But if the economy is heading south in those final weeks, the challenger—Mr. Kerry—is more likely to be our next president.

"Ordinary people don't have a good sense of what the president can and cannot do about the economy," said Andrew Kohut, director of the Pew Research Center, which surveys public opinion. "Their perception is that he is responsible for how they are faring, and if he does not acknowledge their complaints, they judge him as indifferent and not doing a good job."

The first President Bush was a victim of this perception. The 1992 election came 16 months into a recovery that was still too weak to be distinguished in people's minds from the 1990-1991 recession, and Bill Clinton capitalized on that perception with his endlessly repeated slogan, "It's the economy, stupid." Now, Mr. Bush's son is promising more of the strong economic growth and job creation that was so evident in the spring, while keeping his fingers crossed that the nation is not in for another slide, as recent data about the economy increasingly suggest.

The Federal Reserve, of course, has become the true hero—or culprit—for what happens in the near term. A president can have only limited influence. The Bush tax cuts, for example, put money into the pockets of low- and middle-income people, and that contributed to the recovery, although it would have come sooner and been stronger, many economists say, if the tax cuts had been directed much more than they were at lower-income people likely to spend every dollar of such windfalls. Still, despite the shortcomings, the Bush tax cuts helped.

The Kerry formula seeks to recreate the prosperity of the 1990's largely by moving the country back toward the budget surpluses of the Clinton era. As part of the process, Mr. Kerry would rescind the Bush tax cuts on incomes of more than $200,000 annually. The Clinton surpluses, however, were not just President Clinton's doing. Military spending, for example, declined after the cold war, and there was a contribution from tax increases enacted while Republicans still occupied the White House, in addition to a Clinton tax increase.

The deficit reduction and budget surpluses, however, came during Mr. Clinton's watch, and he got the credit. He, in turn, credited deficit reduction and its favorable impact on the bond market as the defining features of the late 1990's prosperity. The president's good luck came to be known as Clintonomics, which Mr. Kerry promises to bring back, although he is realistic about its causes. Ask him about the 90's boom and he cites contributing factors beyond any president's control.

High on his list are the rapid advances in computer technology and the unanticipated surge in labor productivity. "I believe that you had a combination of circumstances in the 1990's, some of which you don't have today repeatable," Mr. Kerry said in a recent telephone interview. Among them, he said, were the fact that "we were coming out of the banking crisis of the late 1980's, early 90's, and we had gone through a consolidation of banks and a certain re-establishment of confidence in the financial sector."

Booms and busts, in sum, do not come and go in response to finger-snapping by presidents. "Where the economy is going to be six months from now is beyond anyone's knowledge or control," said Peter L. Bernstein, a Wall Street economist who has been tracking business cycles for more than 40 years.

True, the nation's presidents are not helpless spectators, certainly not as helpless as their constituents. But they are not masters of the business cycle, either—although that is what most voters expect them to be, the polls tell us. And that is the role that presidential candidates embrace in their campaign oratory.

WE do not hear as much about the great influence that presidents do exercise in shaping the economy in a different way. Booms and busts are largely beyond their control, but distribution of the national income is not. And here, the Bush and Kerry approaches are radically different.

Through tax cuts and other policies, the Bush administration is channeling more income to the wealthiest Americans—record amounts, in fact. The Kerry camp, in contrast, would redistribute income down the social ladder, through practices like a higher minimum wage, extended unemployment insurance, stepped-up spending for education and, above all, subsidized health insurance for millions of Americans who now have no health insurance at all. Both candidates say that, as a spinoff, their approaches will strengthen the economy, but what stands out is who gets what share of the pie.

Income distribution is what a president can control. The news media report this issue, of course, but not nearly as often as the musical chairs.

GREED IS NOT GOOD

Robert Skidelsky

"The Roaring Nineties" is the story of the forces driving the American economy to frenzy in the 1990s and collapse in 2000. It is a much better book than Joseph Stiglitz's previous offering, "Globalization and Its Discontents." That was largely a rant against the International Monetary Fund and the World Bank. Diatribe is not absent from this book. But it is much more solidly rooted in his own path-breaking work on the economics of risk and information, for which he received a Nobel prize in 2001. Stiglitz is not an elegant or even punchy writer. But when he can relate the politics of the 1990s to the economics he knows well, the discussion becomes exciting.

In Stiglitz's view, markets suffer from pervasive "failures," mainly to do with "imperfect and particularly asymmetric information," which, unless corrected by governments, can make them seriously unstable. His account of the roaring '90s focuses on the failure of the Clinton administration to put the right incentives in place to curb these misshaps.

Instead, misguided deregulation, misguided accounting practices, and misguided tax policies all produced perverse incentives to boost the prices of stocks ahead of their real value, thus fueling a bubble that was bound to collapse. The chief gains from this fraudulent bonanza accrued to corporate executives, whose compensation packages skyrocketed while those of their employees stagnated. The stock market "correction" of 2000–2002—with the bankruptcy of giant companies like Enron and the exposure of huge accounting frauds—marked the belated onset of reality.

This is not the whole story. There was also an element of what Alan Greenspan in 1996 called "irrational exuberance," which was largely independent of any particular set of incentives. In this respect, the dot-com bubble of the late 1990s resembles the South Sea Bubble of 1720 and the railway booms of the 19th century.

Since Stiglitz was a member and later chairman of President Clinton's Council of Economic Advisers throughout the roaring nineties', he cannot absolve himself, or the president he was proud to serve, from all blame for what went wrong. His defense is that the political and economic forces in favor of letting the market rip were too strong to contain. The old balances in the economy, particularly markets and government, were swept away by the ideology of the free market, the capture of commanding positions in politics by the Republicans, and, of course, by the explosive force of the new economy itself. There is something else. While an unsustainable boom is building up, there are any number of people who know it cannot last, but to say so publicly and or, even more, to do something which that might moderate it, seems a kind of treason against prosperity. So, as in the 1920s, almost everyone was complicit in the fantasy till the moment of its collapse.

Stiglitz's main attack is directed against the deregulation mania that swept through the United States in the '80s and '90s. Deregulation of telecommunications in 1996 led to an overinvestment bubble, which burst in 2001. Deregulation of electricity in California led to market manipulation, which hugely inflated energy prices to consumers (and Enron's profits) at the expense of Silicon Valley, heart of US innovation. Deregulation of banking—notably the repeal of the Glass-Steagall Act of 1933, which had separated investment from commercial banking—set up conflicts of interest between the two branches and led to corrupt synergies between banks and companies, highly profitable to both sets of executives, but often damaging to their depositors and shareholders. Lax regulation of the accounting sector led to the boom in share options, which greatly boosted managers' pay and artificially inflated company profits. (By 2000, American CEOs were being paid 500 times more than the average employee, up from 85 times in 1990.)

Finally, the frenzy was fed by the temporary cut in capital gains tax of 1997, which Stiglitz calls "one of the most regressive tax cuts in America's history." All in all it is a sorry tale, in which the retreat of the state from social protection made it more difficult to shield people from the consequences of collapse, even as business deregulation made collapse more likely.

The indictment seems damning, but one must remember that this is the case for the prosecution. Stiglitz is a strongly partisan Democrat, and it is often hard to separate the scientist from the preacher. Thus he attributes the failure of energy deregulation in California to bring down consumer prices to market manipulation by Enron, but fails to note that this was a predictable consequence of deregulating wholesale, but not retail, prices. This was a government, not market, failure. In Britain, a better-managed deregulation caused prices to consumers to plummet. There is no reason to think up fancy explanations whenever the market works more or less as common sense would lead one to suppose it would.

The preacher is very much in evidence when Stiglitz contemplates the effects of US advice and policy to developing countries. His theme is that America (often via the IMF and World Bank) pushed free-market policies on the rest of the world—"Cut that budget. Lower that trade barrier. Privatize that utility"—that it would not have dreamt of following itself. The indictment is partly true. But there is another side. Stiglitz talks about what government needs to do, but there is no such thing as government, only particular governments, which differ enormously in their capacity. Things governments can and should do in some countries would be the road to ruin if they did them in others. The right balance between government and markets shifts between countries and also from period to period. Stiglitz's chapter on Russia in his previous book is vitiated by a failure to understand this point.

Like Keynes, to whom he has been likened, Stiglitz overemphasizes stability at the expense of dynamism. The ability of capitalism to "roar" is part of its virtue, even if the roaring does contain the "seeds of disaster." And we should not be misled by such mixed metaphors to exaggerate the scale of the "disaster" that struck in the new millennium. Between 1929 and 1931, the US gross domestic product contracted by over 25 percent. Between 2001 and 2003 the US GDP grew by 1.8 percent. Even subliminal comparison with the Great Depression is way off target.

Nevertheless, corporate executives should take a break from analysts' reports to read Stiglitz's book. It explains how so many of them became fabulously rich; and it warns them that they have been rumbled.

The Deficit: America's Credibility GAP

Growing deficits. Out-of-control federal spending. Rising debt. With the budget suddenly an election issue, it's time for some straight talk.

By Shawn Tully

WHEN ALAN GREENSPAN TESTIFIED BEFORE CONGRESS IN mid-February, the Fed chairman delivered a Valentine's Day garland to the recent performance of the U.S. economy, lauding the "stunning increases in productivity" that have fueled the recovery. But that same testimony included a far darker message: Greenspan reminded Americans that the U.S. economy faces a giant threat in the guise of big budget deficits stretching far into the future. In the past, Greenspan had mainly warned of the looming dangers of deficits in a decade or so, when the baby-boomers start retiring en masse. This time he hinted strongly that raging deficits could derail today's recovery. "Deficits could cause difficulties even in the relatively near term," intoned the chairman in his usual courtly style. In Greenspan-speak, that means the wolf is at the door, and he could start biting in months, not years.

It is astonishing how quickly we've gone from big budget surpluses to massive budget deficits. Between 1998 and 2001, the U.S. generated some $560 billion in surpluses—including a $236 billion surplus in 2000—and it was widely assumed that the era of big deficits was over. Indeed, in 2000 the Clinton administration was giddily predicting that the country would pay off all of the debt held by the public—some $3.4 trillion—by 2010.

But a year later the budget fell into deficit, and it's been spiraling downward ever since. Last year the deficit was $375 billion, and this year it is projected to be a staggering $521 billion. (The government's fiscal year ends in September.) Not surprisingly, the deficit is quickly becoming a hot election-year issue. Which is to say, there's not a lot of straight talk on the subject. Democrats invoke the need to balance the budget, but they never mention the source of half our fiscal mess, that government spending is now largely out of control. The Bush administration, meanwhile, has projected that the deficit will shrink in half by 2009. But to get to that number, the administration had to make a series of assumptions that are nothing short of laughable, as we shall see. Add to those bogus assumptions the administration's steely determination to not raise taxes, and, well, we've got a big problem.

At every step, this administration has EXACERBATED THE BUDGET DEFICIT with its shocking lack of fiscal restraint.

What's truly scary—what makes this deficit problem different from past deficits—is the trend: huge budget deficits from here to eternity. There is simply no way, with current government spending patterns, that the budget will ever be back in balance—not without tax hikes that would be unacceptably high and ruinous to the economy.

What is also scary, though, is the seeming indifference of this administration to the looming deficit problem. In a widely quoted passage from the new book *The Price of Loyalty*, Bush's former Treasury Secretary, Paul O'Neill—the one real deficit hawk in the administration—quotes Vice President Dick Cheney as telling him, "Reagan proved that deficits don't matter." If that is really what the Bush administration believes—and to be fair, Cheney denies it—then we're in a lot more trouble than we realize.

Deficits matter for three reasons. First, they increase the national debt, which in turn drives government spending even higher by tacking on ever-increasing interest expenses each year. Second, they put our economy at the mercy of foreign governments and investors, whom we have to count on to buy that debt. And third, they represent an unwillingness to come to terms with government spending. The more the government spends as a percentage of GDP—and right now the federal government absorbs 20% of GDP—the greater the drain on resources available for Americans to spend and invest in the private sector. As legendary economist Milton Friedman told Fortune, "What really matters is spending. Whether you finance the increased spending by borrowing or by raising taxes, you're leaving less resources for the private sector."

That is not to say the deficits are always bad. Think of the government like a household: If it borrows to meet an emergency, and if the borrowing is temporary—and creditors know it's temporary—the dollars generated by the debt can prove a boon by sparking economic growth. To put it another way, deficits aren't a problem if they're cyclical—if the creditors believe that as soon as the economy rebounds, the U.S. can bring its revenues back in line with spending.

Right now America is leaning heavily on foreign investors and governments, especially Japan and China, to buy the government debt that funds the deficits. At the moment, those investors are giving us the benefit of the doubt: They're still convinced that we'll get a grip on our deficits. That's the reason they're still buying our 30-year Treasuries for a rock-bottom 5% yield. But if the rest of the world loses confidence in our fiscal management—and that is now a legitimate fear—interest rates will spike. As Greenspan says, America must take action toward "restoring fiscal sanity."

We have, of course, been down this road before. In the late 1970s, deficit spending and, most of all, too much monetary stimulus by the Fed helped push up interest rates to the point where, by the early 1980s, they were wreaking enormous havoc on the economy. Then-Fed chairman Paul Volcker succeeded in squeezing inflation out of the economy, though in the process we had to endure a terrible recession and double-digit unemployment in parts of the country. But deficit spending soared under Ronald Reagan's presidency—and interest rates remained relatively high. Still, even during the Reagan era, the deficit began coming down—in part because Reagan signed a series of tax hikes into law.

In retrospect, the presidencies of George H.W. Bush and Bill Clinton represent something of a golden age of fiscal management. In 1991, displaying the kind of admirable political will that it could use now, Congress passed the hugely important Budget Enforcement Act, which clamped tight caps on discretionary spending, which includes all the money that Congress has to authorize each year—as opposed to mandatory spending, which includes big-ticket entitlement programs like Social Security and Medicare. The law also forced Congress to pay for the new entitlement spending with cuts in other entitlements, notably Medicare. That same year Bush signed into law his own tax hike—a move that helped doom his presidency, because it went back on his infamous "Read my lips" pledge, but which also helped bring the deficit under control.

The effect of the Budget Enforcement Act was quite stunning: From 1995 to 1998, outlays for nondefense discretionary spending grew by an astoundingly modest 1% a year. By 2000, government outlays had dropped to 18% of GDP, from 22% in 1992. By any measure, that was a heroic accomplishment, though strong growth helped a lot.

"Deficits could cause difficulty even in the short term," says the Fed chairman. IN GREENSPAN-SPEAK, THE WOLF IS AT THE DOOR

The combination of spending restraint and tax hikes helped revenues take off. But there was also some luck involved. First, the peace dividend at the end of the Cold War enabled the U.S. to vastly shrink spending on defense. Between 1990 and 1999, military outlays dropped from $300 billion to $275 billion. Second, in the late 1990s, entitlements still weren't growing as fast as GDP—thanks to a moderation in health-care costs and the slow rate of increase in Social Security beneficiaries. Amazingly, between 1996 and 2000, spending on Social Security, Medicare, and Medicaid actually *fell*, from 8.2% of GDP to 7.6%. And finally there was the effect of the bull market and the Internet bubble. In 2000 and 2001, for instance, receipts from capital gains jumped to more than $100 billion a year after averaging less than $50 billion in the mid-1990s.

Today, of course, the situation is virtually the opposite. Most of the uncontrollable factors that helped create a surplus in the late 1990s pushed us toward a deficit by 2002. Take capital gains. With the market in the doldrums, revenues from capital gains have shrunk from $119 billion in 2000 to $45 billion just three years later. In the wake of 9/11, Bush has understandably ramped up defense spending far above what Clinton planned. Bush's forecasts for future defense spending don't look big until you consider that he's leaving out future appropriations for Iraq, which are estimated at $50 billion next year alone. Homeland security accounts for billions more. Rising health-care charges have driven up the cost of Medicare and Medicaid. By 2010, shifting demographics will cause a steep rise in Social Security payouts. Today those three huge entitlements are up to 8% of GDP and are due to grow to 10% by 2014—and an intolerable 14% by 2030.

But at every step along the way, this administration has exacerbated the deficit problem with its shocking lack of fiscal restraint. One example was the steep tax cuts President Bush first proposed in 2001. The original rationale was that taxpayers should get a portion of the surplus rebated to them. Then the economy started faltering, and the surplus began shrinking. In the face of these changing circumstances, Treasury Secretary O'Neill argued that the tax cuts should be abandoned or at least pared back. But the administration pushed them through anyway, arguing that the weak economy needed the stimulus. By 2003, receipts as a percentage of GDP slumped to 16.5%, a postwar low; this year they're expected to fall even lower.

What's more, although the administration gives lip service to the Republican credo of smaller government, its actions suggest otherwise. Just look at the numbers: From 2001 to 2004, in a mere three years, spending outside defense and homeland security and defense-oriented foreign aid has jumped 23%, or more than 7% annually. In the same period, federal aid to education, for example, rose almost 50%, to $57 billion. Discretionary spending on health care, a category that includes the budgets of the NIH and CDC, rose 44% in those three years. The result? Federal spending is back up to 20% of GDP, and the Brookings Institution estimates that it is on track to reach 22% of GDP by 2014. "Within only a few years," concluded a recent report by the International Monetary Fund, "the hard-won gains of the previous decade have been lost." That same report concluded that about half of the big swing from surplus to deficit was due to the stock market crash and the economy's slowdown. The other 50% was a product of the Bush tax cuts and the big ramp-up in federal spending.

Perhaps the best single example of lack of spending discipline was the Medicare prescription-drug benefit Congress passed—and the President eagerly signed—in late 2003. By the administration's own (undoubtedly conservative) calculations, the new Medicare drug benefit will cost $60 billion a year by 2009. Without it, Medicare spending was expected to rise around 6% annually. With the drug benefit, Medicare spending is likely to jump over 10% a year. It's a budget breaker if ever there was one.

SO WHAT IS THE BUSH ADMINISTRATION PROPOSING TO GET THE deficit back under control? So far, not much—which is precisely what has to make our creditors nervous. White House budget projections over the next five years call for the deficit to shrink in half—but many of the assumptions upon which that number is based are simply not realistic. For instance, it assumes that the economy will grow at an average rate of 3.5% from 2004 to 2009, which is pretty optimistic. ("Achieving 3.5% would be a record worth crowing over," says Robert Reischauer, former chief of the Congressional Budget Office.) It also assumes that

Bush's Budget Man Tries to Explain His Numbers

Even partisan Republicans have expressed deep skepticism about President Bush's budget's fiscal responsibility—or lack thereof. **Joshua Bolten**, *the director of the Office of Management and Budget, took some time to speak with* FORTUNE *writer Jeremy Kahn about President Bush's budget. For a man in the hot seat, he sounds awfully serene. Here are edited excerpts. (For a longer version, see foriune.com.)*

What parts of the budget demonstrate hard-nosed fiscal responsibility?

There are a number of tough calls to be made. For example, while we are substantially increasing the federal commitment to homeland-security spending, we have shifted our emphasis to high-threat areas. So the bulk of our federal assistance will go to those areas that the Department of Homeland Security operation thinks are most under threat. Now that's a politically difficult thing to do. On its merits it's absolutely the right thing to do.

Can the administration really persuade Congress to hold nondefense discretionary spending growth to 0.5% a year?

There is always pressure in Congress to spend more, but we've heard from some members in the Republican caucus that they would like to be even slightly more restrained than the President has been. So we think we've hit it about straight down the middle of the fairway as far as what is both sensible and realistic. We'll see what Congress does with it. I think there is a good prospect of achieving an '05 budget that is very close to, if not exactly on, the numbers the President has sent up.

If Congress does not hold spending to those levels, is the President going to start vetoing spending bills?

The President hasn't needed to veto bills in the past because the leadership in Congress has ensured that bills fall within his parameters. Last year is a good example. The President set some limits, and it was agreed to by the Republican leadership [of the House and Senate]. There are plenty of complaints about the priorities chosen by Congress in some of those bills, but in terms of the overall spending restraints, Congress lived within the limits the President asked for. And I am very optimistic that we'll be able to do the same or better this year.

There's criticism that the administration's revenue projections are unrealistic too.

I think the revenue projections in the budget are realistic. If anything they're conservative. We've chosen a conservative growth rate of 4.4% for this year. Blue Chip [an organization that pools the forecasts of Wall Street economists] is now at 4.6% and CBO [the Congressional Budget Office] is now at 4.8%, so the growth rates are conservative.

Some argue that the U.S. has always managed to grow itself out of deficits. Can we simply grow ourselves out of this one?

History tells us that the projections are often wrong, and it could well be that we have underestimated economic growth and therefore the revenues coming in. But I don't think we should count on just growing ourselves out of this deficit. We also need to exercise serious fiscal restraint. I think that is well reflected in the budget that's been presented in '05 and in our assumptions going forward.

nondefense discretionary spending, excluding Homeland Security, will drop in actual dollars, from $454 billion to $430 billion, from 2005 to 2009. This isn't just optimistic, it's implausible; over the past 40 years, discretionary spending has never dropped for a sustained period. What dropped was the rate of increase.

It gets worse. The Bush budget offers $65 billion in refunds to help uninsured Americans purchase health-care coverage—but doesn't include a concomitant $65 billion rise in spending. Why? Because it promises to find $65 billion in offsetting spending cuts. How? It doesn't say.

Or take the alternative minimum tax, a complicated levy that imposes a surcharge on high-earning taxpayers with lots of itemized deductions. In 2001 and 2003, Congress lifted the amount of income excepted from AMT from $45,000 to $58,000 until 2004. But though the administration swears it is dedicated to reforming and reducing the AMT, its budget assumes just the opposite: that the AMT exemption will revert to $45,000 from 2006 to 2009—which would result in 30 million Americans paying the tax by 2009. It's hard to imagine that the administration would allow that to happen—and yet without it, tax revenues will fall by 3% from current White House forecasts.

The Brookings Institution ran numbers using more realistic forecasts for spending increases (higher) and tax receipts (lower) than in the President's highly optimistic budget. Though Brookings is a liberal think tank, its spending numbers are fairly conservative; if anything, they could get far worse. Brookings reckons that even if Congress imposes relatively spartan restraint on discretionary spending, the deficit will still stand at $500 billion in 2009, precisely where it is today.

IT'S NOT JUST THE BROOKINGS INSTITUTION EITHER. MOST TOP Republicans don't believe the White House numbers. "It will be extremely difficult to reduce the deficit below today's dollar levels at all over the next five years," says Bill Hoagland, budget advisor to Senate Majority Leader Bill Frist.

And that's the real problem. It's not so much the current size of the deficit—which at 4.5% of GDP is actually smaller than the Reagan deficits of the mid-1980s—it's the trend. Put simply, using reasonable assumptions, spending is slated to remain far higher than revenues into the blue horizon. That's what has to be reversed—and quickly. Otherwise, America's fiscal credibility is at risk.

So what should we do? For starters, we need to bring back the Budget Enforcement Act, which expired in 2002. What was so important about the BEA is that it forced Congress and the White House to make tough choices: If politicians wanted to up spending in one area, they had to find offsetting cuts in another area.

To its credit, the Bush administration has suggested reviving the BEA. Under its plan, the law would cap increases in all discretionary spending at less than 1% a year, while requiring that all new spending legislation be offset by cuts of equal size in other entitlements. Bush's plan doesn't go far enough, though. It should also include another set of sharp teeth in the original BEA: Any new tax cuts should also trigger equal cuts in spending or tax hikes somewhere else.

Ultimately, the goal should be to keep federal spending right where it is now, at about 20% of GDP, while balancing the budget over, say, a ten-year span. To do so will require more than just controlling spending, important though that is. It will also mean imposing some tax increases—or rolling back recent tax cuts.

Most painful of all, it will require regaining control over entitlements, especially Social Security and Medicare. "They're America's exploding cigar," says Bill Gale, a senior fellow at Brookings. According to the OMB, if entitlements are left alone, federal spending as a share of GDP will grow from 20% to 28% by 2035. Though they remain America's biggest sacred cows, entitlement programs will break us if we remain unwilling to wrestle them to the ground.

Two possible ideas: Social Security benefits are currently indexed to the consumer price index, despite strong evidence that the CPI overstates cost-of-living increases. Greenspan recommends moving to a more accurate index, which would lower the annual benefit increases. Another good idea: Raise the eligibility age to 68, reflecting the greater longevity of Americans nearing retirement.

If the deficits keep running, America's total debt will hit $9.7 trillion by 2014. That's 54% of GDP, the highest number in 50 years and a major red flag for the foreign investors buying our debt. By then we'd be drowning in $500 billion a year in interest payments, three times the current amount.

That's the bad news. The good news is that Americans are starting to pay attention to the growing deficit. It's beginning to feel a little like 1992, when Ross Perot ran for President using his famous charts that illustrated the nation's growing sea of red ink. "I've seen the budget issue swing from big attention to lack of attention," says Hoagland, Senator Frist's budget expert. "I'm a deficit hawk. Now I'm back in vogue." Not a moment too soon.

REPORTER ASSOCIATE: *Christopher Tkaczyk*
FEEDBACK stully@fortunemail.com

Bush: *Grow Slowly and Carry a Big Debt*

Promising too much? By relentlessly dismantling the programs that fostered the best economic performance in decades, Bush has revived supply-side policies that produce slower growth and exploding debt.

by **Robert J. Shapiro**

When George W. Bush became president in January 2001, the American economy was showing some weakness and some strength, much as it had when Bill Clinton took office in 1993. This time, housing was strong, and retail and services were still healthy, but manufacturing was depressed, and business investment was falling. Coming off the record expansion of the 1990s, President Bush's first economic challenge was not to fine-tune the end of a successful cycle or change the policies that produced that success. His task was, and is, to ensure that when the next business cycle begins, the economy is able to generate the strong investment, job gains, business starts, and productivity advances that drove up American growth and incomes in the 1990s.

Instead, President Bush has led a counterrevolution, relentlessly dismantling the program that fostered America's best economic performance in three decades. In less than one year, he has revived the supply-side, big business-oriented program of the 1980s that produced slower growth, much more modest productivity gains and virtually stagnating incomes for average Americans. In so doing, he has replaced a mainstream, market-based approach to fiscal discipline, competition, and innovation with rising budget deficits, a partial retreat from open trade, and a wink and a nudge to anti-competitive practices by giant companies.

To understand how wrong-headed this program is, we need to remember just what happened over the last decade. The driving forces of the great 1990s boom—muscular business investment and productivity, waves of technological and organizational innovation, seamless capital flows, and fast-rising incomes—grew out of economic imperatives and scientific dynamics, not politics. Yet public policies in the 1990s fostered an environment that actively encouraged private investment, ingenuity, and personal initiative.

Good luck also played a key role: Energy prices stayed low until 1999, the real price of information technologies fell sharply, a strong dollar and foreign currency crises drove down import prices, and managed care took the wind out of health-care inflation. The convergence of key technological advances in computer power and storage, data communications speed and capacity, and software power was also fortuitous. Beyond that, decades of progress in enhancing competition had produced an economy that was highly efficient, innovative, and flexible enough to take good advantage of low inflation and rapid technological progress.

Yet, policy decisions also made critical differences. Key initiatives to open domestic and foreign markets helped maintain competitive pressures to develop and deploy new technologies, along with unusually strong demand. These initiatives included the North American Free Trade Agreement; the Uruguay Round of GATT, including creation of the World Trade Organization; free-trade initiatives with the Caribbean Basin, Israel and Jordan; and hundreds of bilateral trade agreements. Continuing deregulation of telecommunications, including wireless spectrum, paired with tight antitrust supervision of giant information-technologies firms, reinforced falling prices to help keep business investment strong, especially in new technologies and new firms.

But the most critical policy shift was a sea change in fiscal policy. With a strong assist in 1990 from the first President Bush, President Clinton and a succession of Democratic and Republican Congresses spent a decade slowing the growth of federal spending to half its 1980s rate and rebuilding the revenue base eroded in the 1980s. When the 1990s began, the economy faced large and rising deficits for as long as anyone could reasonably forecast; by the decade's end, the budget deficit was gone and rising surpluses loomed as far as anyone could see.

Clinton boom. This was a historic turnaround not seen in more than a half-century. The shift to surpluses dramatically expanded the pool of domestic capital, fostering more business investment by reducing short-term borrowing costs. Credible expectations of future surpluses further spurred business investment by keeping down long-term borrowing costs. The improved fiscal climate also allowed the Federal Reserve Board to run more relaxed monetary policies, fueling demand, growth, and higher corporate-retained earnings for more business investment. And as business and consumer confidence rose, entrepreneurs became more willing to create new businesses, and entrepreneurial managers became more disposed to develop or deploy new products, methods and technologies. These forces came together to produce what can fairly be called the Clinton boom—more than a half-decade of strong growth, investment and income gains, accompanied by low inflation, falling unemployment, and declining poverty rates.

"The signature economic policy, and **policy shift**, of the early administration is the sharp **U-turn** on the budget that has replaced the prospect of growing surpluses with **expanding deficits**."

Against this backdrop, the dimensions of the Bush counterrevolution are clear. The signature economic policy, and policy shift, of the early administration is the sharp U-turn on the budget that has replaced the prospect of growing surpluses with expanding deficits. Its underlying logic and precedent lie in the Reagan experiment, pressed on Mr. Bush by Lawrence Lindsay, his chief economic adviser since 1999 and an unyielding advocate of supply-side economics. Supply-side theory holds that fiscal discipline is a minor force, but growth can be assured when incentives to invest are increased by cutting the marginal tax rates on income and inheritances for high-income people, who have long dominated personal investment. In this view, the fiscal shift of the 1990s, which included higher tax rates on wealthy individuals, was unrelated to the strong investment, productivity and growth that followed.

History dealt a body blow to this theory. The lesson of the strong performance of the 1990s, and of its weaker counterparts in the 1970s and 1980s, is that the real economy and its pretax returns affect people's performance and incentives much more than the tax code. Investment and incomes grew much faster in the 1990s after the top tax rate increased, and in the 1950s and 1960s when the top marginal tax rate was 70 to 90 percent, than they did after the sharp income tax cuts of the early 1980s.

Though it's too early to know just how fast investment, productivity and incomes will grow as the president's multitrillion-dollar tax cut takes full effect, it's clear and certain that investors don't generally favor large structural deficits.

The cost of borrowing. One of the key factors for investment rates is the price of long-term business borrowing. In the 1990s, long-term interest rates trended downward—became less expensive—even as growth accelerated. This dynamic reversed itself after Congress approved Mr. Bush's program. Even as the Federal Reserve repeatedly pushed down short-term interest rates last year to combat the slowdown, the cost of long-term borrowing went up. For example, while the yield on six-month Treasury bills fell from 5.7 percent in December 2000 to 1.8 percent in December 2001, the yield on 20-year securities rose from 5.6 percent to 5.8 percent.

The rising cost for business to borrow long-term is not surprising, given the difference between the budget picture projected in May 2001—before the Bush budget program passed—and the deficits now expected. For example, a $400 billion surplus projected last year for 2004 has now become a small projected deficit. The implications of a $400 billion shift in the fiscal balance, considered against a backdrop of business investment, are huge. The $400 billion projected reduction in the domestic capital available for investment in 2004 is equivalent to nearly one-third of all business fixed investment in 2000, the last year of the boom, and more than 40 percent of business investment in equipment and software that year. Much of this projected shortfall in domestic capital can be replaced by capital from abroad, as it was in the 1980s, but the price of borrowing it will be higher, and therefore overall investment will be lower.

HOLDING PATTERN: The recession has driven up unemployment, and Bush's supply-side policies will hamper investment and slow the recovery.

To be sure, the recession, not the new tax cuts, caused last year's deep slump in most areas of business fixed investment. But the Bush budget deficits will keep a lid on business investment as the economy recovers over the next few years, and that will spell the difference between the Clinton boom and the more disappointing performance that could mark the Bush years. This is because administration policies are undermining the conditions that fostered the strong New Economy growth of the 1990s—when low interest rates helped fuel more R&D, and new technologies, once developed, helped fuel strong business investment in new equipment, again financed at low interest rates. These investments helped raise productivity, which enabled the Federal Reserve to continue to keep interest rates low and the expansion going. Now, with forecasts of rising budget deficits driving up long-term interest rates, the president's program has begun to unravel this virtuous cycle of investment, innovation, productivity and growth.

These new policies also threaten a dynamic that was crucial to America's sense of vitality, self-confidence, and above all, positive change in the 1990s—the dynamic of cascading innovation. This phenomenon begins with economics: Productivity and income gains rose in the 1990s, as they had in the 1950s and 1960s, not just because firms bought new labor-saving technologies, but also, and mainly, because firms across the economy used these technologies to change the way they operate. Most workplaces became less hierarchical, and most workers became a little more independent. Some of these firms applied their new technologies in their new organizations and came up with new goods or services—including wireless devices like BlackBerry, on-board driving directions, digital films, custom bicycles, Napster, and online auctions. Competitors, recognizing the potential of the new technologies tapped by their rivals, demanded more; that produced another round of technological advance, which brought everything from the generations of Pentiums to wireless applications and broadband. The new technologies create the potential for more rounds of innovation in how companies conduct themselves and the products they produce. The clearest example of such cascading innovation, with its countless social and economic effects, is the evolution of the Internet itself.

SUSTAINING THE BOOM: In the tech-heavy 1990s, budget surpluses fueled strong growth, income gains, and high employment. Then came the counterrevolution.

Other administration policies could also slow the investment and innovation bandwagon. There may be less prospect of finding new foreign markets, not only because most of the world is slowing down, but also because the Bush administration is showing less commitment to free trade. Already, the White House has supported new trade protections for domestic steel and a rollback of part of the free-trade agreement with Caribbean nations. Even in the area of deregulation and competition, the administration has supported bailouts for large firms, shelved active antitrust action in the information technology sector, and stalled the drive to open up spectrum for third-generation wireless communications. The administration may further dampen market competition by directing much of its energy and environmental policy to the plans and interests of the largest energy and chemical corporations—even setting aside Enron.

The politics. The principle and purpose behind the Bush counterrevolution lie not in economics, but in politics—sometimes avowedly so. Throughout his campaign, Mr. Bush insisted that the good times of the 1990s had little to do with his predecessor's policies, and that government is ethically obliged to respect people's "right" to keep more of what they earn by lowering taxes. This neatly blended appeal to public morality and self-interest shielded Mr. Bush from the political sins of his father, who lost conservative support when he raised taxes in 1990 to help contain the deficit. Behind the moralizing also lies the political strategy of Reaganomics: By bringing back large budget deficits, Mr. Bush can force most Democrats, some moderate Republicans, and anyone else opposed to his approach, to choose between "higher" taxes or putting aside much of their own agenda.

Mr. Bush is wrong in suggesting that mainstream economic policies had little to do with the good times of the 1990s, and he is wrong in holding that his supply-side revival will produce prosperity. In truth, the Bush program is a ticking bomb. Its greatest costs begin a half-decade and more from now, and retiring baby boomers may find themselves at ground zero.

The fact is, the centerpiece of the president's economic program—large tax cuts—is antithetical to Social Security reform, the centerpiece of his domestic agenda. Social Security faces a cash-flow deficit a decade from now, so any reform must involve additional resources—usually from general revenues or more borrowing. This shortfall would come sooner and loom larger under Bush's favorite reform, partial privatization, because it would slash payroll tax receipts, and the need for additional resources would mount more sharply.

The Bush economic program will make these resources scarcer and more expensive. As the decade wears on, the tax cuts will reduce general revenues at an accelerating rate. Furthermore, the grim fiscal outlook will continue to mean higher interest rates, which will not only raise the cost of borrowing those resources, but also will increase the need for them, because it will slow growth and, with it, payroll tax revenues. Long after President Bush's term ends, his economic policies will leave both baby boomers and the American economy in a bind.

Robert J. Shapiro is managing director of Sonecon, a consulting and investment banking firm, and a fellow at the Progressive Policy Institute. He was an undersecretary of commerce in the Clinton administration.

The Deficit That Didn't Just Happen

A Sober Perspective on the Budget

It took the federal government 28 years (1970–98) to produce a budget surplus, but only 4 years to return to deficit. President Bush's 2003 budget promises that the government will have a surplus in 2005, but the revenue and spending policies it pursues risk another long spell of red ink that may extend well into the next decade, when the front edge of the baby boom generation reaches retirement age and both health and pension costs escalate.

By Allen Schick

Why the asymmetry in budget cycles? Why is the vicious circle of deficits so much longer than the virtuous circle of balanced budgets? If economic weakness impels government to spend more than it takes in, shouldn't the reverse also occur, that economic good times rescue the budget from red ink?

Part of the answer is that adverse budgetary effects of recession linger after the economy recovers. Recession lowers the trend line of economic growth, and it therefore takes a number of years to recover the lost output. Just a 1 percent drop-off in the 2002 growth rate would add $50 billion to the deficit a decade later, even if full growth were to resume in 2003.

This is the no-fault part of the deficit story that the Bush budget emphasizes. But it is far from the whole picture. In fact, the Congressional Budget Office has estimated that less than one-quarter of the $4 trillion in lost surpluses over the next decade is due to current economic difficulties. Most of the remainder is the result of political decisions to spend more and tax less. Two years ago in these pages, in "A Surplus, If We Can Keep It," I argued that policy mistakes caused the deficit surge in the 1980s and policy corrections stabilized federal finances in the 1990s. Critical turning points in budgeting don't just happen; they are the products of sound or flawed policies. No less than in the past, policy matters in budgeting. And policy mistakes are the reason why the fiscal outlook has rapidly deteriorated.

Policy mistakes are not simply matters of disagreement. They are inconsistent actions that cannot achieve purported objectives. Cutting taxes while steeply boosting defense spending in the early 1980s was mistaken because it generated huge deficits. Raising taxes in the early 1990s while constraining spending growth was sound policy because it enabled the government to successfully implement its deficit elimination strategy.

The government may now be at the cusp of another major policy error. It is not yet as big as the error two decades ago, but it risks becoming more damaging. The Bush budget story has three interlocking chapters: spending decisions, tax legislation, and White House attitudes concerning surpluses.

Spending Our Way Out of the Surplus

The arrival of a surplus a few years ago triggered a spending frenzy that vitiated the discretionary spending caps established by the 1990 Budget Enforcement Act and made a mockery of the BEA requirement that increased spending be offset by cuts in other spending or by revenue increases. In 2000 and 2001, discretionary spending soared more than $200 billion above the legal limits on annual appropriations. The caps expire at the end of 2002—which will at least enable politicians to be more honest about what they are doing. They no longer have to pretend that the census and other ongoing operations of government are national emergencies.

Defense is leading the spending parade, but it is not the only winner. In a replay of the policies of Ronald Reagan, Bush proposes to boost defense spending by $85 billion over three years, with additional tens of billions for homeland security. In dollar terms, this defense buildup is bigger than the one undertaken in the early 1980s, but it is a significantly smaller share of GDP or of total federal spending. The odds are, however, that defense costs are understated in the budget. On the one hand, the president's State of the Union Address declares that "our nation is at war... and the civilized world faces unprecedented dangers." On the other hand, his budget projects that defense spending will decline by mid-decade as a share of GDP. Military leaders have already complained that the additional money is insufficient; they will not have to wait long to get more.

Bush has not proposed the wholesale elimination of domestic programs, preferring instead to hold many to approximately the previous year's spending level. This way, inflation does the cutting and the president can claim credit for some well-publicized increases. But the discretionary budget may be tighter than it appears, for it includes billions for homeland security and for the health care and pensions of federal employees, which have been shifted from the mandatory to the discretionary budget. The CBO's baseline, which shows domestic spending keeping pace with GDP, would eat up most of the budget surplus promised by the president for the next decade.

Entitlements are also likely to add to budget pressures. Congress must reenact welfare and agriculture legislation during the 2002 session, and advocates are demanding hefty increases. The president's Medicare numbers are $300 billion (over the next 10 years) below CBO's baseline. He expects the rise in Medicare spending to decelerate despite the increase in the number of older Americans covered by Medicare.

Summing up the expenditure story, in the next decade the government will spend more than it did in the recent past and more than the president has projected in the budget. The era of big government may be over; the era of big spending is not. The question is, will government have the money to pay for it?

The Power Not to Tax

Judging from the Bush budget, the clear answer is "no." George W. Bush may be the first president in American history to declare war and demand tax cuts. He wants almost $700 billion in tax cuts over the next 10 years, on top of the $1.3 trillion cut enacted last year. The true size of that cut was masked by artfully placed phase-ins and phase-outs. Some cuts were scheduled to take effect near the end of the 10-year period; most would phase out during or at the end of it. Fully implemented, over the course of a decade the cuts would subtract almost $2 trillion from federal revenue.

Despite its search and destroy mission to find and liquidate provisions of the tax code, the administration would allow the alternative minimum tax (AMT), which may be the most disliked feature of the tax code, to ensnare millions of Americans in coming years. The AMT was originally designed to curb aggressive tax avoidance, but because it is not indexed for inflation, increasing numbers of people will face the AMT in future years for reasons completely unrelated to tax sheltering. Last year's tax cut granted taxpayers a temporary reprieve from the AMT, but that relief expires in 2004. Apparently, even the White House could not afford the $500 billion (over 10 years) price tag of fixing the AMT problem. An alternative take is that the president knows Congress will be pressured to act and that if he gets his additional tax cuts and Congress fixes AMT, the combined revenue loss would be even higher. A final spin on the administration's oversight is that once millions of taxpayers have to pay AMT, they will be so angry as to undermine public support for taxes. Whatever the true motive, the downstream loss in revenue may be even higher than the administration has forecast.

One need not wait long to see the effects. The 2003 budget shows two consecutive years—2001 and 2002—of decline in federal revenues, the first time that has happened since the end of World War II, when the United States shifted from full mobilization to peacetime. Even if no new tax cuts are enacted beyond those already adopted, the federal government faces a structural imbalance that is being masked in the short run by Social Security surpluses but will become apparent less than a decade from now. The administration has ignored the dire future by departing from past budget practice and shortening the budget's time horizon from 10 years to 5. Of course, this does not stop it from promoting permanent tax cuts whose budget impact will be fully felt after the foreshortened 5-year period has ended

The Political Logic of Unbalanced Budgets

The White House is not clueless as to the fiscal course it has charted. This is not a case of ignorance aforethought. The administration knows what it wants and is setting out to get it.

During the Reagan era, when serious policy mistakes led to a fivefold escalation in public debt from $700 billion to $3.5 trillion, Senator Daniel Patrick Moynihan accused the administration of creating the deficit to starve the government of revenue. Moynihan did not have a smoking gun to confirm his hypothesis, but George W. Bush has supplied one. Several weeks after taking office, the Bush White House published *A Blueprint for a New Beginning*, with a chart titled "Budget Surpluses Lead to Bigger Government." If this is so, the prudent thing to do is to get rid of surpluses; otherwise, government will grow bigger. Many conservatives have accepted as an article of faith that government spends any money it has and that the only effective way to constrain spending is to take away the surplus. In their mind, it is better to have a smaller government with a bigger deficit than a bigger government with a smaller deficit.

The problem with this point of view is that even if the government is broke, it will spend more. One reason is that big government includes big defense. In an age of terrorism, the Pentagon will not spend less because the government has red ink. Another is that, as David Stockman, Reagan's budget director, discovered two decades ago, Republicans also beat the drums for more spending. Stockman labeled this phenomenon "the triumph of politics," which became the title of his surly memoirs on his service in the U.S. government.

The third, most compelling reason for more government spending is that higher spending is built into the demographics of American life. We are now two decades closer in time, but no closer in solution, to the baby boom surge. These costs will have to be faced, regardless of the government's financial position. Some cynics think that the White House understands the mammoth costs that lie only a few years ahead, but that it is driven by the conviction that only a full-blown financial crisis will build support for privatizing all or a big portion of Social Security and Medicare. It believes that as long as Uncle Sam can afford to pick up the tab, there will be no pressure to fundamentally restructure these retirement programs.

We may, however, get only the crisis part of this scenario, in which case the administration is taking truly enormous risks with the future well-being of the United States. As the title of this article says, this deficit didn't have to happen. And it shouldn't.

Allen Schick is a visiting fellow in the Brookings Governmental Studies program and professor of public affairs at the University of Maryland.

Notes from underground:

money that people earn and spend outside the realm of official economic calculations is nonetheless real.

Elia Kacapyr

Money that people earn and spend outside the realm of official economic calculations is nonetheless real.

The Department of Commerce estimates that the U.S. produced $7.6 trillion worth of goods and services in 1996. This is the official assessment of Gross Domestic Product (GDP). Yet, everyone involved with the collection and dissemination of this figure understands that it is a vast underestimate. The Department of Commerce traditionally ignores the wide array of goods and services produced in the *underground* economy.

For instance, illegal gambling and prostitution are not included in the official estimate of GDP. Because of the criminal nature of these activities, it is understandably hard to get a handle on their dollar volume. It's also hard to estimate the value of legal goods and services provided in an illegal fashion, i.e., "off the books." The house painter who insists on being paid in cash to avoid claiming income and paying taxes does not contribute these dollars to the official GDP. Products produced and exchanged through casual or formal barter systems also fly under the department of Commerce's radar.

But by far the largest type of production not included in official accounts is both legal and ethical. It falls under the category of "housework." This includes any goods or services that households provide for themselves. Do-it-yourself auto repairs, cooking and cleaning, vegetable gardening, and much more fall into this classification—virtually everything we do that could be done by someone else if we paid them enough.

The "underground" economy includes all production not accounted for in the official GDP. Estimates of its scope range from 3 percent to 40 percent of the "aboveground" economy. The wide range of estimates is the result of different definitions. For instance, most studies of the underground do not include housework. That is, many researchers, like Edgar Feige, consider the underground to be only illegal and "off-the-books" production. Even so, his estimates suggest that the underground is about 20 percent of the above-board economy. One estimate of the economic value of unpaid housework sits at 31 percent of official 1981 GDP, according to Robert Eisner, in The Total Incomes System of Accounts. Piling other types of underground activity on top of this boosts the size of the underground economy to as much as half of the official total.

Underground money has implications for other economic statistics and economic policy. The official unemployment and poverty rates may be overestimated because of the employment and earnings people make but don't report. The federal government also loses out on at least $100 billion in lost tax revenues. On the other hand, the fact that the money's in consumers' hands means it's flowing somewhere.

If the proportional size of the underground economy remains relatively constant, then economic data expressed in rates, such as the growth rate in GDP, will be accurate despite the fact that they ignore the underground. But such a consistency is unlikely, evidence indicates that when tax rates rise, so does underground activity.

Some statistics that go into the American Demographics Index of Well-Being, such as the employment rate and after-tax income, exclude the underground economy. In their absence, the best we can do is note the inaccuracy. In August 1997, the Well-Being Index stood at 102.47, down about a tenth of a percent from July's revised reading of 102.56. These figures indicate that the typical American has enjoyed an increase in well-being of almost 2.5 percent since April 1990, the base month for the Index.

The decline in August is due to a drop in labor productivity that lowered the productivity and technology component, as well as an increase in the average work week that cut into leisure time. The social and physical environment also gave up ground as a result of increases in crime, divorce, and the number of endangered species. On the upside, income and consumer attitudes improved. The income figures don't account for our under-the-table dealings. But our attitudes might to some extent reflect them.

WHY ARE TAXES SO COMPLICATED

AND WHAT CAN WE DO ABOUT IT?

The time, money, and aggravation that tens of millions of Americans expend to understand and comply with the income tax is, it turns out, nothing new. In his 1776 *The Wealth of Nations*, Adam Smith noted that "subjecting the people to the frequent visits and the odious examination of the tax gatherers ... may expose them to much unnecessary trouble, vexation, and oppression: and though vexation is not, strictly speaking, expence, it is certainly equivalent to expence at which every man would be willing to redeem himself from it." For Americans today, the "expence" includes maintaining records, learning the law, preparing the return or hiring a preparer, corresponding with the IRS, and learning how to reduce (or cheat on) taxes.

BY WILLIAM GALE

How Bad Is It?

For low-income households, headaches can arise from issues regarding filing status, abandoned spouses, dependency tests, the child and dependent care tax credit, and the earned income tax credit. For individuals with higher income, complexity arises in itemizing deductions, the treatment of capital income (particularly capital gains, interest deductions, and passive losses), and the alternative minimum tax. For small business owners, issues relating to inventory, depreciation, and distinguishing various expenses can be complicated. For large corporations, tax complexity is centered on depreciation, international income, the alternative minimum tax, and coordinating with state taxes. In addition, large firms are almost continually audited; one tax expert has described the basic corporate tax return as nothing more than an "opening bid."

Stories of income tax complexity are legion. The internal revenue code contains more than five million words. In *Money Magazine*'s, recent surveys, every one of 40 to 50 tax preparers came up with a different estimate of the tax liability due on a complex, hypothetical return. The share of taxpayers who pay tax professionals to complete their tax returns rose from 42 percent in 1981 to 51 percent in 1997.

Yet the costs can easily be overblown or distorted. For many people, the tax system is not that complicated. Almost 40 percent file simplified 1040A or 1040EZ forms, and about 18 percent file the 1040 but have no itemized deductions or business income. Many people go to preparers to expedite refunds or because they prefer to spend their time on other things rather than on preparing taxes. Marsha Blumenthal and Joel Slemrod found that while the average taxpayer spent 27.4 hours on filing income tax returns and related activities, 30 percent spent less than 5 hours, and another 15 percent spent between 5 and 10 hours. About 11 percent spent 50-100 hours, and 5 percent spent more than 100 hours. About half had no out-of-pocket expenses, and 17 percent paid less than $50. Costs were highest among high-income and self-employed taxpayers.

Estimates of the total cost of complying with and running the individual and corporate income tax systems in 1995 go as high as $600 billion, but the most reasonable estimates range between $75 billion and $150 billion, or about 10–20 percent of income tax revenue. Even at $75 billion—or $386 per adult per year—tax complexity imposes significant costs. Resources lost to compliance and administrative costs could be productively devoted to other activities. Complexity also generates confusion and aggravation among taxpayers, which can reduce confidence in the system. Thus, *other things equal*, social welfare would be improved by having a tax system that is simpler to comply with, administer, and enforce. Of course, other things are never equal.

Tax Trade-offs

Since virtually everyone agrees that taxes should be easy to understand, administer, and enforce, why are taxes so complicated? The answer is that people also agree that taxes should be fair, should be conducive to economic prosperity, should raise sufficient revenue to finance government spending, and should respect individuals' privacy. Many people also think tax incentives should be used to pursue social or economic policies for the poor, housing, health, the environment, and small businesses.

Trading off these goals is difficult. Sometimes the meaning of a goal is unclear. Fairness, for example, is clearly "in the eyes of the beholder." Sometimes people differ about the best way to reach a goal. Is it best to help the poor via cash payments, tax incentives to work, direct provision of health care and education, or some other way? Finally, and most importantly, the goals are mutually inconsistent, and people disagree about which goals deserve the greatest weight.

As a result, tax policy involves tradeoffs—and complexity is the result. In the end, complexity resembles pollution. Some of it is undoubtedly unnecessary, but much of it is the unfortunate byproduct of the production of goods that many people want.

For reasons of fairness, most tax systems tailor tax burdens to depend on individual characteristics. This creates complexity in several ways. It requires tracing income from the business sector to individuals. It requires reporting and documenting individual characteristics such as marital status, dependents, each person's level and composition of income and spending, and so on. And it requires tax rates that vary with individual characteristics, creating incentives to shift income to other people with lower income, such as children, or to other time periods when income might be lower.

Complexity also derives from using the tax system to house social programs that subsidize what Congress and a significant portion of the population consider to be desired activities: housing, charity, health insurance, higher education, child care, state and local governments, retirement saving, entrepreneurial activity.

Closing tax loopholes also increases complexity. Any time a provision for special treatment or social engineering arises, it must be limited. If the child care credit, for example, is not intended to subsidize ski lessons in Aspen, some line has to be drawn concerning what is allowed and what is not. The taxation of financial income is particularly difficult in this regard.

Clamping down on tax evasion often increases complexity. Given the opportunity, people sometimes cheat on their taxes. Taxes on income from wages, for example, are withheld and sent to the government by the employer. The evasion rate is around 1 percent. Taxes on income from sole proprietorships are neither withheld nor sent in by a third party. The evasion rate here exceeds 30 percent. Many tax complexities exist to limit opportunities to cheat. In the late 1980s, a new law required people who claimed the child care credit to provide the Social Security number of the care provider. This both reduced the number of child care credit claims and raised by 65 percent the amount of income reported by child care providers.

While trade-offs among consensus policy goals are an important source of complexity, political factors are another. That is, complexity can also be the result of the production of goods that only a few of us want. Politicians and interest groups have a vested interest in certain types of subsidies that reduce taxes on favored constituencies. The lavish campaign contributions received by members of the House Ways and Means Committee do not come from lobbyists deeply respectful of a tax code clean of special subsidies. There is no lobby for simplicity.

Campaign gifts received by members of the House Ways and Means Committee do not come from lobbyists respectful of a tax code clean of special subsidies.

Sometimes the tax code is used to hide subsidies that would not be supported as outright spending. Consider a "homeowner welfare program" in which taxpayers earned an entitlement to help pay their mortgages. The entitlement grew in proportion to mortgage size, interest rate, and tax rate, but anyone whose entitlement was less than $6,000 received nothing from the program. Obviously, not a very appealing idea, but not that different from the mortgage interest deduction.

And let's face it: taxpayers *like* complexity that reduces their taxes. It's just complexity that raises taxes that annoys. Thus, people will grump about the new filing requirements for capital gains or child credits, but few will volunteer to give up those cuts.

The real question is not the total amount of compliance costs, but whether society gets good value for income tax complexity. My view is that, generally, we do not. The economy-wide perspective is important here. Suppose people had to fill out ten extra lines of the tax form to receive a $1,000 tax cut. Each might regard that as "good complexity," well worth the added cost of providing a few extra pieces of information. But in the aggregate, the revenues would have to [be] raised from taxpayers, so everyone's tax "cut" would be from a higher initial tax liability and net taxes would be the same. Thus, from a social perspective, the sum of all individuals' "good complexity" would be zero or negative.

Many existing provisions designed to encourage certain activities end up either largely subsidizing activity that would have occurred anyway or creating new problems. Many of the reasons for complexity are completely inappropriate: hiding unpopular programs, special loopholes that fuel campaign contributions. It is hard to see any impact on economic growth, and the "fairness" that occurs is a very strange kind. The subsidies help one group, but at the expense of all others.

Fundamental Tax Reform and Simplicity

The complexity of existing taxes is a powerful force behind the movement to replace the income tax with a flat tax or sales tax. The new systems would shift the tax base to consumption, rather than income, flatten tax rates, eliminate all deductions and credits, and collect most or all taxes at the business level. Plan advocates promise great simplification, and it is clear that pure versions of either plan would be much simpler than the existing system. But, well, it's not that simple.

Just as the income tax has deviated from a low-rate tax, with a one-page form and three pages of instructions, the flat tax or sales tax would also be under pressure to depart from its pure form. The thousands of lobbyists now working in Washington are unlikely to pack up and go home. In short, you can repeal the tax code, but you can't repeal politics.

On paper, for example, the sales tax would be vastly simpler than the current system. But the 45 existing state sales taxes are nothing like the single-rate, no-exemption sales tax that is proposed at the national level. The states feature numerous exemptions for goods and especially services, as well as different rates for different goods.

Moreover, as Joel Slemrod has shown, it is inappropriate to analyze simplicity independently of evasion and enforcement. The sales tax rate required to replace federal taxes would be well above the 23 percent rate claimed by advocates. After correcting for mistakes in the way the proposal treats government spending, and adjusting for political factors that would erode the tax base and for a reasonable amount of tax avoidance activity, a federal sales tax could result in mark-ups at the cash register in excess of 70 percent. At these rates, the incentive to evade sales taxes (which, unlike the income tax, feature no third-party withholding to aid in compliance) and the political pressure to exempt certain goods from taxes would be strong.

No country has ever successfully run a high-rate national retail sales tax. Many have tried to implement some variant of a sales tax and have given up. European governments, and numerous conservative and liberal scholars, have concluded that sales taxes at the required rates would be unworkable.

How about the flat tax? Under such a tax, businesses pay taxes on gross sales minus the cost of materials, services, capital goods, wages, and pension contributions. Individuals pay taxes on wages and pensions, less personal exemptions. No other income is taxed, and no other deductions are allowed. Flat tax advocates claim that individual and business returns will fit on a post card. In theory, the flat tax promises to be as simple as the sales tax.

But flat tax proponents have already acknowledged the need to provide transition relief to businesses that bought assets under the old system. Various flat tax plans include deductions for mortgage interest, charity, and payroll taxes. Deductions for health insurance and state and local taxes, the earned income credit, and graduated tax rates on wage income cannot be far behind. Allowing for these items would raise the required flat tax rate to about 32 percent and complicate taxes.

More fundamentally, the flat tax makes different distinctions than the existing system does. This will create new "pressure points," and so could create a host of new compliance and sheltering issues and accentuate problems created by existing regulations. For example, the differential treatment of "interest income" and "sales" under the flat tax has led tax experts Charles McLure and George Zodrow to conclude that the business tax "contains unacceptable opportunities for abuse." As attorney Alan Feld notes, the flat tax will either generate complicated business transactions (to skirt the simple rules) or complicated tax laws (to reduce the gaming possibilities), or both.

The flat tax would cause huge changes in tax liabilities for businesses across the country. It would create situations where some businesses with large economic profits would pay no taxes and others with economic losses would face steep taxes. Amending the tax to address these issues would create complexity.

At the individual level, the flat tax would renegotiate every alimony agreement in the country. Under the flat tax, alimony payments would no longer be deductible and receipts would no longer be taxable. Another difficulty would arise from earnings that are subsequently stolen. Under the flat tax, a robbery victim is still liable for taxes—and the robber is not. Under the income tax, it is the other way around. Additional anomalies will no doubt be discovered. Each of these problems with the individual tax could be fixed— but each solution would require a bigger postcard. Even a flat tax modified along these lines would be simpler than the current system. But with a rate of 30 percent or more, a realistic flat tax may not be politically appealing.

Simplifying the Income Tax

What about tax simplification options in the existing system? To begin with, procedural changes could raise the visibility and explicit consideration of simplicity and enforcement issues in the making of tax policy. For example, the recent IRS restructuring legislation requires the IRS to report to Congress each year regarding sources of complexity in the administration of federal taxes. The Joint Committee on Taxation is required to prepare complexity analysis of new tax legislation that affects individuals or small businesses.

It is also possible to eliminate the need for certain taxpayers to file tax returns. Thirty-six countries already use a return-free system for some of their taxpayers, replacing end-of-year filing requirements with withholding throughout the year and end-of-year reconciliation by the tax agency. In recent work, Janet Holtzblatt of the Treasury Department and I found that 52 million U.S. taxpayers could be placed on a return-free system with minor changes in the structure of taxes. These families have income only from wages, pensions, Social Security, interest, dividends, and unemployment compensation; they do not itemize deductions; and they face at most a 15 percent tax rate. Although the net compliance and administrative savings may not be great (because these people already have simple returns), a return-free system could reduce the psychic costs (fear and aggravation) associated with tax filing for the affected taxpayers.

Structural reforms could also reduce complexity. Broadening the tax base by eliminating deductions and preferences and taxing capital gains as ordinary income directly removes complexity. Increased standard deductions remove many people from the tax system. Lower tax rates would reduce the value of sheltering and cheating. Increasing the number of people who face the same "basic" rate facilitates the withholding of taxes on interest and dividends at the source, further simplifying taxes and increasing compliance. In short, broadening the base and reducing the rates can be revenue-neutral, fair, and efficient, as well as simplifying. Such reforms make taxes simpler for many taxpayers and could reduce compliance costs by 10–15 percent.

Getting Serious about Simplicity

We could have much simpler taxes if we were willing to change our preferences and forgo common notions of fairness, reduce our concern with tax evasion and loopholes, eliminate a raft of targeted social and economic incentives, and reduce the extent to which taxes depend on individual characteristics. Retaining those preferences, however, does not condemn us to much of the seemingly needless complexity of the current code. While the goal of fundamental tax reform is both more distant and less likely to resolve current problems than its advocates might care to admit, the existing system could be improved and simplified with a concerted effort to take simplicity seriously as a distinct policy goal.

Tax Reform R.I.P.

By Robert J. Samuelson

Eugene Steuerle is one of Washington's ranking policy wonks—a term used here with respect. He's forgotten more about taxes in the past 15 seconds than most of us will ever know. He arrived in Washington in 1974, worked for years at the Treasury and moved in 1989 to the Urban Institute, a think tank. Steuerle has just written a book, "Contemporary U.S. Tax Policy," that addresses the insistent question: Why is the federal tax system such a mess? The answer, in a word, is democracy.

In theory, it's easy to imagine a simple tax system with low rates, a broad tax base—the amount of taxable income—and substantial "progressivity," meaning that the rich pay higher rates. But in practice it has been elusive. Democrats and Republicans alike are too eager to use tax breaks to advance various social, economic and political agendas. The resulting tax code is so confusing, complex and contradictory that it costs taxpayers (in accounting fees and the value of their time) about $100 billion annually to complete their returns, estimates economist Joel Slemrod of the University of Michigan. In 2003 that roughly equaled the combined spending of the departments of education ($57.4 billion), homeland security ($32 billion) and state ($9.3 billion).

The appeal of tax breaks is that they give "the appearance of reducing the government's size ... even as government interference in the economy increases," writes Steuerle. But a tax system that promotes various causes (more saving, more health insurance, college attendance) cannot be simple. It brims with provisions. Goals conflict; contradictions are unavoidable. Similarly, a system that favors some taxpayers (homeowners, the elderly) must disfavor others. "Fairness" suffers.

Of course, the rich often try to skirt taxes through abusive shelters. But it's a myth that legal tax breaks mainly benefit the wealthy. The government publishes a yearly list of "tax expenditures," indicating the costs in forgone taxes of different breaks. These favor the middle and upper-middle classes. Here are some of the biggest for 2004: tax-free employer contributions to pensions and 401(k) plans, $123 billion; tax-free employer payments for health insurance, $120 billion; the deductibility of interest on home mortgages, $68 billion; charitable deductions, $43 billion; the exclusion of some Social Security benefits from income taxes, $27 billion. For the wealthy, the biggest break involves preferences for capital gains (mainly profits on stocks); in 2004, they're worth $82 billion.

All these tax breaks are immensely popular. They would be more defensible if they always made economic sense. Unfortunately, they don't. One reason Americans are building ever-larger homes for ever-smaller families is that housing is subsidized through the tax code. Similarly, the tax code subsidizes health insurance and, by shielding covered patients from many routine costs, promotes higher health spending. "The United States should have a tax system which looks like someone designed it on purpose," the late William E. Simon, Treasury secretary from 1974 to 1977, once said. Dream on.

Actually, Congress and President Reagan once made a stab at a better system. The Tax Reform Act of 1986 reduced tax rates and broadened the tax base. But the new system could survive only if politicians exercised self-restraint. It wasn't to be. Bill Clinton raised tax rates and expanded tax breaks. President Bush has gone one better. He's lowered rates and expanded preferences.

Sometimes this ceaseless competition for new tax breaks implodes. Congress is now considering a bill to repeal a provision of the corporate tax that, because it violates international trade rules, is subjecting $4 billion of U.S. exports to European tariffs. But the House and Senate versions of the bill are so stuffed with conflicting tax breaks (including ones for cruise ships, ranchers and oil companies) that the legislation has stalled.

As Steuerle notes, taxes cannot be divorced from broader budget questions. What should government do? For whom? Who pays? How much might new taxes hurt economic growth? But this is a debate we resolutely avoid. Republicans and Democrats merely echo their supporters' fondest hopes. Republicans reject any tax increases—ever. Democrats indicate that taxes need rise only on the wealthy. Considering existing budget deficits and future spending commitments, especially for retiring baby boomers, neither message is realistic.

Well, that's democracy. Tell 'em what they want to hear, not what they need to hear. Steuerle suggests that budgetary pressures—including more taxpayers triggering the alternative minimum tax—will promote sober solutions. "The grand budget compromise that must take place," he writes, "is between those who would allow retirement and health programs to continue to grow without bound and those who would continually prescribe tax cuts into the future." Based on history, that seems a triumph of hope over experience.

Link Between Taxation, Unemployment Is Absent

By Jonathan Weisman

When President Bill Clinton raised taxes in 1993, the unemployment rate dropped, from 6.9 to 6.1 percent, and kept falling each of the next seven years. When President Bush cut taxes in 2001, the unemployment rate rose, from 4.7 to 5.8 percent, then drifted to 6 percent last year when taxes were cut again.

It has become conventional wisdom in Washington that rising tax burdens crush labor markets. Bush castigated his political opponents last week for "that old policy of tax and spend" that would be "the enemy of job creation."

Yet an examination of historical tax levels and unemployment rates reveals no obvious correlation.

"The fact of the matter is, we have much higher rates of employment today than we did in 1954, but our level of taxation is considerably higher," said Gary Burtless, a labor economist at the Brookings Institution. "You simply can't look at total taxation to find employment levels."

The issue has become particularly relevant as Congress debates budget resolutions that would extend tax cuts that otherwise would expire over the next five years, and as Bush clashes daily with Sen. John F. Kerry (Mass.), his Democratic rival, over tax policies and job creation. The Senate voted Wednesday night to place new barriers on future tax cuts.

Republican economists—and White House officials—contend that higher marginal tax rates stifle business investment, hiring and the desire to work.

Senior Treasury Department officials said the correlation is "standard macroeconomics" dating to the Kennedy administration. Last year's surge in economic growth can be timed to the week that tax refunds arrived in American mailboxes, they said.

"The bottom line is, cuts in taxes lead to economic growth, which leads to improvements in the labor market to levels that are better than they otherwise would have been," said Mark J. Warshawsky, acting assistant Treasury secretary for economic policy.

But finding the proof in historical data is difficult, conceded Eric M. Engen, a Republican economist at the American Enterprise Institute.

"If you could hold everything else constant, yes," the correlation would be there, he said. "But everything else isn't the same. That's the big problem that economists have always had."

Engen cautioned that total tax takes are affected by economic growth as well as tax levels. A booming economy—driven not just by tax issues but also by interest rates, trade policies, inflation rates and other factors—will pump money into the government's coffers as it pushes unemployment down, he said.

Still, Burtless noted, some prominent conservative economists, including Harvard University's Martin S. Feldstein, predicted wrongly that the Clinton tax cuts would choke off the 1990s recovery and kill jobs, while the millions of new jobs that Bush said his $1.7 trillion in tax cuts would generate have not materialized. The historical disconnect does not stop there.

In 1964, federal taxation as a share of the economy stood at 17.5 percent, while unemployment was at 5.2 percent. That year, income taxes were slashed, lowering the tax rate in 1965 to 17 percent of the economy. Unemployment dropped as well, to 4.5 percent.

But then tax levels rose sharply, to 19.7 percent of the economy in 1969, while unemployment fell steadily, to 3.5 percent.

In 1981, President Ronald Reagan again slashed taxes. Taxation fell from 19.6 percent of the economy that year to 17.4 percent in 1983. The unemployment rate, however, rose over that period, from 7.6 percent to 9.6 percent. By 1989, taxation had drifted upward again, to 18.3 percent of the economy, but unemployment had fallen to 5.3 percent.

Total taxation in Sweden, including local taxes, is equal to 59.2 percent of that country's economy, the highest level in the 27-member Organization for Economic Cooperation and Development. In contrast, the U.S. total tax burden is 30.6 percent, lowest among the OECD members. Yet unemployment for the past two years in Sweden has been considerably lower than U.S. levels.

Burtless suggested that the issue is not tax levels but tax structures. Sweden has high taxation, but its generous social welfare system rewards citizens for the number of years spent working.

The Clinton tax increase was focused on upper-income households, but it included a sizable increase in the earned income credit for low-wage workers, making it more profitable for them to find and keep jobs.

Go Figure

THE GOOD NEWS is that you might be in for a tax cut. The bad news is that you'll only get it if you behave properly. And what is the required behavior? Never fear. Congress and the White House, with the help of the Internal Revenue Service's rule writers, will be glad to detail it for you. It won't take more than a few thousand pages.

Over the past few weeks, Congress has been hard at work marking up tax bills intended to reward key groups of voters, such as married couples and heirs to substantial estates. And, while some of these bills are likely (even designed) to be vetoed, others will ultimately make it into law—if not under this administration then under the next. With projected budget surpluses mounting with every recount, it's a near certainty that Congress will sooner or later return a big chunk of that extra revenue to taxpayers.

There is, of course, some chance that the tax cut we ultimately see will be straightforward: a decrease in income tax rates plus the elimination of some of the anomalies that make the tax code so complex and so often unfair. Some chance—but not much.

The tax code, you see, has become the lawmakers' code of good conduct. Way back during the reigns of FDR, Kennedy, Johnson, and, yes, even Nixon, if the government wanted to support some worthy purpose, it funded a program—along with some (often inadequate) mechanism for administering it and judging its success. But that was before "spending" became a curse and "tax cuts" a blessing. Spending has been deemed woefully inefficient, resulting in large, unresponsive government bureaucracies that consume much of their money in overhead and redundant activity. Tax cuts, by comparison, are simplicity itself—the money stays right in your pocket, and you can spend it as you please, with maximum flexibility and efficiency. So these days if politicians want, for instance, to increase the supply of affordable, quality child care, they don't fund and license day care centers. Instead, they give parents a tax credit so that they can make arrangements on their own. True, in a momentary lapse in 1986, Congress dumped a lot of older tax preferences, making the code both simpler and fairer. But that, as it turned out, just cleared the way for a glut of new gimmicks—embedded in some 78 subsequent tax laws—all engineered to reward the right kind of behavior.

Here is a sample of things the current tax code encourages you to do: Get married (if your spouse doesn't hold a job); have kids (or adopt some); educate said kids (or send them to day care); get old; save money (take your choice here of seven different types of IRA accounts, including "Traditional IRA," "Spousal IRA," "SEP IRA," and the euphemistic "Simple IRA"); enjoy capital gains; suffer passive losses; and inherit a family business or farm.

If Al Gore becomes president, look for new or bigger breaks for caring for kids or disabled relatives, running a small business, pursuing "lifelong learning," and saving for retirement. If George W. Bush takes over, he'll push an across-the-board rate cut, as well as special breaks for farmers, ranchers, adopted and foster kids, donors to churches and charities, and families setting aside money for private kindergarten and grade school.

Which would all be well and good—these are, after all, mostly worthy purposes—if tax breaks really were as simple and efficient as today's politicians would have you believe. But they're not. Take their alleged simplicity. Democrats, in particular, try to ensure that any new tax subsidy is "means-tested"—that is, targeted to low- and middle-bracket taxpayers (or paid directly to those owing no taxes). But that means creating for each new tax benefit what the Urban Institute's Eugene Steuerle dubs a "mini-tax system," with its own rules for determining eligibility and measuring income. When, for example, does a child count as a child for tax purposes? That depends on whether you want to claim a dependent-care credit, a Hope credit, or any of a host of other credits on his or her behalf. Will getting married cut or increase your tax bill? Better check out the 60-plus provisions of the tax code that depend on marital status.

Things don't get any better higher up the income spectrum. The fact that so many tax breaks are phased out as income increases produces a wildly erratic tax-rate schedule. If your family earnings total around $100,000 and you get a modest pay raise, for example, you could end up forking over more of your gain to the feds than if you were earning $1 million. That's because you may face cutbacks in the amount you can now deduct for Hope, child, or adoption credits, for example. With somewhat more income, you'll start losing your itemized deductions and personal exemptions, too. At higher levels of income, however, the phaseouts have all been completed, so Bill Gates can probably keep more of his next dollar than you can. "People have no idea what their marginal rate is," says Stephen Corrick, a tax partner at Arthur Andersen.

And if tax breaks aren't very simple, neither are they very efficient. It has been well-documented that tax preferences mostly subsidize activities—such as saving money, hiring workers, or having kids—that would have occurred anyway. And much of the money doesn't go toward the intended purpose at all. Shocking as it may seem, people cheat. They take advantage of even the most high-minded tax breaks—exaggerating, for example, their contributions to the collection plate each Sunday—if they think they can get away with it. And the more complicated the tax laws, the more people can get away with. Back in 1990, Congress was horrified to discover that some 40 percent of the Earned Income Tax Credit, a refundable payment to low-earning breadwinners, was going to families not entitled to it. (This did not, however, deter Congress from subsequently expanding and further complicating the EITC.) In response, the IRS was forced to step up EITC audits—enforcement being yet another casualty of a complicated tax code. As Representative Amo Houghton, chair of the Ways and Means Oversight Committee, noted at a recent hearing, "A provision we pass may make good sense in terms of fairness and equity but may be absolutely unworkable in the real world."

All this well-meaning complexity doesn't just breed tax evasion; it breeds cynicism. Taxpayers know the system is irrational, and they suspect, often correctly, that they're getting screwed. This is a prime factor—Democrats, take note—in the public's support for replacing the income tax with a far less progressive but presumably simpler "flat" tax.

Congress, of course, is not insensitive to these problems. Only two years ago it added a provision to the tax code requiring the IRS to prepare an annual report pinpointing "sources of complexity in the administration of the Federal tax laws." (Simply handing out mirrors to each of the 535 members was not considered.) Then, having duly noted its concern, Congress returned to the more congenial business of conjuring up new sources of complexity for the IRS to document.

JODIE ALLEN

JODIE ALLEN is a senior writer at *U.S. News & World Report* covering political economy.

What Should Central Banks Do?

This paper was prepared for the Homer Jones Lecture, Federal Reserve Bank of St. Louis, March 30, 2000. Frederic S. Mishkin is a professor at the Graduate School of Business, Columbia University and a scholar at the National Bureau of Economic Research. He thanks Dan Thornton, Bill Poole, Lars Svensson, and the participants in the Macro Lunch at Columbia University for their helpful comments. Any views expressed in this paper are those of the author only and not those of Columbia University or the National Bureau of Economic Research.

Frederic S. Mishkin

INTRODUCTION

In the last twenty years, there has been substantial rethinking about how central banks should do their job. This rethinking has led to major changes in how central banks operate, and we are now in an era in which central banks in many countries throughout the world have had notable success—keeping inflation low, while their economies experience rapid economic growth. In this lecture, I outline what we think we have learned about how central banks should be set up to conduct monetary policy and then apply these lessons to see if there is room for institutional improvement in the way the Federal Reserve operates.

The lecture begins by discussing seven guiding principles for central banks and then uses these principles to outline what the role of central banks should be. This framework is then used to see how the institutional features of the Fed measure up. I will take the view that despite the Fed's extraordinarily successful performance in recent years, we should not be complacent. Changes in the way the Fed is set up to conduct its business may be needed to help ensure that the Fed continues to be as successful in the future.

GUIDING PRINCIPLES FOR CENTRAL BANKS

Recent theorizing in monetary economics suggests seven basic principles that can serve as useful guides for central banks to help them achieve successful outcomes in their conduct of monetary policy. These are:

- Price stability provides substantial benefits;
- Fiscal policy should be aligned with monetary policy;
- Time inconsistency is a serious problem to be avoided;
- Monetary policy should be forward looking;
- Accountability is a basic principle of democracy;
- Monetary policy should be concerned about output as well as price fluctuations; and
- The most serious economic downturns are associated with financial instability.

We will look at each of these principles in turn.

Price Stability Provides Substantial Benefits to the Economy

In recent years a growing consensus has emerged that price stability—a low and stable inflation rate—provides substantial benefits to the economy. Price stability prevents overinvestment in the financial sector, which in a high-inflation environment expands to profitably act as a middleman to help individuals and businesses escape some of the costs of inflation.[1] Price stability lowers the uncertainty about relative prices and the future price level, making it easier for firms and individuals to make appropriate decisions, thereby increasing economic efficiency.[2]

Price stability also lowers the distortions from the interaction of the tax system and inflation.[3] Price stability lowers the uncertainty about relative prices and the future price level, making it easier for firms and individuals to make appropriate decisions, thereby increasing economic efficiency.[2] Price stability also lowers the distortions from the interaction of the tax system and inflation.[3]

All of these benefits of price stability suggest that low and stable inflation can increase the level of resources productively employed in the economy, and might even help increase the rate of economic growth. While time-series studies of individual countries and cross-national comparisons of growth rates are not in total agreement, there is a consensus that inflation is detrimental to economic growth, particularly when inflation is at high levels.[4] Therefore, both theory and evidence suggest that monetary policy should focus on promoting price stability.

Align Fiscal Policy with Monetary Policy

One lesson from the "unpleasant monetarist arithmetic" discussed in Sargent and Wallace (1981) and the recent literature on fiscal theories of the price level (Woodford, 1994 and 1995) is that irresponsible fiscal policy may make it more difficult for the monetary authorities to pursue price stability. Large government deficits may put pressure on the monetary authorities to monetize the debt, thereby producing rapid money growth and inflation. Restraining the fiscal authorities from engaging in excessive deficit financing thus aligns fiscal policy with monetary policy and makes it easier for the monetary authorities to keep inflation under control.

Time Inconsistency Is a Serious Problem To Be Avoided

One of the key problems facing monetary policymakers is the time-inconsistency problem described by Calvo (1978), Kydland and Prescott (1977), and Barro and Gordon (1983). The time-inconsistency problem arises because there are incentives for a policymaker to try to exploit the short-run tradeoff between employment and inflation to pursue short-run employment objectives, even though the result is poor long-run outcomes. Expansionary monetary policy will produce higher growth and employment in the short-run. Therefore, policymakers will be tempted to pursue this policy even though it will not produce higher growth and employment in the long-run because economic agents adjust their wage and price expectations upward to reflect the expansionary policy. Unfortunately, however, expansionary monetary policy will lead to higher inflation in the long-run, with its negative consequences for the economy.

McCallum (1995) points out that the time-inconsistency problem by itself does not imply that a central bank will pursue expansionary monetary policy that leads to inflation. Simply by recognizing the problem that forward-looking expectations in the wage- and price-setting process promotes a strategy of pursuing expansionary monetary policy, central banks can decide not to play that game. From my first-hand experience as a central banker, I can testify that central bankers are very aware of the time-inconsistency problem and are, indeed, extremely averse to falling into a time-inconsistency trap. However, even if central bankers recognize the problem, there still will be pressures on the central bank to pursue overly expansionary monetary policy and inflation may result, so that the time-inconsistency problem remains. The time-inconsistency problem is just shifted back one step; its source is not in the central bank, but rather, resides in the political process.

The time-inconsistency literature points out both why there will be pressures on central banks to pursue overly expansionary monetary policy and why central banks whose commitment to price stability is in doubt are more likely to experience higher inflation. In order to prevent high inflation and the pursuit of a suboptimal monetary policy, monetary policy institutions need to be designed in order to avoid the time-inconsistency trap.

Monetary Policy Should Be Forward Looking

The existence of long lags from monetary policy actions to their intended effects on output and inflation suggests that monetary policy should be forward looking. If policymakers wait until undesirable outcomes on inflation and output fluctuations actually arise, their policy actions are likely to be counterproductive. For example, by waiting until inflation has already appeared before tightening monetary policy, the monetary authorities will be too late; inflation expectations will already be embedded into the wage- and price-setting process, creating an inflation momentum that will be hard to contain. Once the inflation process has gotten rolling, the process of stopping it will be slower and costlier. Similarly, by waiting until the economy is already in recession, expansionary policy may kick in well after the economy has recovered, thus promoting unnecessary output fluctuations and possible inflation.

To avoid these problems, monetary authorities must behave in a forward-looking fashion and act preemptively. For example, assume that it takes two years for monetary policy to have a significant effect on inflation. Under these circumstances, even if inflation is quiescent currently (with an unchanged stance of monetary policy) and policymakers forecast inflation to rise in two years time, they must act immediately to head off the inflationary surge.

Policymakers Should Be Accountable

A basic principle of democracy is that the public should have the right to control the actions of the government: In other and more famous words, "The government should be of the people, by the people and for the people." Thus, the public in a democracy must have the capability to "throw the bums out" or punish incompetent policymakers through other methods in order to control their actions. If policymakers cannot be removed from office or punished in some other way, this basic principle of democracy is violated. In a democracy, government policymakers need to be held accountable to the public.

A second reason why accountability of policymakers is important is that it helps to promote efficiency in government. Making policymakers subject to punishment makes it more likely that incompetent policymakers will be replaced by competent ones and creates better incentives for policymakers to do their jobs well. Knowing that they are subject to punishment when performance is poor, policymakers will strive to get policy right. If policymakers are able to avoid accountability, then their incentives to do a good job drop appreciably, making poor policy outcomes more likely.

Monetary Policy Should Be Concerned with Output as well as Price Fluctuations

Price stability is a means to an end—a healthy economy—and should not be treated as an end in itself. Thus, central bankers should not be obsessed with inflation control and become what Mervyn King (1997) has characterized as "inflation nutters." Clearly, the public cares about output as well as inflation fluctuations, and so the objectives for a central bank in the context of a long-run strategy should not only include minimizing inflation fluctuations, but should also include minimizing output fluctuations. Objective functions with these characteristics have now become standard in the monetary economics literature, which focuses on the conduct of monetary policy (e.g., see the papers in Taylor, 1999).

The Most Serious Economic Downturns Are Associated with Financial Instability

A reading of U.S. monetary history (Friedman and Schwartz, 1963, Bernanke, 1983, and Mishkin, 1991) indicates that the most serious economic contractions in U.S. history, including the Great Depression, have all been associated with financial instability. Indeed, this literature suggests that financial instability is a key reason for the depth of these economic contractions. The recent financial crises and depressions in Mexico and East Asia also support this view (Mishkin, 1996, 1999a and Corsetti, Pesenti, and Roubini, 1998). Preventing financial instability is, therefore, crucial to promoting a healthy economy and reducing output fluctuations, an important objective for central banks, as we have seen above.

IMPLICATIONS FOR THE ROLE OF A CENTRAL BANK

Armed with these seven guiding principles, we can now look at what institutional features a central bank should have in conducting its operations. We derive the following implications/criteria for the role of a central bank:

- Price stability should be the overriding, long-run goal of monetary policy;
- An explicit nominal anchor should be adopted;
- A central bank should be goal dependent;
- A central bank should be instrument independent;
- A central bank should be accountable;
- A central bank should stress transparency and communication;
- A central bank should also have the goal of financial stability.

Price Stability Should Be the Overriding, Long-Run Goal of Monetary Policy

Together, the first three principles for monetary policy outlined above suggest that the overriding, long-run goal of monetary policy should be price stability. A goal of price stability immediately follows from the benefits of low and stable inflation, which promote higher economic output. Furthermore, an institutional commitment to price stability is one way to make time-inconsistency of monetary policy less likely. An institutional commitment to the price stability goal provides a counter to time-inconsistency because it makes it clear that the central bank must focus on the long-run and thus resist the temptation to pursue short-run expansionary policies that are inconsistent with the long-run, price stability goal.

The third principle, that fiscal policy should be aligned with monetary policy, provides another reason why price stability should be the overriding, long-run goal of monetary policy. As McCallum (1990) has pointed out, "unpleasant monetarist arithmetic" only arises if the fiscal authorities are the first mover. In other words, if the fiscal authorities are the dominant player and can move first—thus setting fiscal policy exogenously, knowing that the monetary authorities will be forced to accommodate their policies to maintain the long-run government budget constraint—then fiscal policy will determine the inflation rate. Indeed, this is the essence of the fiscal theory of the price level. On the other hand, as McCallum (1990) points out, if the monetary authorities are the dominant player and move first, then it will be fiscal policy that will accommodate in order to satisfy the long-run government budget constraint and monetary policy will determine the inflation rate. An institutional commitment to price stability as the overriding, long-run goal, is just one way to ensure that monetary policy moves first and dominates, forcing fiscal policy to align with monetary policy.

The sixth guiding principle, that output fluctuations should also be a concern of monetary policy, suggests that a fanatic pursuit of price stability could be problematic because policymakers should see not only price fluctuations, but also output fluctuations as undesirable. This is why the price stability goal should be seen as overriding in the long-run but not in the short-run. As Lars Svensson (1999) states, central banks should pursue what he calls "flexible inflation targeting," in which the speed at which a central bank tries to get to price stability reflects their concerns about output fluctuations. The more heavily a central bank cares about output fluctuations, the more time it should take to return to price stability when it is not already there. However, because a "flexible inflation targeter" always sets a long-term price stability goal for inflation, the fact that a central bank cares about output fluctuations is entirely consistent with price stability as the long-run, overriding goal.

An Explicit Nominal Anchor Should Be Adopted

Although an institutional commitment to price stability helps solve time-inconsistency and fiscal alignment problems, it does not go far enough because price stability is not a clearly defined concept. Typical definitions of price stability have many elements in common with the commonly used legal definition of pornography in the United States—you know it when you see it. Thus, constraints on fiscal policy and discretionary monetary policy to avoid inflation might end up being quite weak because not everyone will agree on what price stability means in practice, providing both monetary policymakers and politicians a loophole to avoid making tough decisions to keep inflation under control. A solution to this problem, which supports the first three guiding principles, is to adopt an explicit nominal anchor that ties down exactly what the commitment to price stability means.

There are several forms that an explicit nominal anchor can take. One is a commitment to a fixed exchange rate. For example, in 1991, Argentina established a currency board that required the central bank to exchange U.S. dollars for new pesos at a fixed exchange rate of one to one. A second nominal anchor is for the central bank to have a money-growth target, as was the case in Germany. A third nominal anchor is for there to be an explicit numerical inflation goal as in inflation-targeting countries such as New Zealand, Canada, the United Kingdom, Australia, and Brazil, among others. All these forms of explicit nominal anchors can help reduce the time-inconsistency problem, as the success of countries using them in lowering and controlling inflation demonstrates (Mishkin, 1999b). These nominal anchors also help restrain fiscal policy and also are seen as an important benefit of inflation targeting in countries such as New Zealand and Canada (Mishkin and Posen, 1997, and Bernanke, Laubach, Mishkin, and Posen, 1999).

One criticism of adopting an explicit nominal anchor, such as an inflation target, is that it will necessarily result in too little emphasis on reducing output fluctuations, which is inconsistent with the guiding principle that monetary policy should be concerned with output as well as price fluctuations. However, this view is mistaken. Inflation targeting, as it has actually been practiced (Mishkin and Posen, 1997, and Bernanke, Laubach, Mishkin, and Posen, 1999), has been quite flexible and has not led to larger output fluctuations. Indeed, adoption of an inflation target can actually make it easier for central banks to deal with negative shocks to the aggregate economy. Because a decline in aggregate demand also leads to lower-than-expected inflation, a central bank is able to respond with a monetary easing, without causing the public to question its anti-inflationary resolve. Furthermore, inflation targeting can make it less likely that deflation, a fall in the price level, would occur. There are particularly valid reasons for fearing deflation in today's world, including the possibility that it might promote financial instability and precipitate a severe economic contraction. Indeed, deflation has been associated with deep recessions or even depressions, as in the 1930s, and the recent deflation in Japan has been one factor that has weakened the financial system and the economy. Targeting inflation rates of above zero, as all inflation targeters have done, makes periods of deflation less likely. The evidence on inflation expectations from surveys and interest rate levels suggest that maintaining a target for inflation above zero (but not too far above) for an extended period does not lead to instability in inflation expectations or to a decline in the central bank's credibility.

Central Banks Should Be Goal Dependent

Although there is a strong rationale for the price stability goal and an explicit nominal anchor, who should make the institutional commitment? Should the central bank independently announce its commitment to the price stability goal or would it be better to have this commitment be mandated by the government?

Here the distinction between goal independence and instrument independence made by Debelle and Fischer (1994) and Fischer (1994) is quite useful. Goal independence is the ability of the central bank to set its own goals for monetary policy, while instrument independence is the ability of the central bank to independently set the instruments of monetary policy to achieve the goals. The fifth guiding principle that the public must be able to exercise control over government actions and that policymakers must be accountable, so basic to democracy, strongly suggests that the goals of monetary policy should be set by the elected government. In other words, a central bank should not be goal independent. The corollary of this view is that the institutional commitment to price stability should come from the government in the form of an explicit, legislated mandate for the central bank to pursue price stability as its overriding, long-run goal.

Not only is the principle of a legislated mandate and goal dependence of the central bank consistent with basic principles of democracy, but it has the further advantage that it is consistent with the second and third guiding principles—it makes time-inconsistency less likely, while making alignment of fiscal policy with monetary policy more likely. As we discussed above, the source of the time-inconsistency problem is more likely to be embedded in the political process than it is in the central bank. Once politicians commit to the price stability goal by passing central bank legislation with a price stability mandate, it becomes harder for them to put pressure on the central bank to pursue short-run expansionary policies that are inconsistent with the price stability goal. Furthermore, a government commitment to price stability also is a commitment to making monetary policy dominant over fiscal policy, ensuring a better alignment of fiscal policy with monetary policy.

An alternative way to solve time-inconsistency problems has been suggested by Rogoff (1985): Grant both goal and instrument independence to a central bank and then appoint conservative central bankers to run it, who put more weight on controlling inflation (relative to output) than does the general public. The result will be low inflation, but at the cost of higher output variability than the public desires.

There are two problems with this solution. First, having "conservative" central bankers impose different preferences from those of the public on the conduct of monetary policy is inherently undemocratic. Basic democratic principles indicate that the preferences of policymaking should be aligned with those of the society at large. Second, in the long run, a central bank cannot operate without the support of the public. If the central bank is seen to be pursuing goals that are not what the public wants, support for central bank independence is likely to erode. Thus appointment of "conservative" central bankers may not be stable in the long run and will not provide a permanent solution to the time-inconsistency problem.

The same principles that suggest that the central bank should be goal dependent, with the commitment to the price stability goal mandated by the government, also suggest that the commitment to an explicit nominal anchor should be made by the government. In the case of an exchange-rate target, the government should set the target, as in Argentina, or in the case of an inflation target, the government should set the numerical inflation goal. The fact that the government sets these targets so that the central bank as goal dependent does not mean that the central bank should be cut out of the decision-making process. Because the central bank has both prestige and expertise in the conduct of monetary policy, governments will almost always be better served by setting these targets in consultation with the central bank.

Although it is clear that the government should set the goal for the explicit nominal anchor in the long-run, it is more controversial whether it should set it in the short-run or intermediate-run. If a government, for example, set a short-run inflation or exchange rate target that was changed every month or every quarter, this could easily lead to time inconsistency in which short-run objectives would dominate. In many countries that target inflation, the Ministry of Finance, as the representative of the government, does set an annual inflation target; however, as documented in Bernanke, Laubach, Mishkin, and Posen (1999), the target rarely is changed once price stability is achieved. Thus, even though (in theory) governments could manipulate an annual inflation target to pursue short-run objectives, the transparency of goal-setting leads to a long-run approach to setting inflation targets even when it is done on an annual basis. The situation for the United States is even more complicated. Because of our congressional system, the Treasury Secretary is not the representative of Congress, in contrast to the Minister of Finance who does represent parliament in a parliamentary system. Instead the Treasury Secretary represents the executive branch. Thus, who represents the American government in setting a short- or intermediate-term target for monetary policy is not clear cut. This problem is not as severe for setting the long-run goal of monetary policy, which could be done by a congressional commission with representatives from both the executive and legislative branches, as well as from the public and the central bank. However, the difficulties of delegating the setting of shorter run targets for monetary policy in a congressional system may require that the central bank keep this responsibility.[5]

Central Banks Should Be Instrument Independent

Although the arguments above suggest that central banks should be goal dependent, the guiding principles in the previous section provide a strong case that central banks should be instrument independent. Allowing central banks to control the setting of monetary policy instruments provides additional insulation from political pressures to exploit short-run tradeoffs between employment and inflation. Instrument independence means that the central bank is better able to avoid the pursuit of time-inconsistent policies in line with the third guiding principle.

The fourth guiding principle, that monetary policy needs to be forward looking in order to take account of the long lags in the effect of monetary policy on inflation, provides another rationale for instrument independence. Instrument independence insulates the central bank from the myopia that is frequently a feature of the political process arising from politicians' concerns about getting elected in the near future. Thus, instrument independence makes it more likely that the central bank will be forward looking and adequately allow for the long lags from monetary policy actions to inflation in setting their policy instruments.

Recent evidence seems to support the conjecture that macroeconomic performance is improved when central banks are more independent. When central banks in industrialized countries are ranked from least legally independent to most legally independent, the inflation performance is found to be the best for countries with the most independent central banks (see Alesina and Summers, 1993, Cukierman, 1992, and Fischer, 1994, among others). However, there is some question whether causality runs from central bank independence to low inflation or, rather, whether a third factor is involved, such as the general public's preferences for low inflation that create both central bank independence and low inflation (Posen, 1995).

The bottom line is that basic principles for monetary policy and democracy suggests that central banks should have instrument but not goal independence. This degree of independence for central banks is analogous to the relationship between the U.S. military and the government during the successfully prosecuted Gulf War in 1991. The military had instrument independence. It had complete control over the prosecution of the war with little interference from the government (in contrast to the less successfully waged Vietnam War). On the other hand, the military did not have goal independence. It was the Commander in Chief, George Bush, who made the decisions as to what the objectives and goals of the war would be.

Central Banks Should Be Accountable

The fifth guiding principle, that policymakers should be accountable, indicates that the central bank should be subject to government and public scrutiny. One way of ensuring accountability is to make the independence of the central bank subject to legislative change by allowing the act that created the central bank to be modified by legislation at any time. Another way is to mandate periodic reporting requirements to the government. For example, as was done in the Humphrey-Hawkins legislation which requires the Chairman of the Federal Reserve to testify to Congress twice a year.

The need for central banks to be accountable provides an additional reason why central banks should have an explicit nominal anchor. If there is no explicit nominal anchor, it is far less clear upon what criterion the central bank should be judged, and thus it is harder to hold it accountable. On the other hand, with an explicit nominal anchor, like a target for inflation or the exchange rate, the public and the politicians have a clear cut benchmark to assess the performance of the central bank. Thus, an explicit nominal anchor enhances the accountability of the central bank. Indeed, with an explicit nominal anchor, accountability can be enforced by making the central bank governor subject to dismissal if he or she breaches the goals set by the government, as is the case in New Zealand.

Central Banks Should Stress Transparency and Communication

Increased transparency of monetary policymaking is another important way to increase central bank accountability in line with the fifth guiding principle. Central banks need to communicate clearly their monetary policy strategy in order to explain their objectives and how they plan to achieve them. Each time they change their policy instruments, such as the interbank interest rate, they also need to clearly state the decision and then explain the rationale for it. Transparency can be further increased by publication of the central bank's forecast and the minutes of the discussion of monetary policy.

In addition, central banks need to pursue many outreach vehicles to communicate with the public. These include the continual making of speeches to all elements of society, more openness with the press and media, and the development of brochures and reports that are accessible to the public. Particularly noteworthy in this regard are the "Inflation Report" type documents initially developed by the Bank of England and now emulated by many other central banks. These documents depart from the usual dull-looking, formal reports of central banks to take on the best elements of textbook writing (fancy graphics, use of boxes) in order to better communicate with the public.

Increasing transparency and accountability not only helps to align central banks with democratic principles, and is thus worthy of its own right, but it also has benefits for the ability of central banks to conduct monetary policy successfully. Transparency reduces the uncertainty about monetary policy, interest rates, and inflation, thus making private-sector planning easier. Transparency and communication also promote a better public understanding of what central banks can do—promote price stability which, as suggested by the first guiding principle, has the potential to enhance economic growth in the long run—and what central banks cannot do—create permanent increases in output and employment through expansionary policy. Better public understanding of what central banks can and cannot do is then likely to help generate more public support for monetary policy, which is focused on price stability, becoming the long-run, overriding goal.

Although central bankers find their life to be a more comfortable one when they are not accountable and can avoid intense public scrutiny, increased transparency and accountability have important benefits for central bankers, helping them to adhere to the first five guiding principles outlined in the previous section. Because transparency and accountability can increase the public support for the price stability goal and longer-term thinking on the part of the central bank, they can reduce political pressures on the central bank to pursue inflationary monetary policy and, thus, limit the time-inconsistency problem, while generating more support for forward-looking policy by the central bank. Also, greater transparency and communication can help the central bank convince the public that fiscal policy needs to be aligned with monetary policy.

In addition, transparency and accountability can increase support for independence of the central bank.[6] An instructive example is provided by the granting of instrument independence to the Bank of England in May 1997. Prior to this date, monetary-policy decisions in the United Kingdom were made by the government (the Chancellor of the Exchequer) rather than by the Bank of England. When, on May 6, 1997, the Chancellor of the Exchequer, Gordon Brown, announced the granting of instrument independence to the Bank of England, giving it the power to set the overnight interest rate, he made it particularly clear at the press conference that, in his view, the action had been made possible by the increased transparency and accountability of policy under the recently adopted inflation-targeting regime.

Central Banks Should also Have a Financial Stability Goal

Because central banks should care about output fluctuations (Principle 6) and the most serious economic contractions arise when there is financial instability (Principle 7), central banks also need to focus on preventing financial instability. The primary way that central banks prevent financial instability is by acting as a lender of last resort, that is, by supplying liquidity to the financial system to keep a financial crisis from spinning out of control. Because acting as a lender of last resort, in effect, provides a safety net for financial institutions to whom the funds will be channeled, it creates a moral hazard problem in which these institutions who are potential borrowers have incentives to take on excessive risk, which can make financial instability more likely. Thus, central banks need to consider the tradeoff between the moral hazard cost of the role as lender of last resort and the benefit of preventing financial crises. Keeping moral hazard from getting out of hand indicates that central banks should not perform the role of lender of last resort unless it is absolutely necessary; and, therefore, this role should occur very infrequently.

Because lender-of-last-resort lending should be directed at providing funds to solvent, but illiquid, financial institutions and not to insolvent institutions, in order to reduce incentives to take on too much risk by these institutions, the central bank needs to have information regarding to whom it might have to extend loans when it performs this role. One way for the central bank to get this information is for it to have a supervisory role over these institutions. This is an argument for giving central banks a role in prudential supervision (see, e.g., Mishkin, 1992, and Bernanke, 2000). In addition, a supervisory role for the central bank can help it obtain information about whether a situation really is likely to lead to a financial crisis and, thus, requires a lender-of-last-resort intervention. Without this information, the central bank may either intervene too frequently or fail to do so when it is really needed, thus making financial instability more likely. It is possible that central banks can acquire the information they need from supervisory agencies which are separate from the central bank, but some central bank officials doubt this (see Peek, Rosengren, and Tootell, 2000). Thus, there is an argument for the central bank to have a role in prudential supervision, but it is by no means clear cut. Furthermore, there are arguments against central bank involvement in prudential supervision because it may cause a central bank to lose its focus on the price-stability objective.

A FEDERAL RESERVE SCORECARD

Now that we have outlined what the role of a central bank should be, we can assess how the institutional features of the Federal Reserve measure up. We provide an assessment of whether the way the Fed is set up to conduct its operations is consistent with each of the seven criteria discussed in the previous section.

Price Stability Should Be the Overriding, Long-Run Goal of Monetary Policy

Through their testimony and speeches, high officials in the Federal Reserve System, and especially Alan Greenspan, have made it quite clear that the overriding long-run goal for Fed monetary policy is price stability. However, there is no clear mandate from the U.S. government that price stability should be a long-run, overriding goal. The Humphrey-Hawkins Act passed in 1978, with the revealing title, "Full Employment and Balanced Growth Act," stipulates that monetary policy should have goals of full employment and economic growth, as well as price stability. It is true that the Humphrey-Hawkins Act could be interpreted as allowing for price stability to be the overriding, long-run goal because, as was indicated previously, price stability is a means of promoting high economic growth and full employment in the long-run. However, it is even easier to interpret the legislation as supporting an emphasis on pursuit of full employment and economic growth in the short-run, which is inconsistent with the pursuit of price stability. The lack of a clear mandate for price stability can lead to the time-inconsistency problem in which political pressure is put on the Fed to engage in expansionary policy to pursue short-run goals.

In contrast to the United States, many other countries now have legislation which mandates price stability as the overriding, long-run goal of monetary policy, and this is a growing trend. For example, a mandate for price stability as the overriding, long-run goal for monetary policy was a requirement for entry into the European Monetary Union, and the Maastricht Treaty gives this mandate to the central banking system for the European Monetary Union, which most accurately referred to as the Eurosystem.[7] This trend also has been evident even in emerging market countries, where many central banks have had their mandate revised to focus on price stability.

On the first criterion of the need for an institutional commitment to price stability, as the overriding long-run goal, the United States does not score well.

An Explicit Nominal Anchor Should Be Adopted

Not only has the U.S. government not committed to price stability as the overriding, long-run goal, but also neither it nor the Fed has adopted an explicit nominal anchor. The actions and rhetoric of the Greenspan Fed have made it clear that it will fight to keep inflation from rising from the current level of around 2 percent, and it is fair to characterize the Fed as having an implicit nominal anchor. Nonetheless, the Federal Reserve has not come out and articulated an explicit goal for inflation and has, instead, stated its commitment to price stability. This has been loosely defined by Alan Greenspan as a situation in which changes in the price level are not a major consideration for businesses and households. At the present time, the public (and maybe even members of the FOMC) have no idea of whether the Fed's goal for inflation is 1 percent, 2 percent, or possibly higher. I think it is fair to say that right now the nominal anchor in the United States is Alan Greenspan. The problem is that this leaves some ambiguity as to what the Fed's target is. Even more importantly, the existence of this implicit nominal anchor depends on personalities. Alan Greenspan, despite his recent reappointment, will not be around forever. When he steps down, will the public believe that there is sufficient commitment to a nominal anchor to keep inflation from appearing again?

On the criterion of having an explicit nominal anchor, the institutional set up of the Fed also does not score well.

Central Banks Should Be Instrument Independent

The Federal Reserve has been set up to be far more independent than other government agencies in the United States. Members of the Board of Governors are appointed by the government by 14-year terms, insulating them from political pressure, while Reserve Bank presidents, who also sit on the FOMC, are appointed by the boards of directors at each Reserve Bank and are not subject to Congressional review. Even more important is that the Federal Reserve generates substantial profits, on the order of $20 billion per year, most of which it returns to the U.S. Treasury, so that it has its own revenue base and is not dependent on funds from the government. Indeed, by law the Federal Reserve is exempt from General Accounting Office (GAO) audits of deliberations, decisions, or actions on monetary policy matters.

Given its insulation from the political process and its financial independence, it should be no surprise that the Fed has complete control over setting its monetary policy instruments. This has the benefits of enabling the Fed to resist political pressure to engage in time-inconsistent expansionary policy and to be forward-looking in the setting of its policy instruments.

On the criteria of instrument independence the Fed scores well.

Central Banks Should Be Goal Dependent

We have already seen that independence can go too far. Instrument independence is desirable but goal independence is problematic. The independence of the Fed—described above—and the lack of a clear mandate from the government allows the Fed to make the decisions on what the goals of its policies should be. Thus the Fed has a high degree of goal independence. In some ways goal independence makes the Fed's job easier because it insulates it from political pressure, but it does have a downside. The substantial goal independence of the Federal reserve creates a fair amount of tension in a democratic society because it allows an elite group to set the goals of monetary policy. Indeed, recent criticism of the Federal Reserve may have been prompted by the impression that the Federal Reserve, and particularly its Chairman, has become too powerful.

The goal independence of the Federal Reserve should not be seen as total, however. Politicians do have the ability to influence the goals of the Fed because the Congress can modify the Federal Reserve Act at any time. Also, the Fed has a great interest in other legislation that affects its operations. A case in point is the recent Gramm-Bliley-Leach Financial Services Modernization Act, passed in 1999, which had major implications for whether the Federal Reserve would continue to have supervisory responsibilities over large banking organizations (which it continued to keep). Furthermore, Congress can criticize the budget of the Fed for items that are unrelated to monetary policy or foreign-exchange operations. As an example, in 1996 Senators Dorgan and Reid called for Congress to exercise budgetary authority over the nonmonetary activities of the Federal Reserve because they were concerned that the Fed was too focused on fighting inflation and not enough on reducing unemployment.

As a comparison, the Eurosystem should be seen in some ways as more goal independent than the Federal Reserve System and in other ways less. The Maastricht Treaty specifies that the overriding, long-run goal of the ECB is price stability, so that the goal for the Eurosystem is more clearly specified than it is for the Federal Reserve System. However, Maastricht did not specify exactly what this price stability means so the Eurosystem has defined the quantitative goal for monetary policy, an inflation rate between 0 and 2 percent. From this perspective, the Federal Reserve System is slightly less goal dependent than the Eurosystem. On the other hand, the Eurosystem's statutes cannot be changed by legislation, but only by alterations to the Maastricht Treaty. From this perspective, the Eurosystem is much less goal dependent than the Federal Reserve System because its statutes are specified in a treaty and thus are far harder to change than statutes that are embedded in legislation.

As the examples above indicate, the Federal Reserve is not goal dependent, but we should not take this view too far. Thus, on the goal dependence criteria, the Fed's score is mixed.

Central Banks Should Be Accountable

Closely related to goal dependence is the accountability of the central bank to meet its goals. There are formal accountability mechanisms for the Fed. For example, the Chairman of the Board of Governors has been required to testify twice a year to Congress about the conduct of monetary policy under the Humphrey-Hawkins legislation. Also, as we have seen, the Fed is subject to punitive actions by the Congress if it so chooses, either by amending the Federal Reserve Act or through passage of other legislation that affects the Fed.

On these grounds the Federal Reserve System is more accountable than the Eurosystem. As we have seen, the Eurosystem's statutes cannot be modified by legislation but, rather, requires amendment to a treaty, a far more difficult process. Moreover, although the President of the European Central Bank is required to testify once a year to the European Parliament, this requirement may not guarantee sufficient oversight of the Eurosystem's policies. Since the European Parliament is currently significantly less powerful than the national parliaments of the countries that make up the Monetary Union, scrutiny by that organization would not influence the Eurosystem's behavior as strongly as would oversight by a more powerful body, such as a consortium of national parliaments or the individual parliaments themselves. It is not clear to whom the Eurosystem would be accountable.

However, the absence of an explicit nominal anchor means that there is no benchmark against which the public or Congress can measure the performance of the Federal Reserve System. In contrast, the Eurosystem has outlined its price-stability goal of inflation between 0 and 2 percent, so there is a predetermined criterion to judge its performance. Thus, despite the requirement that the Fed testify to Congress, the accountability of the Fed is not very strong. The Federal Reserve is able to obscure what its strategy and goals are and has indeed done this in the past. This leaves open the possibility that there could be a political backlash against a "high-handed" Federal Reserve that could have adverse consequences on its independence and ability to successfully conduct monetary policy in the future.

On the accountability criteria, the Fed also does not score very well.

Central Banks Should Stress Transparency and Communication

In recent years, the Fed has come a long way on the transparency and communication front. In the past, the Fed had a reputation for not only being unclear about its goals and strategy, but for keeping markets in the dark about its setting of policy instruments. This has changed dramatically in recent years. Starting in 1994, the Fed began to announce its policy actions after every FOMC meeting. It then moved in 1999 to announcing the bias in the direction of future moves in the federal funds rate, which caused some confusion, and so replaced this announcement at the beginning of this year with one that indicates the balance of risks for the future—whether toward higher inflation or toward a weaker economy. Fed officials also have been more active in articulating the strategy of monetary policy, its need to be preemptive, and the importance of the pursuit of price stability.

Despite improved transparency and communication, the lack of explicit goals has meant that Fed transparency is still much less than at many other central banks. In contrast to central banks that have adopted inflation targeting, the Fed produces nothing like an "Inflation Report" in which it clearly lays out in plain English the strategy for monetary policy and how well the central bank has been doing. One consequence of the weakness of Fed transparency and communication is that the public debate on monetary policy in the United States still has a tendency to focus on short-run considerations, as reflected in politicians' focus on "jobs, jobs, jobs" when discussing monetary policy. This focus on short-run considerations is substantially less in countries where central banks use communication vehicles such as "Inflation Reports" to refocus the public debate on longer-run considerations such as price stability.

It is interesting to contrast the way public debate is conducted with what has occurred in Canada, which has adopted an inflation-targeting regime with high transparency and accountability. In 1996, the president of the Canadian Economic Association made a speech criticizing the Bank of Canada for pursuing monetary policy that (he claimed) was too contractionary. His speech sparked off a widespread public debate. Instead of degenerating into calls for the immediate expansion of monetary policy with little reference to the long-run consequences of such a policy change, the debate was channeled into a substantive discussion over what should be the appropriate target for inflation, with both the Bank and its critics obliged to make explicit their assumptions and estimates of the costs and benefits of different levels of inflation. Indeed, the debate and the Bank of Canada's record and responsiveness led to increased support for the Bank of Canada, with the result that criticism of the Bank and its conduct of monetary policy was not a major issue in the 1997 elections as it had been during the 1993 elections.

On the transparency and communication criteria, the Fed's score is mixed, although it has been improving over time.

Central Banks Should also Have a Financial Stability Goal

Here the Fed's performance has been very strong. The Greenspan Fed has made it very clear that it will act decisively to prevent financial crises and has done so not only with words but with actions. The Fed's actions immediately after the October 19, 1987, stock market crash are a textbook case of how a lender-of-last-resort role can be performed brilliantly.[8] The Fed's action was immediate, with Greenspan announcing right before the market opened on October 20 of the Federal Reserve System's "readiness to serve as a source of liquidity to support the economic and financial system," which operated to decrease uncertainty in the marketplace. Reserves were injected into the system, but once the crisis was over, they were withdrawn. Not only was a crisis averted so that the business cycle expansion continued, but also the inflationary consequences of this exercise of the lender-of-last-resort role were small. The 75 basis point decrease in the federal funds rate in the Fall of 1998 immediately after the Russian financial crisis and the near-failure of Long-Term Capital Management, which roiled U.S. capital markets, also illustrated the Fed's commitment to act decisively to prevent financial instability. The aftermath was an economy that continued to expand, with inflation staying at the 2 percent level.

On the criteria of the commitment to the financial stability goal, the Fed's score is excellent.

CONCLUSION: WHAT SHOULD THE FED DO?

Our scorecard for the Fed indicates that although the institutional set up of the Fed scores well on some criteria, there is room for improvement in others. But, is there a need for the Fed as an institution to change? The Fed's performance in recent years has been extraordinary. It has been able to bring down inflation in the United States to the 2 percent level, which can reasonably be characterized as being consistent with price stability, while the economy has been experiencing the longest business cycle expansion in U.S. history, with very high rates of economic growth. As my son likes to say, "It don't get no better than this." The natural question then arises: If it ain't broke, why fix it?

However, our Fed scorecard suggests that we do need to consider institutional improvements in the way the central bank operates. The absence of an institutional commitment to price stability, along with weak Fed transparency, which stems from the absence of an explicit nominal anchor, leaves the Fed open to political pressure to pursue short-run objectives (i.e., job creation). This might lead to time-inconsistent expansionary policy and would produce inflation. In the past, after a successful period of low inflation, the Federal Reserve has "fallen off the wagon" and reverted to inflationary monetary policy—the 1970s are one example—and, without an explicit nominal anchor, this could certainly happen again in the future.

Indeed, the most serious problem with the Fed's institutional framework and the way it currently operates is the strong dependence on the preferences, skills, and trustworthiness of the individuals in charge of the central bank. Yes, the Fed under Alan Greenspan has been doing a great job, and so the Fed's prestige and creditability with the public have risen accordingly. But the Fed's leadership will eventually change, and there is no guarantee that the new leadership will be committed to the same approach. Nor is there any guarantee that the relatively good working relationship that now exists between the Fed and the executive branch will continue. In a different economic or political environment—and considering the possibility for a backlash against the Fed's lack of accountability—the Fed might face far stronger attacks on its independence and increased pressure to engage in over-expansionary policies, further raising the possibility that inflation will shoot up again.

So what should the Fed do? The answer is that the Fed should continue in the direction that it has already begun to increase its transparency and accountability. First, it should advocate a change in its mandate to put price stability as the overriding, long-run goal of monetary policy. Second, it should advocate that the price-stability goal should be made explicit, with a numerical long-run inflation goal. Government involvement in setting this explicit goal would be highly desirable, making the Fed goal independent, which should help retain public support for the Fed's instrument independence. Third, the Fed should produce an "Inflation Report" type of document that clearly explains its strategy for monetary policy and how well it has been doing in achieving its announced inflation goal.

The outcome of these changes is that the Fed would be moving to an inflation-targeting regime of the type described in our book, which has been recently published by the Princeton University Press (Bernanke, Laubach, Mishkin, and Posen, 1999). Clearly, the U.S. Congress and executive branch need to play an important role in encouraging the Fed to move toward inflation targeting. A detailed outline of a proposal for how this might be done can be found in our book. I leave you to read it on your own. Otherwise, you will be subjected to another full lecture.

References

Alesina, Alberto, and Lawrence H. Summers. "Central Bank Independence and Macroeconomic Performance: Some comparative Evidence," *Journal of Money, Credit, and Banking* (May 1993), pp. 151–62.

Andersen, Palle, and David Gruen. "Macroeconomic Policies and Growth," in *Productivity and Growth*, Palle Andersen, Jacqueline Dwyer, and David Gruen, eds., Reserve Bank of Australia, 1995, pp. 279–319.

Barro, Robert J., and David Gordon. "A Positive Theory of Monetary Policy in a Natural Rate Model," *Journal of Political Economy* (August 1983), pp. 589–610.

Bernanke, Ben S. "Non-Monetary Effects of the Financial Crisis in the Propagation of the Great Depression," *American Economic Review* (March 1983), pp. 257–76.

_____. "Comment on 'The Synergies Between Bank Supervision and Monetary Policy: Implications for the Design of Bank Regulatory Structure'," in *Prudential Supervision: What Works and What Doesn't*, Frederick S. Mishkin, ed., University of Chicago Press, forthcoming.

_____. Thomas Laubach, Frederic S. Mishkin, and Adam S. Posen. *Inflation Targeting: Lessons from the International Experience*, Princeton University Press, 1999.

Blinder, Alan S. *Central Banking in Theory and Practice*, MIT Press, 1998.

Briault, Clive. "The Costs of Inflation," *Bank of England Quarterly Bulletin* (February 1995), pp. 33–45.

Calvo, Guillermo. "On the Time Consistency of Optimal Policy in the Monetary Economy," *Econometrica* (November 1978), pp. 1411–28.

Corsetti, Giorgio, Paolo Pesenti, and Noriel Roubini. "What Caused the Asian Currency and Financial Crisis? Part I and II," NBER Working Papers, nos. 6833 and 6834, 1998.

Cukierman, Alex. *Central Bank Strategy, Credibility, and Independence: Theory and Evidence*, MIT Press, 1992.

Debelle, Guy, and Stanley Fischer. "How Independent Should a Central Bank Be?" in *Goals, Guidelines, and Constraints Facing Monetary Policymakers*, Jeffrey C. Fuhrer, ed., Federal Reserve Bank of Boston, 1994, pp. 195–221.

English, William B. "Inflation and Financial Sector Size," Finance and Economics Discussion Series No. 96-16, Board of Governors of the Federal Reserve System, April 1996.

Feldstein, Martin. "Capital Income Taxes and the Benefits of Price Stabilization," NBER Working Paper 6200, September 1997.

Fischer, Stanley. "Modern Central Banking," in *The Future of Central Banking*, Forrest Capie, Charles A. E. Goodhart, Stanley Fischer, and Norbert Schnadt, eds., Cambridge University Press, 1994, pp. 262–308.

Friedman, Milton, and Anna J. Schwartz. *A Monetary History of the United States, 1867–1960*, Princeton University Press, 1963.

King, Mervyn, "Changes in UK Monetary Policy: Rules and Discretion in Practice," *Journal of Monetary Economics*, (June 1997), pp. 81–97.

Kydland, Finn, and Edward Prescott. "Rules Rather than Discretion: The Inconsistency of Optimal Plans," *Journal of Political Economy* (June 1977), pp. 473–91.

McCallum, Bennett T. "Inflation: Theory and Evidence," in *Handbook of Monetary Economics*, Ben M. Friedman and Frank H. Hahn, eds., Elsevier Press, 1990, pp. 963–1012.

_____. "Two Fallacies Concerning Central-Bank Independence," *American Economic Review* (May 1995), pp. 207–11.

Mishkin, Frederic S. "Asymmetric Information and Financial Crises: A Historical Perspective," in *Financial Markets and Financial Crises*, R. Glenn Hubbard, ed., University of Chicago Press, 1991, pp. 69–108.

_____. "An evaluation of the Treasury Plan for Banking Reform," *Journal of Economic Perspectives* (Winter 1992), pp. 133–53.

_____. "Understanding Financial Crises: A Developing Country Perspective," in *Annual World Bank Conference on Development Economics*, 1996, pp. 29–62.

_____. *The Economics of Money, Banking, and Financial Markets*, 5th ed., Addison-Wesley Publishing Co., 1998.

_____. "Lessons from the Asian Crisis," *Journal of International Money and Finance* (August 1999a), pp. 709–23.

_____. "International Experiences with Different Monetary Policy Regimes," *Journal of Monetary Economics* (June 1999b), pp. 579–605.

_____, and Adam S. Posen. "Inflation Targeting: Lessons from Four Countries," *Economic Policy Review*. Federal Reserve Bank of New York (August 1997), pp. 9–110.

Peek, Joe, Eric Rosengren, and Geoffrey Tootell, "The Synergies Between Bank Supervision and Monetary Policy: Implications for the Design of Bank Regulatory Structure," in *Prudential Supervision: What Works and What Doesn't*, Frederic S. Mishkin, ed., University of Chicago Press, forthcoming.

Posen, Adam S. "Declarations Are Not Enough: Financial Sector Sources of Central Bank Independence," in *NBER Macroeconomics Annual*, Ben S. Bernanke and Julio J. Rotemberg, eds., MIT Press, 1995, pp. 253–74.

Rogoff, Kenneth. "The Optimal Degree of Commitment to an Intermediate Monetary Target," *Quarterly Journal of Economics* (November 1985), pp. 1169–89.

Sargent, Thomas, and Neil Wallace. "Some Unpleasant Monetarist Arithmetic," *Quarterly Review*, Federal Reserve Bank of Minneapolis (Fall 1981), pp. 1–17.

Svensson, Lars. "Inflation Targeting as Monetary Policy Rule," *Journal of Monetary Economics* (June 1999), pp. 607–54.

Taylor, John, ed. *Monetary Policy Rules*, University of Chicago Press, Chicago, 1999.

Woodford, Michael. "Monetary Policy and Price Level Determinacy in a Cash-in-Advance Economy," *Economic Theory*, vol. 4, no. 3 (1994), pp. 345–80.

_____. "Price-Level Determinacy with Control of a Monetary Aggregate." *Carnegie-Rochester Conference Series on Public Policy* (December 1995), pp. 1–46.

Notes

1. E.g., see English (1996).
2. E.g., see Briault (1995).
3. E. G., see Fischer (1994) and Feldstein (1997).
4. See the survey in Andersen and Gruen (1995).
5. For further discussion of who should set an inflation target in the United States, see Bernanke, Laubach, Mishkin, and Posen (1999).
6. Blinder (1998) also makes a strong case for increased transparency and accountability of central banks.
7. The Eurosystem currently is made up of the eleven national central banks of the countries that have joined EMU, with the European Central Bank (ECB) at the center having a role similar to that of the Board of Governors in the Federal Reserve System.
8. Indeed, this example appears in my textbook (Mishkin, 1998).

The Science (and Art) of Monetary Policy

During most of the 1990s, the United States experienced exceptionally good times, and the Federal Reserve received some of the credit for the booming economy and low inflation. Figure 1 shows the marked decline in the civilian unemployment rate from a peak of 7.8% in June 1992 to a low of 3.9% in September 2000. In May 1997, the unemployment rate fell below 5% for the first time since 1973—and it stayed there for the rest of the decade. Although some were concerned that inflation would re-ignite because of tight labor markets, instead it remained in check. In fact, the inflation rate, measured by the Consumer Price Index (CPI), actually *declined* through most of the 1990s. When the more volatile food and energy components of the CPI are removed, the resulting measure of inflation has remained below 3% since 1993.

The last eighteen months, however, have presented the Federal Reserve with particularly difficult policy decisions. In the summer of 1999, concerned that inflation was threatening, the Fed raised its target for the federal funds interest rate. From a level of 4.74% in May 1999, the funds rate rose as a result of Fed policy until it peaked at 6.54% in August 2000. As 2000 drew to a close, increasing signs of economic slowing led the Fed to cut interest rates, lowering its target for the funds rate twice in January, once in March, and once in April.

This swing in interest rates, together with some criticism that the Fed might have raised rates too much in 2000 and not cut them enough in 2001, raises the question of whether there are any guiding principles that the Fed has followed, or could have followed, in making its decisions. Are there rules for designing and implementing good monetary policy that all economists agree on? Or is policymaking inherently a subjective task, one that depends critically on combining both good economics and insightful judgment?

Is monetary policy a science?

A recent article by three leading monetary economists, Rich Clarida, Jordi Gali, and Mark Gertler, is titled "The Science of Monetary Policy." The word "science" in the title suggests that economists now have all the knowledge they need to design and implement good monetary policy. If that were so, the public's focus on Alan Greenspan as the Chairman of the Federal Reserve would be misplaced—monetary policy would not depend on an individual's judgment. Instead, just as sending a rocket to Mars or building a bridge depends critically on the input from scientists and engineers, implementing the science of monetary policy would require only a staff of good economists.

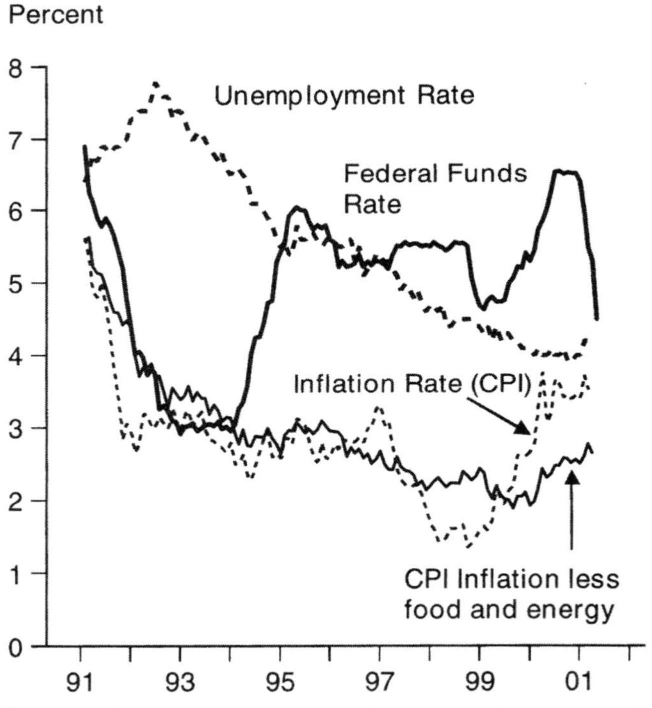

Figure 1 Unemployment, inflation, and the funds rate

Currently, many economists are in agreement with three basic principles that form the core of the "scientific" approach to monetary policy. Each of these principles is designed to guide central bankers.

Principle 1: Focus on the output gap. A huge literature in the 1980s and 1990s showed how excessive inflation can result if a central bank aims for output objectives that are too ambitious. If, for example, the central bank engages in expansionary policies in an attempt to keep output above potential, the net result will only be a higher average rate of inflation. Well-meaning central banks could find themselves generating rates of inflation well above what they had wanted without any gains in long-term output.

Many solutions to this problem have been suggested. The simplest is to have the central bank adopt a realistic output objective. Specifically, the central bank should strive to stabilize output around potential output, sometimes also called full-employment output. This objective is usually expressed by saying the central bank should stabilize the *output gap*, the difference between actual real output and potential. In the words of economist Lars Svensson, "...there is considerable agreement among academics and central bankers that the appropriate [monetary policy objective] both involves stabilizing inflation around an inflation target and stabilizing the real economy, represented by the output gap" (Svensson 1999).

Principle 2: Follow the Taylor Principle. The second principle in the "scientific" approach to monetary policy is to follow the Taylor Principle. This principle states that the central bank's policy interest rate should be increased more than one for one with increases in the inflation rate. Named after Stanford University economist John Taylor, the Taylor Principle ensures that an increase in the inflation rate produces a policy reaction that increases the real rate of interest—the interest rate corrected for inflation. The rise in the real interest rate reduces private spending, slows the economy down, and brings inflation back to the central bank's inflation target. Conversely, if inflation falls below the central bank's target, the Taylor Principle calls for a more than one for one cut in the central bank's policy interest rate. This reduces the real rate of interest, stimulates private spending, and pushes inflation back to its target level.

Policies that violate the Taylor Principle can lead to serious problems. If a rise in inflation is met by a less than one for one increase in the policy rate, then real interest rates actually fall. This fuels further economic expansion, pushing inflation even higher. Rather than acting to bring inflation back down to its target level, such a policy can cause inflation to spiral out of control.

One way to implement the Taylor Principle is to follow a Taylor Rule, also named after John Taylor, which specifies exactly how much to change the federal funds rate in response to changes in inflation and the output gap.

Principle 3: Be forward-looking. Monetary policy actions affect the economy with a lag. An interest rate cut may not have its maximum impact on real output for twelve or even eighteen months, and the effects on inflation may take longer still. Central banks cannot wait to act until inflation has increased or the economy has gone into a recession. These lags mean that central banks must be forward-looking. For example, when the Fed raised interest rates in 2000, inflation was still quite low, once the volatile food and energy components were removed. The Fed acted because it was concerned that inflation would otherwise begin to rise.

The public clearly believes that implementing monetary policy is not something that can be delegated to unknown government economists in Washington.

One policy framework that satisfies these three principles is *inflation forecast targeting*. Under an inflation forecast targeting procedure, the central bank is concerned with stabilizing inflation at low levels and with stabilizing the output gap. Because of the lags in policy, the emphasis is on responding to the central bank's forecast of future inflation. If the forecast says inflation will rise, the central bank should act to slow the economy down—it doesn't wait until inflation actually has increased. Because inflation forecast targeting is based on the three policy principles, it has gained many adherents among academic and central bank economists.

Economists have significantly advanced their understanding of the principles of good monetary policy in recent years. Yet the public clearly believes that implementing monetary policy is not something that can be delegated to unknown government economists in Washington. The public believes leadership matters, and that it matters that Federal Reserve Chairman Alan Greenspan is in charge of policy. Is there more to achieving good monetary policies than simply following the economist's scientific principles?

Is monetary policy an art?

Perhaps the public believes Alan Greenspan's leadership matters because they believe monetary policy is, in part, an art. It requires the fine touch of a master policymaker, one whose feel for the correct moment to change interest rates cannot be reduced to a few scientific principles. But if making policy isn't a science, what exactly is nonscientific about it? The best way to understand the "art" of policymaking is to revisit our three policy principles.

How can we focus on the output gap when we don't know what it is? It's all very well to tell central banks to focus on the output gap, but how are they supposed to know what the gap is? When major shifts in productivity growth occur—as happened in the 1970s with the productivity slowdown and again in the 1990s with the productivity speedup, measuring the output gap can be difficult. The output gap is the difference between something we can measure (real GDP) and something we can't (the economy's potential output level). Trying to determine how new information technologies would affect productivity growth and whether the growth speedup would be sustained was a major issue confronting policymakers in the 1990s. As the economy grew rapidly during the second half of the decade, economists were uncertain whether real output was rising above potential, in which case interest rate hikes would be called for, or whether both actual and potential output were growing more rapidly, leaving the output gap stable.

A similar problem had beset the Fed during the 1970s. Then, the problem was the productivity slowdown. Some economists have argued that the Fed failed to recognize at the time that potential was growing more slowly than before. As a consequence, the Fed interpreted the slowdown in actual growth as a reflection that output was falling below potential. In fact, both actual and potential declined relative to their previous trends. Because the gap had not fallen, policy was too expansionary in the early 1970s, helping to fuel inflation.

Implementing the Taylor Principle. The Taylor Principle calls for adjusting the policy interest rate more than one for one with changes in inflation. But how much more? If inflation rises by 1 percentage point, should the federal funds rate be increased by 1.5 percentage points? 2 percentage points? Or 1.01 percentage points? The Taylor Principle alone does not offer guidance.

The art of conducting policy lies in the ability to translate the general principles into actual policy decisions.

Responding strongly to changes in inflation will help keep inflation more stable around a low average level, but it also will result in larger fluctuations in output and employment. A weaker response results in greater fluctuations in the inflation rate but more stable output and employment. Hence, there is a trade-off between inflation stability and employment stability. Making the right trade-off requires good judgment.

The art of forecasting. Implementing inflation forecast targeting means the central bank has to be able to forecast future economic conditions. This is not an easy task. Last summer, economic forecasts did not foresee the growth slowdown that began during the third quarter. The Fed had to respond quickly in early 2001 as signs of an economic slowdown developed.

Good forecasts are based on good data, good economic models, *and* good judgment. Mechanical forecasts based on a few key indicators inevitably ignore information that might be relevant. While statistical models provide a baseline for developing economic forecasts, good forecasters always supplement the models' predictions with judgmental adjustment.

Conclusion

Economists have contributed much to making the design of monetary policy more scientific. From the articulation of general principles for good policy to the construction of small models that can be used to simulate the impacts of alternative policies, recent research by academic and central bank economists has contributed to our knowledge about monetary policy. Despite these advances, however, conducting policy is far from routine. General principles are important, but they're not sufficient—policymakers also need quantifiable guidance. They need to know whether the current output gap is +2% or -2%. They need to know whether the funds rate should be increased by 150 basis points or 200 for every 1 percentage point rise in inflation. And they need to know how much inflation will rise or fall over the next six months. This level of guidance is still missing from the science of monetary policy. The art of conducting policy lies in the ability to translate the general principles into actual policy decisions.

There is a long tradition of trying to take discretion out of monetary policy—Milton Friedman's proposal that the Fed should just ensure a constant annual growth rate for the money supply was an example of a policy designed to remove the role of the individual policymaker. While economists have identified broad principles to guide policymakers, making policy is not a science. Good policy will probably always require good policymakers, as it requires combining the science of the economist with the art of the practitioner.

Carl E. Walsh
Professor of Economics, UC Santa Cruz, and Visiting Scholar, FRBSF

References

Clarida, Richard, Jordi Galí, and Mark Gertler. 1999. "The Science of Monetary Policy: A New Keynesian Perspective." *Journal of Economic Literature* 37 (December) pp. 1,661–1,707.

Svensson, Lars E. O. 1999. "How Should Monetary Policy Be Conducted in an Era of Price Stability?" In *New Challenges for Monetary Policy*, pp. 195–259. Federal Reserve Bank of Kansas City.

Reprinted with permission from the Federal Reserve Bank of San Francisco *Economic Letter*, May 4, 2001, pp. 1–4. The opinions expressed in this article do not necessarily reflect the views of the management of the FRBSF, or of the Board of Governors of the Federal Reserve System.

How does monetary policy affect the U.S. economy?

This is the third of four consecutive issues devoted to our updated and expanded Q&A on monetary policy: (1) "How is the Federal Reserve structured?" and "What are the tools of U.S. monetary policy?" (2) "What are the goals of U.S. monetary policy?" (3) "How does monetary policy affect the U.S. economy?" and (4) "How does the Fed decide the appropriate setting for the policy instrument?" The revised text will appear in a pamphlet soon.

The point of implementing policy through raising or lowering interest rates is to affect people's and firms' demand for goods and services. This section discusses how policy actions affect real interest rates, which in turn affect demand and ultimately output, employment, and inflation.

What are real interest rates and why do they matter?

For the most part, the demand for goods and services is not related to the market interest rates quoted in the financial pages of newspapers, known as nominal rates. Instead, it is related to *real* interest rates—that is, nominal interest rates minus the expected rate of inflation.

For example, a borrower is likely to feel a lot happier about a car loan at 8% when the inflation rate is close to 10% (as it was in the late 1970s) than when the inflation rate is close to 2% (as it was in the late 1990s). In the first case, the real (or inflation-adjusted) value of the money that the borrower would pay back would actually be lower than the real value of the money when it was borrowed. Borrowers, of course, would love this situation, while lenders would be disinclined to make any loans.

So why doesn't the Fed just set the real interest rate on loans?

Remember, the Fed operates only in the market for bank reserves. Because it is the sole supplier of reserves, it can set the nominal funds rate. The Fed can't set real interest rates directly because it can't set inflation expectations directly, even though expected inflation is closely tied to what the Fed is expected to do in the future. Also, in general, the Fed has stayed out of the business of setting nominal rates for longer-term instruments and instead allows financial markets to determine longer-term interest rates.

How can the Fed influence long-term rates then?

Long-term interest rates reflect, in part, what people in financial markets expect the Fed to do in the future. For instance, if they think the Fed isn't focused on containing inflation, they'll be concerned that inflation might move up over the next few years. So they'll add a risk premium to long-term rates, which will make them higher. In other words, the markets' expectations about monetary policy tomorrow have a substantial impact on long-term interest rates today. Researchers have pointed out that the Fed could inform markets about future values of the funds rate in a number of ways. For example, the Fed could follow a policy of moving gradually once it starts changing interest rates. Or, the Fed could issue statements about what kinds of developments the FOMC is likely to focus on in the foreseeable future; the Fed even could make more explicit statements about the future stance of policy.

How do these policy-induced changes in real interest rates affect the economy?

Changes in real interest rates affect the public's demand for goods and services mainly by altering borrowing costs, the availability of bank loans, the wealth of households, and foreign exchange rates.

For example, a decrease in real interest rates lowers the cost of borrowing; that leads businesses to increase investment spending, and it leads households to buy durable goods, such as autos and new homes.

In addition, lower real rates and a healthy economy may increase banks' willingness to lend to businesses and households. This may increase spending, especially by smaller borrowers who have few sources of credit other than banks.

Lower real rates also make common stocks and other such investments more attractive than bonds and other debt instruments; as a result, common stock prices tend to rise. Households with stocks in their portfolios find that the value of their holdings is higher, and this increase in wealth makes them willing to spend more. Higher stock prices also make it more attractive for businesses to invest in plant and equipment by issuing stock.

In the short run, lower real interest rates in the U.S. also tend to reduce the foreign exchange value of the dollar, which lowers the prices of the U.S.-produced goods we sell abroad and raises the prices we pay for foreign-produced goods. This leads to higher aggregate spending on goods and services produced in the U.S.

The increase in aggregate demand for the economy's output through these different channels leads firms to raise production and employment, which in turn increases business spending on capital goods even further by making greater demands on existing factory capacity. It also boosts consumption further because of the income gains that result from the higher level of economic output.

How does monetary policy affect inflation?

Wages and prices will begin to rise at faster rates if monetary policy stimulates aggregate demand enough to push labor and capital markets beyond their long-run capacities. In fact, a monetary policy that persistently attempts to keep short-term real rates low will lead eventually to higher inflation and higher nominal interest rates, with no permanent increases in the growth of output or decreases in unemployment. As noted earlier, in the long run, output and employment cannot be set by monetary policy. In other words, while there is a trade-off between higher inflation and lower unemployment in the short run, the trade-off disappears in the long run.

Policy also affects inflation directly through people's expectations about future inflation. For example, suppose the Fed eases monetary policy. If consumers and businesspeople figure that will mean higher inflation in the future, they'll ask for bigger increases in wages and prices. That in itself will raise inflation without big changes in employment and output.

Doesn't U.S. inflation depend on worldwide capacity, not just U.S. capacity?

In this era of intense global competition, it might seem parochial to focus on U.S. capacity as a determinant of U.S. inflation, rather than on world capacity. For example, some argue that even if unemployment in the U.S. drops to very low levels, U.S. workers wouldn't be able to push for higher wages because they're competing for jobs with workers abroad, who are willing to accept much lower wages. The implication is that inflation is unlikely to rise even if the Fed adopts an easier monetary policy.

This reasoning doesn't hold up too well, however, for a couple of reasons. First, a large proportion of what we consume in the U.S. isn't affected very much by foreign trade. One example is health care, which isn't traded internationally and which amounts to nearly 15% of U.S. GDP.

More important, perhaps, is the fact that such arguments ignore the role of flexible exchange rates. If the Fed were to adopt an easier policy, it would tend to increase the supply of U.S. dollars in the market. Ultimately, this would tend to drive down the value of the dollar relative to other countries, as U.S. consumers and firms used some of this increased money supply to buy foreign goods and foreigners got rid of the additional U.S. currency they did not want. Thus, the price of foreign goods in terms of U.S. dollars would go up—even though they would not in terms of the foreign currency. The higher prices of imported goods would, in turn, tend to raise the prices of U.S. goods.

How long does it take a policy action to affect the economy and inflation?

It can take a fairly long time for a monetary policy action to affect the economy and inflation. And the lags can vary a lot, too. For example, the major effects on output can take anywhere from three months to two years. And the effects on inflation tend to involve even longer lags, perhaps one to three years, or more.

Why are the lags so hard to predict?

So far, we've described a complex chain of events that links a change in the funds rate with subsequent changes in output and inflation. Developments anywhere along this chain can alter how much a policy action will affect the economy and when.

For example, one link in the chain is long-term interest rates, and they can respond differently to a policy action, depending on the market's expectations about future Fed policy. If markets expect a change in the funds rate to be the beginning of a series of moves in the same direction, they'll factor in those future changes right away, and long-term rates will react by more than if markets had expected the Fed to take no further action. In contrast, if markets had anticipated the policy action, long-term rates may not move much at all because they would have factored it into the rates already. As a result, the same policy move can appear to have different effects on financial markets and, through them, on output and inflation.

Similarly, the effect of a policy action on the economy also depends on what people and firms outside the financial sector think the Fed action means for inflation in the future. If people believe that a tightening of policy means the Fed is determined to keep inflation under control, they'll immediately expect low inflation in the future, so they're likely to ask for smaller wage and price increases, and this will help achieve low inflation. But if people aren't convinced that the Fed is going to contain inflation, they're likely to ask for bigger wage and price increases, and that means that inflation is likely to rise. In this case, the only way to bring inflation down is to tighten so much and for so long that there are significant losses in employment and output.

What problems do lags cause?

The Fed's job would be much easier if monetary policy had swift and sure effects. Policymakers could set policy, see its effects, and then adjust the settings until they eliminated any discrepancy between economic developments and the goals.

But with the long lags associated with monetary policy actions, the Fed must try to anticipate the effects of its policy actions into the distant future.

To see why, suppose the Fed waits to shift its policy stance until it actually sees an increase in inflation. That would mean that inflationary momentum already had developed, so the task of reducing inflation would be that much harder and more costly in terms of job losses. Not surprisingly, anticipating policy effects in the future is one of the more difficult parts of conducting monetary policy, and it's a key issue in the next and final *Economic Letter* in this series, "How does the Fed decide the appropriate setting for the policy instrument?"

Suggested reading

For further discussion of the topics in this article, see the following issues of the *FRBSF Economic Letter*.

93–38 "Real Interest Rates," by Bharat Trehan. `http://www.frbsf.org/publications/economics/letter/1993/el93-38.pdf`

95–35 "What Are the Lags in Monetary Policy?" by Glenn Rudebusch. `http://www.frbsf.org/publications/economics/letter/1995/el1995-05.pdf`

95–23 "Federal Reserve Policy and the Predictability of Interest Rates," by Glenn Rudebusch. `http://www.frbsf.org/publications/economics/letter/1995/el1995-23.pdf`

97–18 "Interest Rates and Monetary Policy," by Glenn Rudebusch `http://www.frbsf.org/econrsrch/wklyltr/el97-18.html`

2002–30 "Setting the Interest Rates," by Milton Marquis. `http://www.frbsf.org/publications/economics/letter/2002/el2002-30.pdf`

The Maestro Slips Out of Tune

By PAUL KRUGMAN

"The time has come, in my judgment, to consider a budgetary strategy that is consistent with a pre-emptive smoothing of the glide path to zero federal debt or, more realistically, to the level of federal debt that is an effective irreducible minimum." Translation: Go ahead and cut taxes.

With those words, delivered in Senate testimony on Jan. 25, 2001, Alan Greenspan—revered during the 1990's as the nonpartisan architect of America's prosperity—inserted himself decisively into politics, on the side of George W. Bush. The chairman of the Federal Reserve didn't specifically endorse Bush's plans, but his words were exactly what Bush needed. Before Greenspan's testimony, many political observers questioned whether the victor in a disputed election could get an enormous, controversial tax cut through Congress. After Greenspan spoke, much of the resistance collapsed.

Yet in retrospect we know that Greenspan's "judgment"—that tax cuts were needed to prevent excessive budget surpluses—was a misjudgment of Rumsfeldian proportions. In fact, the United States is headed for a budget deficit of more than $400 billion this year, more than half of it a result of tax cuts passed since Greenspan gave Bush his support.

Greenspan is still a figure of enormous prestige and power; he is to economic policy what J. Edgar Hoover once was to law enforcement. After 17 years as Fed chairman, Greenspan has become an icon, and it's hard to imagine America without him; indeed, last month the president nominated him for a fifth term. Yet his reputation is not what it once was. At the height of the boom, he was the monetary maestro whose advice was sought on many aspects of economic policy. Now his record as a monetary leader has been called into question, and his judgment on fiscal policy has been proved disastrously wrong. Worse, he seems to have abandoned the long tradition that places the Fed above the political fray.

The Making of a Maestro Greenspan is, without question, a very smart man. He has also been very lucky.

He had the good fortune to follow an illustrious predecessor. Paul Volcker assumed office at a time of double-digit inflation. During Volcker's eight years as Fed chairman, he tamed inflation and steered the world through a major financial crisis, then oversaw a powerful economic recovery. On becoming chairman in August 1987, Greenspan inherited both a healthy economy and an office whose prestige had never been higher.

He enhanced that prestige with his deft handling of the stock market crash of October 1987. Still, in the early 1990's few would have considered Greenspan a great Fed chairman. When the economy stalled in 1990, Greenspan's Fed was caught by surprise and was too slow to react by cutting interest rates. What resulted was a nasty if brief recession that, among other things, ensured the first George Bush's electoral defeat. (Some Wall Street analysts suggest that the second George Bush delayed Greenspan's latest reappointment to pressure him to keep interest rates low until after the election.)

But then came the great boom.

Greenspan jump-started that boom by cutting interest rates once he realized that the economy was weakening, but any Fed chairman would have done the same thing. After the recovery began, he again followed standard operating procedure. William McChesney Martin, who was Fed chairman from 1951 to 1970, famously said that the Fed's job is to take away the punch bowl just when the party really gets going—that is, to raise interest rates and slow down a booming economy before the boom turns into an inflationary spiral. Greenspan dutifully raised interest rates through 1994.

But as the boom continued and the unemployment rate dropped to new lows, he did something unexpected: nothing.

Around 1994, some businessmen began talking about a "new economy," in which old rules no longer applied. In the 70's and 80's, an unemployment rate below 6 percent signaled an overheating economy, on the verge of inflation. The new-economy advocates claimed, however, that this was no longer true—that thanks to accelerating productivity growth and increased competition, it was possible to run much closer to full employment without a takeoff in inflation.

Unlike most economists at the time, Greenspan took those claims seriously. And sure enough, the optimists were right. Over the next six years unemployment fell to 4 percent, a level not seen in 30 years, yet inflation remained quiescent. Greenspan didn't create the economic miracle of the 90's, but—to his great credit—he didn't stand in its way. And his name therefore became associated with the boom.

Bubble Trouble "But how do we know when irrational exuberance has unduly escalated asset values, which then become subject to unexpected and prolonged contractions, as they have in Japan over the past decade?" Greenspan asked this question in December 1996, expressing his concern that a bubble was developing in the stock market. He had reason to think so: traditional measures of stock valuation, like the price-earnings ratio, were rapidly moving off the charts, and investor psychology was already starting to remind those who knew economic history of the 20's.

Greenspan's "irrational exuberance" speech was clearly intended to caution the markets. Soon afterward, he raised interest rates slightly, again with the clear intention of sending a warning signal to investors. But then he backed off. There were no more rate increases, and Greenspan began lauding the economy's achievements. Bad call: his first instinct was right. It was a bubble, after all.

Critics say that by letting the bubble develop unchecked, Greenspan set the stage not just for future market losses but also for trouble in the economy as a whole. Greenspan counters that the Fed can't target stock prices the way it targets inflation, because you can't know whether a bull market is a bubble until it bursts. The Fed, he says, should not consider asset prices part of its brief. Is he right?

When the bubble burst, the United States' economy went into recession, just as critics of Greenspan's inaction feared. Still, if he had been able to lead our economy into a quick, decisive recovery, his position would have been clearly vindicated. But though recovery was quick—the recession of 2001 officially lasted only eight months—it wasn't decisive. On the other hand, if the economy had fallen into a Japan-type deflationary trap, Greenspan would have been proved clearly wrong. That didn't happen, either. Over the last few months, the recovery has finally started to look like the real thing. We seem to have avoided a Japan syndrome, at least this time.

On balance, I think the critics are right and Greenspan is wrong. We avoided becoming Japan after the bubble burst, but it was a near miss: with interest rates down to 1 percent, the Fed had almost run out of ammunition before the economy turned around. And even if the economy is finally on the mend, over the last three years millions of American workers lost their savings or suffered the indignity and financial hardship of prolonged unemployment—pain that could have been avoided if Greenspan had burst the bubble before it grew so big.

But this argument will probably go on forever. Fifty years from now, economic historians will still be arguing over whether Greenspan's performance as monetary manager deserves an A or a B-. What they won't argue about is Greenspan's culpability for America's plunge into deficit.

The Partisan Chairman In the first days of the Bush administration, as we've seen, Greenspan gave decisive aid and comfort to the new president, urging Congress to cut taxes in order to prevent excessive budget surpluses. Three years and at least $900 billion in additional debt later, that argument seems ludicrous. And besides giving bad advice, Greenspan was engaging in highly questionable behavior. Since then, rather than make amends, he has compounded the sin.

As an institution, the Federal Reserve is set up more like the Supreme Court than like an ordinary government agency. Members of the Federal Reserve Board serve for long terms; chairmen typically serve across several administrations from both parties. There's a reason for this: economists often argue that the Fed, like the Supreme Court, must be insulated from the political process so that it can make necessary but unpopular decisions. The quid pro quo for this insulation, however, is that the Fed must stand above the political fray. Like Supreme Court justices, the members of the Fed board undermine the rationale for their independence if they use their power for partisan purposes.

So was that 2001 testimony partisan? Yes. Greenspan argued on the basis of budget projections—which he must have known are notoriously unreliable—that the federal government would pay off all its debt in a few years. If this happened, the government would be forced to invest future surpluses in the financial markets—which, he argued, would be a bad thing. To avoid this outcome, he claimed, surpluses had to be reduced with tax cuts.

It was a peculiar, tortured argument, full of holes. For example, partial privatization of Social Security—which Greenspan supports—would impose "transition costs" in the trillions of dollars, easily taking care of the supposed problem of excessive budget surpluses. As many warned at the time, Greenspan was also completely wrong about the budget prospect—projections of huge surpluses quickly gave way to projections of huge deficits.

Above all, Greenspan's fear-of-surpluses argument was at complete odds with what he had said in the past. All through the Clinton years, Greenspan preached the virtues of fiscal restraint, and he did not change his views when the budget deficits of the 80's and early 90's vanished. Just six months before his 2001 testimony, Greenspan saw no problem with large projected budget surpluses. "The Congress and the administration," he said in July 2000, "have wisely avoided steps that would materially reduce these budget surpluses. Continued fiscal discipline will contribute to maintaining robust expansion of the American economy in the future." But then a Republican entered the White House, brandishing a tax-cut proposal—and Greenspan suddenly developed an elaborate theory of why it was necessary to reduce those surpluses, after all.

Any doubts that Greenspan holds George Bush to different standards than he held Bill Clinton were dispelled in the years that followed. He didn't call for a reconsideration of the 2001 tax cut when the budget surplus evaporated. He didn't even offer strong objections to a second major round of tax cuts in 2003, when the budget was already deep in deficit.

Since then, Greenspan has gone back to warning against the evils of budget deficits. But he still hasn't called for a reconsideration of recent tax cuts; on the contrary, he has endorsed Bush's plan to make the tax cuts permanent. Instead he calls for spending cuts, emphasizing the need to trim Social Security benefits. I went back to testimony Greenspan gave in February 2001; sure enough, he assured nervous senators that tax cuts would not threaten future Social Security benefits.

But it's even worse than that. Before Greenspan became Fed chairman, he headed a commission that recommended changes in Social Security to secure its future. The most important recommendation, adopted by Congress, was for an increase in the payroll tax—a regressive tax that falls much more heavily on lower- and middle-income families than it does on the well-off. The ostensible purpose was to generate a surplus within the Social Security system, building up a trust fund to pay benefits once the baby boomers retire.

That was the bait; now Greenspan has pulled the switch. The sequence looks like this: he pushed through an increase in taxes on working Americans, generating a Social Security surplus. Then he used the overall surplus, mainly coming from Social Security, to argue for tax cuts that deliver very little relief to most people but are worth a lot to those making more than $300,000 a year. And now that those tax cuts have contributed to a soaring deficit, he wants to maintain the tax cuts while cutting Social Security benefits. He never said, "Let's raise taxes and cut benefits for working families so that we can give big tax cuts to the rich!" But that's the end result of his advice.

Greenspan never said, 'Let's raise taxes and cut benefits for working families so that we can give big tax cuts to the rich!' But that's the end result of his advice.

Why did he do it? There are two possible interpretations. The more generous one is that he never gave up the ideals of his younger days. Into his 40's, Greenspan was an acolyte of Ayn Rand, the libertarian novelist and philosopher, and Greenspan has never repudiated his Randian association. Nonetheless, during the Clinton years he came to be viewed as a moderate. Maybe that was a mask, and all those years he was just waiting for an opportunity to use the prestige of his office to undermine the hated institutions of the welfare state.

The less generous interpretation is that Greenspan simply abused his position to help his friends. Kenneth Thomas, a finance professor at the Wharton School, has calculated that Greenspan visits the White House about once a week, as The Christian Science Monitor reported last month, and that is almost four times as often as he did when Clinton was president.

Part of the genius of George Bush's political operatives is their ability to persuade people (Colin Powell, Tony Blair) to betray their principles, to say and do things they will later regret, in support of a presumed shared cause. Paul O'Neill, Bush's first treasury secretary, falls into the same category: he was a moderate Republican who for a time played good soldier, defending the Bush tax cuts despite private qualms, to help the new president—a man he thought shared his values—by giving him an early political victory. And guess what: O'Neill was a close friend of Greenspan's.

According to Ron Suskind's book "The Price of Loyalty," written with O'Neill's cooperation, Greenspan told O'Neill that a tax cut without triggers—that is, conditions that would cancel the cut if projected surpluses didn't materialize—was "irresponsible fiscal policy." Yet Greenspan never made a forceful public case against a trigger-free tax cut, perhaps because he did not want to make trouble for his friend O'Neill. And by the time he realized just how irresponsible the tax cut really was, he was trapped—too deeply associated with the administration's policies to change course without losing face.

Either way, Greenspan did something remarkable. After becoming a symbol of America's economic turnaround in the 90's, and anointing himself the nation's high priest of fiscal probity, he lent crucial aid and comfort to the most fiscally irresponsible administration in history. In the end, that will be his most important legacy.

Paul Krugman is a Times columnist and a professor at Princeton. His latest book is "The Great Unraveling: Losing Our Way in the New Century."

The Cycles of Financial Scandal

Will an era of reform follow a decade of excess?

By Kevin Phillips

GOSHEN, Conn.

America is at a turning point. Corporate scandals, the fall of the stock markets, the sudden mobilizations in Washington of the last few weeks to legislate against some of the more egregious corporate abuses: they all indicate that the nation's attitude toward business is changing. It is potentially a bigger change than many politicians realize. What's unnerving them is that the payback from the market bubble of the late 1990's is becoming apparent to Main Street. The charts of the downside since March 2000 are starting to match the slope of the earlier three-year upside.

Not that it's a new phenomenon. In the Gilded Age of the late 19th century and again in the Roaring Twenties, wealth momentum surged, the rich pulled away from everyone else and financial and technological innovation built a boom. Then it went partially or largely bust in the securities markets. Digging out is never easy. But this time, the deep-rooted nature of "financialization" in the United States that developed in the 1980's and 90's may make it even tougher.

Near the peak of the great booms, old economic cautions are dismissed, financial and managerial operators sidestep increasingly inadequate regulations and ethics surrender to greed. Then, after the collapse, the dirty linen falls out of the closet. Public muttering usually swells into a powerful chorus for reform—deep, systemic changes designed to catch up with a whole new range and capacity for frauds and finagles and bring them under regulatory control.

Even so, correction is difficult, in part because the big wealth momentum booms leave behind a triple corruption: financial, political and philosophic. Besides the swindles and frauds that crest with the great speculative booms, historians have noted a parallel tendency: cash moving into politics also rises with market fevers.

During the Gilded Age, the railroad barons bought legislatures and business leaders bought seats in the United States Senate. In the last years of the 19th century, one senator naïvely proposed a bill to unseat those senators whose offices were found to have been purchased. This prompted a colleague to reply, in all seriousness, "We might lose a quorum here, waiting for the courts to act."

Over the last two decades, the cost of winning a seat in Congress has more than quadrupled. Legislators casting votes on business or financial regulation cannot forget the richest 1 percent of Americans, who make 40 percent of the individual federal campaign donations over $200. Money is buying policy.

Speculative markets and growing wealth momentum also corrupt philosophy and ideology, reshaping them toward familiar justifications of greed and ruthlessness. The 1980's and 1990's have imitated the Gilded Age in intellectual excesses of market worship, laissez-faire and social Darwinism. Notions of commonwealth, civic purpose and fairness have been crowded out of the public debate.

Part of the new clout and behavior of finance is so deep-rooted, however, that it raises questions that go far beyond the excesses of the bubble. In the last few decades, the United States economy has been transformed through what I call financialization. The processes of money movement, securities management, corporate reorganization, securitization of assets, derivatives trading and other forms of financial packaging are steadily replacing the act of making, growing and transporting things.

That transformation has many roots. Finance surged in the 80's partly because deregulation removed old ceilings on interest rates and let financial institutions offer new services. The rising stock market, in turn, drew money from savings accounts into money market funds and mutual funds, turning the securities industry into a huge profit center. Computers underpinned the expansion of everything from A.T.M.'s to scores of new derivative instruments by which traders could gamble with such dice as Treasury note futures or Eurodollar swaps. Meanwhile, the Federal Reserve and Treasury Department proved during the 80's and 90's that nothing too bad could happen in the financial sector, because Washington was always ready with a bailout.

Supported so openly, rescued from the stupid decisions and market forces that pulled down other industries, the finance, insurance and real estate sector of the economy overtook manufacturing, pulling ahead in the G.D.P. and national income charts in 1995. By 2000, this sector also moved out front in profits. It also became the biggest federal elections donor and the biggest spender on Washington lobbying.

The effects have been profoundly inegalitarian—and not just in the loss of manufacturing's blue-collar middle class. In the last two decades, as money shifted from savings accounts into mutual funds, promoting the stock markets and the money culture, corporate executives became preoccupied with stock options, compensation packages and golden parachutes. "More" became the byword.

In the new management handbook as rewritten by finance, the concerns of employees, shareholders and even communities could be jettisoned to raise stock prices. Major companies could make (or fake) larger profits by financial devices: writing futures contracts, investing in stocks, juggling pension funds, moving low-return assets into separate partnerships and substituting stock options for salary expenses. Enron was only the well-publicized tip of a large iceberg.

A century ago, putting a new regulatory framework around abuses of the emergent railroad and industrial sectors became a priority. This effort largely succeeded. Whether another such framework must be put in place around finance in order to safeguard household economic security is a question that at the very least calls for a national debate. Whether the current proposals are the beginnings of that debate or mere window dressing remains to be seen.

Kevin Phillips is the author of "Wealth and Democracy: A Political History of the American Rich."

Bank Mergers Don't Win All Raves

About 20% in Survey Say They Are Worse Off, Citing High Fees, Drop in Service

By KATHY CHU

NEW YORK—A wave of bank mergers has left many consumers feeling shortchanged.

The majority of Americans who have been through a bank merger say it has made little difference to them, but about 20% say they are worse off, according to an online study of 1,001 consumers by Maritz Research. Only about 14% feel they are better off.

In the poll, which has a margin of error of plus or minus three percentage points, consumers cited new or higher fees and a decrease in service as the main reasons why they feel harmed by bank mergers.

"People aren't seeing the economies of scale," said Eric Levy, a research director at Maritz in St. Louis. "They don't know what to expect."

Consumers may have reason to be concerned. A 2003 Federal Reserve study revealed that banks with operations in more than one state tend to charge higher fees on average—for services such as stop-payment orders, overdrafts and cash withdrawals—than those banks operating only in one state.

In the current wave of consolidation, however, banks may be more careful about slapping customers with fees, for fear that they will flee to competitors.

"By measure of inertia, fees are still going to rise, but it's not going to be just because of these mergers," said Greg McBride, a senior analyst at Bankrate.com, a rate-monitoring site. "I don't think we're going to see as many changes in fee structures as a few years ago."

Of course, consumers will see some benefits, including access to a greater number of automatic-teller machines and bank branches. For instance, the recent combination of FleetBoston Financial Corp. and Bank of America Corp. has expanded the network of ATMs to more than 16,000 and bank locations to about 5,700.

In the past five years, more than half of all U.S. households have gone through a bank merger, according to the Maritz poll, conducted between April 7 and 12. One in four has been through this experience in the past year.

Consolidation has changed the landscape, providing fewer choices for consumers of where to bank. At the end of 2003, about 7,769 commercial banks were insured by the Federal Deposit Insurance Corp., a significant decrease from the nearly 11,000 commercial banks out there a decade ago. This is mainly due to mergers and corporate reorganizations, according to David Barr, a FDIC spokesman.

The biggest challenge banks face when undergoing a merger is keeping customers informed and satisfied. The danger of not doing so is that some customers may flee to competitors, including smaller banks that tend to offer more personal service.

While the majority of consumers currently affected by a merger plan to stay with their banks, about 13% of consumers are looking to change banks, according to Maritz. Another 35% plan to see what the combinations bring.

Customers often leave for multiple reasons, some of which can be hard to measure by surveys, say experts. These include not wanting to pay new fees, as well as frustration over the higher number of sales pitches and technology-integration issues.

"I don't have any hard data, but anecdotally, from talking with many of our members, they feel that they gain market share and customers every time there's consolidation in their market," said Robert Davis, executive vice president of America's Community Bankers, a Washington, D.C., trade group whose members have a median of $140 million in assets and two or three bank branches.

Write to Kathy Chu at kathy.chu@dowjones.com

UNIT 5

The Changing Global Economy

Unit Selections

Key Points to Consider

- How should the United States respond to the challenges of the global economy?
- Should we be concerned about the large U.S. current account deficit?
- Will efforts at economic integration such as NAFTA and the European Monetary Union succeed?
- Where is the Chinese economy heading?
- How do today's consumption patterns affect tomorrow's human development?

DUSHKIN ONLINE

Links: www.dushkin.com/online/

These sites are annotated in the World Wide Web pages.

The European Union in the U.S.
http://www.eurunion.org

Institute for International Economics
http://www.iie.com

Inter-American Development Bank (IDB)
http://www.iadb.org

North American Free Trade Association (NAFTA)
http://www.nafta-sec-alena.org

Organization for Economic Co-operation and Development (OECD)
http://www.oecd.org

Sustainable Development.Org
http://www.sustainabledevelopment.org

United Nations Development Programme (UNDP)
http://www.undp.org

World Resources Institute
http://www.wri.org

The world economy is in a period of rapid change. Over the last decade we have witnessed a series of unforeseen events: aftershocks of the September 11, 2001 terrorist attacks; ambitious market reforms in what were formerly centrally planned economies; an acceleration of the process of economic integration in Western Europe and North America; and the impoverishment of many small, less developed countries burdened by staggering international obligations. Simultaneously with these developments has come the "globalization" of trade, reflecting America's increasing economic interdependence with the rest of the world.

The U.S. economic system is extraordinarily resilient. Historically, it has consistently demonstrated an ability to adjust to change, adapt to new technologies, and create new jobs. In absolute terms, the United States is presently the world's most important international trader: total U.S. exports and imports each exceed $1 trillion annually. In addition, the United States has for many years been able to enjoy the advantages of remaining relatively self-sufficient. Whereas Canada and most Western European countries derive roughly a quarter of their national income from trade, the United States obtains only about 10 percent of all income from this source.

This unit explores key issues in the global economy. C. Fred Bergsten spells out a foreign economic policy for the next U.S. president. He says that while the U.S. may be in a position to undertake unilateral initiatives for the sake of national security, in economic policy unilateralism is simply not an option. Lael Brainart and Robert E. Litan show why, in a post 9/11 world, it is even more important for the U.S. to combat international poverty and promote vibrant international trade. Then, Nancy Birdsall considers the implications of market-led globalization for the world's poor nations.

The next two articles deal with the economics of "free trade." Virginia Postrel shows how trade results not only in lower prices for the same goods, but also a greater range of goods to choose from. But Jeff Madrik warns that the benefit of lower prices gained from free trade may be less than the cost of lost jobs or lower wages. Then, Joseph Stiglitz, a Nobel Prize winner and formerly chief economist of the World Bank, argues that while, in theory, the International Monetary Fund supports democractic institutions in the nations it assists, in practice it undermines the democratic process by imposing policies on them.

The unit concludes with a United Nations study that examines implications of the rapid growth of world consumption in the twentieth century for human development in the twenty-first century.

Managing a Globalizing World

AN OVERVIEW

By Barry Bosworth and Philip H. Gordon

The massive street protests at last July's G-8 summit in Genoa, Italy—following similar demonstrations at other international gatherings in Gotenberg, Prague, Washington, Davos, and Seattle—have focused the world's attention as never before on the phenomenon now known as globalization. The issues raised under the heading of globalization are controversial in part because the term has different meanings for different people. Most broadly, globalization is the expansion and intensification of linkages and flows—of people, goods, capital, ideas, and cultures—across national borders. To some this process implies the need for an element of global governance—a decline in the importance of national entities as they are replaced by global institutions. A more integrated global system has also increased awareness of a set of common problems—pollution, disease, and crime—that many have come to believe can only be addressed collectively. The result has been growing controversy about how to ensure a safer, more prosperous world to the benefit of all. In this issue of the *Brookings Review*, experts from inside and outside Brookings address the impact of globalization on a range of international issues.

In some respects, globalization is an old story. Transnational banks and trading enterprises have been important features of international commerce since the Middle Ages in Europe. By some measures, trade between nations was higher at the beginning of the 20th century than at the beginning of the 21st. The gold standard constituted a de facto common monetary system that linked national financial markets more closely than today's array of floating and semi-floating exchange rates. The movement of people across national borders also peaked in the 19th century, when travelers had no need for passports or visas. But globalization was set back in the first half of the 20th century, as two world wars and a severe world depression led to a breakup of the international monetary system and a series of national actions to curb trade. Much of the remainder of the century was devoted to restoring the trade and financial linkages that existed before 1914.

Though some analysts have used past examples of international integration to play down the significance of developments today, in fact global linkages at the opening of the 21st century far exceed those of earlier eras in degree, intensity, speed, volume, and geographic reach. Over the past decade globalization has been driven by technological advances, which have dramatically cut the costs of international shipping, transportation, travel, communication, and financial interaction, as well as of computing and information exchange. But globalization has also been driven by policies and ideas, as governments around the world, particularly since the 1980s, have increasingly come to believe that opening their borders to outside capital, competition, and ideas is good for their societies as a whole. One result has been an increase in openness in the already fairly integrated industrialized regions of North America, Europe, and East Asia. Another has been the incorporation of China, Russia, Eastern Europe, and Latin America into a more integrated international political and economic system.

In an economic sense, globalization is most evident in the expansion of international commerce. A recent book by Angus Madison estimates that the export share of world output has grown about fourfold since 1870. Growth has been particularly rapid in the past half century (figure 1). Today the total value of annual international exports is almost $7 trillion. For the United States, total trade (exports and imports) has increased from 11 percent of GDP in 1929 to today's 25 percent, but all that growth has come about in the past quarter century.

Global capital markets have also grown rapidly, with private capital flows rising from less than 5 percent of world GDP in 1975 to about 20 percent today. And foreigners play a critical role in financing the U.S. economy.

Figure 1. World Trade and Production, 1950–99

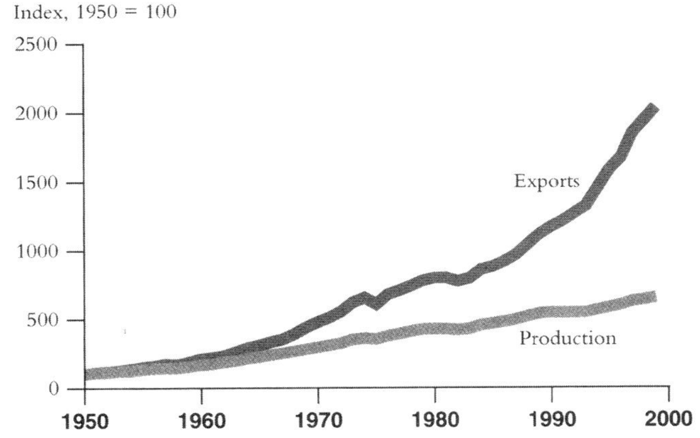

Source: WTO

Figure 2. Share of U.S. Population That Is Foreign-Born, 1900–2000

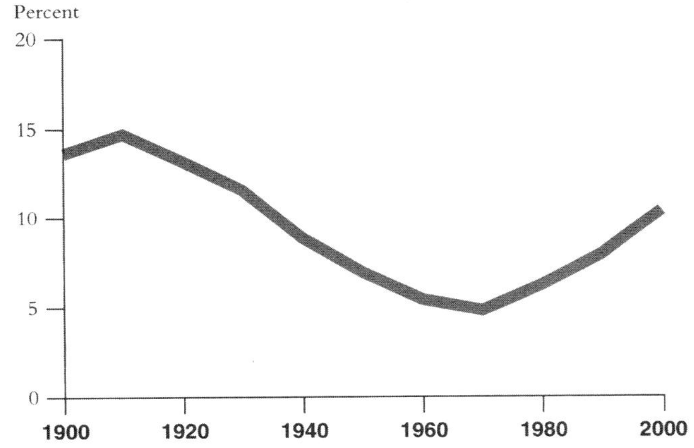

Source: *Department od Commerce Historical Statistics of the United States Colonial Times to 1970, US Statistical Abstract 2000.*

Figure 3. Global Inequality of Individual Incomes, 1820–1992

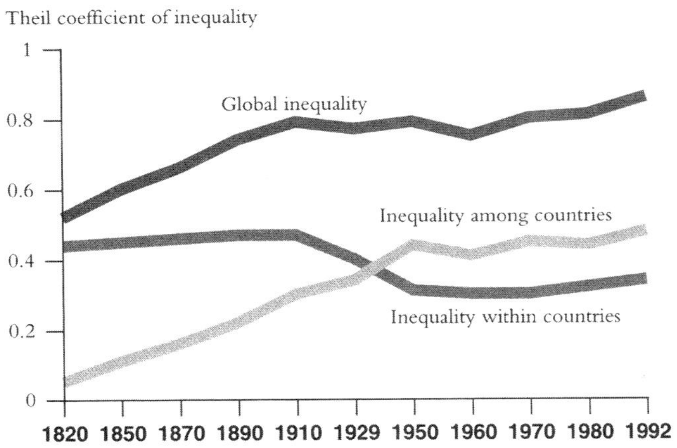

Source: François Bourguignon and Christian Morrisson, unpublished paper written for the World Bank, 2000. The "countries" here consist of 15 single countries with abundant data and large populations plus 18 other country groups. The 18 groups were aggregates of geographical neighbors having similar levels of GDP per capita.

At the end of 2000, Americans, with a national income of $8 trillion, had investments in the rest of the world worth about $3.7 trillion, while foreign claims on the United States totaled $7.4 trillion.

And while the share of the global population migrating across national borders has remained roughly stable over the past half century, its composition has changed: a growing proportion moves from very poor to rich countries. In the United States, the share of the population that is foreign-born has increased dramatically in the past 40 years, though it remains below that of the early 1900s (see figure 2).

Finally, the falling cost of travel, as well as technological innovations in communications, has greatly increased contact between people of disparate cultures. Today, some 250 million people worldwide have access to the Internet, putting them in touch with ideas and information from literally anywhere else in the world at any time. Global television and radio broadcasts and other media have also helped promote unprecedented contact among people of different nations. Those contacts have promoted extensive cultural interaction, offering people around the world the many benefits of access to different cultures, but have also stoked resentment in some quarters as people worry about apparent "threats" to their way of life, often equating "globalization" with "Americanization."

Why is globalization so controversial? Concerns vary. First, within any country, the liberalization of trade creates both winners and losers. Although economists can demonstrate that the gains to the winners will exceed the losses—the benefits of increased specialization and economies of scale—some losses can be substantial. Within U.S. manufacturing, for example, workers whose jobs are displaced through trade will ultimately suffer reductions in annual income that average about 16 percent when they find new jobs. Most countries make only minimal efforts to compensate the losers. Such domestic conflicts have long been evident in the United States in the textile, steel, and automobile industries, but their importance increases as the pace of globalization accelerates. More generally, a more open, competitive global economy can be expected to harm the welfare of low-skilled workers in the industrialized countries.

Second, a substantial portion of the globe's population has thus far failed to gain from globalization, and poverty remains a severe problem for many. More than a billion people, roughly a quarter of the world's population, exist on less than $1 a day; and more than half the world's people live on less than $2 a day. Critics charge that the gains from globalization are too sharply skewed toward the already prosperous industrial countries. Most economic analysis suggests that poor countries need to be more, not less, integrated with the global economy if they are to have access to the capital, technology, and infrastructure required to raise productivity and living standards. But some analysts object that the industrial countries are erecting ever more barriers to new entrants in the form of

Figure 4. CO_2 Emissions Per Capita, Annual Average, 1995–97

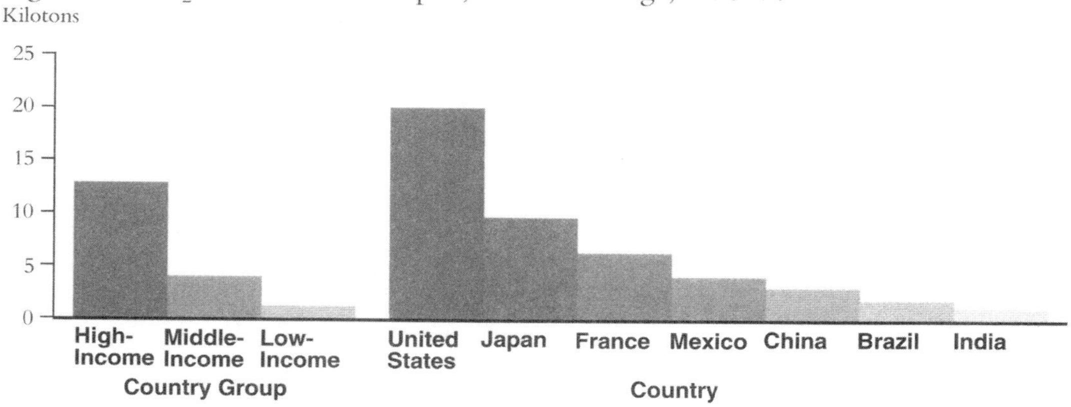

Source: *World Development Indicators 2001.*

Figure 5. CO_2 Emissions Levels by Country Group, 1960–95

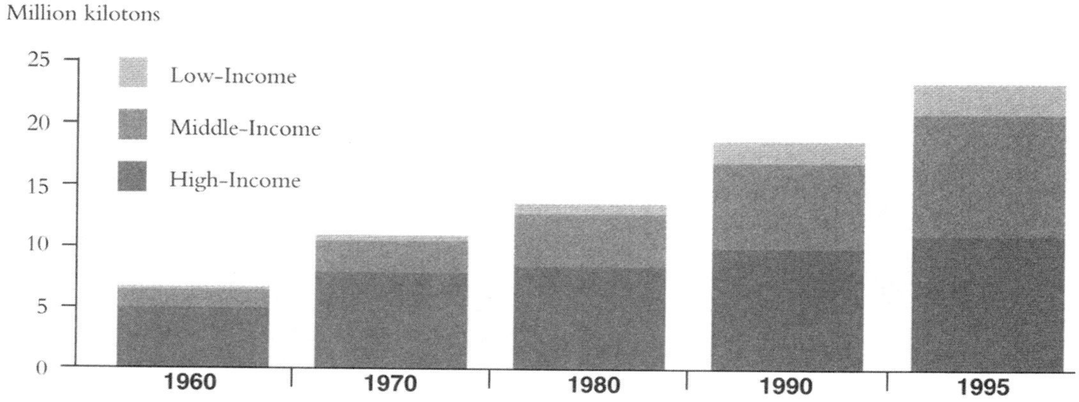

Source: *World Development Indicators 2001.*

restrictions on the use of new technologies, as well as labor and environmental standards higher than those followed by the industrial countries at similar stages of development.

In the debate over the distribution of globalization's benefits it is important to distinguish between the change in the distribution of income within and among countries. Before World War I, incomes in countries now considered industrialized—Europe, the United States, Canada, Australia, and Japan—tended to converge because of expanding trade and the mass migration of people out of Europe. Since World War II, a similar convergence can be traced in large part to reconstruction of war-damaged economies. Several Asian economies also moved out of the ranks of severe poverty to achieve standards of living comparable to those of the industrialized economies of Europe.

The record is more disappointing when more countries are included (see figure 3). Over the span of a century or more, the income gap between the richest and poorest countries has widened. For the most recent decades, conclusions depend on specific methodologies and whether fast-growing economies, such as China, India, and Indonesia, are included. On balance, there has been little change in the aggregate, though some evidence suggests that significant involvement in the global trading system helps improve growth in the high performers.

Third, environmental concerns have emerged as a new source of conflict. As shown in figure 4, carbon emissions, believed to be a cause of global warming, are strongly tied to economic development. On a per capita basis Americans generate the most emissions—roughly seven times those of China. But the developing countries are helping to boost growth in emissions (figure 5). The United States has refused to join in cooperative efforts to reduce carbon emissions unless constraints are placed on the developing countries, and it has rejected a standard that equalizes emissions per capita.

Other forms of pollution also rise with economic development, but as countries become wealthier they can afford to make the investments required to reduce pollution. Thus, some environmental problems will worsen with development, others will decline, and still others will initially worsen and then improve. Environmental quality becomes an important goal only in societies that have escaped grinding poverty. The transfer of pollution-control technologies from the rich to the poor nations also helps the poor countries achieve lower pollution goals than did the rich countries at comparable stages of development. It is sometimes argued that competition among countries to attract multinational firms and jobs might lead to a competitive race to the bottom in terms of environmental standards. The available evidence, however, suggests the opposite, as the more open economies have been quicker to adopt the cleaner technologies and foreign-owned firms tend to pollute less than national firms.

Finally, globalization is controversial because although open borders increase flows of less expensive and better-quality goods, well-allocated capital investments, and new ideas and information, they may also invite narcotics, laundered money, terrorists, weapons of mass destruction, and diseases like tuberculosis and AIDS. These less welcome consequences pose huge challenges to an international community more interconnected—and therefore more vulnerable to developments taking place all around the world—than ever before.

Can globalization be harnessed so that all citizens and countries benefit and not just the lucky few? Is it a force for spreading democracy and individual freedom, or does it help authoritarian governments to maintain control? Are global regimes and institutions—financial, commercial, environmental, and political—the best ways to cope with the challenges posed by globalization, or should each country fend primarily for itself? There are no easy answers, but these are some of the critical questions that our contributors address.

Barry Bosworth is a senior fellow in the Brookings Economic Studies program. Philip H. Gordon, a senior fellow in the Brookings Foreign Policy Studies program, is director of the Brookings Center on the United States and France and the author, with Sophie Meunier, of The French Challenge: Adapting to Globalization *(Brookings, 2001).*

Foreign Economic Policy for the Next President

C. Fred Bergsten

The Dangers of Rollback

At a time when U.S. foreign policy is dominated by war, terrorism, and weapons of mass destruction, economic concerns are often relegated to the back burner. But in reality, economic policy must be an integral component of any successful foreign policy. Some of its elements, such as the suppression of terrorist financing and support for reconstruction efforts in Iraq and Afghanistan, bear directly on the most central national security concerns. The linkage, however, is much broader, because most countries, rich or poor, large or small, depend heavily on the global economy for their prosperity and their stability. Hence, economics ranks at the top of their list of concerns. To continue to be relevant to the rest of the world, the United States must engage effectively on these issues.

As the sole military superpower, the United States may often be able to undertake unilateral initiatives for the sake of national security. But in economic policy, unilateralism is simply not an option. No government, Washington included, can ignore market forces. The European Union's economy is now as large as that of the United States, and the euro has begun to challenge the dollar for global financial leadership. The United States relies on foreign investors—including the monetary authorities of competitor Asian economies—to finance massive external deficits, and it depends on oil imported at prices set by producers in other countries. Cooperation is therefore a necessity in the realm of international economics. Indeed, because of the close connection between economics and other international issues, economic policy often restrains the unilateralist tendencies in U.S. foreign policy as a whole.

Foreign economic policy is also critical to the health of the domestic economy. Over the past generation, the share of trade in U.S. GDP has tripled, to about 30 percent, and over the past decade, the competitive stimulus provided by rapid globalization has helped spur a dramatic increase in productivity, thus contributing to faster growth and job creation as well. On the financial side, foreigners' willingness to invest more than $500 billion a year in the United States funds massive trade deficits and makes up for low domestic savings rates. Overall, the reduction of trade barriers over the past 50 years has raised the annual income of the average family by $2,000.

But for the past decade, U.S. foreign economic policy has been mired in stalemate. For eight years, Congress refused to authorize the president to negotiate new trade agreements. When it finally did so in 2002, it was thanks only to a series of protectionist concessions on the part of the Bush administration. Legislation to replenish the International Monetary Fund (IMF), meanwhile, languished for more than a year at the height of the Asian financial crisis. It was rescued only by the intervention of a farm bloc seeking new funding for sales to major overseas markets.

The main reason for this stalemate is that global economic developments have harmed many individuals in the United States even as they have benefited the economy as a whole. Changes driven by technological advance and globalization have disrupted firms, communities, and workers, and a small but significant number of workers—perhaps 150,000 a year—suffer dislocations and significant earnings losses due to trade. Many others fear that "there but for the grace of God go I." It is now becoming clear that white-collar jobs can be "outsourced" just as blue-collar jobs have been.

U.S. policymakers must decisively overcome the domestic backlash against globalization to create a firm political foundation for a sustainable and constructive foreign economic policy. But the outlook is worrisome, despite the current economic recovery. Overvalued exchange rates and the massive trade deficits they create—characteristics of the current U.S. economy—have historically caused a retreat from openness. The admirable efforts of the Bush administration to revive liberalization have mostly run aground: the Doha Round of World Trade Organization (WTO) negotiations stalled at Cancún in September 2003; the Free Trade Area of the Americas fared similarly poorly at Miami in November 2003; and bilateral free trade agreements are facing stiff congressional resistance and may have to be shelved. Moreover, disputes between Europe and the United States could spark a transatlantic trade war, and a vicious round of China-bashing has erupted over the past year. These developments have put U.S. trade policy, and hence the global trading system, in deep jeopardy and could start to reverse the profound benefits of globalization.

Stopping the advance of globalization would be very dangerous to U.S. foreign policy because globalization—more than terrorism or the end of the Cold War—has been the dominant force for change in international affairs in the past 50 years. And rightly or wrongly, it is equated with Americanization in much of the world. Debates over globalization are often debates over the role of the United States itself. A significant rollback of globalization, or a halt in its continued advance, would therefore represent a major defeat for the United States on the world stage. The next administration must recognize the urgency of the situation and make foreign economic policy a top priority.

A New Global Order

More and more, "emerging market economies"—China and India, most notably—are becoming world-class competitors in a range of sectors. This development will require even more rapid improvement in the skills of U.S. workers and the flexibility of U.S.-based companies. It will require more effective safety nets to cushion the inevitable victims of transition. It will necessitate continuing U.S. policy reforms to increase the country's competitiveness and diligent negotiations on trade and other international issues to assure a level playing field.

But new competitors also offer attractive markets for U.S. exports and investment. They are valuable suppliers of high-quality, low-cost goods. And if properly incorporated into the global economy—and paired with effective domestic policies in the United States—they will lead to new gains in global growth, as well as improvements in U.S. productivity that will further magnify the benefits of globalization for the United States.

> Washington will have to navigate in very unfamiliar economic waters.

The most difficult challenge facing the next administration stems instead from fundamental changes in the structure of the global economy. Since World War II, the United States has been able to dominate the world economy, even during periods of poor performance and dreadful policy, because it has been the only economic superpower. (U.S. military supremacy may have helped on occasion, but there is, in reality, little day-to-day spillover from security to economic affairs.) Japan has never played a major role in global economic policy, and Europe, even after the creation of the EU, has failed to consolidate its decision-making and speak with a single voice. The notable, and highly instructive, exception has been trade policy: Europe did centralize its policy and so forced Washington to deal with it as an equal.

All of this is now changing rapidly. When it expands to 25 members this year, the EU will have a total output (not to mention a population) greater than that of the United States; it is already the world's largest trading entity, and the euro has become a key currency along with the dollar. Europe has not yet consolidated its decision-making or external representation, but it is sure to do so over time.

Even more dramatic changes could come across the Pacific. China is likely to continue growing rapidly for at least two more decades, becoming an economic superpower in its own right. In addition, East Asia is in the process of creating an economic bloc that could eventually comprise both a regional free trade area and an Asian monetary fund. Such a bloc would claim about one-fifth of the world economy, 20 percent of global trade, and $1.5 trillion in monetary (mostly dollar) reserves—about ten times those of the United States. Such an East Asian group would be a third economic superpower.

This confluence of events could convert the unipolar economic order of the past half-century into a bipolar or tripolar one, forcing Washington to navigate in very unfamiliar waters. U.S. foreign economic policy will have to overcome the challenges of integrating emerging powers into existing global structures and of managing the world economy by committee. It will have to forge new techniques of cooperation among near-equals, as well as compete in increasingly fierce global markets. It will have to draw on its strong ties with both Europe and Asia (which are far stronger than links between the two) to promote its own interests and secure the place of the United States as the pivotal actor in shaping new multilateral regimes.

A reelected President Bush or his successor will have to design and implement new initiatives to address global economic challenges of the highest national and international priority: forging a new domestic consensus in support of globalization; restoring and maintaining a sustainable external financial position; reviving trade liberalization; and freeing the world economy from the manipulation of energy markets by leading producers. He will have to do all of this in a new global economic context, in which a unified Europe, a rising China, and a new Asian bloc are shattering the final vestiges of U.S. economic hegemony.

Credit Check

The United States is by far the world's largest deficit and debtor nation. Both the U.S. economy and U.S. foreign policy are thus put at serious risk by the prospect of an outbreak of trade protectionism, foreign unwillingness to finance the $4 billion needed every working day to balance U.S. books, or even dumping of large portions of the

$10 trillion in U.S. currency held abroad (driving interest rates up and the U.S. economy down). The continued buildup of debt owed to foreigners, moreover, will steadily erode national income over time. The next administration must work to restore a sustainable current account and international financial position.

The goal should be to cut the external deficit in half, from its present level of $550 billion (or more than 5 percent of GDP). This reduction would have the important effect of stabilizing the ratio of foreign debt (already more than $3 trillion) to GDP. The only lasting way to do so is to sharply increase the savings rate in the U.S. economy, so that massive foreign capital inflows no longer push the dollar to overvalued levels and generate huge trade deficits. There is, unfortunately, no proven policy to increase private saving. Hence the government must convert its own budget deficit into a modest surplus, at least in periods of robust growth as at present.

Unfortunately, budget correction will not likely come soon enough to reduce the vulnerability created by external deficits. More immediate, if less fundamental, remedies are also required. The only feasible option is reducing the value of the dollar by 25 percent from its early 2002 peak. That decline has already begun, in a gradual and orderly manner, and it is probable that markets will also generate the rest of the correction. Because the U.S. economy is performing well relative to other large economies, there is little risk of a "hard landing." U.S. policymakers should thus make sure that market forces are allowed to prevail in lowering the dollar's value, threatening direct intervention if necessary to offset intervention by other countries (especially China and Japan) seeking to block the adjustment.

The problem of U.S. external deficits has been a recurring one over the past 30 years. Therefore, in addition to restoring sustainable trade and current account balances now, U.S. policymakers must recognize the need to revamp the institutional arrangements that govern exchange rates and overall economic relationships between countries. For all the talk of "reforming the international financial architecture" over the past decade, little has been done. The Treasury Department under both Presidents Bill Clinton and Bush—and the group of seven highly industrialized countries (G-7) and the IMF as well—have allowed countries such as China and Japan to violate existing rules while ignoring the need for basic improvements in such rules.

The next administration should negotiate fundamental improvements in the international monetary system, in order both to protect the United States against a return to unsustainable deficit levels and to provide a more stable foundation for the global economy as a whole. The most promising approach would be to implement new mechanisms limiting the deviation of exchange rates from their equilibrium values through close cooperation between economic policymakers in major countries.

New Paths to Open Markets

Trade liberalization, an integral aspect of globalization over the past half-century, has dramatically helped the U.S. economy and contributed mightily to Washington's global leadership position. Further efforts in this direction will bring further benefits. Foreign economic policy must therefore remain devoted to the goals pursued by every U.S. administration in the past 70 years: reducing barriers at home and abroad to international exchange, and developing a rules-based trading system built around strong international institutions.

The United States has a strong interest in further opening international markets, moving as close as possible to global free trade, and strengthening the enforcement machinery of the WTO. Its comparative advantage in services and agriculture means that wholesale liberalization of those sectors, through aggressive U.S.-sponsored initiatives, would bring significant benefits. U.S. markets are already quite open, whereas other countries—particularly rapidly growing developing economies—maintain much higher barriers that can be reduced only through new international negotiations. Policymakers should work to eliminate the discrimination inherent in preferential trade deals engineered by Europe and, prospectively, by Asia.

In its first two years, the Bush administration achieved two notable successes in trade policy: the passage of fast-track negotiating authority and the launch of the Doha Round of WTO negotiations. Overall, it has pursued a coherent strategy of "competitive liberalization" in which multilateral, regional, and bilateral agreements reinforce and catalyze one another. These efforts, however, have recently run aground, and potential conflicts with Europe and China darken the picture even more.

The next administration must therefore attach high priority to reviving an effective trade policy. Most urgent is a more forthcoming offer of liberalization by the United States itself, especially in agriculture, to revive the Doha Round that broke down in Cancún. Washington must reverse the subsidy increases of the 2002 farm bill—contingent, of course, on fully reciprocal liberalization by other developed economies (chiefly the EU, Japan, and South Korea) and partial liberalization by the more advanced developing countries (chiefly Brazil and India). The United States should also repeat its offer to eliminate, again on a reciprocal basis, all duties on nonagricultural trade. The breakdown at Cancún proved that developing countries, united in a new G-22, can block multilateral trade progress on their own. Policymakers must recognize this fact and work constructively with the coalition, rather than trying to ignore or dismantle it. A successful Doha Round would then provide a firm foundation for a new "WTO plus" agreement in the western hemisphere.

The next administration must also revise trade policy as it relates to bilateral agreements. The list of bilateral partners chosen to date by the Bush administration (including Australia, Bahrain, Bolivia, Central America, Colombia, Ecuador, Morocco, Peru, the Southern African Customs Union, and Thailand, in addition to existing agreements with Canada, Chile, Israel, Jordan, Mexico, and Singapore) is arbitrary, offering modest benefits and little impetus to "competitive liberalization." Because of their limited benefits, these initiatives attract little support in Congress or the U.S. business community. Some of them have in fact attracted opposition sufficient to make their passage through Congress unlikely (at least in election year 2004). The Bush administration made the same mistake in selecting free trade partners that the Clinton administration made in pursuing fast-track negotiating authority in 1997: attempting to minimize domestic opposition instead of maximizing domestic support.

The next administration should, in close consultation with Congress, spell out four clear criteria for choosing free trade partners, in the following order of priority: net economic gains to the United States, promotion of constructive economic reforms in the partner country, importance for broader U.S. trade policy, and significance for overall U.S. foreign policy objectives. A few of the current candidates for agreements pass this test, but several others not on the list should be top priorities: Brazil (especially if the Free Trade Area of the Americas fails to move forward), South Korea, and, pending necessary internal reforms, Egypt and Indonesia. Washington should also offer a regional free trade agreement to Africa, as it has to Latin America, the Middle East, and Southeast Asia.

A revitalization of the Asia-Pacific Economic Cooperation forum (APEC) should also be part of the U.S. response to any European stalling and to the prospect of a new East Asian bloc. Just as President George H.W. Bush insisted on full U.S. participation when APEC was created in 1989 and President Clinton used APEC to pressure Europe to complete the Uruguay round, the United States should use strengthened transpacific ties as a counterweight to such developments. APEC can once again promote major U.S. foreign policy and economic objectives.

Domestic Backlash

THE BIGGEST BARRIER to a constructive and consistent policy on trade and globalization is domestic. The U.S. public is split virtually down the middle on these issues. Congress' rejection of fast track in 1994, 1997, and 1998, and its near-rejection of it in 2002, was an accurate reflection of divided public opinion, not an aberration by deviant legislators.

The country divides along educational lines. Workers with college degrees, or at least some college experience, support globalization because they think they can take advantage of the opportunities it offers. Workers who have not gone beyond high school—half of the U.S. labor force—oppose further globalization because they fear they cannot adjust to it. The only long-term strategy for achieving domestic consensus, therefore, is to improve education and raise the overall skill level of the population. In the short term, effective governmental assistance to workers who are displaced by increased trade flows can help considerably. This assistance should have two components: stronger safety nets to cushion the transitional costs of job displacement, and more effective training and other adjustment programs to help workers qualify for new positions.

Acting on such evidence, Congress insisted that its authorization of new trade negotiations in 2002 be linked to substantial improvement in the Trade Adjustment Assistance program, which has pursued these goals since 1962. The new legislation broadened eligibility for the program, provided more generous levels of aid (especially for job-search and relocation expenditures), and established innovative wage insurance (to cover lost income when workers accept lower-paying jobs) and health insurance improvements. Unfortunately, in its first term the Bush administration (like its predecessors) has failed to implement these programs aggressively. The next administration must do so, in addition to developing other programs to alleviate the negative impacts of liberalization. Coverage should be broadened and benefits increased. There should be more effective support for adjustment, such as lifelong learning programs. Other innovations should include asset-value insurance, full portability of health and pension benefits, and a new "Human Capital Investment Tax Credit" to induce companies to provide more on-the-job training.

The economic gains from globalization to the United States are so large that it can readily afford to set aside a small portion of the proceeds to take care of those who lose out in the process—and basic norms of justice require that it do so. The United States will be unable to build a sustainable political base for a constructive foreign economic policy until it decisively addresses the adverse domestic consequences of globalization.

Energy Drain

Energy is another area in which the United States is vulnerable, in both economic and foreign policy terms. The lack of an effective energy policy—highlighted once again by the recent failure of Congress to pass adequate legislation after three years of effort—keeps U.S. foreign policy beholden to a few key producers and will probably force the United States to continue to launch periodic military interventions to satisfy its tremendous appetite for energy.

The leaders of the Organization of Petroleum Exporting Countries (OPEC) are allowed to manipulate world energy prices, holding them 50 to 75 percent above market levels in recent years. As a result, the cost of energy as a share of U.S. GDP has tripled since 1997. Since the oil shocks of the 1970s, prices have ranged from 15 to 300 percent of competitive levels, averaging almost double the competitive price. (In addition, as Alan Greenspan noted, the three major U.S. recessions prior to the shallow decline in 2001 "have all been preceded by spikes in the price of oil.") Over this period, inflated energy costs have depressed the U.S. GDP, and those of other oil-importing countries, by 15 to 30 percent. Restoration of market energy prices could alone boost economic growth by one percent a year.

Fortunately, as energy economist Philip Verleger has pointed out, consuming countries now have the capacity to counter the influence of producers. Strategic inventories now exceed 1.2 million barrels, including over 600 million held by the United States alone. These holdings make it possible for consumers to drive prices down until they better reflect the market and to keep them there, by using inventories as price stabilizers rather than thinking of them solely as protection against supply disruptions (which did not occur during either of the wars with Iraq). It is sheer folly for the United States to invest billions of dollars in its petroleum reserves only to sit on them as producers drive up prices.

> Disregard for rigged oil prices is a drain on the economy and a gap in the war on terrorism.

Any new campaign to cut world oil prices would inevitably invite charges of being part of a broader anti-Islamic crusade. It would be essential, for political as well as economic reasons, that the initiative be multilateral. The Organization for Economic Cooperation and Development's International Energy Agency (IEA) could manage the effort, with maximum efforts to include China and other oil-importing nations. It should, moreover, be emphasized loudly and repeatedly that large Muslim countries, notably Pakistan and Turkey, would also benefit from lower energy prices.

Oil-consuming countries should offer OPEC a producer-consumer agreement before threatening it with the prospect of sales from strategic stockpiles. The lead producers limit supply and push for higher prices in part because they fear a future loss of market share to Russia, Iraq, and western African countries. The IEA could agree to create mechanisms to provide OPEC countries, particularly those in the Persian Gulf, with a guaranteed market while at the same time offering oil to consumers at prices much lower than what they currently pay. Such an agreement should include larger global oil inventories and a system to share future production cuts, should prices drop too far, among all the major suppliers (rather than just a few cartel members).

The U.S. position would obviously be strengthened greatly if the United States finally took serious steps to limit its own consumption of energy. The most straightforward way to do so would be to target the most energy-intensive sector, transportation, by raising corporate average fuel economy standards, particularly as they apply to SUVs and light trucks. A sizeable carbon or gasoline tax would help enormously and also reduce the budget deficit.

There is, of course, a direct link between these energy proposals and the war on terrorism. A large portion of terrorist financing comes from Middle Eastern countries that benefit from the institutional arrangements that keep oil prices high. The United States' disregard for rigged oil prices is a gap in the antiterrorism campaign, as well as a major drain on the U.S. economy, and it should be remedied as soon as possible.

INSTITUTING CHANGE

NEW INSTITUTIONS will be needed to conceptualize and implement new policies. At the international level, one key requirement is for the United States and the EU, the world's two economic superpowers (together accounting for well more than half of the global economy), to create a "G-2"—an informal steering committee to manage the world economy and their bilateral relationship.

Although a transatlantic free trade area would be a bad idea, discriminating against the world's poorest countries, close and continuing cooperation between the United States and the EU is necessary for global economic progress. The G-2 would operate informally and would not undermine any other multilateral institutions or associations. Indeed, it would even contribute to a revitalization of such institutions. The G-7 nations, for example, could become the G-3 (the United States, the EU, and Japan) or, eventually, the G-4 (when China is ready to join).

To start, both the United States and the EU should be much more forthcoming with offers to liberalize trade in order to restart the Doha Round. (Their grossly inadequate positions at Cancún led to the current breakdown.) Conflicts over other bilateral issues could also be resolved more easily if they saw themselves as responsible co-leaders of the world economy rather than tit-for-tat antagonists. And cooperation on new economic initiatives would help patch up the political rift opened by the Iraq war. It would serve as a response to a new economic bloc in East Asia, and it could help strengthen the ability of global institutions such as the IMF and the WTO to maintain a multilateral check on new regional steps. The deep economic interpenetration of the United States and Europe—with $500 billion in direct investment in each direction and $400 billion in annual trade—is the main force holding them together. A G-2 initiative would thus have broad benefits for overall foreign policy.

A new institutional approach is needed at home as well. In recent years, foreign economic policy has devolved into a series of uncoordinated, ad hoc decisions, despite the obvious need to coordinate foreign policy with economic policy. Taxes are slashed and vast budget deficits created with little thought for their impact on the U.S. global economic position or international financial vulnerability. The Treasury Department fulminates against bailouts of emerging market economies before meekly complying with White House orders to support the same bailouts for foreign policy reasons (as in Argentina, Brazil, and Turkey). The U.S. Trade Representative is relegated to the sidelines in creating new steel tariffs or shaping the farm bill, despite their centrality to trade policy. Energy legislation is pursued with nary a word about how producer countries rig global prices and levy huge costs on our economy.

The Clinton administration created a National Economic Council to address such issues but never institutionalized the mechanism; it quickly fell into disuse when key personnel changed. A well-managed council, eventually written into law to parallel the National Security Council (NSC), is badly needed now. It would also help if at least one of the two top officials at the State Department and the NSC brought some economic expertise to their positions and were more cognizant of the importance of international economic issues to their broader mandates.

Congress must also get its act together on foreign economic policy. In an earlier era, similar global imperatives, the salience of which is underlined by current events, prompted the creation of the Senate and House intelligence committees to amalgamate foreign policy, national security, and related domestic concerns. The creation of similar committees on globalization could bring together the leadership of the trade committees (Ways and Means in the House, Finance in the Senate), those responsible for international finance, some of the relevant special committees (agriculture and commerce), and the foreign policy committees.

The Prospects for Progress

The United States has great economic strengths. It remains by far the world's largest national economy. Its sharp growth in productivity over the past decade appears likely to continue and perhaps accelerate again, generating very rapid expansion for a mature industrialized country. Moreover, it is growing much faster than other industrialized economies. The dollar will continue to be the main global currency for some time, and the U.S. model of capitalism and globalization dominates thinking around the world.

Yet the next president will face unprecedented challenges in the conduct of foreign economic policy. The case for globalization will have to be made persuasively, forcefully, and repeatedly. Domestic support could crumble if the president fails to address its internal costs with new safety nets and opportunities for skill enhancement; international support could dissolve if the White House's strategy fails to offer reciprocal benefits to other countries or is conducted without full consideration of their concerns. Such an outcome would be extremely costly. The economy would suffer from trade restrictions and a plummeting dollar in the short term and from reduced productivity growth in the long term. Foreign policy, meanwhile, would be jeopardized if the United States retreated from constructive cooperation with other nations on issues at the top of their agendas.

Most important, foreign economic policy could rescue overall U.S. foreign policy. The United States' biggest problem in the international arena is its tendency to act unilaterally on a range of issues. Such unilateralism is demonstrably ineffective and thus thankfully rare in the economic domain. The international economic initiatives proposed in this essay would convey a new image of U.S. foreign policy while furthering U.S. national interests. They should rank high on the agenda of the next U.S. president.

C. FRED BERGSTEN is Director of the Institute for International Economics. He was Assistant Secretary of the Treasury for International Affairs from 1977 to 1981 and Assistant for Economic Policy to the National Security Council from 1969 to 1971.

No Stepping Back: America's International Economic Agenda for 2003-05

by Lael Brainard , Robert E. Litan

September 11 was a defining event for America's international economic posture. International engagement, we now know, is not a matter up for debate but a fact of our times. Securing the U.S. homeland will require extensive cooperation from nations around the world and a sustained effort to strengthen the perceived legitimacy of America's preeminence in the international economic order. Now more than ever, it is important to demonstrate that combating international poverty and promoting vibrant international trade and capital flows are in the mutual self-interest of America and its foreign partners.

Fighting International Poverty

U.S. spending to fight world poverty plummeted during the 1990s. With the Cold War's end, policymakers lost interest in using foreign aid to fight communism. And disillusionment about aid's effectiveness was widespread. Aid critics contrasted the stunning economic success of East Asia, where aid has amounted to less than 2 percent of GDP, with the poor performance of the aid-dependent states of sub-Saharan Africa, where aid flows have exceeded 10 percent of GNP for several decades. This seeming contradiction may help explain why U.S. development aid, which had been more than 3 percent of total budget outlays in 1962, had fallen to roughly one-half of 1 percent by 2001.

Now the pendulum may be swinging the other way. Aid activists have learned to mobilize public support by using celebrities to back a simple, compelling goal—as when the global rock star Bono, of U2, made common cause with the pope in 1998 to persuade leaders of the richest nations to forgive the debt of the poorest nations. And the campaign against terrorism has provided a potentially powerful political rationale for foreign assistance—namely, that by strengthening foreign economies, aid may help weaken incentives for their residents to turn to terrorism.

The shift in the politics of aid and its heightened public salience present a tantalizing opportunity to make real progress in fighting global poverty. But it is critical to invest aid funds effectively and to be realistic about what aid can accomplish. The post-September 11 security rationale for development aid, for example, is far from airtight. The masterminds and key actors in the attacks were largely from middle-class backgrounds in the relatively more affluent societies of the Middle East. Their dissatisfaction is more likely rooted in frustration with the political and economic paralysis in their societies than in poverty per se. Yet poverty surely is a critical ingredient in failed states such as Afghanistan and Somalia that host terrorist training camps, and poor education coupled with despair helps explain the resonance of terrorist ideology in the Islamic world.

In the future, aid allocations should be driven primarily by an economic rationale—whether aid is likely to generate economic growth. Experience suggests that aid is most likely to spur growth when national leaders are committed to reform, governance is transparent and accountable, macroeconomic policies are sound, and the aid is more likely to add to national investment than merely to substitute for local investment.

Moreover, aid works best when it respects the power of the market. Previous "silver bullet" approaches that sought to supplant market mechanisms—forced industrialization, investing in industrial infrastructure—proved disappointing. Effective aid policies address market failures and align market returns with social returns.

In recent years, the share of total world aid devoted to investments in health, education, and sanitation has risen to nearly one-third (and nearly one-half for U.S. bilateral aid)—an emphasis consistent with both good economics and development experience. Aid is effective in these arenas because the market underprovides these socially valuable "public goods" whose benefits are spread so broadly that individuals do not have the incentive to pay the costs. Thus, the strong humanitarian case for development aid in providing public goods in the poorest nations is joined by a compelling economic case for action.

A strong public-goods case can also be made for aid that advances scientific knowledge in areas such as agriculture and medicine, where weak demand for innovations in the poorest nations leads to large gaps between their potential social value and their apparent market value. In wealthy nations, governments combine public funding for basic research and development with targeted protection for resulting intellectual property to encourage the development of scientific knowledge commensurate with its social value. But poor nations have few public resources to subsidize research, and intellectual property investments offer little promise of private returns. Thus, a key challenge for international development is to establish incentives for the global production of scientific knowledge tailored to the needs of poor nations.

For example, the United States may need to fine-tune intellectual property protection for pharmaceuticals. Intellectual property laws are designed to strike a balance between two competing needs—encouraging innovation and making valuable knowledge widely accessible. In recent years, efforts by the United States to extend these protections to the international level have come under attack for denying lifesaving medicines to the poorest nations. Indeed, there is some tension between boosting research on diseases disproportionately afflicting the poor and making medicines more accessible to poor nations. Extending the time a given producer enjoys an intellectual property monopoly on a particular drug encourages greater research effort. But making the drug broadly accessible requires pricing it at cost, which undercuts the value of the monopoly. For a limited class of internationally agreed health emergencies, where medicines are already in production in response to demand in rich nations, these goals can be reconciled by segmenting markets in rich and poor nations. Pharmaceutical producers could maintain their profit margins in wealthier markets if their governments prohibited "parallel" imports of their drugs from poor countries. And poor countries could get medicines at close to cost directly from the pharmaceutical company or from local or third-country generic producers.

Emerging International Consensus on Aid

Aid programs historically have been driven by the diverse agendas of donor countries. In a break with tradition, broad international agreement has recently emerged that aid is most effective when beneficiary countries are heavily involved in shaping development programs and priorities. It may now be possible to reorient the aid process around comprehensive national strategies designed by beneficiary governments in an open process involving key stakeholders. The World Bank's new Poverty Reduction and Growth Framework, established to direct resources freed up by debt forgiveness toward nationally determined social investments, reflects this new orientation. In the new framework, beneficiary nations present spending plans and assistance needs as part of an overall strategy to reduce poverty, thus ensuring that domestic budget resources reinforce the same priorities as aid.

Recent years have also seen an emerging consensus on the highest-priority programmatic areas for development aid. The consensus is broadly reflected in the eight development goals adopted in September 2000 at the United Nations Millennium Summit, for achievement by 2015. The goals—to eradicate extreme poverty and hunger; promote gender equality; achieve universal primary education; reduce child mortality; improve maternal health; combat HIV/AIDS, malaria, and other diseases; ensure environmental sustainability; and develop a global partnership for development—were specified in terms of 18 targets linked in turn to measurable results. One target, for example, was to halve the share of people whose income is less than one dollar a day.

Achieving these goals will be expensive. A group chaired by former Mexican President Ernesto Zedillo has put the price tag at an additional $50 billion a year—roughly double the current annual aid contributions of $53 billion, $30 billion of which goes to the world's poorest nations. Of the added resources, $12 billion would go for education, $10 billion for health, and $20 billion to fighting poverty. The U.S. share would range somewhere between $8.5 billion and $20.7 billion a year—the low end based on the U.S. share of IMF and World Bank capital, the high end reflecting the 41.3 percent U.S. share of the total GDP of industrialized donor countries.

> After September 11, U.S. Trade Representative Robert Zoellick lost no time in proclaiming trade to be central to America's campaign against terror.

The Bush administration has pledged to increase bilateral development aid by $5 billion a year by 2006 and to provide the new funding through a Millennium Challenge Account. Recipients would have to meet eligibility criteria in the areas of good governance, economic freedom, and investment in health and education. Continued access to funds would be contingent on measurable results. The administration's announcement of the new aid was greeted by applause from aid advocates and officials from poor nations—but also by an undercurrent of skepticism along the lines of "Show me the money." Some advocates have suggested a fiscal year 2003 down payment. Aid requests from the administration, however, have essentially held steady at historically low shares of the budget in the past two fiscal years. And the few areas that have seen increased funding—such as combating international HIV/AIDS—have come partly at the expense of spending on malaria and tuberculosis, rather than as net increases. Even on HIV/AIDS, the administration has resisted funding increases proposed by Congress.

Strengthening the Trading System

After growing a record 12.5 percent in 2000, world trade grew less than 2 percent in 2001. Foreign direct investment flows, which reached a record $1.3 trillion in 2000, are estimated to have fallen by half in 2001, the sharpest drop in three decades. Most experts see little or no link between these sharp declines and the events of September 11 and attribute them instead to economic slowdowns in the United States, European Union, and Japan, as Well as the information technology collapse.

Nonetheless, September 11 was a wake-up call for many trade supporters worldwide. It reinforced the direct interest of the wealthier nations in strengthening the trading system by rectifying the perceived inequities that prevent millions of the world's poor from reaping the potential benefits of globalization.

A key question now is whether the new security environment will signal a sustained shift in the terms of the U.S. debate to a broader definition of America's national interest. Sensing the opportunity, U.S. Trade Representative Robert Zoellick lost no time in proclaiming trade to be central to America's campaign against terror. President Bush used even stronger terms: "The terrorists attacked the World Trade Center, and we will defeat them by expanding and encouraging world trade."

But together, the terrorist attacks and the deepening of recession in the United States and around the world upped the ante on both sides of the trade debate. With the United States experiencing the first surge of unemployment in years and with the manufacturing sector hit particularly hard, domestic concerns moved front and center.

The post–September 11 emphasis on international coalition building created enormous momentum for the successful launch of global trade talks at the World Trade Organization meeting in Doha, Qatar, in November 2001. Success became a political imperative. Although the decision to hold the talks in Qatar, one of a handful of WTO member-states from the Middle East, had been made long before, the determination to follow through was courageous and symbolically important. Moreover, as evidenced by the term used to describe the outcome, "the Doha Development Agenda," the tenor of discussions at Doha tipped the balance on the margins toward the developing world. Both the European Union and the United States made important concessions to the developing countries to ensure a successful launch. But the advanced nations will be hard-pressed to deliver on their promises, given the high domestic sensitivities of the sectors likely to be affected by most controversial subject areas—the farm sector, textiles, and environmental and labor standards.

In 2002, following eight years of stalemate, Congress granted the president trade promotion authority—whereby Congress agrees to streamline its approval process for future trade agreements in return for enhanced oversight of negotiations. But the vote by the House of Representatives was highly partisan and won by a razor-thin margin of three votes, purchased at the expense of concrete up-front concessions in the form of trade-restrictive measures. The process left a deep divide at home and left foreign trading partners questioning the value of the U.S. promise to negotiate future trade opening in the face of immediate trade rollbacks.

Still, both the Doha agreement and TPA are important commitments to proceed with trade negotiations—which will inevitably require concessions in specific sectors where identifiable jobs and livelihoods are directly on the line. And so far, whenever concrete sectoral trade-offs have arisen—whether on farm subsidies, steel safeguards, Canadian lumber, or textiles access—the Bush administration has decided in favor of domestic sectoral interests.

The United States is by no means unique in this gap between its broader geostrategic aims and its willingness to accept painful sectoral dislocation when the economy is under stress. Both the European Union and Japan have been under tremendous pressure from their farm sectors to oppose opening agriculture to international competition.

Sustaining a focus on smoothing the rough edges of the global trading system, addressing inequities in global governance, and helping to give the world's poorest citizens a stake in the international system is as difficult as it is important. Even the compelling national security rationale of vanquishing terrorism may not be enough to overcome the intense domestic pressures. Trade policy presents knotty trade-offs between the losses faced by those whose jobs and companies are vulnerable to international competition and the greater but more diffuse national interest in a more competitive and productive economy—and in promoting a more peaceful, prosperous, and equitable world.

The potential worldwide gains from trade are quite impressive. The IMF puts the gains from eliminating all barriers to merchandise trade in a range from $250 billion to $680 billion a year. Developing countries would stand to gain the most in relation to GDP, with one-third of the total gains accruing to the poorest countries. The World Bank values comprehensive trade reform at $350 billion overall, with half accruing to developing nations. The value of total agricultural support by governments in industrialized countries is more than $300 billion a year, more than five times higher than spending on foreign development aid and more than the entire GNP of sub-Saharan Africa. Cuts in these subsidies could materially improve the livelihoods of the three-quarters of the world's poor who live in rural areas. Cutting barriers to services trade would produce a further annual global gain of $250 billion, most of it accruing to the developing world. The World Bank's chief economist estimates that trade protection in the rich nations costs' the developing nations more than $100 billion a year—twice the value of the international aid they receive.

International Finance

The first half of the 1990s saw remarkable progress in integrating the so-called emerging markets and transition economies into the international financial system. Private capital flows to emerging markets rose from $46 billion in 1990 to $235 billion in 1996. But as a series of damaging financial crises—Mexico in 1995; Southeast Asia, Russia, and Brazil in 1997-99; and Argentina, Turkey, and Brazil, among others, in 2002—make clear, sustaining that progress will not be easy. Important challenges are yet to be resolved.

The issues arising out of these crises are of direct interest to U.S. policymakers and citizens for several reasons. First, with world financial markets tightly linked and shifts in investor sentiment sudden and sharp, the U.S. economy can be adversely affected by instability far from our shores. Second, the United States has a strong national security interest in avoiding financial and often political crises in key allies, such as South Korea and Thailand in 1998 and Turkey and Argentina in 2001. Third, the United States is the principal financial supporter of the two international financial institutions—the International Monetary Fund and the World Bank—whose resources have been mobilized to prevent these crises from spinning out of control.

The typical policy reaction to financial crises—hard currency loans from the IMF and other sources coupled with broad conditions on how recipient governments must operate their economies—has become increasingly controversial. In 2000, a congressional commission, headed by Alan Meltzer of Carnegie Mellon University, concluded that the "bailout with conditionality" policy was making things worse rather than better by encouraging lenders and borrowers to believe that an international rescue effort always would be mounted to prevent lenders from suffering any loss. The commission recommended radically scaling back IMF lending and cutting back on the conditions accompanying loans.

Policy has, in fits and starts, moved in this direction—though driven more by the complex realities of the financial markets than by the commission's recommendations. The IMF has adopted policy reforms to reduce the likelihood and severity of crises and their potential worldwide impact. Perhaps most important, countries that have undergone crisis have abandoned fixed exchange rates and now allow the market (more or less) to determine the rate of exchange. Flexible rates require both borrowers and lenders to take account of the risk of future currency movements as well as the risk of nonrepayment.

The financial crises also led to institutional reforms. The IMF is better funded and somewhat more transparent. The governance of the international financial system has been strengthened by the creation of a new steering group that includes important emerging markets and the largest advanced economies. Several key creditor governments are pressing the IMF to narrow its focus to crisis prevention and response and to scale back the medium-term balance-of-payments financing that has made too many countries virtual dependents of the Fund.

Policymakers have continued to debate whether financial crises should be resolved by bailing out borrowing countries or by "bailing in" private investors by suspending debt payments. During the second half of the 1990s, policymakers tried many approaches to private-sector involvement, mostly out of desperation rather than by design and only after substantial sums had been spent. The bail-ins ranged from purely "voluntary" exchanges (which failed) to "concerted" rollovers blessed and orchestrated by the international financial authorities to unilateral exchanges dictated by debtor governments without an international seal of approval. Increasingly, private-sector involvement is being acknowledged as a vital lever in crisis resolution—a recognition that official resources are more and more outgunned by private capital.

Institutionalizing this new presumption is proving thorny. The absence of a world bankruptcy regime makes it difficult to develop rules that would encourage investors to make better risk assessments but not exacerbate creditor panic at moments of financial precariousness. Since 1999, private-sector involvement has been a prominent feature of most sizable stabilization programs, with the particulars being worked out on a case-by-case basis.

Meanwhile, investor expectations have shifted to incorporate a higher probability that their claims will be restructured in the event of losses. Indeed, the dominant concern by 2002 was no longer that too much money is sloshing around the emerging markets but that capital flows have been drastically, perhaps excessively, reduced.

Adjustment among the Advanced Economies

Today risks are also being posed by the industrial countries—a problem that no amount of IMF reform is likely to fix, for the Fund has no leverage over countries that are not borrowers.

The potential for disorderly adjustment in America's growing external imbalance cannot be lightly dismissed. During the late 1990s, the United States was a magnet for foreign capital, attracting much of the world's international capital flows. With strong productivity growth and a booming stock market, America seemed like a great investment. Against a backdrop of stagnation in Japan, slower growth in Europe, and diminishing appetite for exposure to emerging markets, the dollar strengthened by 30 percent against the yen between late 1999 and early 2002 and by 36 percent against the euro between its introduction in early 1999 and early 2002. The flip side of this equation is a growing current account deficit, which has remained at or above 3.9 percent of GDP since 2000, reaching 5 percent in the second quarter of 2002.

When the current account deficit last exceeded 3.4 percent of GDP (in 1987), it precipitated a sharp drop in the dollar and a delayed fall in the current account, which returned below 2 percent in 1989. The current circumstances could likewise presage volatility and a sharp adjustment at a time when weakness in the U.S. stock market threatens recovery and causes foreign investors to flee. At the same time, projected financing needs of the federal government have increased sharply, with a $236 billion surplus turning to a $106 billion deficit in just two years and continued deficits projected through 2004. Meanwhile the dollar tumbled roughly 12 percent against the yen and the euro between February and July of 2002. The share of foreign capital coming into the U.S. market as direct investment or committed capital fell from 39 percent in 1998 to 17 percent in 2001, suggesting that a much larger share of external borrowing is being financed by short-term capital or "hot money" that can reverse direction rapidly.

The World Bank's chief economist estimates that trade protection in the rich nations costs the developing nations more than $100 billion a year—twice the value of the international aid they receive.

In late 2001 and throughout 2002 the United States found itself at the center of one of the worst crises in corporate governance and transparency since the Great Depression. The crisis—reflected most graphically in a steep fall in stock prices during much of 2002—was triggered by the failure of Enron and followed shortly thereafter by disclosures of accounting errors at WorldCom, Xerox, Merck, Bristol-Myers Squibb, and other companies. With each new disclosure, investors, commentators, and the public seemed to lose ever more confidence in the system of corporate disclosure and governance that only a few years back had seemed to be the best in the world. After serving as a safe haven for foreign investors throughout the 1980s and 1990s, U.S. markets suddenly lost their appeal. Portfolio and direct investment from abroad plummeted by nearly half, from annual rates of $686 billion in 2000 to $361 billion in the first quarter of 2002.

By last summer, Congress had enacted and the president had signed sweeping reform legislation that created a new quasi-government agency to oversee the auditing profession; restricted auditors from engaging in nonaudit businesses; toughened criminal and other penalties for corporate fraud and misrepresentations; speeded up disclosure of insider trading of securities; and prohibited corporate loans to executives. Earlier the Securities and Exchange Commission had implemented new disclosure requirements, and the New York Stock Exchange had proposed sweeping corporate governance reforms for companies listed on the exchange that required a majority of board directors to be independent; shareholders to approve executive compensation packages; and audit committees of boards of directors to hire and fire outside auditors.

One key unresolved issue is whether the United States will continue to require all publicly held companies whose shares are traded here to report their financial condition according to Generally Accepted Accounting Principles (GAAP) or permit foreign (and domestic) companies to use the International Accounting Standards (IAS) that are being accepted elsewhere around the world. The Enron affair gave impetus to advocates of IAS, who claimed that Enron would not have been able to expand so rapidly—and take on so much debt—had it been required by IAS to consolidate its many off-balance sheet entities. The growing globalization of capital markets also seems to strengthen the case for a single set of reporting standards worldwide, which is what IAS is well on the way to becoming.

There are two views on what should be done. The dominant one is that the two standards should continue to coexist but more closely approach one another. A minority view (to which one of us subscribes) is that competition between the two is healthy and if allowed to proceed—for example, by governments or exchanges allowing companies to use either standard without restriction—then demand by investors for useful disclosure would keep both standard-setting bodies on their toes. Perhaps most important, competition between the standards could reduce the role of political influence, which has been apparent in the setting of U.S. GAAP for some time.

An Urgent Question

September 11 brought a new urgency and heightened focus to the debate over America's international engagement—its roles in development assistance, world trade, and the international financial system. Today the question is not *whether* the United States should remain engaged, politically and economically, with the rest of the world in all these areas. The question—which urgently needs answering—is *how*.

Lael Brainard is a senior fellow in the Brooking Economic Studies and Foreign Policy Studies programs. Robert E. Litan is vice president and director of the Brooking Economic Studies program.

ASYMMETRIC Globalization

Global Markets Require Good Global Politics

by Nancy Birdsall

The globalization of markets can benefit—and has benefited—rich and poor alike. But the integration of the global economy is outpacing the development of a healthy global polity. To realize the values and rules critical to a secure and just world—and to make the full benefits of a global market available to all—will require a better global politics.

The debate about the implications of market-led globalization for the poor has taken on new urgency in the past several years. On one side are most mainstream economists, international institutions such as the United Nations and the World Bank, most finance ministers and central bank governors in poor and rich nations alike, and most professional students of development. They argue that globalization is not to blame for any increase in world poverty and inequality—and point out that the world's poorest people, those living in rural Africa and South Asia, are those least touched by globalization. On the other side of the debate are most social activists, members of nonprofit civil society groups who work on environmental issues, human rights, and relief programs, most of the popular press, and many sensible, well-educated observers. To them, the issue seems self-evident. Globalization may be good for the rich countries and the rich within countries, but it is bad news for the poorest countries and especially for the poor in those countries.

One central issue is whether the current distribution of economic and political power in the world is just or fair—whether it provides for equal opportunities to those who are poor and, in global affairs, relatively powerless. On this score, I believe it is time for the first group to internalize the arguments of the second and recognize the need for an improved global politics, in which more democratic and legitimate representation of the poor and the disenfranchised in managing the global economy mediates the downside of more integrated and productive global markets.

Globalization, Poverty, Inequality

Most developing countries began to be tied into the world economy only in the 1980s. Before that, although they participated in some multilateral trade agreements, special preferences permitted them to protect their own markets. In the 1980s, however, and increasingly in the 1990s, most developing countries took steps to open and liberalize their markets. In addition to reducing and eliminating tariffs and nontariff barriers, they made fiscal and monetary reforms, privatized and deregulated their economies, eliminated interest rate ceilings, and, in the 1990s, opened capital markets—a package that came to be known as the Washington Consensus. These market reforms and accompanying, often socially painful, structural changes were encouraged and supported by the International Monetary Fund, the World Bank, and the U.S. Treasury with large loans typically conditioned on countries' adopting and implementing agreed policies. The increasing reliance on markets in the developing world and, in the 1990s, in the countries of the former Soviet empire is with good reason seen as part and parcel of globalization. And because of the conditioned loans, many opponents of globalization today see the turn to the market—and thus to global capitalism—as imposed on the developing countries. (Ironically, the loans often were disbursed even when agreed conditions were not implemented.)

With the growing influence of markets in the past two decades have come changes in global inequality and world poverty. Over the past century, global inequality by most measures has been growing. At the end of the 19th century, the ratio of the average income of the richest to the poorest country in the world was 9 to 1. Today the average family in the United States is 60 times richer than the average family in Ethiopia or Bangladesh (in terms of purchasing power). The increase in inequality is the result of a simple reality. Today's rich countries, already richer 100 years ago (thanks to the Industrial Revolution), have been blessed with economic growth and have gotten a whole lot richer. Poorer countries, poor to start with, have grown little if at all.

In the past two decades, the picture has changed a bit. Some developing countries, including China and more recently India, have grown faster than the already rich countries. Incomes in China and India will not soon equal those in rich countries—it would take them almost a century of faster growth even to reach current U.S. levels. Still, some developing countries have done some dramatic catching up.

And the rapid growth in India and China has caused world poverty to decline. Between 1987 and 1998, the share of the world's population that is poor (using World Bank figures and the Bank's poverty line of $1 a day in 1985 dollars) fell from about 25 percent to 21 percent; the absolute number fell from an estimated 1.2 billion to 1.1 billion. The decline was concentrated in India and China; elsewhere in the developing world, numbers rose.

Measured in yet another way—by a "world" distribution of income that ranks all individuals or households around the world according to income, giving each person (or household) the same weight in the distribution—world inequality is extremely high but is leveling off. Although today the richest fifth of world households is about 25 times richer than the poorest fifth, in the past 20 years the rapid growth of India and China has slowed increases in world inequality. (The world distribution of course gives much greater weight to these high-population countries.)

At the world level, then, it is fair to say that poverty is declining and inequality is not increasing. Today's global inequality is mostly a matter of differences between rich and poor countries in past rates of growth. That brings us back to the main argument of globalization's proponents: countries that have successfully entered the global market and participated in globalization have grown most. Historically, that included Japan, beginning in the Meiji era between 1868 and 1912, the poorer countries of Western Europe during the 19th century and then again after World War II, and the so-called miracle economies of East Asia between about 1970 and 1998. More recently, it has included China and India, as well as Bangladesh, Brazil, Malaysia, Mexico, Mozambique, the Philippines, Thailand, Uganda, and Vietnam. Poverty remains highest in the countries, including many in Africa and some in South Asia, and among people, especially in the rural areas of China, India, and Latin America, that are marginal to global markets. To the extent that globalization has "caused" increasing inequality, it is not because some have benefited a lot—a good thing—but because others have been left out altogether.

Globalization Is Not the Solution

But if globalization is not the cause, neither is it the solution to the world's continuing poverty and haunting inequality. Consider the plight of many of the world's poorest countries. Highly dependent on primary commodity and natural resource exports in the early 1980s, they have been "open" for at least two decades, as measured by their ratio of imports and exports to GDP. But unable to diversify into manufacturing (despite reducing their own import tariffs), they have seen the relative world prices of their commodity exports fall—and have been left behind. Despite rising exports, tariff reductions, and market-oriented reforms including greater fiscal and monetary discipline and the divestiture of unproductive state enterprises, they have been unable to increase their export income, failed to attract foreign investment, and grown little if at all.

Many of these countries in sub-Saharan Africa, as well as Haiti, Nepal, and Nicaragua, seem trapped in a vicious circle of low or unstable export revenue, weak and sometimes predatory government, terrible disease burdens (the HIV/AIDS pandemic being only one recent example), and failure to deliver to their children education and the other services that are critical to sustainable growth. For these countries, despite efforts by their governments to enter global markets, globalization has not worked. Success in global markets might come with success in growth and development itself, but it is not likely to come on its own.

For better-off emerging market economies, globalization has failed to work in a second way. For them global trade has been generally a boom, but global financial markets pretty much a bust. In the past decade, Mexico, Korea, Thailand, Indonesia, Russia, Brazil, Ecuador, and Turkey, and this year Argentina, were all hit by financial crises triggered or made worse by their exposure to global financial markets. Weak local financial markets and wary local and foreign creditors made these countries highly vulnerable to the panicked withdrawal of capital typical of bank runs. And the resulting financial instability was especially costly for the working poor and the emerging middle class. In Turkey, Argentina, and Mexico, hit repeatedly by inflation and currency devaluations in the past two decades, wealthy citizens move substantial financial assets abroad, often simultaneously acquiring bank and corporate debt that is then socialized and paid by taxpayers, worsening inequality—and certainly appearing unfair. In parts of Asia and much of Latin America, inequality had already increased during the mid-1990s boom as portfolio inflows and high bank lending fueled demand for assets, such as land and stocks, owned by the rich.

In both regions the poor and working class gained the least during the boom and then lost the most, certainly relative to their most basic needs, in the post-crisis bust. The high interest rates that the affected countries used to stabilize their currencies also hurt most small capital-starved enterprises and their low-wage employees. The bank bailouts that often follow financial crises create public debt that again implies a transfer from taxpayers to rentiers. China and India, whose capital markets remained relatively closed, survived the financial crises of the late 1990s better than did Mexico, Argentina, and Thailand. More open trade is good for growth and benefits the poor, but the effects of the rapid and near-complete opening of capital markets pushed by the IMF and the U.S. Treasury throughout the 1990s were not so benign. No wonder social activists are suspicious of corporate and financial influence in global markets.

A third problem with globalization has been that privatizing and liberalizing financial markets in the absence of adequate regulatory institutions and banking standards and supervision invite corruption. Russia is only the most visible example. Open

> Opportunities in the global economy are not equal.

capital markets make it easier for corrupt leaders to burden their own taxpayers with official and private debt while padding their own foreign bank accounts. Unregulated markets make money laundering and tax evasion easier and raise the costs asymmetrically for poor countries to defend their own tax systems. Global capital markets do not cause all these problems, but like an occasion of sin they increase the likelihood that human failings will corrupt the system, usually at a cost to the poor and powerless.

Unequal Opportunities

Not all the suspicions of the activists are necessarily warranted. But the activists are right in one important respect. The opportunities in the global economy are not equal.

In the global market, those without the right training and equipment can easily lose. That is because markets that are bigger and deeper reward more efficiently those countries and those people who already have productive assets. For people the relevant assets include financial, physical, and, perhaps most crucial today, human capital. For countries what matters are healthy and stable country institutions—established political systems, secure property rights, adequate banking supervision, reasonable public services. It is no accident that 80 percent of all foreign investment occurs among the industrialized countries—and that just 0.1 percent of all U.S. foreign investment went to sub-Saharan Africa last year.

At the individual level, the best example of how healthy markets can generate unequal opportunities is the rising returns to higher education throughout the world. In the high-tech global economy, the supply of university-educated people has not been keeping up with ever-increasing demand, leading to wage gains for college graduates and wage losses for those with high school education or less. Just about everywhere in the world (Cuba, China, Kerala state in India, all socialist entities being exceptions), education reinforces initial advantages instead of compensating for initial handicaps.

The global market for skilled and talented people is another illustration of the asymmetrical effect of markets. The highly skilled are highly mobile. Indian engineers can quadruple their earnings by moving from Kerala to Silicon Valley. For the individuals concerned, this "brain drain" is a good thing, and eventually it can generate offsetting remittances and return investments if the institutional and policy setting in India and other poor countries improves. But in the short run, it makes it harder for the poorer countries to build those institutions and improve those policies. The annual loss to India of its brain drain to the United States is estimated at $2 billion. The farmers and workers whose taxes finance education in poor countries are subsidizing the citizens of the rich countries—whose tax revenues are boosted by the immigrants' contributions.

The efficiency gains and increased potential for growth of a global market economy are not to be disdained. Rising wage gaps in open and competitive markets should not surprise or alarm us: they may be the short-term price worth paying for higher long-run sustainable growth. They create the right incentives for more people to acquire more education, in principle eventually reducing inequality. But in modern market economies, a well-defined social contract tempers the excess inequalities of income and opportunity that efficient markets easily generate. Progressive tax systems provide for some redistribution, with the state financing at least minimal educational opportunities for all and some social and old-age insurance. There is no global analogue.

When the Market Fails

Global market failures also raise new costs for the vulnerable and compound the risks faced by the already weak and disadvantaged. The rich countries that historically have the highest per capita greenhouse gas emissions have not internalized the costs of their pollution but have imposed them on the poor countries, whose citizens have few resources to protect themselves.

Financial contagion across countries, affecting even those emerging market economies with relatively sound domestic policies, can also hit hardest the already vulnerable. Financial contagion has not only brought instability and slower growth to Latin America and East Asia; it has weakened their capacity to develop and sustain institutions and programs to protect their own poor. With global market players doubting the commitment of nonindustrialized countries to fiscal rectitude at the time of any shock, countries are forced to tighten fiscal and monetary policy to reestablish market confidence, rather than stimulate their economies to combat recession. These austerity policies are the opposite of the policies the industrial economies implement—reduced interest rates, unemployment insurance, increased availability of food stamps and public works employment. All these are fundamental ingredients of a modern social contract. And the effects of unemployment and bankruptcy can be permanent for the poor. In Mexico, increases in child labor that cut school enrollment during the 1995 crisis were not reversed: some children did not return to school when growth resumed.

Contagious diseases, transnational crime, and potentially beneficial but risky new technologies such as genetically modified foods also entail asymmetric costs and risks for poor countries and poor people. Similarly, poor countries that protect

> Those concerned with global justice face a daunting problem of global collective action.

global resources such as tropical forests and biological diversity are paying the full costs but are unable to capture the full benefits of these global goods. Within countries, governments temper market failures through regulations, taxes and subsidies, and fines; and they share the benefits of such public goods as security, military defense, management of natural disasters, and public health through their tax and expenditure decisions. Ideally those decisions are made in a democratic system with fair and legitimate representation of all people, independent of their wealth. In nations, such political systems seldom work perfectly. In the global community, a comparable political system just barely exists.

Economic Power and Global Rules

Unequal opportunities for the poor, and the risk they bear when the market fails, are not the whole story. In the global game, economic power matters. The rich and powerful can influence the design and implementation of global rules to their own advantage. Political constraints in rich and powerful countries dominate, for example, the design of global trade rules. The resulting protection in the United States and Europe of agriculture and textiles—both sectors that could generate jobs for the unskilled—locks many of the world's poorest countries out of potential markets. The U.S. African Growth and Opportunity Act and the European Union's recent initiative to eliminate all barriers to imports from the world's 49 poorest countries are steps in the right direction—but very small steps indeed since the countries that can benefit make up only a minuscule proportion of all world production. And even those initiatives were watered down considerably by domestic political pressures and include complicated rules that create uncertainty and limit big increases in poor-country exports.

Political constraints also affect the way trade rules are implemented. Complicated negotiations and dispute resolution put countries with limited resources at a disadvantage. The use of antidumping actions by U.S. producers, even when they are unlikely to win a dispute on its merits, creates onerous legal and other costs to producers in developing countries and chills new job-creating investment in affected sectors. About half of antidumping actions are directed against developing country producers, who account for 8 percent of all exports.

International migration too is governed by rules stacked against the developing countries, especially their poor and unskilled citizens. Permanent migration has slowed because higher-income countries restrict immigration. In the 25 years before World War I, 10 percent of the world's people changed their permanent country residence; in the past 25 years, that figure has fallen to 2 percent. Yet just as the huge influx of Europeans to the Americas in the 19th century reduced inequality, more migration today would do the same. An auto mechanic in Ghana can quintuple his income just by moving to Italy. During the recent information technology boom, the United States allowed highly skilled workers to enter with temporary visas—a boom, no doubt, for the beneficiaries, but also a drain on the working taxpayers in poorer countries who helped educate them and yet another example of the capacity of the already rich to exploit their power.

Economic power also affects the rules and conduct of the international institutions. The International Monetary Fund is meant to help countries manage macroeconomic imbalances and minimize the risks of financial shocks. But in the 1990s the IMF, heavily influenced by its richer members, was too enthusiastic in urging developing countries to open their capital accounts. Even when the policies supported by the IMF and the World Bank have made sense—and I believe for the most part they have—the policymakers have no real accountability to the people in developing countries most affected by them. Developing countries are poorly represented in these institutions' voting and other forms of governance.

A New Agenda of Good Global Politics

That poverty is declining worldwide and inequality is leveling off are not signs that all is well in our new globalized economy. Proponents of market-led globalization must recognize that the global economy is not addressing the problems of poverty and inequality and is ridden with asymmetries that add up to unequal opportunities. Social activists must rethink their demands for dismantling the limited institutions for managing globalization's downside. Both groups must join forces to push a new global agenda, aiming for a new global politics to accompany the global economy.

Statements of social and economic rights in the United Nations and relatively minor transfers of financial and technical resources from rich to poor countries are as close as we have come to anything like a global social contract. Anyone arriving from another planet into our highly unequal global economy would have to conclude that rich countries have no interest in doing anything much to help the poor in poor countries—surprising given what could be their enlightened self-interest in a more secure and prosperous global economy. The logic of a global social contract is clear, but it cannot be constructed out of nothing. As is the case within countries, a social contract involves some transfers—for investments in the human capital and the local institutions that can ensure equal opportunities for the poor.

Past mistakes in foreign aid policy—multiple and onerous standards of different donors, conditionality that doesn't work—should not be an excuse for the rich countries' minimal spending on foreign aid. With many poor countries consolidating reforms, their ability to spend resources productively now far exceeds the amount of aid available. In the industrialized economies, domestic social contracts—public transfers for investing in education, health, and housing and for social-safety-net programs such as unemployment and disability insurance and welfare and pension programs—usually amount to more than 10 percent of GDP. Foreign aid for a global social contract is below 0.5 percent of rich countries' combined GDPs.

Most important, the global and regional institutions that are the world's most obvious mechanisms for managing a global social contract must be reformed, not dismantled. It is ironic that the World Bank and the IMF have been the lightning rods for antiglobalization protests. Accused of being too powerful, they may well be too limited in their resources and insufficiently effective to manage a global contract that would bring equal education, health, and other opportunities to the poor in poor countries. Making these institutions more representative and more accountable to those most affected by their programs, and thus more effective, has to be on the agenda of better global politics.

That agenda must also include opening rich-country markets to developing countries and rethinking the rich world's restrictions on immigration of the unskilled. Developing countries should also be more fully and fairly represented in international institutions, especially the financial institutions, whose policies and programs are so central to their development prospects.

Those concerned with global justice, whether economists and finance ministers or activists, face a daunting problem of global collective action. They need to make a common agenda for a global social contract. In practical terms that means working together in the short run to build a more level playing field in global governance. It means insisting that a new global development architecture be based on good global politics and not just expanded global markets.

Nancy Birdsall is president of the Center for Global Development. This article is drawn from a speech given at the Carter Center in February 2002.

Variety, the Spice of Life, Has Measurable Value. But It's Not Easy to Determine.

By Virginia Postrel

CHAMPAGNE from France. Silk sweaters from China. Winter blueberries from Chile. Video games from Japan. Beer from Ireland. Silver jewelry from India. Cellphones from South Korea. Shoes from Italy.

International trade does not just offer consumers the same goods at lower prices, which is the traditional economic story. It also brings us goods we wouldn't otherwise have access to. Trade increases the number of varieties in the marketplace. It gives consumers more choices.

"The U.S. used to import coffee from around 25 countries," says David E. Weinstein, an economist at Columbia University. "Now we import it from 52 countries. Beer we import from three times more countries than we used to."

Consider Starbucks. Its Web site lists coffee varieties from Brazil, Colombia, Costa Rica, Ethiopia, Guatemala, Indonesia, Mexico, New Guinea, Panama, Yemen and Zimbabwe. Consumers value this variety for its own sake, not just because of lower prices or higher quality.

"When you compare two types of coffee, you may not think one is necessarily better," Professor Weinstein says. "But sometimes you'd like to drink a certain type of coffee, and other times you'd like to drink another type of coffee."

Being able to get exactly the coffee you're in the mood for makes you, in a sense, better off. But this improvement in consumer welfare has tended to go unmeasured. In most economic statistics, coffee is coffee, beer is beer and shoes are shoes.

In a recent working paper for the National Bureau of Economic Research, Professor Weinstein and Christian Broda, an economist with the Federal Reserve Bank of New York, estimate how much international trade has benefited consumers simply by increasing variety. (The paper is available at `www.ny.frb.org/research/staff_reports/sr180.html`.)

The results are striking. Consumers, they estimate, would be willing to pay $280 billion a year, or about 3 percent of gross domestic product, to have access to the variety of goods that were available in 2001, rather than what they could have bought in 1972.

That represents a huge, previously uncounted rise in the standard of living. It also suggests that measurements of real price increases, like the Consumer Price Index, are overstated.

The economists looked at the number of goods, like red wine, and varieties, which they defined as goods from a certain country, like red wine from France. For thousands of goods, they calculated how much an increase in variety mattered to consumers—how "substitutable" the varieties were.

Consumers do not generally care what country a commodity like crude oil comes from, for example. They care much more about varieties of wine, automobiles or cheese, and they value some varieties more than others. Access to French wine is more important to most people than access to Japanese or Australian wine.

"The nasty mathematics," Professor Weinstein says about the paper, "is all about trying to make adjustments for the fact that qualities of varieties may vary across countries."

Economists generally use the term "variety" to mean the least aggregated version of a good in their data, but not necessarily a specific brand, much less an individual item. To a consumer, of course, variety has increased even more than the economists' data indicate—not all red wine from France is the same. As a result, the paper's calculations probably understate the gains from increasing variety.

The calculations took about four days, using four computers. Ten years ago, the economists estimate, the same calculations, also using four computers, would have taken more than four months. Little wonder that nobody has done this calculation before.

Once the economists determined how much variety mattered for each good, they looked at how much variety had increased. From 1972 to 2001, the number of varieties increased from 74,667 (7,731 goods, from an average of 9.7 countries) to 259,215 (16,390 goods, from an average of 15.8 countries).

Using this information, they calculated a price index that measured how much each variety increase was worth to consumers.

The conventional import price index, they estimate, overstates the price of imports by about 1.2 percent a year, because it does not take the higher value of variety into account.

Interestingly, the greatest gains took place not in the 1990's but from 1972 to 1988, a period when conventional measures show a relatively stagnant standard of living. During this period, major exporters, notably South Korea and China, liberalized their economies.

"Those countries flooded the U.S. market with a lot of varieties that we really liked," Professor Weinstein says.

Americans are not the only consumers who are better off. In an article published in The American Economic Review in May, the economists use less detailed data to estimate the worldwide benefits of variety growth.

"Countries like China, Mexico, the former U.S.S.R., and Singapore have welfare gains that are double digits—three to five times larger than those for the U.S.," Dr. Broda says. "This is really a world phenomenon, beyond the U.S."

The benefits of variety also help explain why many people are willing to pay more to live in big cities. Thanks to greater variety, urban dwellers get more for their money.

Professor Weinstein, who used to teach at the University of Michigan, explains it this way: "In Ann Arbor, you have maybe a dozen good restaurants to choose from, and in New York you probably have several thousand good restaurants to choose from. Yet when you compute the price of a meal, you don't take that at all into account."

Virginia Postrel (www.dynamist.com) is author of The Substance of Style: How the Rise of Aesthetic Value Is Remaking Commerce, Culture, and Consciousness *(HarperCollins).*

As Job Exports Rise, Some Economists Rethink the Mathematics of Free Trade.

By Jeff Madrick

FREE trade theory has a growing number of detractors, and one of their traditional concerns has understandably moved to center stage in this presidential election year. How much has the exporting of jobs to foreign nations contributed to the lack of jobs and the absence of wage growth in the current expansion at home?

The standard tenets of free trade theory strongly support the case for outsourcing. Generally, as business finds cheaper ways to make products, it reduces prices to consumers. And some businesses may not survive unless they can reduce labor costs.

In general, most economists believe that the "consumer surplus" that results from lower prices far outweighs the cost of lost jobs or lower wages. In other words, there are many more winners than losers. But recent research suggests that the magnitude of this advantage has been exaggerated. Also, the plight of the losers has clearly been sorely neglected in the economic literature.

And if sending jobs abroad turns from its current relative trickle to a fast-flowing stream, as it well might, the costs of job dislocation will be still higher.

It is more than a little interesting how frequently past research understated the costs of jobs lost to free trade. A literature search published in a 2003 monograph by the economists Michael W. Klein, Scott Schuh and Robert K. Triest, called "Job Creation, Job Destruction and International Competition" (Upjohn Institute), provides a useful summary of this work.

A 1972 study by Stephen P. Magee, for example, toted up the welfare benefits of trade and set them against the costs of unemployment. The study purportedly showed that the benefits of hypothetically eliminating all trade restrictions outweighed the costs of unemployment induced by international competition by a ratio of 100 to 1.

It is hard to argue with such a lopsided benefit. But Mr. Klein, Mr. Schuh and Mr. Triest note that Mr. Magee neglected crucial costs of job dislocation, like the likelihood of displaced workers being paid a lower wage when they got new jobs. A 1980 study took into account more job dislocation costs, but found that benefits from a 50 percent cut in global tariffs still exceeded dislocation costs 20 to 1. Such results understandably led economists to neglect the costs of job dislocation.

The 1980 adjustments were still not nearly enough, however, Mr. Klein, Mr. Schuh and Mr. Triest argue. The main reason is that such early studies assumed that net changes in jobs—the difference between those destroyed and those created—were a good proxy for those who suffered from job dislocations. But in fact, many more jobs are destroyed and created in the United States than is immediately apparent.

For example, the authors find that in a large sample of manufacturers, 1.3 jobs per 100 were lost on balance each year from 1973 to 1993. But 10.2 jobs per 100 were destroyed, while 8.8 were created. (The discrepancy is a result of rounding.)

Such a high rate of job destruction carries serious costs for workers, even when they eventually find new jobs. There are long periods of unemployment, retraining costs and costs of searching for a job. And the new jobs usually pay less than the old ones. In the meantime, skills are lost as well.

The authors estimate that if some of these costs of job dislocation were taken into account, the benefits of trade would outweigh the costs by a far smaller margin. For example, the ratio in the 1980 study would be reduced from 20 to 1 to only 2 to 1.

The authors remain advocates of free trade; a benefit of 2 to 1 is still hefty. But the findings suggest at the very least that a sizable number of workers are inevitably hurt by free trade.

Are protective tariffs an answer? One valuable contribution of Mr. Klein, Mr. Schuh and Mr. Triest is to show that job losses are rarely if ever uniform in an industry. As a consequence, tariffs may often be too broad a policy tool because they will protect companies that would not fire workers anyway.

Moreover, trade and the exporting of jobs are not the only sources of dislocation. Technological changes that may rapidly make existing products obsolete have the same consequences. Mr. Klein, a professor at Tufts University, says a better policy is to make unemployment insurance more generous. He adds that portability of corporate benefits like pensions and health insurance would also more directly address some costs of job dislocation.

Other economists are beginning to think about policies that efficiently compensate those who lose jobs for the costs of dislocation. Carl Davidson and Steven J. Matusz, in a monograph called "International Trade and Labor Markets" (Upjohn Institute), also argue that such policies must not sweep across industries and the labor force. They favor wage and employment subsidies over broader measures.

Such an analysis by no means tells us everything we have to know about free trade and outsourcing. On the one hand, the benefits of free trade are not necessarily limited to the consumer surplus. For example, to the extent that free trade expands markets, as even Adam Smith might have argued, it stimulates productivity growth because it makes possible enormous economies of scale in manufacturing, services and marketing, and enhances competition.

On the other hand, keeping domestic wages high adds to the demand that can generate productivity gains. Moreover, the basic tenets of free trade assume that the economy is operating at full employment—in other words, almost everyone who wants a job can find one. Not enough research has been done on the trade effects in an economy with persistent unemployment, which has characterized most of the last 30 years.

What is entirely clear, however, is that the losers from free trade require more of the nation's attention. And their numbers are growing as trade and job migration expand.

Jeff Madrick is the editor of Challenge Magazine, and he teaches at Cooper Union and New School University. His new book is "Why Economies Grow," from Basic Books and the Century Foundation.
E-mail: challenge@mesharpe.com

BOOKS

MASTER OF DISASTER

A leading economist says the protesters have a point about the I.M.F.

BY JOHN CASSIDY

In 1998, Joseph Stiglitz, a Columbia professor who shared last year's Nobel Prize in Economics, visited a village in rural Morocco where aid workers had been encouraging local women to raise chickens. At the time, Stiglitz was the chief economist of the World Bank, the Washington-based lending agency, which was supporting the project. It had started out well. The Moroccan government supplied the villagers with as many newly hatched chicks as they needed. But at some point, Stiglitz says, the International Monetary Fund, the World Banks' sister organization, told the Moroccan government to leave the task of distributing chicks to private enterprise. A for-profit firm agreed to supply the villagers, but it refused to guarantee the chicks' survival—a policy that had calamitous consequences. The impoverished peasants refused to risk what little money they had on livestock that were likely to die in large numbers in infancy, and the nascent industry withered. When Stiglitz arrived in Morocco, the chicken coops were empty. A promising attempt to alleviate poverty had failed.

It may seem like a long way from Moroccan chickens to the economic crisis in Argentina, the recent financial upheavals in Southeast Asia, the failures of post-Soviet capitalism, and anti-globalization protests on the streets of Seattle and Genoa, but in "Globalization and Its Discontents" (Norton; $24.95) Stiglitz argues that all these matters are related. In promoting private enterprise wherever it can, the I.M.F. was following the so-called Washington Consensus view of economic development, which sees the expansion of free market capitalism as the route to prosperity. With the backing of the United States Department of the Treasury, the I.M.F. urges governments everywhere to privatize, liberalize, and retrench. In the past twenty-five years, many developing countries have followed this advice, dismantling their public-sector enterprises and opening up their economies to international trade and investment. As a result, the world has become more interconnected than ever, with the level of exports, imports, and cross-border investment all increasing sharply.

According to Joseph Stiglitz, globalization has been hijacked by the rich.

According to classic economic theory, this expansion of trade and commerce should have made humanity a lot better off. Ever since Adam Smith, economists have generally agreed that trade is a good thing, because it allows countries to specialize in what they do best. This "division of labor" (Smith's phrase) raises productivity, which results in more income to spend on food, health, education, and consumer goods. Although some people lose their jobs as the pattern of trade changes, the winners gain enough to compensate the losers and still have some left over for themselves.

During the nineteen-seventies and eighties, when countries like South Korea and Singapore were exporting their way out of poverty, the theory seemed to be working as advertised. Globalization, in Stiglitz's words, "helped hundreds of millions of people attain higher standards of living, beyond what they, or most economists, thought imaginable." During the past decade, however, something has gone wrong. Since 1990, the number of people living on less than two dollars a day has risen by more than a hundred million, to three billion. The gap between rich and poor countries has turned into a chasm. Even relatively prosperous parts of the developing world, such as Southeast Asia and Eastern Europe, have fallen into unprecedented slumps. "Globalization today is not working for many of the world's poor," Stiglitz declares. "It is not working for much of the environment. It is not working for the stability of the global economy."

Why not? According to Stiglitz, the rich countries have hijacked globalization, using as weapons the I.M.F., the World Trade Organization, and other international bodies that are supposed to act in the interests of all countries. These institutions are "all too often closely aligned with the commercial and financial interests of those in the advanced industrial countries," Stiglitz writes, and the net effect of the policies they promote is "to benefit the few at the expense of the many, the well-off at the expense of the poor." The governments of the rich countries have pushed developing nations to open their borders to computers and banking services but continued to protect their own farmers and textile workers from the cheap food and clothes that poor countries produce. They have supported the extension of patent agreements that guarantee high profits for Western pharmaceutical companies like Pfizer and Merck while depriving African governments of the drugs they need to fight an AIDS epidemic. "The critics of globalization accuse Western countries of hypocrisy," Stiglitz writes, "and the critics are right."

If this argument brings to mind the young protesters who have made a business of disrupting international summits, Stiglitz is unapologetic. Until the anti-globalization movement came along, "there was little hope for change and no outlets for complaint," he writes. "*Some* of the protestors went to excesses; *some* of the protestors were arguing for higher protectionist barriers against the developing countries, which would have made their plight even worse. But despite these problems, it is the trade unionists, students, environmentalists—ordinary citizens—marching in the streets of Prague, Seattle, Washington, and Genoa who have put the need for reform on the agenda of the developed world."

As this passage suggests, Stiglitz is part of a growing heterodoxy that seeks to define a middle ground between the Washington Consensus and the more radical elements of the anti-globalization movement. The financier and philanthropist George Soros is part of the dissenting movement, too, and he has written a pithy little book, "On Globalization" (Public Affairs; $20), setting out his views and his recommendations for reform. Like Stiglitz, Soros supports globalization in principle but is dismayed at the narrow focus among policymakers on expanding trade and industry. "International trade and global financial markets are very good at generating wealth, but they cannot take care of other social needs, such as the preservation of peace, alleviation of poverty, protection of the environment, labor conditions, or human rights," he maintains.

Soros's book is clearly written, but it doesn't carry as much weight as Stiglitz's. As a leading economic theorist and someone who has served in senior government positions, Stiglitz has a perspective on his subject which can hardly be ignored. Within four years of obtaining his Ph.D., from M.I.T., in 1967, he had published more than fifteen academic papers, several of which are now regarded as seminal. He has since established himself as an expert in many areas of economics, including finance, development, and the public sector.

The common theme running through Stiglitz's academic work is that markets often don't work in the simplistic way that is taught in Econ. 101. Because of complications like asymmetries of information between buyers and sellers, markets sometimes fail to work at all, and the government has to step in. (It was Stiglitz's work on asymmetric information that won him a Nobel Prize.) In 1993, when Stiglitz joined the White House Council of Economic Advisers, at the start of the Clinton Administration, he naïvely thought he saw the chance to "forge an economic policy and philosophy that viewed the relationship between government and markets as complementary." Instead, he found that "decisions were often made because of ideology and politics. As a result many wrong-headed actions were taken."

Stiglitz stayed at the council for four years, eventually becoming its chairman. In 1997, he moved a few hundred yards along Pennsylvania Avenue to the World Bank. The World Bank and the I.M.F. had been founded at the end of the Second World War to promote expansionary Keynesian policies around the globe, with the bank focussing on long-term development and the fund on short-term crisis management, but they long ago converted to the tenets of what Stiglitz calls free-market fundamentalism. The I.M.F., in particular, seems to revel in its role as enforcer of the Washington Consensus. Since countries approach the I.M.F. only when they are desperate for money, the fund has a good deal of leverage, which it uses to force governments to cut budget deficits, raise taxes, and close down or sell off state enterprises. Though these reforms are sometimes necessary, Stiglitz maintains that the I.M.F.'s representatives are often oblivious of the human suffering they cause. "Modern high-tech warfare is designed to remove physical contact: dropping bombs from 50,000 feet ensures that one does not 'feel' what one does," he writes. "Modern economic management is similar: from one's luxury hotel, one can callously impose policies about which one would think twice if one knew the people whose lives one was destroying."

The centerpiece of "Globalization and Its Discontents" is a critical account of the I.M.F.'s role in the Asian financial crisis and the Russian transition. The Asian crisis began in July, 1997, when Thailand devalued its currency, and it quickly spread throughout Southeast Asia, plunging the region into the deepest recession it had seen for decades. Stiglitz argues that the underlying cause of the collapse was the misguided financial liberalization that Washington had urged upon the Asian countries during the previous few years.

Countries like Singapore and South Korea hardly needed economic advice from anybody. Through a combination of hard work, high savings rates, and extensive government intervention, they had turned themselves into universally admired models for development. Between 1950 and 1990, South Korea raised its gross domestic product per capita from ninety dollars to forty-four hundred dollars. As part of the "Asian model" of development, governments prevented foreign investors (and domestic residents) from moving money in and out of their countries freely. These restrictions helped prevent damaging swings in exchange rates; they also kept out American financial firms, which were eager to expand in Asia. Beginning in the early nineteen-nineties, the I.M.F. and the Treasury Department encouraged the Asians to remove the restriction on capital movements. Stiglitz viewed this policy as an unnecessary sop to Wall Street, but the Treasury Department overruled his objections. By the middle of the nineteen-nineties, South Korea, Thailand, and most other Asian countries had heeded Washington's advice and abolished controls on money flows. The result was a speculative boom, with foreign capital pouring into risky investments. For a while, the region seemed to be growing even faster than usual. But, once the Thai crisis erupted, overseas investors pulled out their money en masse, causing financial markets to collapse.

The I.M.F. made the downturn worse by ordering the stricken countries to raise interest rates and balance their budgets in order to restore the confidence of investors. These austerity policies had been designed for profligate countries in Latin America, which ran big budget deficits and printed too much money. Most of the Asian countries, by contrast, had balanced budgets, or even surpluses, when the crisis struck. The fact that monetary policy was being tightened during a recession only spooked investors more, and the conflagration spread to other countries, including Malaysia and Indonesia. Suharto's government was forced to cut food and fuel subsidies in order to meet the I.M.F.'s fiscal targets, and the subsequent riots ended up bringing down the dictator. Mahathir bin Mohamad, the Malaysian Prime Minister, managed to escape Suharto's fate only by ignoring the I.M.F.'s advice. In the face of bitter opposition from Washington, he introduced laws that made it difficult for Malaysians and foreign investors to send their money abroad. Far from destroying the Malaysian economy, as some free-market economists had predicted, these "capital controls" allowed the country to recover more quickly than most of its neighbors.

The Asian financial crisis never came any closer to most Americans than the business pages. Yet it was so severe that some people in the region concluded that the I.M.F. and the American government had set out deliberately to weaken a potential economic rival. Stiglitz doesn't go that far, but his judgment is almost as damning: "The I.M.F. was not participating in a conspiracy, but it was reflecting the interests and ideology of the Western financial community."

Stiglitz's analysis of what happened in Russia will be more controversial. As he details, the I.M.F. advanced the country billions of dollars in loans to support the "shock therapy" that Boris Yeltsin's government administered after the collapse of the Soviet Union. The therapy involved freeing prices, hawking state-owned enterprises to private investors at a discount, and trying to maintain a strong currency. Stiglitz argues that these policies were misguided, and he marshals some depressing statistics to support his case. Between 1940 and 1946, a period when Hitler's Army laid waste to Russia, total industrial production in the Soviet Union fell by about a quarter. Between 1990 and 1999, Russian industrial production fell by more than half. Though the economy has recovered somewhat in the past couple of years, the Russian gross domestic product is still well below where it was when the Berlin Wall came down. Poverty rates are much higher, life expectancy has fallen (almost unprecedented in a developed country), and much of Russia's industry is in the hands of former Communists and gangsters. For Stiglitz, the Russians' attempt to build capitalism virtually overnight was reminiscent of the Bolsheviks' failed attempt to impose Socialism after November, 1917. Just as chaos forced Lenin to retreat to the halfway station of the "New Economic Policy," the dramatic collapse of the post-Soviet economy forced the modern-day reformers to back off. In 1998, the ruble collapsed (despite another I.M.F. loan) and the Yeltsinites were eventually replaced by a former K.G.B. agent, Vladimir Putin.

Is Stiglitz overstating the case against the I.M.F. here? The proponents of shock therapy, such as the Harvard economist Andrei Shleifer, who advised the Russian government during the mid-nineteen-nineties, argued that moving rapidly was the only way to prevent a Communist resurgence, and that the policy wasn't enforced vigorously enough. Instead of consistently promoting radical change, Yeltsin vacillated, one moment supporting reformers like Anatoly Chubais, the next moment backing conservatives like Viktor Chernomyrdin. Whatever the merits of such political considerations, though, the strictly economic case for the shock therapy is underwhelming. Indeed, there is now a consensus among economists that it is a mistake to try to create a market economy without first developing the institutions necessary for capitalism to function properly, such as enforceable laws and a working tax system. Under Putin, the Russian government is now concentrating on building just that sort of infrastructure, and the results are encouraging. Even the I.M.F. has come to acknowledge the wisdom of this strategy; almost everyone agrees that there is no shortcut to building a modern economy.

Stiglitz commends the gradual approach that China and Poland have taken toward liberalizing their economies. In Poland, one of the best-performing economies in Eastern Europe in recent years, the government rejected a key element of the Washington Consensus: rapid privatization. Instead of rushing to sell off state enterprises, the Poles concentrated on creating a modern legal system and a social safety net. Only then did they allow private investors to take over banks and the like. In China, too, the government left most of the big state-owned firms in place, but it created new firms alongside them by allowing villages and towns to set up their own enterprises, often in partnership with foreign companies. During the nineteen-nineties, China's G.D.P. grew at an average annual rate of about ten per cent, and its poverty rate dropped dramatically. "The contrast between what happened in China and what has happened in countries like Russia, which bowed to I.M.F. ideology, could not be starker," Stiglitz writes. "In case after case, it seemed that China, a newcomer to market economies, was more sensitive to the incentive effects of its policy decisions than the I.M.F. was to its."

"Globalization and Its Discontents" does have some disappointing omissions, especially concerning the author's own experiences. In the Clinton Administration, Stiglitz clashed frequently with Lawrence Summers, the Harvard economist who served in the Treasury Department and eventually became the Secretary of the Treasury. Summers was far more sympathetic to the Washington Consensus than Stiglitz was, and he worked closely with the I.M.F. According to some people in

Washington, Summers forced Stiglitz out of the World Bank by demanding his departure as the price of supporting the reappointment of James Wolfensohn as the institution's president. Yet, apart from a few derogatory references to Summers's role in specific policy debates, Stiglitz makes no mention of their rivalry, or of the circumstances surrounding his resignation from the World Bank.

All of this raises the inevitable question of how much of the book is score-settling. It will not escape I.M.F. officials that Stiglitz is overly reluctant to criticize the governments of developing countries for making bad policies, which have done at least as much as the I.M.F. to keep poor people poor. And he surely understates the difficulties facing the I.M.F. when it goes into a country where the stock market and the currency are both plummeting. What's more, I.M.F.-led bailouts can sometimes work, as they did in Mexico.

Still, there is no disputing Stiglitz and Soros's central point that global capitalism has outgrown its institutional framework. Both authors suggest reforms that might go some way toward remedying this situation. First and foremost, they advocate restructuring the international institutions, so that they are more democratic and effective. The I.M.F.'s voting structure dates back decades and makes no sense—the Netherlands has about as many votes as China has. Stiglitz also recommends improving banking supervision, changing the international bankruptcy laws, reducing the number of I.M.F. bailouts, and increasing the amount of aid and debt relief that developing countries receive, especially those in Africa. Soros, for his part, thinks international aid should be increased and that the World Trade Organization ought to take more account of issues like workers' rights, health and safety, and the environment.

One can debate the particulars of reform but not the need for it. "Without reform, the backlash that has already started will mount and discontent with globalization will grow," Stiglitz writes. "This will be a tragedy for all of us, and especially for the billions who might otherwise have benefited."

Workers' Rights
LABOR STANDARDS AND GLOBAL TRADE

by Gary Burtless

Of all the debates surrounding globalization, one of the most contentious involves trade and workers' rights.

Proponents of workers' rights argue that trading nations should be held to strict labor standards—and they offer two quite different justifications for their view. The first is a moral argument whose premise is that many labor standards, such as freedom of association and the prohibition of forced labor, protect basic human rights. Foreign nations that wish to be granted free access to the world's biggest and richest markets should be required to observe fundamental human values, including labor rights. In short, the lure of market access to the United States and the European Union should be used to expand the domain of human rights.

The key consideration here is the efficacy of labor standards policies. Will they improve human rights among would-be trading partners? Or will they slow progress toward human rights by keeping politically powerless workers mired in poverty? Some countries, including China, might reject otherwise appealing trade deals that contain enforceable labor standards. By insisting on tough labor standards, the wealthy democracies could lay claim to the moral high ground. But they might have to forgo a trade pact that could help their own producers and consumers while boosting the incomes and political power of impoverished Chinese workers.

The second argument for strict labor standards stresses not the welfare of poor workers, but simple economic self-interest. A trading partner that fails to enforce basic protections for its workers can gain an unfair trade advantage, boosting its market competitiveness against countries with stronger labor safeguards. Including labor standards in trade deals can encourage countries in a free trade zone to maintain worker protections rather than abandoning them in a race to the bottom. If each country must observe a common set of minimum standards, member countries can offer and enforce worker protections at a more nearly optimal level. This second argument, unlike the first, can be assessed with economic theory and evidence.

Evaluating these arguments requires answering three questions. First, what labor standards are important to U.S. trade and foreign policy? Second, how can labor standards, once negotiated, be enforced? Finally, does it make sense to insist that our trade partners adhere to a common set of core labor standards—and if so, which standards?

Which Labor Standards Matter Most?

Although the international community agrees broadly on the need to respect labor standards, agreement does not extend to what those standards should be. Forced labor and slavery are almost universally regarded as repugnant, but other labor safeguards thought vital in the world's richest countries are not widely observed elsewhere.

The International Labor Organization, created by the Treaty of Versailles after World War I, has published labor standards in dozens of areas, but it has identified eight essential core standards (see box), most of which refer to basic human rights. Of the 175 ILO member countries, overwhelming majorities have ratified most of the eight standards. More than 150 have ratified the four treating forced labor and discrimination in employment and wages. Washington has ratified just two standards, one abolishing forced labor and the other eliminating the worst forms of child labor, placing the United States in the company of only eight other ILO member countries, including China, Myanmar, and Oman.

Many proponents of labor standards would expand the core list of ILO protections to cover workplace safety, working conditions, and wages. The U.S. Trade Act of 1974 defines "internationally recognized worker rights" to include "acceptable conditions of work with respect to minimum wages, hours of work, and occupational safety and health." The University of Michigan, for example,

Core ILO Labor Standards

Freedom of association. Workers and employers shall have the right to form and join organizations of their own choosing without interference from public authorities. Where multiple organizations are established, workers and employers shall be free to join any of them. (Convention #97, adopted 1948)

Right to organize and bargain collectively. Workers shall enjoy protection against antiunion discrimination, both when hired and throughout their term of employment. Member states shall promote voluntary negotiations between unions and employers on the terms and conditions of employment. (Convention #98, 1949)

Prohibition on forced labor. Member states shall prohibit compulsory labor in all forms. Forced labor is that "exacted from any person under the menace of any penalty and for which the said person has not offered himself voluntarily." (Convention #29, 1930)

Abolition of forced labor. Member states shall not use compulsory labor as political coercion, punishment for political views, retaliation for union activity, workforce mobilization, labor discipline, or racial or other forms of discrimination. (Convention #105, 1957)

Prohibition of employment discrimination. Member states shall eliminate discrimination in access to employment and training on the basis of race, gender, national origin, and religious or political belief. (Convention #111, 1951)

Equal pay for men and women. Member states shall promote equal pay for men and women who perform work of equal value. (Convention #100, 1958)

Minimum age of work. Ordinary work should not be performed by children younger than the last age of compulsory schooling, and in no event by children under 15. (A temporary exception allowing light work as early as age 12 is permitted for very poor countries with underdeveloped educational systems.) (Convention #138, 1973)

Prompt elimination of the worst forms of child labor. The worst forms of child exploitation, including slavery, debt bondage, all forced or compulsory labor, and the sale or trafficking of children, particularly for illegal activities, is prohibited. (Convention #182, 1999)

obliges producers of goods bearing its insignia to respect the core ILO standards and also requires them to pay minimum wages and to offer a "safe and healthy working environment."

The labor standards that might be covered by a trade agreement fall along a continuum from those that focus on basic human rights to those that stress working conditions and pay. On the whole, the case for the former is more persuasive. Insisting that other nations respect workers' right of free association reflects our moral view that this right is fundamental to human dignity. Workers may also have a "right" to a safe and healthy workplace, but that right comes at some cost to productive efficiency. Insisting that other nations adopt American standards for a safe and healthy workplace means that they must also adopt our view of the appropriate trade-off between health and safety, on the one hand, and productive efficiency, on the other.

Enforcing Labor Standards: The Status Quo

The principal global institution enforcing labor standards today is the ILO, which reports regularly and periodically on the steps each nation takes to implement the standards it has ratified. If complaints are lodged, the ILO investigates the alleged violation and publicizes its findings. Even if a member nation has not ratified the freedom-of-association conventions, the ILO may investigate alleged violations of those conventions. The ILO cannot, however, authorize retaliatory trade measures or sanctions. Instead it provides technical assistance to member countries to bring their labor laws and enforcement procedures into compliance.

Although the work of the ILO has been recognized with a Nobel Peace Prize, many labor sympathizers are skeptical that it can protect workers using its existing enforcement tools since they impose little penalty besides bad publicity.

Putting Teeth into Standards Enforcement

Labor advocates favor strengthening enforcement by expanding the role of the World Trade Organization or using bilateral trade agreements.

WTO rules do not apply to labor standards; they govern members' treatment of the goods, services, and intellectual property of other member countries. In those areas the WTO has developed elaborate dispute settlement procedures to investigate complaints. If a WTO panel finds that a member country has violated WTO rules, it may allow the complaining country to retaliate.

At the 1996 WTO ministerial meeting, developing countries strongly resisted efforts to allow the WTO to enforce labor standards, and the meeting concluded by affirming the ILO's role in determining and dealing with labor standards. Similarly, when President Clinton and some EU leaders tried to bring workers' rights into the next round of multilateral trade negotiations at the 1999 WTO ministerial meeting in Seattle, developing countries rejected the initiative.

In a recent free trade pact, Jordan and the United States agreed to protect core ILO workers' rights. They also spelled out how to resolve disputes over labor standards: if one country weakens its labor laws or fails to bring its laws or enforcement into compliance with the ILO core standards, the other may take appropriate measures, including withdrawal of trade benefits.

The AFL-CIO has endorsed the labor provisions of the Jordan trade pact, while the U.S. Chamber of Commerce has denounced them. The Chamber favors free trade agreements, and it fears that most countries will resist including enforceable labor standards in any new agreement. This view is almost certainly correct, at least in the developing world.

Practical Difficulties

Some Americans may fear that including enforceable labor standards in trade agreements will open the United States to charges that it fails to enforce ILO core standards, exposing it to possible trade penalties. But U.S. civil rights and labor laws already contain the fundamental protections demanded by the ILO conventions.

Citizens in developing countries might be less confident that their laws and enforcement procedures will meet the tests implied by the ILO conventions, especially as construed by observers from affluent countries. Interpretations devised in the drawing rooms of Paris or the recreation rooms of suburban Washington might seem out of touch with conditions in countries where half or more of the population lives on less than $2 a day.

Two of the most troublesome ILO standards involve child labor. Rich countries—very sensibly—restrict children's participation in the job market so that youngsters can attend school and prepare to become workers. But in poor countries, where children's earnings are a crucial family resource and schooling may be unavailable, the restrictions may not be appropriate. Of course, children in poor countries deserve protection and education too, but the standard of protection and the resources available for schooling will be far below those in a wealthy country.

A standard of protection that is appropriate in rich countries can impose excessive burdens on poor ones. Third-world leaders fear, understandably, that including enforceable labor standards in trade treaties will expose their countries to constant challenge in the WTO—and that the standards will be used mainly to protect workers and businesses in developed countries from competition from third-world workers.

AFL-CIO President John Sweeney denies that enforcing labor standards can have a protectionist impact. The ILO standards, he notes, are designed to protect the interests of workers in low-income as well as high-income countries. The WTO and United States strongly defend intellectual property (IP) rights and enforce trade penalties when developing countries violate those rights. Extending the same protections to workers' rights, he reasons, cannot be protectionist.

While it is easy to sympathize with Sweeney's view, there is a big difference between worker rights in another country and the IP rights of a country's own citizens. If Burma denies its workers the right to organize independent unions, its actions are deplorable but do not directly injure me. If Burma allows publishers and recording companies to reproduce my copyrighted books and songs without compensating me, the theft of my creative efforts injures me directly. It is hardly surprising that U.S. voters would insist on remedies for injuries to themselves before fixing the problems of workers overseas. Sweeney may object that the injury to Burmese workers from human rights abuses is much more serious than the monetary losses from copyright infringement suffered by a handful of artists, inventors, and U.S. corporations. And he may well be right. But American artists, inventors, and corporate shareholders can vote in U.S. elections; Burmese workers cannot.

How to Assess WTO Penalties?

If the WTO is to be used to assess penalties against countries violating international labor norms, its member countries must devise a new way to assign penalties for violations. Under current procedures, a country found to have a valid trade complaint may retaliate against the offending country by withholding a trade benefit roughly equivalent to the benefit denied it by the offender as a result of the violation of WTO rules. It is not obvious how to calculate the penalty when the violation involves a labor standard. There the injury has been suffered by workers in the offending country, and residents of the complaining country may have enjoyed a net benefit.

Suppose, for example, the United States accuses another country of employing underage children in its apparel industry. The violation increases the offending country's supply of low-wage workers, thus reducing producers' wage costs and the prices charged to domestic and overseas consumers. The adult workers in the offending country have clearly suffered injury, as have the children if their work has deprived them of schooling that was otherwise available.

How did the violation affect Americans? U.S. apparel workers probably lost wages and jobs. But their losses are counterbalanced by gains to U.S. consumers, who bought clothing more cheaply because of child labor in the offending country. Since all American workers, including those in the apparel industry, are themselves consumers, it is not clear whether the violation injured U.S. workers as a class. Last year apparel imports into the United States exceeded exports by about $55 billion. If the use of child labor overseas cut the cost of imports, Americans spent less for clothing than they otherwise would have. While most Americans deplore child labor, at home or abroad, it is hard to see how an overseas violation of the child labor standard has injured them. Nor is the United States likely to weaken its own child labor laws because it has benefited from the availability of cheaper imported clothes.

Private Sanctions

As a final option for enforcing labor standards, American consumers can apply their own private sanctions. Anyone who finds child labor or forced labor reprehensible can refuse to buy products made in countries that tolerate those practices. The ILO could push consumers into action by publishing information about offending countries and their violations. It could also publicize any country's refusal to cooperate with ILO investigations. If voters want more information about imported goods and services from countries that comply with ILO standards, their own national governments can provide it. Washington can help American consumers increase pressure on offending countries by requiring sellers to label products with the country of origin. It could also encourage or require sellers to identify goods and services produced in countries that fully comply with ILO's core labor standards.

Should Uncle Sam Enforce Labor Standards?

The case for enforcing labor standards is strongest when it involves basic human rights, such as freedom of association or freedom from slavery, and when it rests on moral grounds rather than economic calculation. If Washington wants to require its trading partners to respect basic human rights, it must be prepared to accept the real costs it will thereby impose on its own producers and consumers—and occasionally on the victims overseas whom it is trying to help. Economic theory and evidence may be useful in calculating the potential cost of trade sanctions to the United States and its trading partners. It is not helpful in determining whether the potential gains to human rights are worth the income sacrifice. Nor is social science very informative about whether a policy of trade sanctions is likely to improve victims' rights.

The case for requiring U.S. trade partners to respect international labor standards is least compelling when it involves the terms and conditions of employment. If a country respects ILO core standards, then workers will be able to negotiate for the best combination of pay, fringe benefits, work hours, and workplace amenities that their level of productivity allows. If we insist that the resulting compensation package meet minimum international standards, we are substituting our own judgment for that of the affected workers and their employers.

Readers may object, rightly, that the weak bargaining position of workers in poor countries makes it unlikely that their negotiations with employers will secure decent compensation and safe working conditions. But their weak bargaining position is linked to their low productivity and skills. Today U.S. and European labor standards are much higher, and labor regulation enforced more rigorously, than was the case 50 years ago. The improvement is closely associated with workers' increased skill and productivity. Even in the developing world, the better-off countries are more likely than the poorest to conform to ILO labor standards. In countries with per capita income of $500 a year or less, 30–60 percent of children between the ages of 10 and 14 work. In countries with per capita income of $500–1,000, just 10–30 percent of youngsters work. As productivity improves, so too will the bargaining position and wages of industrial workers. If history is any guide, national labor standards will improve as well.

The most reliable way to improve the condition of third-world workers is to boost their average productivity. Concerned voters in rich countries can help make this happen by pressing to open up their own markets to third-world products. Many low-income countries have a comparative advantage in manufacturing apparel, textiles, and footwear and in producing staple foods, fruits, and vegetables. Rich countries often impose high tariffs or quotas on these products, and nearly all provide generous subsidies to their farmers—thus denying third-world producers and farmers access to a huge potential market. The World Bank estimates that tariff and nontariff barriers, together with subsidies lavished on U.S. and European farmers, cost third-world countries more in lost trade than they get in foreign aid.

If we insist that developing countries meet immediately the labor standards that the richest countries achieved only gradually, we will keep some of them out of the world's best markets. The poor countries that agree to abide by ILO standards will occasionally be challenged—sometimes by representatives of rich countries more intent on protecting their own workers from "unfair" overseas competition than on improving the lot of third-world workers. While the moral case for requiring our trading partners to respect labor rights is compelling, the case for removing trade barriers that limit the product markets and incomes of the world's poorest workers is just as powerful.

Gary Burtless is a senior fellow in the Brookings Economic Studies program and co-author, with Robert Litan, of Globaphobia Revisited: Open Trade and Its Critics (*Brookings*, forthcoming).

The fall and rise of the global economy

Anyone who follows the news, even casually, or reads product labels, is aware that the world economy has become more interdependent in recent decades. Indeed, the worldwide integration of national economies—through goods and services trade, capital flows, and operational linkages among firms—has never before been as broad or as deep.[1]

Nevertheless, the course of globalization has not always been smooth. At the start of the 20th century, the global economy was highly integrated. In some regards, it was nearly as integrated as it is today. Yet two decades later, a noteworthy commentator lamented the apparent end of this economic integration. John Maynard Keynes wrote an eloquent and oft-cited description of the pre–World War I economy.[2]

> What an extraordinary episode in the economic progress of man that age was which came to an end in August, 1914!... life offered, at a low cost and with the least trouble, conveniences, comforts, and amenities beyond the compass of the richest and most powerful monarchs of other ages. The inhabitant of London could order by telephone, sipping his morning tea in bed, the various products of the whole earth... he could at the same moment and by the same means adventure his wealth in the natural resources and new enterprises of any quarter of the world.... But, most important of all, he regarded this state of affairs as normal, certain, and permanent, except in the direction of further improvement, and any deviation from it as aberrant, scandalous, and avoidable.

In the decades that followed, two world wars, the Great Depression, and protectionist policies seemed to bring economic integration to an end. Since then, however, advances in technology and changes in policy have worked to reopen borders. Despite Keynes' characterization of the pre–World War I period as an "extraordinary episode," the economic globalization and buoyancy of that period was not an aberration. Rather, it was the 1913–50 period that stands out for its uncharacteristically weak growth in both output and trade. After 1950, the world economy resumed its trend toward globalization. But it took time to make up the ground lost: In the U.S. and elsewhere, the level of trade relative to output has consistently exceeded early 20th century levels only in the past few decades. Indeed, just a few years ago, academic papers debated whether the world economy in the 1980s and early 1990s was more, or less, integrated than it was in 1900.[3]

1. U.S. trade relative to GNP since 1900

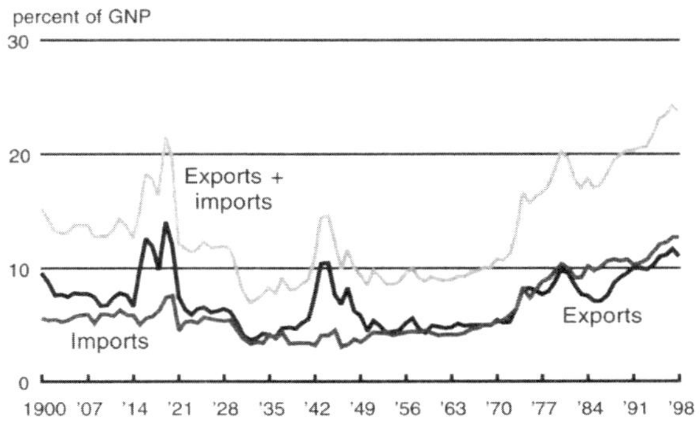

Sources: U.S. Department of Commerce, Bureau of the Census, 1975, *Historical Statistics of the United States*, Washington; and U.S. Department of Commerce, Bureau of Economic Analysis, various years.

This *Chicago Fed Letter* reviews the ebbs and flows of globalization during the past century, and argues that a continuing commitment to open markets is worth pursuing as a way to raise living standards both at home and abroad.

Growing importance of trade and capital flows in the U.S.

Trade and, to a much lesser extent, investment links were well established a century or more ago, but both deteriorated during the interwar period. Today, global economic ties have rebounded and are generally more extensive and intensive than ever before.

Figure 1 illustrates the historical ebb and flow of U.S. trade. Except briefly around the time of each world war, the ratio of trade (exports plus imports) to gross national product (GNP) did not return to turn-of-the-century levels until the 1970s. Recently, however, this ratio has approached 25%, its highest point in at least a century.

During much of the 19th and early 20th centuries, the U.S. participated actively in a generally vibrant world trade.[4] Internationally, there were few nontariff trade barriers. The interwar period that followed, however, was largely one of rising tariff and nontariff barriers—in the U.S. and elsewhere—and global disintegration rather than integration. Since World War II, technological developments and the gradual liberalization of international trade and capital flows have put integration on the upswing.

Some of this rising trade can be attributed to "two-way" intra-industry trade. Anecdotal evidence and recent studies document how production processes have been increasingly divided up and reallocated, either domestically or globally.[5] Tasks, such as research and development, design, assembly, and packaging, are performed by firms in the U.S. and elsewhere, based on countries' relative strengths in completing them. Consider the computer industry. According to a recent report, in 1998 an estimated 43% of domestic producers' total shipments was exported, and an estimated 58% of final and intermediate domestic consumption was imported; some 60%, by value, of the hardware in a typical U.S. personal computer system comes from Asia.[6]

Cross-border capital flows have likewise grown to unprecedented levels, reflecting reduced barriers to capital, an increased desire of investors to diversify their portfolios internationally, and a plethora of new financial instruments and technologies.[7] One survey reports that average daily turnover on world foreign exchange markets rose from $0.6 trillion in April 1989 to about $1.5 trillion in April 1998.[8]

Official balance of payments data provide a measure of capital flows that, roughly speaking, measure the change in cross-border ownership claims. Figure 2 shows data on inflows of capital to the U.S. by foreigners and outflows of capital sent abroad by U.S. residents. Although U.S. outflows abroad have been rising, foreign inflows have been rising even faster. These cross-border flows typically were no more than 1% of GNP through the 1960s. By contrast, from 1995 through 1998, inflows averaged 7% of GNP.

2. U.S. capital inflows and outflows

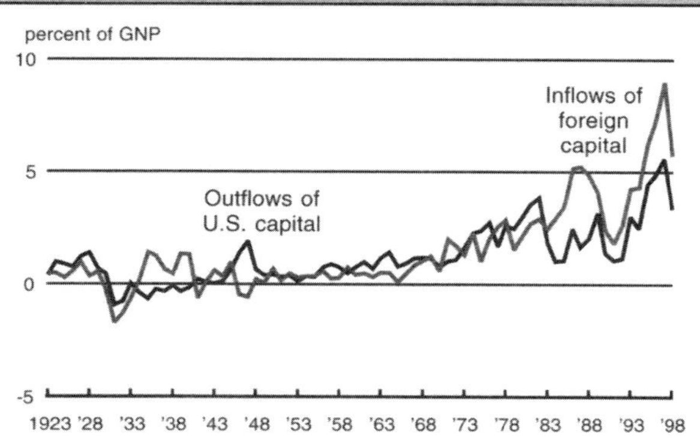

Note: Outflows of U.S. capital are the net increase in U.S.-owned assets abroad. Inflows of foreign capital are the net increase in foreign-owned assets in the United States.

Sources: Data from 1923 to 1959 are from U.S. Department of Commerce, Bureau of the Census, 1975, *Historical Statistics of the United States*, Washington. Data from 1960 to 1999 are from U.S. Department of Commerce, Bureau of Economic Analysis, various years.

Role of technology and policy

The forces driving globalization include technology and policy. Technological improvements have reduced the costs of doing business internationally; they have also created opportunities for new kinds of commercial transactions, particularly in financial markets and online. At the same time, policy has worked actively to open markets around the world. Together, technology and policy have helped to lower barriers to trade and investment.

Improved transportation technologies have reduced the cost of moving products. For example, the advent of *containerization* in land- and sea-based shipping has reduced both handling requirements and transit time for deliveries.[9] In addition, air transport has become more economical. Worldwide, the cost of air freight, measured as average revenue per ton-kilometer, dropped by 78% between 1955 and 1996.[10] At the same time, the share of world trade in high-value-to-weight products such as pharmaceuticals has risen. Reflecting the falling cost of air freight as well as the shifting composition of trade, air shipments in 1998 accounted for 28% of the value of U.S. international trade—up from 7% in 1965 and a negligible share in 1950.[11]

Improved communications and information technologies have also facilitated international commerce, particularly trade in services. In 1930, a three-minute phone call from New York to London cost $293, measured in 1998 dollars.[12] By 1998, one widely subscribed discount plan charged only 36 cents for a clearer, more reliable three minute call.[13] Firms' ability to provide customer support by telephone or e-mail at relatively low cost, or to transmit digital products electronically via the Internet, has reduced the importance of market proximity in some industries.

Improved communications and information technologies have also underpinned rapid financial market developments. The range of financial instruments has exploded in recent years, contributing to the massive gross flows of financial capital discussed earlier. For example, advances in computing technology enable traders to implement complex analytical models. This in turn allows financial firms to meet demand for new financial instruments, such as swaps, options, and futures, which allow market participants to better manage their risk.

Given the economic and technological forces behind globalization, its rise may seem inevitable. Yet governments have taken on a critically important role in opening markets and removing distortions, thereby allowing market forces to play themselves out. In contrast, policy during the interwar period actively promoted protectionism through high tariff and nontariff barriers.[14] Indeed, rising protectionism in a number of countries—including the U.S. through the Tariff Act of 1930 (Smoot-Hawley)—made the Great Depression more severe. Despite U.S. efforts to begin reducing tariffs at home and abroad in 1934, through the Reciprocal Trade Agreements Act, world tariffs remained high on average.

For the past half century, in contrast, policy has worked actively to remove barriers and distortions to the market forces underpinning trade and investment. For example, the General Agreement on Tariffs and Trade and, more recently, the World Trade Organization have championed trade liberalization. Since the 1970s, most industrial countries have removed most controls on international capital movements, and many developing countries have greatly relaxed theirs.

Globalization and living standards

Economists generally argue that openness to the world makes us more prosperous. The freedom of firms to choose from a wider range of inputs, and of consumers to choose from a wider range of products, improves efficiency, promotes innovation, encourages the transfer of technology, and otherwise enhances productivity growth. Through trade, countries can shift resources into those sectors best able to compete internationally, so reaping the benefits of specialization and scale economies. Countries on both sides of a transaction stand to gain.

Some, but not all, of the benefits of market opening are quantifiable. For example, recent studies that evaluate trade liberalizing measures under the Uruguay Round of multilateral negotiations, completed in 1994, tend to focus on the effects of reducing tariffs and export subsidies and eliminating quotas. These studies, which capture only a narrow range of the possible gains, find that annual global income could rise on the order of $200 billion, measured in 1992 dollars.[15]

Opening domestic markets to global capital can also improve living standards. Global capital markets allow investors to allocate their resources where the returns are highest and to diversify their portfolios, thereby reducing their risk. At the same time, countries receiving capital inflows can develop more quickly, since the inflows allow them to increase their productive capital stock without foregoing current consumption. When the capital inflow takes the form of foreign direct investment, the inflow often improves access to international best practices in production, including managerial, technical, and marketing know-how. Therefore, global investment, like trade, benefits both sides of the transaction. These benefits, in turn, can lead to higher real incomes and wages.

Of course, economic globalization is not an end in itself, but rather a means to raise living standards. Like other sources of economic growth, including technological progress, economic integration involves natural tradeoffs. The same processes that bring about economic growth can force costly adjustments for some firms and their workers. Increased trade re-sorts each country's resources, directing them toward their most productive uses, but some industries and their workers may face sharp competition from other countries. Overall, however, economists generally attribute only a small share of worker dislocation in the U.S. to trade, roughly 10% or less.[16] (Such challenges may, of course, be greater in some other countries, particularly those where entrenched cultural and institutional barriers restrict the mobility of workers.) Nevertheless, crafting sound domestic policy to help ease the transition for those affected poses a significant challenge.

The emphasis here on domestic policy is intentional. Even in an increasingly global economy each nation largely controls its own destiny. Sound domestic policy plays an important role in ensuring that the benefits of international economic integration are shared widely, raising living standards within and across the countries that take part. In large measure, active participation in international markets for goods, services, and capital strengthens the case for domestic policies that make sense even without integration. Among these are policies that encourage a flexible and skilled work force, provide an adequate social safety net, reward innovation, and secure the integrity and depth of the financial system.

Conclusion

For centuries, rising prosperity and rising integration of the global economy have gone hand in hand. The U.S. and much of the rest of the world have never before been as affluent as today. Nor has economic globalization—the worldwide integration of national economies through trade, capital flows, and operational linkages among firms—ever before been as broad or as deep. Keynes' description of London at the beginning of the 20th century rings even truer for the United States and many other countries today. This conjuncture of rising wealth and expanding international ties is no coincidence. The U.S. has gained enormously from these linkages. Indeed, future improvements in Americans' living standards depend in part on our continued willingness to embrace international economic integration.

Over the long term, increasing our standard of living in the U.S. requires that Americans embrace change. It is clearly in our interest to forge ahead, both promoting and guiding the process of international economic integration. Yet even as we actively promote and encourage global economic linkages, we must confront the very real challenges that arise from economic globalization. We must find ways to share its benefits as widely as possible. The key lies in maintaining an economy that is sufficiently flexible and vibrant to meet the challenges of reaping those benefits. Ultimately, our prosperity in the global economy depends primarily on our policies at home.

—John G. Fernald
Senior economist
—Victoria Greenfield
Senior economist, RAND

Notes

1. This *Chicago Fed Letter* draws heavily on chapter 6 of Office of the U.S. President, 2000, Economic *Report of the President*, Washington, DC: United States Government Printing Office, February. The authors wish to thank Yu-Chin Chen, John Goldie, and Robert Lawrence for their assistance and insight in preparing the original text.
2. John Maynard Keynes, 1919, *Economic Consequences of the Peace*, London: Macmillan, available on the Internet at www.socsci.mcmaster.ca/.-econ/ugcm/3113/keynes/peace.htm.
3. See, for example, the discussion and references in Michael Bordo, Barry Eichengreen, and Douglas Irwin, 1999, "Is globalization today really different from globalization a hundred years ago?," *Brookings Trade Forum 1999*, Washington, DC: The Brookings Institution, pp. 1–50.
4. Douglas Irwin, 1985, "The GATT in historical perspective," *American Economic Review*, Vol. 85, No. 2, pp. 323–328, provides an overview of the pre-World War I and interwar periods.
5. See David Hummels, Jun Ishii, and Kei-Mu Yi, 2001, "The nature and growth of vertical specialization in world trade," *Journal of International Economics*, forthcoming; Catherine Mann, 1999, *Is the U.S. Trade Deficit Sustainable?*, Washington, DC: Institute for International Economics, pp. 39–41; Robert Feenstra, 1998, "Integration of trade and disintegration of production in the global economy," *Journal of Economic Perspectives*, Vol. 12, No. 4, pp. 31–50; and others.
6. McGraw-Companies and the U.S. Department of Commerce, International Trade Administration, 1999, U.S. *Industry and Trade Outlook '99*, p. 27–1 and p. 27–5.
7. Maurice Obsfeld and Alan Taylor, 1998, "The Great Depression as a watershed: International capital mobility over the long run," in *The Defining Moment: The Great Depression and the American Economy in the Twentieth Century*, Michael D. Bordo, Claudia Goldin, and Eugene N. White (eds.), Chicago: University of Chicago Press, pp. 353–402, emphasize that *net* capital flows across countries (as measured by current account balances relative to GDP) were larger in the late 19th and early 20th centuries than they are today. By contrast, Bordo, Eichengreen, and Irwin, op cit., emphasize that *gross* capital flows—our focus in this *Fed Letter*—are much larger today than ever before.
8. Bank for International Settlements, 1999, *Central Bank Survey of Foreign Exchange and Derivatives Activity*, available on the Internet at www.bis.org, May.
9. Containerization, as it is called, allows a standard-sized container to be hauled by truck or rail and then, if continuing overseas, loaded by crane directly onto a ship. For more on the transformation of shipping, see, The Economist Newspaper Limited, 1997, "Schools brief, delivering the goods," *The Economist*, available on the Internet at www.economist.com, November 13.
10. *Economic Report of the President*, op cit., p. 209, cites data from David Hummels, 1999, "Have international transportation costs declined?," University of Chicago, unpublished paper, as well as personal correspondence from Hummels.
11. David Hummels, 1999, "Have international transportation costs declined?," University of Chicago, unpublished paper, p. 7, and the U.S. Department of Commerce, various publications.
12. For historical data on the nominal price of a telephone call, see U.S. Department of Commerce, 1975, *Historical Statistics of the United States, Colonial Times to 1970, Part 2*, Washington, DC: U.S. Government Printing Office, p. 791.
13. U.S. Federal Communications Commission, 1999, *Trends in the U.S. International Telecommunications Industry*, Washington, DC, table 16.
14. See Irwin, op cit.
15. These estimates cover only a narrow range of the potential benefits from the Uruguay Round. See Council of Economic Advisers, 1999, "America's interest in the WTO," white paper, p. 22, citing results in Glenn W. Harrison, Thomas Rutherford, and David G. Tarr, 1996, "Quantifying the Uruguay Round," p. 238, and Joseph F. Francois, Bradley McDonald, and Hikan Nordstrom, 1996, "The Uruguay Round: A numerically based quantitative assessment," pp. 282–283, both in *The Uruguay Round and the Developing Countries*, Will Martin and L. Alan Winters (eds.), London: World Bank and Cambridge University Press.
16. Council of Economic Advisers, 1999, "America's interest in the World Trade Organization: An economic assessment," p. 14, citing the *Economic Report of the President*, 1998, pp. 244–245, and other sources.

AMERICA'S RECORD TRADE DEFICIT:

A Reflection of Economic Strength

"The contention that trade deficits somehow damage the U.S. economy is directly challenged by its superior performance during times when they are rising."

BY DANIEL T. GRISWOLD

AMERICA'S chronic trade deficit continues to set records, month after month, year after year, not only for its size, but for its share of an expanding gross domestic product (GDP). The large and growing gap between how much the U.S. imports and how much it exports continues to fuel anxiety among policymakers, economic commentators, and critics of American trade policy. However, those worries rest on a fundamental misunderstanding of the trade deficit's causes and consequences.

Although the U.S. has run a trade deficit every year since 1975, those deficits have reached an unprecedented level as the expansion of the 1990s stretches into a new decade. The U.S. ran a deficit on goods and services of more than $360,000,000,000 in 2000. That is up a third from the then-record deficit of $264,000,000,000 in 1999, and more than double the deficit of 1998.

Trade skeptics, a majority of Americans, and a surprising number of trade journalists believe that a trade deficit of such magnitude can be only bad news. They assume that the deficit imposes a drug on growth and a net loss of jobs, because of either lost export opportunities or rising imports that displace domestic production. During the debate in 2000 over granting permanent normal trade relations to China, for example, opponents predicted that the deal would expand America's bilateral trade deficit with China and cost as many as 1,000,000 jobs in the U.S. economy during the next decade.

Immediate worries about the trade deficit have been compounded by more long-term concerns that the deficit is unsustainable. Critics warn that chronic and growing deficits will burden future generations with a crashing foreign debt, leave America vulnerable to foreign pressure, and undermine foreign investor confidence in the U.S., triggering capital flight, a downward spiral of the dollar, and a "hard landing" for the economy.

In 1998, those and other concerns prompted Congress to appropriate $2,000,000 to establish and fund the Trade Deficit Review Commission with a mandate "to study the nature, causes, and consequences of the United States merchandise trade and current account deficits." The

12-member panel of private citizens, half appointed by the Democratic leadership and half by the Republican leadership in Congress, heard testimony in Washington and around the country from economic experts, business and labor leaders, and other witnesses on the alleged causes and consequences of the deficit. The commission issued its final report on Nov. 14, 2000.

The report was really two starkly contrasting documents beneath a single cover—one authored by the Republican-appointed members, the other by those appointed by the Democrats. The Democratic side concluded that the trade deficit poses a threat to the U.S. economy, both immediately and in the long run. The Republican side, while agreeing that large and growing deficits cannot continue indefinitely, concluded that the deficit reflects more positive developments in the U.S. economy, such as relatively strong growth and rising levels of investment.

How policymakers view the deficit will have important implications for U.S. trade policy. If they accept the view that it poses a real danger to the economy, they will be more inclined to impose new trade barriers in an effort to curb imports, and less inclined to support new trade agreements that would open markets at home and abroad. If they accept the view that the deficit is not a real danger, they will be more inclined to pursue further reductions in trade barriers to stimulate global trade.

Congress and the Bush Administration will face political pressure to do something to "fix" the trade deficit. Although it was not a major issue during the 2000 election campaign, both the Republican and Democratic parties cited it as a problem in their platforms. With power in Congress almost evenly divided between the two parties, the deficit could be a major part of the trade policy debate.

Widespread misunderstanding about America's trade deficit tilts the political playing field against further trade liberalization and toward harmful fixes that could include erecting barriers to imports. If new regional or multilateral trade agreements are negotiated during the 107th Congress, opponents of expanding trade will likely raise the same charges they have in the past about the impact of bilateral deficits and the overall trade deficit on jobs, industry, and the economy.

Evaluating claims about the consequences of the deficit requires an understanding of its causes. Not surprisingly, the two factions of the Trade Deficit Review Commission came to widely differing conclusions about the causes of the persistent U.S. trade deficit. The Democratic-appointed members contended that it is caused primarily by high trade barriers abroad, predatory import pricing, declining competitiveness of core U.S. industries and low wages and poor working conditions in less-developed countries. The Republican-appointed members explained the deficit as the result of macroeconomic factors in the U.S. economy—specifically levels of national savings, investment, and economic growth—and exchange rate movements.

Economic theory and experience weigh heavily in favor of the explanation that trade deficits are driven primarily by macroeconomic factors, in particular investment flows, and not by allegedly unfair trade barriers or declining industrial competitiveness. Nations that are net recipients of foreign investment will run current account deficits, while those that are net investors in the rest of the world will run surpluses. (The current account is the broadest measure of international trade, including goods, services, income from international investments, and unilateral transfers such as foreign aid and private remittances. The trade deficit includes only goods and services. For the U.S., the two figures currently are about equal in magnitude, and, for purposes of this discussion, the terms will be used interchangeably.)

The underlying cause of the trade deficit is the fact that domestic savings are insufficient to fund all the available domestic investment opportunities. Any savings gap is filled by a net inflow of foreign investment. Those foreign funds allow Americans to buy more than they sell in the international market for goods and services, resulting in a trade deficit. As long as the pool of domestic savings available for investment is smaller than the actual level of investment, the U.S. will run a trade deficit. Conversely, if the pool of domestic savings exceeds domestic investment, the extra savings will flow abroad, resulting in a trade surplus.

An alternative way to explain the trade deficit is that it represents the gap between what the nation produces and what it spends. If Americans spend more on consumption, investment, and government purchases than they produce in a given period of time, the gap must be filled with a net inflow of goods and services from abroad. The result is a trade deficit. If production exceeds domestic purchases, the extra production will be sold abroad, resulting in a surplus. Whichever approach is used, the variables in the equation are not industrial competitiveness or trade policies, but macroeconomic factors of savings and investment or of production and spending.

The causes of bilateral deficits with specific trading partners are more complex. Bilateral deficits can be driven by factors other than investment flows. They can be determined by natural resource endowments (oil being a prominent example), differing growth rates and levels of development, consumer tastes, and trade barriers. Unless those factors affect the level of savings and investment in the U.S., though, they will not change the overall trade balance. Lowering foreign trade barriers through negotiation, or keeping or raising American barriers to products from specific countries, will not put a dent in the overall U.S. trade deficit. If the U.S. managed, through changes in trade policy, to reduce its bilateral deficit with one trading partner, bilateral balances with others would simply adjust accordingly, leaving the overall trade deficit unchanged.

The very notion of balanced trade as a policy goal betrays a lack of understanding of the trade deficit and how it reflects underlying economic realities. A world of balanced trade would be a strange place indeed. Every nation would save exactly what it needed to finance every economically profitable domestic investment, no more and no less, and each would have the same natural resources, level of development, consumer tastes, trade policy, and business cycle as its trading partners. That is not the world we live in.

Members of the Trade Deficit Review Commission were just as divided in their view of the consequences of the deficit. Republican-appointed members concluded that it reflects economic strength, not weakness. Democrat-appointed members, in contrast, blamed the trade deficit for a number of economic ills they believe afflict the U. S., including job loss and increased economic insecurity for American workers as well as downward pressure on their wages and growing income inequality. The Democrats maintain that persistent trade deficits have also contributed to the erosion of the U.S. manufacturing base and the loss of long-run competitiveness.

The latter, dark assessment of the trade deficit's impact on the economy is difficult to square with America's economic performance during the past decade. Since 1992, while the trade deficit has grown dramatically larger, the U.S. economy enjoyed a record-breaking expansion; the unemployment rate fell to a 30-year low; inflation was down; productivity accelerated; manufacturing output reached new highs; and real compensation and household incomes rose across all income levels.

A survey of the U.S. economy since 1973, when the era of floating exchange rates and free capital flows began, confirms that rising trade deficits generally accompany periods of rising investment and expansion. Since 1973, America's current account deficit as a percentage of GDP has grown larger ("worsened") in 16 years and shrunk ("improved") in 11. By almost any measure, the economy has performed better in years in which the trade deficit rose, compared to those in which it shrank.

GDP growth. During years of rising deficits, the growth of real GDP averaged 3.5% per year, compared to 2.6% during years of shrinking deficits. In other words, the economy typically grows more than one-third faster in years in which the trade deficit expands than in those in which it shrinks. The causation, of course, flows from growth to the trade deficit. In a more rapidly growing economy, demand for investment capital and imports increase. Rising incomes stoke demand for imports, and an inflow of foreign capital provides the means to help pay for them.

Employment. The story of jobs is much the same. During years of "worsening" trade deficits, the unemployment rate has, on average, fallen by 0.4%. During years of "improving" deficits, it has, on average, risen by the same amount. This is not to say that a rising trade deficit causes unemployment to fall. Causation works in the other direction: Expanding payrolls boost total domestic income, which, in turn, raises demand for imports. Once again, the protectionists have it wrong—imports do not destroy jobs; job creation fuels demand for imports.

Manufacturing. Critics of the trade deficit argue that it is causing the "deindustrialization" of America. While the economy may be producing service jobs, the U.S. supposedly is shipping its manufacturing capacity overseas. Again, the evidence of the past three decades points in the opposite direction. During years of rising current account deficits, manufacturing output grew an average of 4.6% a year (December to December). During years of shrinking deficits, the average growth rate was a much less robust one percent—less than one-quarter the rate of growth during years of rising deficits. The automobile industry—long a symbol of American industrial might—saw domestic output of cars and light tracks rise an average of 500,000 units during years of rising deficits, and output typically fell by 600,000 units in years when the deficit shrank.

Employment in the manufacturing sector grew slightly, on average, in years in which the trade deficit worsened. Meanwhile, a net total of more than 100,000 manufacturing jobs was eliminated, on average, in years when the trade deficit improved.

Poverty. Americans on the margins of poverty also appear to fare somewhat better when the trade deficit expands. In years when the deficit grew, the poverty rate in the U.S. fell an average of 0.2% from the year before. In years when it shrank, the poverty rate rose by an average of 0.3%. The same expanding economy that causes the trade deficit to grow lifts a larger share of Americans out of official poverty.

The contention that trade deficits somehow damage the U.S. economy is directly challenged by its superior performance during times when they are rising. If trade deficits drug down growth, destroy jobs, decimate manufacturing, and hurt the poor, why are bigger deficits associated with faster growth, a falling unemployment rate, accelerating industrial output, and fewer people living in poverty?

The long-run impact

With the economy performing so well during a time of record trade deficits, it has become increasingly difficult to argue that trade deficits have an immediate negative impact. As a consequence, concern about the trade deficit has shifted to the question of whether the deficit is "sustainable."

As was the case with the causes and immediate consequences of the deficit, the Trade Deficit Review Commission could not agree on its long-term consequences. The Democrat-appointed members warned that chronically large trade deficits could undermine global confidence in the American economy and U.S. leadership, precipitate a "hard landing" that would end the current expansion and burden the economy with large payments to finance the growing stock of foreign investment.

GOP-appointed members agreed that the trade deficit, as a share of GDP, "cannot continue to increase without end," but must at some point reverse itself. Nonetheless, they concluded that "the fundamental strength and flexibility of the U.S. economy, the attractiveness of the United States as a destination for foreign investment, along with the ability of the U.S. economy and financial markets to adjust to changing circumstances, lead us to conclude that at some point in the future the trade deficits will most likely come down in an orderly way without significant disruption to the U.S. economy."

"Foreign debt" in perspective. One consequence of annual trade deficits is that foreign investors acquire more assets in the U.S. than Americans acquire abroad. The difference between the value of assets Americans own abroad and those foreign investors own in the U.S. is called the net international investment position. For most of the 20th century, the U.S.'s net international investment position was positive—that is, Americans owned a larger stock of investment abroad than foreigners owned in the U.S. Since the late 1980s, however, driven by a surge of foreign capital into the U.S., the nation's net international investment position has turned negative. By the end of 1999, the gap between the current market value of foreign-owned assets in the U.S. and that of American-owned assets abroad reached 1.44 trillion dollars, and it could soon approach two trillion.

This change in status is often described as an ominous transformation of America from the world's largest "creditor nation" to the world's largest "debtor nation." Yet, much of what foreigners have invested in the U.S. cannot accurately be described as imposing any kind of "debt" on American citizens. Almost half of the 8.65 trillion dollars in foreign-owned assets in the U.S. at the end of 1999 was equity investment in American real estate and corporations, with 2.8 trillion dollars in the form of foreign direct investment and another 1.44 trillion in portfolio investment in corporate stock.

None of that equity investment represents debt in the sense of an obligation to repay a fixed amount over a certain time period. When a German firm acquires an American automobile or wireless telephone company, Japanese investors buy real estate in Hawaii, or a British pension fund adds 100,000 shares of Microsoft to its portfolio, no American is under any legal obligation to repay anything. The foreign investor in U.S. equities will receive only what the market determines the asset is worth at the time of resale.

Moreover, the sheer size of America's negative net international investment position is not alarming when compared to the overall size of the U.S. economy. At the end of 1999, America's negative net international investment position of 1.47 trillion dollars represented about 16% of that year's GDP. In other words, Americans were producing enough every two months to buy back the difference between foreign-owned assets in the U.S. and U.S.-owned assets abroad. America's "foreign debt" in 1999 was about four percent of the net wealth of all U.S. households and nonprofit organizations.

A related worry about the net accumulation of foreign assets in the U.S. is the nation's ability to make future payments to the owners of those assets. Like the Federal government's accumulated fiscal debt, this issue arouses intergenerational concerns that Americans might be burdening their children with future obligations in order to support current consumption. By any measure, though, America's net payments on investment are modest and should be manageable for the foreseeable future. In 1999, Americans paid out $294,600,000,000 in dividends and interest to foreign investors and, in turn, received $276,200,000,000 from U.S. investments abroad, causing a net payments deficit of $18,400,000,000.

What may seem to be a large amount in nominal terms proves to be modest when compared to America's 9.3 trillion dollar GDP in 1999. As a share of what the U.S. produces, the net investment payments flowing out in 1999 amounted to less than one-fifth of one percent of GDP. The equivalent net "debt service" payment for a family earning $75,000 a year would be $148.

If trends of the last decade continue, net payments to foreigners will continue to grow, both nominally and as a share of GDP, but not to a burdensome level. If payments on foreign-owned assets in the U.S. and receipts on U.S.-owned assets abroad were to continue to grow at the same annual rate as during the last decade, America's net payments deficit would reach $207,000,000,000 by 2009. Assuming a 5.5% annual growth of nominal GDP during that same period, net payments as a percentage of GDP would amount to 1.3%. For that hypothetical household, net service payments would rise to a still-manageable $960 a year.

Meanwhile, the additional domestic investment made possible by the net inflow of foreign capital raises the underlying growth rate of the U.S. economy. Current and future workers will be more productive because of the larger capital stock, thus expanding the economy and easing the relative burden of servicing the nation's net foreign investment position.

The alternative to the inflow of foreign capital is an outflow, or what is known under certain conditions as "capital flight" Chronic outflows of capital can point to problems far more serious than persistent inflows. Russia, for example, has run a current account surplus every year since records became available in 1994, including a $25,000,000,000 surplus in 1999. Those surpluses are a sign not of economic strength, but of economic weakness.

A stake in America's prosperity. A second, persistent worry is that growing foreign ownership of U.S. assets will leave America vulnerable to foreign influence and manipulation. The fear is that its principal creditors, Japan in particular, could wield influence over U.S. government decisions by threatening to cut off the supply of capital inflows, or by threatening to withdraw capital already invested.

Foreign investors in theory could attempt to exert political pressure on the U.S. by threatening to curtail investment, but such an act would have negative consequences for the investor as well as the host country. Americans would lose, of course, because a withdrawal of capital would drive up domestic interest rates, while the falling dollar would make imports more expensive, reducing the purchasing power of American workers. However, America's creditors would also suffer if their alternative investments were less profitable. Foreign investors would be further harmed if the U.S economy were to tip into a recession. Falling demand in the U.S. would quickly translate into falling exports to the American market, while a depreciating U.S. currency and slumping economy would depreciate the value of foreign-owned assets remaining in the U.S.

No foreign leverage

The foreign-influence scenario assumes that foreign investors would act in concert, but such an orchestrated withdrawal of credit seems unlikely. Private investors in industrialized countries do not usually act at the behest of their governments. Even in Japan, a government decision to dump dollars or withdraw funds from U.S. markets would not mean that private companies and individuals would necessarily do likewise. If the American economy remains fundamentally sound, other global investors would likely see the temporary decline in the dollar and U.S. asset prices as an opportunity to buy. The foreign governments attempting to exert "leverage" over the U.S. would, in the end, inflict merely temporary damage on the U.S. economy at the cost of their own long-term interests.

When an economy is as large and as important to the global economy as that of the U.S., its chief "creditors" have a stake in keeping it healthy. They have a strong incentive to act prudently with their investments so as not to undermine their positions. If any country wields leverage, it is the world's chief "debtor"—the U.S.

The "hard-landing" scenario. A third looming worry about the trade deficit is that it will eventually undermine the confidence of foreign investors. According to this scenario, the rising trade deficit spooks foreign investors into withdrawing funds, starting a downward economic spiral.

Most international investors are savvy enough to understand that America's trade deficit is a reflection of underlying strength, not weakness, for all the reasons outlined above. The U.S. trade deficit, by accommodating an inflow of foreign capital, actually encourages lower interest rates and thus promotes economic growth.

As for exchange rates, the trade deficit is not the cause of a weaker dollar, but is associated with a stronger dollar. Since 1980, the trade deficit as a percentage of GDP has closely tracked the real value of the dollar on the foreign exchange market. When the dollar rises, so does the trade deficit, and vice versa. The real value of the dollar trended upward in the 1990s along with the size of the trade deficit.

A strong dollar and a rising trade deficit are not in conflict. While the trade deficit does increase the supply of dollars abroad, which by itself would put downward pressure on the dollar, the demand by foreign investors for dollars to buy U.S. assets has been even greater, resulting in a net appreciation of the dollar. As long as foreign demand for U.S. assets remains strong, the dollar will remain high, and so will the current account deficit.

Foreign investors could reach a point where they believed their portfolios had become overweighted with investments in the U.S., but there is no reason to think that point has arrived, or will anytime soon. The U.S. remains the world's largest economy, and among the freest and most dynamic. The amount of net foreign investment that flows into the U.S. each year is not out of proportion to the American economy's size in the global economy.

Of course, any nation open to the global economy could, in theory, suffer an exodus of capital. If foreign investors decide to sell off assets, or if domestic investors do the same and send their money abroad, the currency will fall, upward pressure will build on interest rates, growth will slow, and the economy could suffer the proverbial hard landing. Such a scenario could occur whether a country was running a trade deficit or a surplus, whether its net international investment position was negative or positive. As long as capital is not held hostage to government controls, a loss of investor confidence could trigger capital flight and the economic ills that would come with it. That fact is an argument not for capital controls, but for sound economic policies that encourage long-term, profitable investment.

Americans would be even better off in the long run if they saved more of what they produce, thereby reducing the amount of foreign capital needed to fund domestic investment. A larger pool of domestic savings available could fund the investment needed to promote growth while at the same time retaining a larger share of the interest and dividends paid to the owners of the nation's capital stock. As long as domestic savings fall short of domestic investment, though, it is far better to welcome capital from abroad than to be forced to reduce investment to the level of domestic savings.

America's annual trade deficits are sustainable as long as the U.S. remains a safe and profitable destination for the world's savings. The accumulating net foreign ownership of U.S. assets does not threaten America's sovereignty, ability to finance that investment, or continued economic expansion.

Daniel T. Griswold *is associate director, Center for Trade Policy Studies, Cato Institute, Washington, D.C.*

REPORT ON POST COLD WAR LATIN AMERICA

Free Trade Area of the Americas: NAFTA MARCHES SOUTH

BY CLAUDIO KATZ

The U.S. plan to create the Free Trade Area of the Americas (FTAA) as a hemisphere-wide successor to, and expansion of the North America Free Trade Agreement (NAFTA) is a strategic project aimed at consolidating U.S. supremacy in the region by means of increased U.S. exports, more investment controls and sophisticated financial-flow monitoring methods.

Planning for the FTAA began seven years ago, but the project remained at a standstill until 1998. At their meeting last year in Quebec, the region's presidents agreed to speed up the planning process and finish FTAA negotiations by 2005. The initiative has received new impetus from the Bush administration, which, as we write, is trying to convince Congress to approve so-called "fast-track" legislation that would give the U.S. executive branch the authority to negotiate trade agreements while reducing Congress' oversight role. The immediate objective of the United States is to find external trade outlets to compensate for the U.S. economic slowdown. Unlike Asia and Europe, Latin America represents a possible new export niche for North American companies[1] The FTAA would slow down competing European moves into Latin America by obstructing negotiations over alternative free trade agreements, like those promoted by Spain. U.S. officials also hope the agreement would help shore up regional military alliances threatened by the recent deterioration of many Latin American political regimes.

The 500 U.S. companies with the closest links to Latin America are pushing for fast implementation of the FTAA. They want the new pact to be modeled on NAFTA and on World Trade Organization (WTO) provisions on commerce, and to incorporate the types of financial discipline imposed by the International Monetary Fund (IMF).

The FTAA negotiations were initially secret and although they are now public, the pact still faces strong opposition from U.S. industries with few international ties. They believe they would be worse off under the agreement. Representatives of this sector successfully prevented Congress from giving former President Clinton fast track authority.

The importance of the political-military interests behind the FTAA is less obvious, but more decisive. For several years, highly organized popular movements with clear social demands have been growing stronger in both rural and urban areas of many Latin American countries. These movements highlight the erosion of political systems that have become delegitimized because of their inability to meet popular claims. Lack of confidence in existing regimes accelerated the end of a presidential term in Peru and led to government dissolution in Ecuador, the effective collapse of the state in Colombia and the disintegration of traditional political parties in Venezuela and Mexico. Preserving stability in the face of this upheaval is a priority of a U.S. government that identifies these crises with a weakening of its own regional security role. The FTAA would be a means for the United States to strengthen its covert military intervention in Colombia, continue with the regional re-armament associated with the U.S. "war on drugs," conduct more Vieques-style military exercises and use diplomatic pressure to get more Latin American support for sanctions against states the State Department considers pariahs: Cuba, Iraq, Libya, and North Korea. The United States successfully opposed the establishment of independent nuclear programs in Argentina and Brazil and now intends to expand this "discipline" to the rest of the world even as it moves forward its own anti-missile defense system.

Nobody disputes that, at present, the FTAA is a U.S. project aimed at increasing its own hegemony in the region. However, after a decade in which neoliberal ideology has been in the ascendency, some now idealize U.S. supremacy. In the past, great power domination was crit-

Brazil: Neoliberal decades bring down "emerging power"

By Emir Sader

The historical period that began with the fall of the Soviet Union and the advent of the United States as the world's only superpower changed Brazil's international position. Up until then, Brazil had been one of the so-called "emerging intermediate powers." Among these it occupied a special place because of its dynamic economy, one so well-endowed with natural resources and technological capacity that when the 1980s began, Brazil was active in all the important economic sectors, including information technology. But the following two decades were marked by a traumatic turnaround, in which Brazil's international profile was sharply reduced, along with its possibilities for economic expansion and for playing a leading international role.

Brazil had the fastest growing economy in the world between 1930 and 1980, but the "debt crisis" of the 1980s interrupted this five decade-long expansion. Then, beginning in 1990, the productive and competitive capacity that had been built up over previous decades was substantially weakened as a succession of Brazilian governments adopted U.S.-promoted neoliberal policies. Deregulation and the brusque opening of Brazilian economy to the international market promoted the replacement of industrial capital by finance capital as the economy's driving force. This made the economy more fragile and in seven years increased the public debt eleven-fold. Brazil began to be strongly dependent on foreign capital in order to keep its accounts current, and it lost its sovereignty to international financial organizations in which the United States plays a preponderant role.

Mercosur, the regional customs union that might have played a key role in affirming the international power of Brazil and other nations of the region, also ended up as a victim of neoliberal policies. [See "Free Trade Area of the Americas: NAFTA Marches South"] The priority given to fiscal adjustment and monetary stability forced the region's governments to impose artificial exchange policies. When differences between member nations' exchange policies produced a marked economic disequilibrium between member countries instead of their integration, Mercosur's final crisis began. In light of this, the proposal for the Free Trade Area of the Americas (FTAA) may represent a consolidation of Brazil's loss of sovereignty. Brazil could be the principal victim of a form of supposed integration that in reality signifies total subordination to the United States. Brazil's natural resources, labor power and massive potential internal market are the booty to be snatched by the United States and its huge corporations.

Brazil now finds itself at a turning point. The possibilities for fiscal adjustment have been exhausted, and so have the political possibilities of the governments that were on the scene during the 1990s. The 2002 presidential elections will occur in a setting that will either permit an opposition victory or give new life to the current model. This means either a rupture with the neoliberal "Washington Consensus" economic plan which is now in effect in Brazil or a continuation of it. There would be continuity even with the victory of a "third way" candidate in the style of Argentina's de la Rua and Mexico's Fox. Such a government would maintain the current economic program despite promises to re-emphasize economic development, combat unemployment, and implement more social problems.

The main left opposition candidate, Luiz Inacio da Silva, known as Lula, hasn't yet clearly defined an external or foreign policy, but if he wins, the nature of his government will certainly depend on how he chooses to act internationally. Brazil must be reintegrated into the international system, and this would mean renegotiation of the debt, because the current payment schedule would make it impossible for any popular government to implement its program, as de la Rua's current situation in Argentina shows. It would also mean redefining international alliances in order to obtain sufficient power to carry out the renegotiation; this would imply not merely the rejection of FTAA, but also an active international policy aimed at creating diversified alliances, with priority given to closer ties with the big nations of the South China, India and South Africa among others.

Without redefining its own relations with the United States and affirming its sovereignty, Brazil won't be able to build a just society or again take up the task of economic and social development. It needs to do these things at home if it is to take on an international leadership role which would allow it to bring together the great majorities of the world who are today excluded from power and from access to most of the world's goods.

icized and the dominant states were accused of imperialism and colonialism; now there are those who argue that such domination is useful. Some maintain that the FTAA will help counteract a supposed lack of entrepreneurship among Latin Americans; they use anthropological, geographical and racial justifications to back up their claims. Others predict that if the region does not take this opportunity to accept U.S. leadership, it will not escape future poverty and decadence[2] It is, however, very difficult to show that Latin America was ever in the past free from U.S. patronage, especially during the last decade, when previous social and economic progress was being undone in many places. During this period, the region's economies were unbalanced by four factors—growing external debt, export specialization, unequal exchange rates and lower purchasing power. These were not the result of Latin America's moving away from the United States. Rather, they reflect the effects of the consolidation of Latin America's subordinate relation to the United States. The region's economic crises are not a consequence of the built-in defects of Latin Americans, but of Latin America's increasingly dependent role in the world market.[3]

Other analysts argue that "domestic markets are not sufficient to overcome underdevelopment" and claim that the FTAA will help us streamline our export capabilities and will facilitate access to the largest market in the world, that of the United States.[4] Do Latin American consumers already have such vast purchasing power and high levels of consumption that markets at home have been exhausted? How can Latin American exports successfully penetrate what is not just the largest, but also the world's most competitive and demanding market? What will be the effect of the enormous gaps in productivity that have so far thwarted access to this market? Answers to any of these queries bring into question a naive belief in a regional "take-off" based on the FTAA. Opinion makers, however, do not weigh their illusions against actual developments, but reiterate their faith in increased exports and investment inflows.

Many of those promoting the FTAA also support dollarization, that is, the adoption of the U.S. dollar as a legal currency. Nevertheless, dollarization supporters have not provided any proof of its advantages for the Central American economies that have already adopted this policy, Guatemala and El Salvador. They also ignore the fact that in Ecuador dollarization was implemented as an emergency measure in the face of financial collapse. Panama is the only country that has had a dollarized economy for an extended period of time, and it certainly does not represent a model of poverty eradication and adequate employment. Over the last decades, Panama, like any other debtor country in the region, had to abide by 17 IMF stabilization programs.[5]

Dollarization is associated with the FTAA project, but it is not integral to the initiative since there is still heated debate within the United States government about its advantages. Consequently, those Latin American countries that give up control of their national currencies by dollarizing do not get in return any commitment from the U.S. Federal Reserve that the Fed will act as a lender-of-last-resort in case of a banking crisis, as it would do in the United States. And while small economies that are commercially integrated with the United States can tolerate the fact that, under dollarization, U.S. officials have more power over individual Latin American economies than national officials do, such inequality would have disastrous consequences for larger, more independent economies like those of Argentina or Mexico.

For now, however, U.S. interests in FTAA are basically commercial. As with any business initiative, FTAA's introduction has been accompanied by a major marketing campaign that seeks to recreate the fantasies that surrounded privatization plans in the 1990s. But, as with everything neoliberal, the predicted prosperity is a promise for the future, while sacrifices are immediately required for implementation.

As negotiations progress, there is less talk about "brotherhood" and "integration" among Americans, North and South, and more demands by particular groups of U.S. corporations. U.S. corporations that operate in service industries intend to step into the areas of insurance, education and health care in Latin America. These areas are particularly profitable because, given the dire state of Latin America's public services, the upper middle classes tend to use private services. In the area of investments, FTAA negotiators are considering provisions that would grant foreign companies the right to resort to an international court that would have more authority than any national legal system. Such legal entities are already part of NAFTA, and have ruled in favor of companies that filed complaints against several states in Canada and Mexico when the states tried to enforce environmental and other local laws.[6]

In the area of public sector procurement, the elimination of rules that give preference to local suppliers is being discussed. North American consortia will be able to push aside any local competitor that does not have as much access to international credit as they do.[7]

In terms of customs barriers, U.S. negotiators want more open Latin American economies but will not allow for increased imports in return. U.S. non-tariff trade barriers—mainly discriminatory anti-dumping measures—affect 34% of the products on the export list of the regional customs union, Mercosur. Under this mechanism, Argentine honey exports were recently penalized with a 60% tariff.

Agriculture is a key area in the agreement. As "agribusiness" corporations make progress in destroying regulations that protect Latin American small farmers, they also block any traces of free competition at home. U.S. Secretary of Commerce Donald Evans has already declared that the $97 billion in U.S. farm subsidies "will not be discussed in the FTAA negotiations."[8] What's more, the resolution of this issue does not depend on negotiations with Latin America, but on talks with the European Community for the reduction of European agricultural subsidies. If this dispute is not solved, all expectations that Argentine exporters, for instance, might have for the FTAA will be frustrated. Some estimate that the agreement will ultimately result in a 30-35% increase in Argentine imports and a 4% reduction in exports.[9]

The FTAA will once and for all consecrate intellectual property rights which brought a windfall to U.S. high-tech companies after the demise of the Argentine and Brazilian information industries. The most important current patent dispute concerns the pharmaceutical industry's objections to a Brazilian government project that produces cheap, generic versions of patented AIDS drugs without the permission of the patent holders. Though this program saves lives and heals patients, it does not meet the profit requirements of the international laboratories.

Last, but not least, the FTAA will authorize the United States to continue violating environmental protection agreements. As a result of NAFTA, several border regions in Mexico became toxic sewers and it is estimated that 40% of the forests in the Mexican state of Guerrero have been destroyed as a result of pollution.[10] The FTAA will also promote more wage flexibility based on the Mexican maquila model. The overall effect of the agreement will undoubtedly be a regional economic cycle more dependent on the U.S. GNP. This will deepen the vulnerability of the Latin American productive sector to downswings.

As it stands, the FTAA will also signify the demise of Mercosur. This customs union, currently made up of Argentina, Brazil, Paraguay and Uruguay, cannot survive in a general free trade zone.[11] For U.S. corporations competing with European rivals, Mercosur represents an obsolete method of protecting the Europeans via tariffs and national or regional subsidies. The United States has clearly expressed its intention of dissolving the South American association in proposals for bilateral agreements with Chile, recently extended to Argentina. But conditions are very different in these two countries: Chile has a small industrial base and has developed a complementary trade with the United States in mineral, fruit and timber products. Argentina, by contrast, still possesses the sort of industrial sector that would see its final days under the FTAA.[12]

There is no doubt, however, that U.S. efforts are directed mainly against Brazil, which boasts the most coveted market and an industrial sector that is still mostly independent of U.S. corporations. Unlike other countries, Brazil cannot acquiesce to the FTAA without sacrificing the international market shares it has already gained. For this reason, the Brazilian government opposes moving up the agreement's start date and wants to make Venezuela a strategic ally. These pressures are increasing Mercosur's tendency toward internal disintegration. Ten years after its creation, Mercosur promoters acknowledge its deterioration. It failed to make progress in the establishment of a common currency, and in the foundation of regional political and judicial institutions. Neither were customs pacts consolidated because common tariffs were never implemented. No arbitration court for conflict settlement was ever established and disagreements regarding subsidies and government procurement systems were not solved.[13]

These disagreements were deepened by the way each country reacted during the debt crisis. While Brazil decided to devalue its currency and lift tariffs, Argentina opted for convertibility and trade opening. All those economists and politicians that propose "to enter the FTAA from Mercosur" cannot explain how joint talks could succeed if more basic agreements were never reached in ten years.[14]

Unlike the European Community (EC), the FTAA does not seek to create a zone of homogenous economic development—the agreement will encourage no backward member country to move closer to the level of the powerful economy which stands behind the pact. No North-to-South budget transfers are planned and gaps in living standards between Latin American countries and the United States will remain. The differences between the EC and the FTAA are obvious: The EC is constituted as a power bloc seeking to challenge the United States, while the FTAA is a pawn of U.S. supremacy used to confront such a challenge. It is therefore appropriate to define this initiative as an imperialist, neocolonialist project for Latin America. If the agreement is put into effect, it will change the nature of the regional bourgeoisie, ending the debate about whether it is dependent or transnational.[15] What is clear is that the Latin American dominant classes are unable to take on the task of creating an integration project of their own. The Andean and Central American pacts experienced the same defeat that Mercosur is suffering now. While during the twentieth century the regional bourgeoisies were unable to develop their Bolivarian dream of integration, they have now lost any interest in such an objective because their level of association with metropolitan—U.S.—capital is substantially higher than it used to be.

Genuine integration between countries cannot be achieved with the obstacles to sustainable development created by the external debt. Payment defaults obliterate all efforts toward regional development.

Mercosur's ten years of existence were also characterized by unprecedented attacks on worker living conditions. Instead of common labor laws and protection of salaried workers, unemployment rates and labor insecurity soared in member states. This experience demonstrates that any genuine integration project among peoples should be based on different principles. First, it should start from the satisfaction of basic demands, such as increased minimum wages, unemployment insurance, free education and health care. The prerequisites for policy coordination towards these goals are solidarity, promotion of labor stability and improvement of living standards rather than competitiveness, capital mobility, and business efficiency.

Second, genuine integration cannot be achieved under the obstacles to sustainable development imposed by the external debt, as illustrated by the 1995 Mexican, the 1998 Brazilian, and the 2000-2001 Argentine crises. Payment defaults obliterate any regionwide effort towards development, and continuing IMF adjustment programs prevent reconstruction of devastated Latin American economies. Finally, an integration project should be conceived as part of a socialist transformation process given that capitalism poses an impossible barrier for Latin American countries to overcome their periphery status. There is a direct link between the old dreams for Latin American unity and the establishment of new forms of ownership and collective economic management.

The debate on these proposals is now framed within the new international political climate created by recent protests against globalization. FTAA negotiators encountered hostile street demonstrations in Buenos Aires and Quebec. The novelty is that many demonstrators not only proclaim that "an alternative world is possible" but also define such a world and the ways to reach it.

Notes

1. Luis Bilbao, "Democracia amurallada," *Le Monde Diplomatique, Buenos Aires,* May, 2001.
2. Andrés Oppenheimer: "Geografía y cultura: ¿factores de progreso?" August 1, 2000; "La posible partición de las Américas," August 6, 2000; and "Qué se espera para América Latina," January 2, 2001, all in *La Nación*, (Buenos Aires).
3. For more on this topic, see Claudio Katz: "Las nuevas turbulencias de la economía latinoamericana," *Periferias*, No. 8-2, 2000, Buenos Aires.
4. Mariano Grondona: "América Latina: ¿se salvará con el ALCA?" April 12, 2001, *La Nación*, (Buenos Aires).
5. Sebastián Edwards: "El dólar no es la cura mágica,"May 13, 2001, *Clarin* (Buenos Aires).
6. Maude Barlow, "Area de libre comercio y la amenaza para los programas sociales," The Council of Canadians, 2001, www.canadians.org.
7. IDEP, "Los capitales únicos ciudadanos del ALCA," *Nosotros*-ATE, *3/2001, Buenos Aires.*
8. Donald Evans quoted in *Página/12*, April 10, 2001, Buenos Aires.
9. Eduardo Locita, "ALCA un proyecto hegemónico,"*Realidad Económica,* No. 178, 2-3/2001.
10. Document of the Argentine Committee against the FTAA, March 2001, Buenos Aires.
11. Mercosur "emerged as a free trade zone in 1991, and became a customs union in 1995, when common import duties—which currently average 13.5%—went into effect for a list of products entering from outside the bloc." Marcela Valente, "Fissures Appear in Mercosur Trade Bloc," Inter-Press Service, September 28, 2001.
12. The Argentine final position is a mystery because, at this writing, the country is on the verge of a suspension of payments and a potential deflationary collapse. While this chaos subsists, the government will have an undefined position vis-a-vis Mercosur and the FTAA. Under the present crisis, some measures taken point to either option but these are actually improvised measures with no clear objectives.
13. Roberto Bouzas, "El bloque puede desaparecer,"April 12, 2001, *Página/12*.
14. Marcela Bordenave, "Mercosur o ALCA," April 10, 2001, Página/12; Alieto Guadagni, "El ALCA desde el Mercosur,"March 29, 2001, *La Nación*.
15. James Petras suggests that this change has already occurred. See *Rebelión*, March 17, 2001; *Página/12*, May 13, 2001.

Claudio Katz is an economic researcher and professor at the University of Buenos Aires and Conicet. This article originally appeared in Nueva Sociedad, *July-August, 2001. Translated from the Spanish by Carolina Escalona.*

ELIMINATING CHILD LABOR

Today's debates on child labor and international trade echo arguments heard in the United States less than a century ago

BY MIRIAM WASSERMAN

In 1995, when news broke in the United States that the soccer balls used in kids' games were routinely made by children in other countries, many were horrified. It was not the first time such a scandal had hit the spotlight. Reports were frequent in the 1990s of children working in garment factories, shoe shops, and mines producing goods that would ultimately make their way to U.S. markets. Although child labor is not a new problem, increased trade and more widespread information have brought us closer to practices, problems, and institutions that can conflict with our own beliefs. The intensity of the feelings on the issue was highlighted last December during the World Trade Organization's (WTO) ministerial conference in Seattle. Thousands of protesters clamored for tighter rules on labor in international trade. President Clinton chose the setting to sign an international treaty to eliminate the worst forms of child labor and urged other countries to follow his lead. The United States also called on the WTO to make child labor and other labor rights issues part of the agenda. But the measure faced stringent opposition from developing nations. Countries such as Thailand, Brazil, and India feared that mandating higher labor standards could rob them of their comparative advantage in cheap labor, price them out of the market, and block their prospects for greater growth and economic development. They argued, in effect, that the industrialized-country focus on child labor used in exports would not only lead to the loss of jobs, but also end up hurting the very children it was intended to help.

Such arguments echoed the heated debates heard in this country less than a century ago. At the beginning of the twentieth century, pressure for federal legislation covering child labor was growing nationally, but especially in the North. It was greeted with resentment in many segments of southern society. They saw it as interference from a richer North which—after having benefited from child labor in its own industrial development—was trying to limit the South's development.

In spite of the controversy, however, the movement to limit child labor prevailed. Today, the number of American children employed full-time has been vastly reduced. But these changes took almost a century and required a host of changes in family income, education policy, production technologies, and cultural norms.

Although the recent scandals have linked child labor to trade, child labor goes well beyond export industries, is widespread, and deeply rooted. Looking at the U.S. experience in reducing child labor can help us get a better understanding of the profound transformation that the elimination of child labor involves.

THE BALL IS IN WHOSE COURT?

The public outcry in the mid 1990s over child labor used to stitch soccer balls put enormous pressure on soccer ball importers such as Reebok, Nike, and Baden Sports. The changes they and other importers made resulted in one of more successful efforts to eliminate child labor from a specific industry. Consumers can now buy imported soccer balls without feeling as if they are encouraging or benefiting from child labor. But the effect on the children involved is less clear.

The impact was felt most directly in and around the city of Sialkot, Pakistan, a region known for over 80 years for its soccer ball industry. In 1996, 75 percent of the world's soccer balls were made there. The industry was a major source of employment, giving jobs to about 10,000 urban workers and

WORKING CHILDREN AROUND THE GLOBE

These estimates undercount children whose work in the household is not sold in the market. They also include children who work part-time.

	NUMBER OF CHILDREN 5-14 WORKING (MILLIONS)	% OF CHILDREN 5-14 WHO WORK
World	250	24.7
Africa	80	41.4
Asia[1]	152.5	21.5
Latin America & Caribbean	17.5	16.5
Oceania[2]	0.5	29.3

SAMPLE COUNTRIES	(THOUSANDS)		GNP PER CAPITA (US$)	% OF POPULATION UNDER POVERTY	% OF CHILDREN ATTENDING PRIMARY SCHOOL	% OF PRIMARY SCHOOL CHILDREN REACHING 5TH GRADE
Bangladesh	6,584	19.1	350	36	76	61
Nepal	2,596	41.7	210	42	70	52
Pakistan	3,313	8.0	480	34	66	48
Philippines	1,863	10.6	1,050	41	89	70
Turkey	1,495	12.6	3,160	NA	73	89

1. EXCLUDES JAPAN. 2. EXCLUDES AUSTRALIA AND NEW ZEALAND. SOURCES: ILO, WORLD BANK, AND UNICEF
NOTE: SAMPLE COUNTRIES WERE CHOSEN BECAUSE THEY HAD AVAILABLE CHILD LABOR ESTIMATES BASED ON THE SAME ILO METHODOLOGY

30,000 rural workers in the surrounding villages. Among them, more than 7.000 children, the vast majority of them between the ages of 10 and 14 (but some as young as five), stitched balls on a full-time basis, according to the U.S. Department of Labor. Other children worked part-time outside of school hours. Middlemen and subcontractors took soccer ball kits to village workshops or households, where workers hand-stitched individual pieces together, glued the bladder to the material, and sewed in the final piece. Once completed, the balls were taken back by the middlemen to the factories for packing and shipment. Children were paid about $0.50 to $0.55 per ball; and depending upon skill and experience, they could be stitching between one and five balls per day.

As a result of the international uproar and bad publicity, Reebok and Nike both contracted with Pakistani manufacturers to make balls in new facilities where all the production was centralized. External monitoring was setup so that no children entered the factory and no soccer ball kits were taken out. The German firm Baden Sports Inc. moved its manufacturing operations to China.

Although well intentioned, these changes were not wholly beneficial to the former child workers and their families. "While Baden Sports can quite credibly claim that their soccer balls are not sewn by children, the relocation of their production facility undoubtedly did nothing for their former child workers and their families," write economists Drusilla Brown, Alan Deardorif, and Robert Stern. Although Nike, Reebok, and the other firms who switched to centralized stitching centers did not displace work from the region, they reduced the income opportunities for women who formerly stitched soccer balls from home in between other household tasks.

About one-quarter of the world's children work; almost half of them, 120 million, do so full-time

Brown notes that although the children worked long hours (between eight and nine hours a day), the working conditions were better than in other industries. Most of the children could read, and were not exposed to toxic chemicals or hazardous tools. Moreover, there was no evidence of the practice of intergenerational debt bondage—one of the most blatant forms of exploitation, in which children are given to their parents' "creditor" so that they repay the family's debt through work. In a region that specializes in handmade soccer balls, says Brown, "perhaps learning a trade was the most appropriate use of their time."

DOMESTIC RESTRICTIONS ON CHILD LABOR

The evolution of laws regulating child labor in the United States was a slow and uneven process. The industrial Northeastern states started restricting the employment of children much before the more agrarian and poorer states. And opposition was fierce when it came to passing a federal law on child labor. All in all, more than a century went by between the passage of the first state law limiting the employment of youth and the adoption of an effective national standard on child labor.

The first law in the country to place limitations on the employment of children was enacted by Massachusetts in 1836. The driving concern was not the age of working children, the hours they worked, or the danger involved in their occupations. Rather, state legislators were worried about work's impact on children's education. The Massachusetts law stipulated that no children under age 15 could be employed unless they had attended school for at least three months in the preceding year. Education was later made compulsory in Massachusetts in 1852. Compulsory schooling laws were enacted in most of the states outside the South during the last half of the nineteenth century, according to William M. Landes and Lewis C. Solomon.

Massachusetts was also first to limit children's workdays, banning children under 12 from working more than 10 hours in 1842. Pennsylvania established the first minimum age in 1848: 12 years for work in cotton, woolen, and silk mills. The first night-work provision was enacted in 1888, when Massachusetts prohibited children under 14 from working between 7 p.m. and 6 a.m. A few, mostly Northeastern states, followed these legal examples, setting minimum age and other requirements according to their local needs and preferences.

Enforcement of these laws was scant. No proof of age was required for employment, and it wasn't until 1867 that Massachusetts instituted the nation's first factory inspection. Even so, the wording of the laws gave ample space for loopholes. For instance, "in Massachusetts, New Jersey, and Rhode Island, the only punishable violations of child labor were those committed 'knowingly,'" according to historian Walter Trattner.

In 1879, only seven states restricted the age of children in manufacturing, with an average minimum age of 11. The uneven formulation of state laws led reformers to push for a national standard. But this turned out to be a drawn-out fight. Two federal laws, the Keating-Owen Bill of 1916 and the Pomerene's Tax Bill of 1919 were declared unconstitutional in 1918 and 1922, respectively, by the U.S. supreme court, which considered them in violation of states' rights. Beginning in 1922, anti-child-labor reformers pushed for a constitutional amendment intended to grant the Congress specific authority to legislate protections for working children.

Most of the opposing votes in Congress came from southern textile states, and it was the Southern Cotton Manufacturers, an industry group, which contested the constitutionality of the laws. Southern states had a larger agricultural base and, particularly after the Civil War, were afflicted with widespread poverty—both factors associated with a greater incidence of child labor. Also, the textile industry, which relied heavily on children, spread and grew dramatically in the South during the second half of the nineteenth century, particularly in Georgia, Alabama, and the Carolinas.

With the Great Depression, the national mood on federal child labor legislation changed. It seemed to many that adult workers were being replaced by young children at lower wages, and this helped shore up the support for restricting child labor.

In 1938, with the passage of the Fair Labor Standards Act, a national standard on the employment of children was finally set. The FLSA prohibited interstate commerce in goods made by children under 16 years of age and by children under 18 years in particularly hazardous occupations. Exceptions could be made for 14- and 15-year-olds in occupations other than manufacturing and mining, if the work did not interfere with their schooling, health, or well-being. Still, the law did not cover children employed in agriculture during their school vacations or migratory child workers.

WHAT IS THE ALTERNATIVE?

As the soccer ball example illustrates, if the goal is to improve the welfare of the children, removing them from work is only part of the issue. The larger question is how to provide them with better alternatives.

"Stopping child labor without doing anything else could leave children worse off," says former Secretary of Labor Robert Reich. "If they are working out of necessity, as most are, stopping them could force them into prostitution or other employment with greater personal dangers. The most important thing is that they be in school and receive the education to help them leave poverty," he adds.

That children and their families need alternatives was clearly demonstrated in Bangladesh in 1993. Garment employers, fearing the passage of a law in the United States to ban imports made with child labor, summarily fired an estimated 50,000 children from their factories. The Child Labor Deterrence Act did not make it into the law books, but the threat of a boycott was serious enough that garment manufacturers began firing

WHERE DO CHILDREN WORK?

The U.S. Dept. of Labor estimates that less than 5 percent of working children produce manufacturing and mining goods for export

	PERCENT OF TOTAL
Agriculture, hunting, forestry, and fishing	**70.4**
Mining and quarrying	**0.9**
Manufacturing	**8.3**
Electricity, gas, and water	**0**
Construction	**1.9**
Wholesale and retail trade, restaurants, and hotels	**8.3**
Transport, storage, and communication	**3.8**
Financing, insurance, real estate, and business services	**0**
Community, social, and personal services	**6.5**

SOURCE: ILO Bureau of Statistics.

children. Some of the displaced children tried to replace the lost income by engaging in stone crushing, street hustling, and prostitution. In response, international agencies and nongovernmental organizations urged the industry to stop firing underage workers until a safety net was in place. After extended negotiations, the Bangladesh Garment Manufacturers and Exporters Association, the International Labor Organization (ILO) and UNICEF agreed to jointly sponsor schools. They also provided monthly stipends to children to help their families replace lost income. By 1997, over three hundred schools were established that served a total of 9,710 children.

Just banning exports made with child labor can push children into more harmful occupations

This incident set an example that is now being followed in Sialkot, attempts are being made to provide the displaced children with some form of social protection. An agreement modeled after the one drafted in Bangladesh was reached between the Sialkot Chamber of Commerce and Industry, UNICEF, and the ILO to provide children and their families with informal education for the children and help for the adults in finding other opportunities to earn income. As of August 1999, 5,795 children were attending classes at the 176 centers sponsored.

Still, replacing work with education can be a difficult task. In many developing countries, particularly in remote rural areas, schools are often not available or not affordable for the poorest families. Countries where child labor is prevalent have very limited resources, and, in some cases, governments have not invested sufficiently to have adequate schools in place. In both Pakistan and Bangladesh, special schools needed to be created for the children leaving the soccer and garment industries. In Pakistan, according to the latest figures from UNICEF, only 66 percent of children attended primary school and fewer than half of them reached fifth grade. Bangladesh fared somewhat better with 76 percent of children attending primary school and 61 percent of them reaching fifth grade.

And getting the children to attend schools presents its own challenges, since education is not always seen as something that will be useful. In Sialkot, where the children were offered no stipends, it has required considerable mobilization and awareness raising with the children and their families, particularly if the children had significant earnings.

A GLOBAL PICTURE

Children working in the Pakistani soccer ball industry and in the garment sector of Bangladesh received much attention because they were working in industries that produced goods destined

PHOTOGRAPHY FOR CHANGE

Lewis Hine's camera was one of the most powerful weapons mustered by the child labor reformers in the early twentieth century. Employed full-time by the National Child Labor Committee (NCLC) between 1908 and 1918, Hine investigated and photographed the working conditions of children in industries in most states east of the Mississippi River and in Missouri, Colorado, Texas, and California. He was among the first to use photography to promote social change, and his images left a lasting impression.

The match between the NCLC and Hine was rather fortuitous. Hine was born in Oshkosh, Wisconsin, in 1874. He started out his professional career as an educator and began using photography as an educational tool, through his acquaintance with Frank A. Manny, a professor of education and psychology, at the Ethical Culture School in New York City. Both men were interested in studying the immigrant tide flowing through Ellis Island at the turn of the century, and Manny assisted Hine in taking some of his first successful pictures.

In the meantime, Edgar Gardner Murphy, an Episcopal clergyman in Montgomery, Alabama, and the founder of the Alabama Child Labor Committee, had pioneered the use of photography in the anti-child-labor campaign. Around 1901, Murphy had smuggled a camera into some of Alabama's textile mills and produced a powerful pamphlet called *Pictures from the Mills.* When the child labor committees in Alabama and New York joined forces and founded the NCLC in 1904, Murphy was one of the movement's most influential figures. In 1906, Hine began photographing children at work for the NCLC on a freelance basis, and by 1908 his passion for photography replaced his teaching career.

The images Hine captured for the NCLC left a deep impression not just because of the emotional topic, but also thanks to Hine's aesthetic sensibilities. In order to obtain the photographs, Hine defied difficult circumstances. His photographic equipment—a modified box-type 5" x 7" camera—weighed up to 50 pounds and the explosive magnesium flash-powder used in interior settings could be quite dangerous. (Apparently, Jacob Riis, a famous contemporary social reform photographer, twice set the places he was photographing on fire.)

Hine's entry was not welcomed at the mills, mines, or factories. He often had to pass as a fire inspector, an insurance salesman, a Bible salesman, or an industrial photographer. To document the specific cases of child labor, he surreptitiously wrote notes in the notebook he kept in his pocket, and he used the buttons on his jacket to measure the children's height. He directed his attention to the particular industries or trades that the NCLC targeted: coal mines, glass factories, Southern and Northern textile mills, seafood canneries, street trades (newsboys and messengers), and agriculture. All in all, he took over 5,000 photographs for the NCLC.

By 1918, the NCLC decided to focus more on the investigative work than on photography, and Hine moved on to other projects. He photographed the Red Cross's efforts at the end of World War I, created a series on men at work, participated in photography projects during the New Deal, and documented the construction of the Empire State building. But commissions for his work declined in the last decade of his life, and he died in poverty in 1940.

for export to the United States. But children in export manufacturing industries represent only a tiny share of all child labor.

About 120 million children 5 to 14 years of age work full-time in the developing world. If part-time work is included, the number of children working grows to 250 million. Even this figure is probably an underestimate because it excludes unpaid work that does not make its way into the market, such as the work of children—particularly girls—who stay home to do household chores or watch over younger siblings. Probably less than 5 percent of all child workers are employed in export industries in manufacturing and mining, according to the U.S. Department of Labor. The vast majority of children who work—over 70 percent—do so in agriculture.

The best predictor of the incidence of child labor is poverty. Child labor declines steeply as one moves from low-income to high-income countries, notes Princeton economist Alan Krueger. Asia, the most densely populated region of the world, has the largest number of child workers, but it is in poverty-stricken Africa where the highest proportion of children work. About 20 percent of African children aged 5 to 14 work full-time—a little under 40 million children. Eighty million children work if part-time work is included. In countries where 1990 income per capita exceeded $5,000, the employment of children was negligible, says Krueger.

The relationship between poverty and child labor is also true within countries. A range of studies in settings as varied as contemporary Côte d'Ivoire and nineteenth century Philadelphia have found that the incidence of child labor decreases as family income rises. Because of this, many believe that economic growth—if evenly distributed—is a key factor in reducing child labor.

Yet, the issue is not just poverty. Cultural factors also play an important role. In many instances, whether a child works or not depends on such factors as gender, religion, or social caste. In his work on child labor in India, MIT political scientist Myron Weiner pointed out that India's incidence of child labor was higher than that of some countries with lower income per capita. He speculated that religious beliefs and India's hierarchical caste system have prevented education from playing an equalizing role in society. "Those who control the education system are remarkably indifferent to the low enrollment and high dropout rate among the lowest social classes," he writes. "The result is one of the highest child labor rates in the world."

In terms of work hazards, children are more susceptible to injuries or work-related illnesses than adults doing the same type of work. The greatest number of illnesses and injuries occur in agriculture, not surprisingly, given the number of children working in that sector. But the likelihood of injury is by far the greatest for children who work in construction and mining, sectors that employ about 3 percent of working children.

Children also tend to work very long hours, leaving little time for school even when it is available. In surveys of 20 countries, the ILO found that in some countries more than half of the children who worked were doing so for nine or more hours per day and up to four-fifths of them did it seven days a week. But evidence on the relationship between school and work is mixed. In a study of child labor in Côte d'Ivoire, World Bank economist Christian Grootaeert found that working actually allowed many children to attend (afford) school.

LEARNING FROM THE UNITED STATES

The plight of working children in the developing world today is not very different, and in some cases even less harsh, than that prevalent in countries such as the United States and England during the nineteenth and early twentieth centuries. As recently as 1900, the U.S. Census estimated that 1.75 million children between the ages of 10 and 15 were employed—about 18 percent of the population that age. The majority of these children worked in agriculture. But young children also worked long hours in factories and textile mills, in the anthracite coal mines of Pennsylvania, and in many other industries.

Yet, the contrast between then and now is dramatic. Today, we take for granted that full-time work for children is bad; but in the early eighteenth century, work was believed to be beneficial for a child's character and moral upbringing. The work of children was integral to the agricultural and handicraft economy. Children and not wives were the most common source of family income aside from what fathers earned. They not only worked on the family farm, but also were often hired out to other farmers.

By the early 1800s, with the beginning of the Industrial Revolution, children went into the factory. New machines raised their productivity and also generated a growing demand for their labor. Economists Claudia Goldin and Kenneth Sokoloff estimate that boys and girls under 15 years of age accounted for 23 percent of all workers in manufacturing in the Northeast in 1820. The work of minors was so important to rising industry that Goldin and Sokoloff have speculated that the availability of relatively cheaper labor from women and children gave the Northeast a comparative advantage over the South, and was one of the factors that facilitated for the region's greater industrial development. (Women in the preindustrial South earned considerably higher wages than their counterparts in the North, according to Goldin and Sokoloff, because they were more productive in southern crops, such as cotton and tobacco, than in the hay, grains, and dairy products produced in the North.)

Child labor laws have been more effective when combined with compulsory education

But as children started working in the mills, the nature of their work changed dramatically. No longer were children working on family farms or in small workshops, but rather on factory floors in repetitive motions, for extremely long hours, with dangerous machinery and often abusive supervisors. Public acceptance of children in work began to change. At the same time, the social view of children was shifting and people began to believe that child's play and leisure were not vices but important aspects to healthy development. Also, as infant mortality rates diminished, parents moved from having many children to having fewer, but investing more in their success.

By the end of the nineteenth century, child labor was clearly on the decline. Social opposition to child labor became organized and very active in demanding legislation to limit the employment of minors. The National Child Labor Committee, founded in 1904, pioneered techniques of mass political action. It hired photographer Lewis Hine to capture the poor conditions of children at work and widely distributed his influential photographs.

Major legislative change took place between 1880 and 1910, during which time 36 states set legal limits on the minimum age of workers in manufacturing—14 years, on average. Finally, a federal law setting a national minimum standard of employment for children was passed in 1938 (see sidebar).

The relative contribution of laws, economic development, and cultural change in reducing child labor is a matter of debate. Between 1880 and 1900, there was a perception that the proportion of children in manufacturing was increasing and this helped fuel the movement for reform. But even though child labor might have increased in the cotton mills of the South and in industries that employed the growing flow of impoverished European immigrants, economists today believe that the fraction of the industrial labor force composed of youth had actually been declining throughout the latter part of the nineteenth century. They attribute this in part to rising incomes, which had made it possible for families to depend less on the income earned by their children. Additionally, new technologies requiring more highly skilled workers led to a decrease in the demand for the unskilled labor of children and to an increase in the returns to education.

Thus, Ohio State University economist Carolyn Moehling believes today that minimum age limits had relatively little effect on the employment of children at the turn of the century. In this view, increasing wealth and changing technology were more directly responsible for the reduction in child labor. Laws helped to cap a process that was already under way. Indeed, the passage of laws banning child labor was possible because there no longer was fervent opposition from parents and industry groups.

But, regardless of whether laws or economic progress led the change, there is widespread agreement that legislation was more effective in bringing about a decline in child labor when combined with compulsory education. Vanderbilt economists Robert Margo and T. Aldrich Finnegan found that, in turn-of-the century America, compulsory education laws had a significant impact in increasing school attendance only in states that also had child labor laws for children of the same age. They speculate that child labor laws reduced the incentive to seek paid employment and in many cases required children to satisfy educational requirements before starting to work. At the same time, it is easier to monitor and enforce school attendance than to oversee the absence of children from each individual workplace.

The importance of each factor contributing to the decline—laws, rising incomes, and changing production technology—likely varied from region to region and from industry to industry. For example, economists Martin Brown, Jens Christiansen, and Peter Philips found that economic factors played a more significant role than legislation in eliminating child labor in the canning industry in urban areas, but laws had a greater impact in rural ones.

As canneries became more mechanized, they required more steady, reliable labor to maximize the use of the equipment, and children became less desirable as workers. Because of this, child labor declined substantially in urban canneries, which made high investments in capital equipment and whose profitability depended on running the machines continuously and working on a variety of crops year-round. In contrast, rural canneries were smaller-scale and specialized in canning the local crop. They had access to a more limited labor pool and had a much more seasonal schedule of production. Both factors made them highly dependent on child labor during peak production times. Thus, in rural areas more exemptions and qualifications to the laws were passed. But ultimately, the legal restrictions weighed more heavily in reducing child labor there than in urban canneries, where the economics of more capital-intensive production had already diminished its use.

ONE SIZE DOES NOT FIT ALL

Just as the importance of different forces varied across individual industries and regions of the United States, there is a consensus in the field that no one solution to the child labor problem can be applied to all countries. What can be done to eliminate child labor will vary, depending on the level and distribution of income, the availability of education, and the cultural factors that influence child labor.

For the poorest of countries, it maybe impossible to really eliminate child labor without income growth or some form of international aid. But for countries with relatively more resources, a range of policy alternatives can help bring about change. "Government can intervene in the market to create a variety of incentives, such as providing better and more schools, giving school meals, and improving conditions in the adult labor market, which result in a reduction of child labor," says Cornell economist Kaushik Basu.

What is to be done depends on the educational infrastructure in place. The American example clearly showed that education played a key role. Better educated workers in the United States were more productive and thus were better able to provide for their own children, reducing the need for child labor. And, taking children out of the labor force may help them only if you provide them with a better alternative.

Export goods are only the tip of the iceberg when it comes to child labor. Perhaps international pressure will help bring about a change in the perception of child labor in countries where it is accepted as an integral part of life. But, for the permanent elimination of child labor, a cultural change ultimately has to come from within developing countries.

Looking to the past gives hope for the future. Child labor, once endemic in countries like the United States and Great Britain, has been greatly reduced there. The process was long, and involved sustained change on many different fronts. But the payoff was worth the effort, for it is hard to build a strong future with such small hands.

TRADE IN THE AMERICAS: All in the familia

This weekend's summit in Quebec will concentrate on the creation of a Free-Trade Area of the Americas. The Bush administration is all for it; South America's biggest economy, Brazil, is not so sure

Sao Paulo and Washington, DC

AT THEIR meeting last month to prepare for the 34-country summit of the Americas this weekend, President George Bush kept a promise to look a sceptical President Fernando Henrique Cardoso of Brazil in the eye and swear that the United States really wants free trade. Brazil, by far South America's largest economy, has so far shown little enthusiasm for talking about a Free-Trade Area of the Americas (FTAA). It is doubtful, not least, because it does not believe Mr Bush can overcome free trade's opponents in the United States; and because a watered-down or hobbled FTAA might be worse than no agreement at all.

Mr Bush shows every sign of being keen as mustard on free trade. His trade representative, Robert Zoellick, is even keener. Mr Bush wants to pursue free trade on three levels: bilateral deals with single trading partners, regional pacts such as the FTAA, and global negotiations in the World Trade Organisation (WTO). This makes for a lot of irons in the fire. Getting his wish, however, will depend on exactly the things Brazil is worried about: his capacity to stand up to domestic industries begging for protection, and his ability to get fast-track authority—now renamed Trade Promotion Authority, or TPA—from Congress. Getting that will depend on how persuasively he can sell his policies to Americans at large.

Mr Zoellick, who litters his speeches with quotes from his boss as though he were Chairman Mao, sees the FTAA as the key to regaining momentum for trade policy. He thinks Bill Clinton lost it by failing to obtain the renewal of fast-track power and by presiding over the meltdown in the global trade talks in Seattle in 1999. The FTAA is as good a place as any to get trade policy moving forward again—if, that is, the neighbours can be made to agree.

The draft agreement for the FTAA already exists; it was prepared at a meeting of trade ministers in Buenos Aires earlier this month, though it will not be made public until the summit is over. A framework similar to that of the North American Free-Trade Agreement (NAFTA) between the United States, Canada and Mexico would be extended southwards, with negotiations to finish by January 2005 and implementation to follow by the end of that year. The FTAA would open a free-trade umbrella over nearly 800m people who accounted for more than $11 trillion in GDP last year. If its effects proved to be anything like NAFTA's, the whole continent would be in for a trade boom.

It will be quite a challenge, however, to reach an agreement acceptable to all 34 countries. (Cuba is excluded at the United States' insistence and French Guiana, since it is officially part of France, is not taking part.) Historically, the continent's more far-flung countries have not made much effort to trade with each other, tending instead to do business with their former colonial masters in Europe. (The banana war, the most contentious result of that policy, was resolved last week. In the 1990s, economic liberalisation and the formation of regional trade blocks such as NAFTA and Mercosur (Brazil, Argentina, Uruguay and Paraguay) meant that trade within the continent grew faster than GDP and faster than world trade in general (see chart) but South America's markets are still less open than those of the Asian tigers.

Suspicions in Brazil

Until recently, Brazil was trying to get its South American neighbours to join it in foot-dragging over the FTAA, or at least to

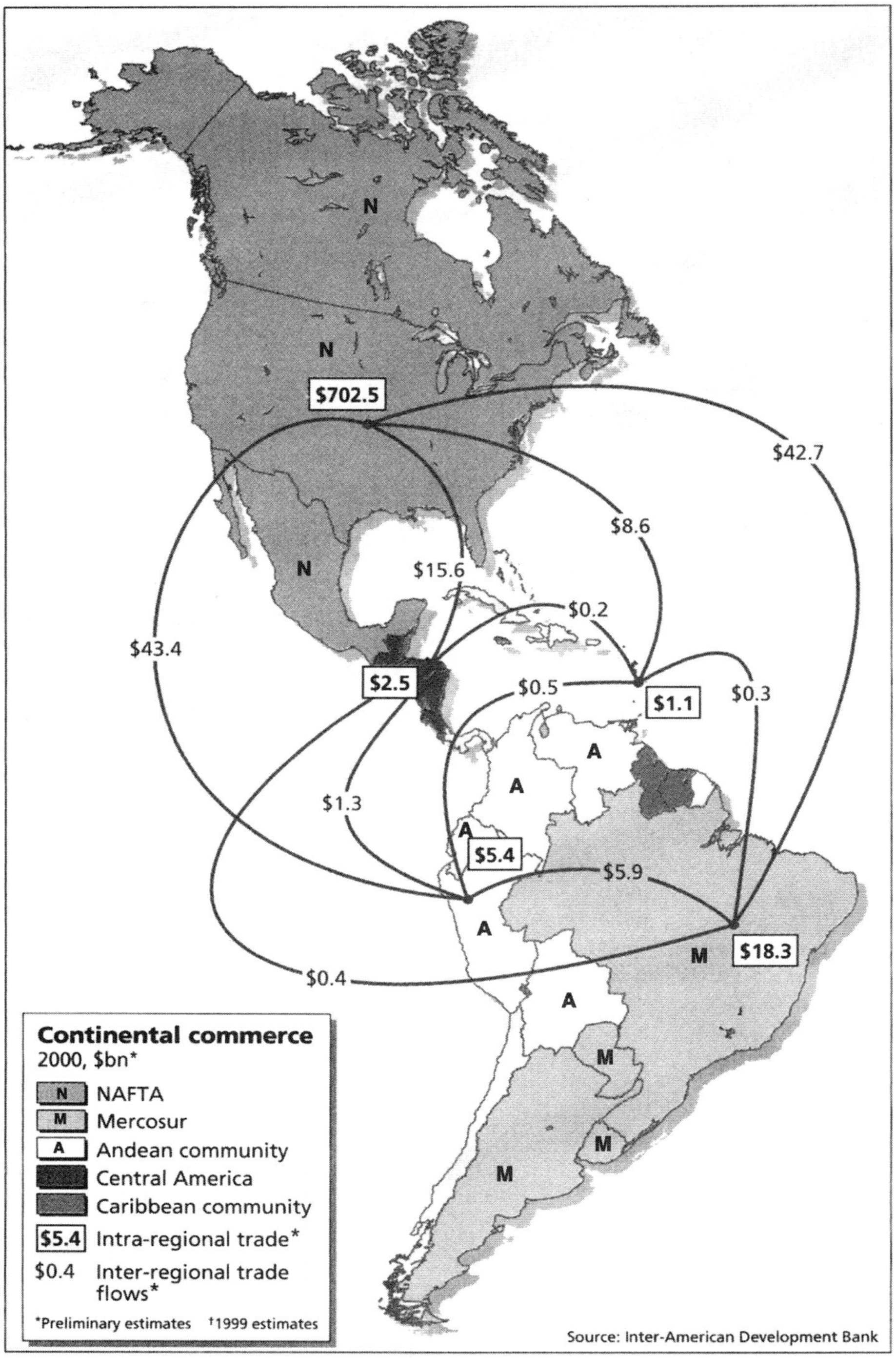

form a united front to take a tough line with the United States. But its strategy has flopped as its neighbours have become ever more enticed by the idea of improved access to the world's biggest consumer market. The United States has been dangling this prospect skilfully in front of the other countries. Chile's president, Ricardo Lagos, was invited to the White House this week to hear from Mr Bush that a bilateral trade deal between them could be signed as early as this year. Argentina and Uruguay have taken the bait, and have made it clear that any blockage in the FTAA talks would not stop them from doing some other sort of deal with the United States.

As a result, Brazil has come round to the view that, since everyone else wants the talks to go ahead, it might as well join in and seek the best deal it can. One of the most important signs of its change of attitude was the sacking, this month, of Samuel Pinheiro Guimaraes, the head of the foreign ministry's think-tank and a fierce critic of the FTAA. This week, Celso Lafer, the foreign minister, attacked the "ostrich mentality" of those in Brazil, such as his former subordinate, who oppose its participation in the talks. And he admitted, more frankly than any senior Brazilian figure has so far, that his country risks losing much of its existing trade if the rest of the Americas rushes to sign a deal without it.

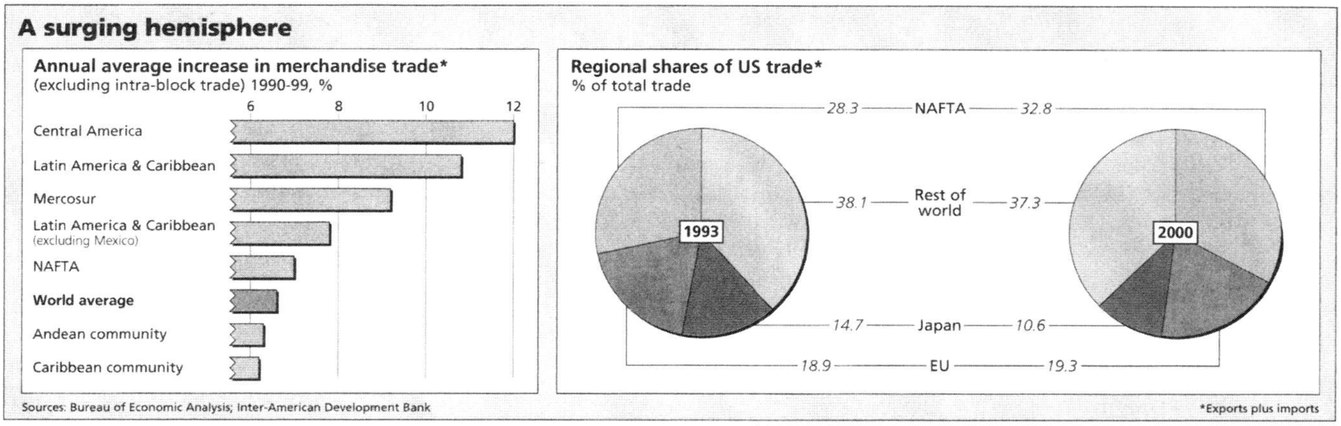

Brazil's businesses have suddenly realised that the FTAA is now more than a remote hypothesis and that they ought to be preparing for it. The country's National Confederation of Industry (CNI) has just completed, though not yet published, its first studies of the impact Americas-wide free trade could have on Brazilian industry. Sandra Rios, an economist at the CNI, says there is not yet a consensus that the FTAA would be good for Brazil overall. But whereas, until recently, only those who feared freer trade were making their voices heard, industries that stand to gain are now speaking up in favour of the talks.

One such is the textile industry, which believes its exports of T-shirts and towels to the United States would be far greater if America lifted its import quotas. The Brazilian Textile Industry Association is so keen on the FTAA that it is calling for it to start sooner than 2006—much to the irritation of the Brazilian government, which successfully fought in Buenos Aires this month to stop the United States from bringing forward the date. Other areas where Brazil is highly competitive, and would thus benefit from freer trade, are agriculture, especially beef and soyabeans, steel-making and ceramics.

Some Brazilian industries that fear being wiped out by North American competitors, such as chemicals and paper-making, have mostly themselves to blame. They have failed to merge and restructure to reach world-class competitiveness. They claim they cannot find affordable finance to do so, but Brazilian companies would find it much easier to attract investors if they undid their complicated holding structures and generally treated minority shareholders better. There is plenty of time to do all this by the FTAA's proposed starting date; just as there is plenty of time for the government to boost the export prospects of all Brazil's industries by pushing reforms of the country's burdensome tax system.

Those industries with most to fear from free trade, such as machinery and electronic goods, are precisely those that successive Brazilian governments have coddled with protectionist tariffs, arguing that this would give them breathing-space to grow big enough to take on foreign rivals. As a result, they have been under little pressure to seek world-class productivity, technology and marketing, and have not bothered. The failure of this strategy is a riposte to the arguments of Mr Guimaraes (the sacked diplomat) and the left-wing Workers' Party, who say that joining the FTAA would mean forgoing independent trade and industrial policies and thus being unable to build competitive industries.

Brazil's neighbours have become increasingly sceptical of such arguments. Argentina is abandoning Mercosur's common tariffs pact and abolishing import duties on machinery because it believes these have served only to prop up inefficient Brazilian firms while preventing Argentine industry from introducing new technology. Francisco Panizza, a Uruguayan political scientist, argues that pleas from Brazilian industries for "time to adjust" are absurd, given that many such industries have been in existence for half a century or more.

Besides, says Heinz-Peter Elstrodt of McKinsey, a management consultancy, many of the Brazilian industries that are, overall, lagging behind include some firms that are close to world-class productivity, and others that are so far behind they may never catch up. The best firms should survive, even with new competition. The worst, unless they adapt, will die out. Brazil's car industry is an example of this, with its newer, more efficient plants expected to drive out older, unproductive ones. But this process is beneficial, and is happening anyway. The FTAA would simply speed it up.

Protective instincts

Brazil's greatest fear is that the United States is plotting to stop it from becoming a big exporter of high-value manufactured goods and to make it return to its historic role of churning out low-value commodities. This is not entirely paranoia. The United States currently applies a whole range of duties, quotas, price restraints and other measures to processed items from Brazil. Some of these will be politically difficult for Mr Bush to negotiate away.

In fact, of course, Mr Bush's America is something less than a bastion of free trade. It gives subsidies to farmers (though these are generally much reduced from their levels of a decade ago) and has imposed "anti-dumping" measures to protect steel-makers. Only last month, the debilitated American steel industry begged for extra protection from foreign competition while it restructures and updates itself. Last week's merger of NKK and Kawasaki Steel, two Japanese giants, will only enhance congressional pressure to enact emergency tariffs.

Even within NAFTA, American protectionism is by no means dead. With the expiration on March 31st of a five-year agreement on trade in softwood lumber between the United States and Canada, which amounts to roughly $10 billion a year, American producers have filed for anti-dumping measures against Canada's government-supported exporters. Disputes on dairy products and sugar could also flare up if import volumes rise. To make matters worse, Canada is embroiled in a lawsuit, brought by its postal workers' union and an anti-globalisation group, that threatens to invalidate NAFTA on the basis that it infringes Canada's sovereignty.

The toughest obstacle to true free trade is public opinion, both in the United States and in its trading partners in the Americas. Radical opposition to globalisation at grassroots level continues to grab headlines; 20,000 demonstrators are expected in Quebec city this weekend. Non-governmental organisations in the United States still shriek about jobs lost to NAFTA, even though unemployment fell to its lowest levels in decades—well below the supposedly "natural" rate—during the life of the agreement. The gap in understanding has not narrowed noticeably since the protests in Seattle.

It is in this climate that Mr Bush and Mr Zoellick must try to extract TPA from Congress. This power would allow Mr Zoellick and his team (when he has finally got it in place) to negotiate trade deals in full and then present them to Congress for a vote. He has pointed enviously to similar powers vested in the European Union's trade commissioner. The EU has signed 20 substantial pacts since 1990, and has 15 more on the way; over the same period the United States has ratified only two, with four more in the works. Although the United States has never shown a predilection for European-style agreements based on customs unions, the contrast is a stark one.

The fight for TPA, though, is likely to be long. Congress wants to attach provisions requiring Mr Zoellick to seek labour and environmental standards as part of trade agreements. These have featured in previous fast-track authorisations, but Mr Bush is dead-set against them. Developing countries also object to these standards, which they say could open avenues to protection against their exports. Cal Dooley, a Democrat in the House of Representatives who worked closely with Mr Zoellick's predecessor, Charlene Barshefsky, thinks that TPA could become a reality in the next 18 months. But he also says that the current Congress is not ready to take any dramatic decisions to promote freer trade.

This week, Mr Zoellick began meeting business and non-governmental interest groups in an effort to start persuading American dissenters. He has promised to use the Internet to spread his message of free trade. The black and Latino media, representing groups who are traditionally wary of losing jobs to cheap foreign labour, are also likely to get visits from Mr Zoellick. Lastly, he promises that the president will address the country about the importance of trade in due time. As Mr Clinton found during the arguments over NAFTA in the early 1990s, it is not a particularly easy pitch to make.

Given these difficulties on the American side, Brazil still talks of the FTAA as merely one of several options. It argues that Mercosur's parallel talks on a free-trade deal with the European Union have at least as much potential to boost Brazil's trade. This is true, but the talks with the EU are at least as likely as the FTAA ones to founder on the issue of farm protection. As for its other option, a deepened and widened Mercosur, this seems a receding prospect: if the FTAA talks were to fail, the main priority for Brazil's current Mercosur partners, as well as potential members such as Chile and the Andean countries, would be to seek the best possible deal with the United States. The alternative would be to fortify a southern trade block that most feel, rightly or wrongly, has brought more benefits to Brazil than to them in the ten years it has been in existence.

The United States, too, has other options. Abandoning the warm and conciliatory (if often empty) rhetoric of the post-Seattle Clinton era, the new administration has adopted a cocky, take-it-or-leave-it attitude towards its trading partners. Messrs Bush and Zoellick hold the keys to the biggest market in the world, and they know it.

Mr Zoellick has repeatedly stated that the United States is interested in working with fast-moving traders, but will leave laggards by the side of the road. With respect to the FTAA, he says, "We will reward good performers, and while we want to bring on others in the region, we won't wait for ever."

The administration's multi-pronged trade policy fits well with this reluctance to curry favour with other countries. Its strategy might be as follows: if WTO negotiations are going too slowly, then concentrate on the FTAA; if the FTAA bogs down, sign bilateral deals with enthusiastic parties such as Chile. Mr Bush's trade policy echoes his overall approach to foreign affairs. Friendly neighbours are welcome; sceptics need not even knock. Brazil, the third-biggest economy in what Mr Bush likes to call "the hemispheric *familia*", will get some sort of trade deal with the United States; but full free trade can wait until Brazil really wants it.

Ready for a Rebound?

Fears of a recession are subsiding but questions linger about Europe's recovery

Bruce Barnard

The European Union's high-risk gamble on a common currency is facing a critical moment as the twelve member countries of the euro zone struggle to grow their economies against the backdrop of a global slowdown that could easily slide into recession. The stakes were raised on January 1 when the euro ceased being a virtual money as bills and coins entered circulation replacing all twelve domestic currencies as legal tender at the end of February.

The EU is embarking on a huge and unprecedented experiment at a time when the national euro-zone economies have almost ground to a halt and are unlikely to start growing again until the second half of the year. After expanding by 3.4 percent in 2000, the fastest rate in a decade, the euro zone grew by only 1.6 percent in 2001 and almost skidded to a halt toward the end of the year. Worse, Germany, the euro zone's locomotive economy accounting for a third of its output, turned in the worst performance, growing a miserly 0.6 percent last year, the smallest rise since the recession of 1993 when its GDP shrank by 1.1 percent.

Fears have eased that the euro zone would slide into recession after the September 11 terrorist attacks in the US deepened the global slowdown that started six months earlier. However, much uncertainty remains about the size, timing, and durability of the recovery.

There are gaping differences between the generally more optimistic government forecasts and the more bearish predictions of private bankers, industrialists, and investment fund managers. The Italian government claims recovery began in January and is forecasting real gross domestic product will grow by 2.3 percent in 2002 following an estimated gain of 1.8 percent in 2001. That is far greater than the Organization for Economic Cooperation and Development's 1.2 percent forecast, which is backed by private economists. France's independent economists reckon the economy will probably expand by 1.3 percent this year, well below government estimates.

The economic slowdown is providing the first big test for the euro zone because its members have given up two key economic instruments—varying domestic interest rates and devaluing national currencies—that were traditionally used to manage and fine-tune national economies. This wasn't a big problem when the euro zone was enjoying relatively strong growth following the euro's launch in January 1999, but the downside has become more apparent as governments watch slowing growth ratchet up jobless rates. The EU average is around 8.5 percent, while Germany and France, the two largest economies, are in danger of heading back toward 10 percent.

The euro zone defused its first potential major crisis earlier in the year after it became clear that Germany's budget deficit in 2002 is moving within an ace of breaching the ceiling of 3 percent of GDP that could trigger massive fines running into billions of euros under the EU's so-called "stability and growth pact." Only four euro-zone countries—Austria, Belgium, Finland, and the Netherlands—backed the attempt by Pedro Solbes, the EU finance commissioner, to issue Germany with a formal "early warning." Portugal, which was also under threat from the Commission, was let off the hook too.

Although the crisis was defused after Germany gave solemn commitments that it will not breach the 3 percent limit, the episode has soured relations between Berlin and Brussels.

Ironically, Germany was the main architect of the stability pact, which was designed to ensure that countries like Italy that have a history of irresponsible fiscal policies and a weak currency would not undermine the euro. However, Germany is the only EU country that has overshot its deficit target, which is agreed upon with the EU, for two successive years. While Germany remains the "sick man" of Europe, signs have emerged recently that its economy finally is recovering from last year's recession, with its export-oriented firms set to benefit from quickening economic growth in the United States.

On the plus side, the changeover to euro notes and coins proceeded almost flawlessly, and the new money is well established with retailers and consumers. The European Central Bank says the switch to euros could have a negative short-term impact on inflation, but increased competition between businesses will lower prices in the longer run.

The arrival of the "real" euro is already having a positive impact on company strategy. For example, Japan's Canon, one of the world's biggest manufacturers of cameras and photocopiers, says it will cut its European distribution costs by 20 percent in the next two years partly due to changes linked to the introduction of the new currency. Using the same currency across most of Europe, coupled with moves to harmonize prices, will allow the firm to halve the number of European warehouses, which, added to lower costs for administration and handling orders, could deliver savings up to $263 million a year.

Many believe the euro likely will strengthen this year, recouping some of its 25 percent loss in value against the dollar since its launch on January 1, 1999. The decline largely was due to the huge outflow of funds across the Atlantic—euro-zone companies and investors spent more than $450 billion making acquisitions or buying bonds and stocks in the US over the past three years. But cash began flowing in the other direction in the second half of 2001, with nearly $90 billion net moving into euro-zone equities between July and November, and the inflow is continuing as investors question whether the US economy has really bottomed out.

Not that a weak euro has done much damage to the euro-zone members. In fact, it has made their products more competitive on world markets, especially compared with dollar-priced goods. Its weaknesses helped German exports grow by 5.1 percent in 2001 when world trade was faltering, following a 13.2 percent surge in 2000.

The struggle to qualify for euro membership also has made several EU countries much better placed to survive the global economic downturn. Spain's radical program of privatization, deregulation, and labor market reform, coupled with cuts in public spending, launched by Prime Minister Jose Maria Aznar when he came to power in 1996 has transformed the country into one of the EU's fastest-growing economies, which is responsible for one of every four new jobs created in Europe over the past five years.

While the euro zone's core economies, especially Germany and Italy, have performed poorly, its smaller members have prospered, partly because they have embraced deregulation and labor market reforms. Ireland remains among the fastest expanding Western economies after a decade of explosive growth, the Netherlands has shaved unemployment to just more than 2 percent, and Finland displaced the US as the world's most competitive economy in the latest annual rankings by the World Economic Forum. Meanwhile, Europe's star economy, the United Kingdom, isn't a member of the euro zone and is unlikely to join for at least four to five years, if at all. It grew faster than the other leading G7 economies in 2001 for the first time since 1986 and looks set to stay ahead in 2002.

A Stronger Euro for Europe?

PARIS—Big financial-services firms almost never air internal disagreements in public. But Morgan Stanley recently published conflicting reports on whether the 12 European nations that use the euro common currency need a dose of "tough love"—specifically a stronger euro—to force the kind of changes that many investors and economists deem are necessary if the Continent is to become more efficient and competitive.

That anyone is calling for a stronger euro might seem incredible, given that European executives have been complaining that the euro's 39% rise against the dollar in the past 2 1/2 years already has put them at a competitive disadvantage in the global marketplace.

Investors in European stocks, too, have been wary. The euro's surge in the past year and the toll it has taken on European corporate profits has been part of the reason why European stock markets haven't done much so far in 2004.

The question of whether a stronger euro ultimately would be good for Europe gets to the heart of an important question for the Continent's future: Can an area of 307 million people plagued by low growth, stubbornly high unemployment, insufficient productivity, rigid labor and product markets and bloated public-pension and health-care systems compete globally?

If it can, investors will reward European companies by purchasing their stock. If not, they'll go elsewhere. Now, some are arguing that one way to push Europe into grappling with its problems before it's too late is a higher euro—unpleasant medicine, in other words, to heal the patient.

"Just as the world learned to live without Japan [in the 1990s], global investors now appear resigned to living without Europe," Morgan Stanley Chief Economist Stephen Roach told clients in a recent report. "Yet another outbreak of 'Eurosclerosis' has left dreams of pan-regional vitality in tatters."

He acknowledges that the 10 new, low-wage EU member countries will increase labor competition in Europe. Still, the Morgan Stanley economist wants to "tighten the noose" further by letting "the markets take over and push the euro up to a level where it hurts, leaving Europe with no choice other than the heavy lifting of structural reforms." A stronger euro would squeeze exports—which have been the bulwark of the euro-zone's fragile recovery—and domestic industries that compete with imports.

Last year, Germany made progress on welfare and labor-market changes, while France pushed through small changes to its pension system. But "since then, the appetite for large-scale reform has waned," says Edward Teather, a European economist at UBS in London. However, on Friday, the German parliament is expected to pass deep cuts in social benefits.

Noting that "European governments are having to run to stand still in the face of pressures from competition globally and demographic change," Mr. Teather, like Mr. Roach, argues that more structural reform is needed. External pressure could aid reform, he says. But he also warns that a stronger euro will hurt "externally exposed industries."

Adds Val Koromzay, director for country studies at the Organization for Economic Development and Cooperation in Paris: "The most realistic reform scenario is to wait for things to get so bad that there is no other option."

The perception that Europe is falling behind has dogged the performance of its stock markets for years. From Nov. 9, 1989, the day the Berlin Wall fell—freeing Western Europe from Communism's long shadow—through Tuesday, the German stock market rallied 106%; French shares rose 136%; and Italian stocks advanced 104%. By contrast, the Dow Jones Industrial Average soared 292%, while the Nasdaq Composite Index surged 332%.

In theory, European Economic and Monetary Union—which formally began on Jan. 1, 1999, but had been in the works for years—was supposed to create an integrated, efficient single market, honed by harmonized regulations and anchored by a common currency, administered by a single central bank.

Reality has turned out to be quite different. From 1989 through 2003, economic growth for the 12 countries averaged 1.95% a year, compared with 2.89% for the U.S. During the past three years, the zone has grown a mere 1% a year, barely more than half Uncle Sam's 1.9% pace. Euro-area seasonally-adjusted unemployment stands at 9%, compared with 5.6% for the U.S.

Meanwhile, Germany, France and Italy's lack of fiscal discipline has made a mockery of the European Union's Stability and Growth Pact, which limits deficits to 3% of gross domestic product.

The explanations for Europe's resistance to change are numerous. For one, the Continent is a very wealthy economy, which isn't yet feeling significant pain from not having changed. There are also many vested interests that would stand to lose from widespread overhauls, such as labor unions, farmers, pensioners, the unemployed and under-employed, recipients of free health care and so on. "Many Europeans are proud of the social-welfare systems that have been built up over the last 50 years or so and are reluctant to see them dismantled," says Mark Cliffe, chief economist at ING Financial Markets in London.

History shows that it usually takes a crisis to prompt broad-based changes. That was the case in Scandinavia at the start of the 1990s and the Netherlands and New Zealand in the 1980s. Noting that it took the 1980-1981 recession for Britain to achieve the full effects of Prime Minister Margaret Thatcher's changes, Mr. Cliffe says many analysts argue European countries need their "Maggie moment."

Still, other economists, including some at Morgan Stanley, are skeptical that Mr. Roach's strong-euro medicine qualifies. Eric Chaney, one of the firm's European economists, contends that a stronger euro would "backfire" by subsidizing sectors of the economy that don't compete with imports, such as government services, the retail industry and consumer services—"precisely where European rigidities are the most deeply rooted."

Stephen Jen, Morgan Stanley's chief currency economist, also disagrees with his boss. "If inflicting pain on Euroland is the best way to kick-start structural reforms, the policy makers could also consider premature fiscal and/or monetary tightening, just to make it more painful for the Europeans," he says.

Adding that Europe's problems partly reflect the different values that Europeans, Americans and Asians place on work and leisure, Mr. Jen says that such biases are very hard to change, "certainly not through an even more overvalued euro."

Write to Michael R. Sesit at michael.sesit@wsj.com

Competition and Business Entry in Russia

Despite privatization, robust competition is still lacking in much of Russia's industrial sector, stifled by excessive concentration, vertical integration, and geographic segmentation. Many established firms enjoy protection from new (and potential) rivals. Reforming anticompetitive business structures and lowering barriers to entry are key to Russia's post-privatization reform program.

Harry G. Broadman

Since the start of reforms in 1992, significant progress has been made in many areas of the Russian economy. Price controls have been lifted on more than 90 percent of wholesale and retail goods, and most state-owned enterprises have been privatized, to varying degrees. But Russia has not yet restructured the dominant firms in its industrial sector (although some restructuring has taken place—especially in the import-substitution sector—since the devaluation of the ruble in 1998). Nor has it eliminated administrative barriers that hinder new domestic and foreign firms from entering the Russian market. Indeed, the scarcity of de novo private firms in Russia is particularly striking in comparison with other transition economies.

There remains considerable potential for abuse of market power, not only in Russia's infrastructure monopoly ("utility") sector (this potential is widely acknowledged, and the government's structural reform agenda includes policy initiatives designed to reduce it) but also in the manufacturing ("nonutility") sector. Many manufacturing firms are shielded from competition because of structural and institutional impediments, including significant seller and buyer concentration—"horizontal dominance"—in regional markets, a high degree of vertical integration and exclusive buyer-seller relationships in certain industrial sectors, geographic segmentation, interregional barriers to trade and investment, and policies that make entry difficult for new firms. These impediments are more pronounced in Russia than in other transition economies. Although the ownership of many enterprises has changed hands thanks to privatization, the industrial configuration established by administrative fiat and central planning during the Soviet era is still largely entrenched, and a new industrial sector in which competitive market forces determine corporate behavior has yet to emerge fully.

Excessive horizontal and vertical consolidation and high entry barriers in Russia's industrial sector have negative consequences for the Russian consumer, for rechanneling enterprise assets to more productive uses, and for the development of the Russian economy: (1) high prices, reduced output, and diminished product and service quality; (2) diminished incentives for transactions between regions, which hampers the development of a unified economic space; (3) reduced foreign investment in business; and (4) the stifling of innovation and technological advancement.

Structural dominance

At the national level, the degree of concentration of industrial output in Russia does not indicate that the lack of competition is a structural problem. The four-firm concentration ratio—that is, the sum of the market shares of the top four producers—in many industries averages about 60 percent, which is similar to that in the United States, and the largest Russian manufacturing enterprises (measured by number of employees) are not unusually large, compared with U.S. firms. However, this aggregate-level analysis of structural dominance masks three underlying attributes of Russia's industrial landscape.

First, large Russian enterprises tend to be configured as single, integrated, multiplant establishments often located in or near the same city, whereas enterprises in industrial countries usually have multiple establishments at several different locations domestically and, often, abroad as well. Thus, the establishments of the largest Russian enterprises are, on average, significantly larger (in terms of number of employees) than their counterparts in other countries, including the United States. Because of the limits of conventional measures of national market share and concentration, the true extent of horizontal dominance in many Russian markets is probably understated. Data on a variety of Russian sectors suggest that, at the oblast (regional) level, the average market share for a typical firm is about 45 percent and the average four-firm concentration ratio is greater than 95 percent. Although the existing level of horizontal integration in Russian manufacturing is largely a legacy of Soviet central planning, such integration appears to be increasing. The increase is due not to new corporate expansion, however, but to mergers and acquisitions.

Second, many of the dominant enterprises in Russia are also highly vertically integrated (or have exclusive buyer-seller relationships). Forty-six percent of the firms participating in a recent survey indicated that their customers purchased supplies from only one or two suppliers and that 23 percent of the suppliers controlled more than 65 percent of the relevant input market. To be sure, putting successive stages of production under one corporate roof can result in economies of scale and reduce transaction costs, as in the case of continuous steel-casting: it would be economically inefficient—if not technologically impossible—to have three separate firms heating iron ore, rolling it into ingots, and then producing the finished steel products. But in most industries, such vertical efficiencies exist only up to a point. Indeed, in many product markets throughout the world, it is increasingly cheaper for a firm to buy inputs (or sell outputs) on the open market or through arm's-length contracts than to produce them internally. In Russia, because the enforceability of contracts still cannot be taken for granted, there are strong incentives for vertical integration. The uncertainties and chronic shortages of the old Soviet supply system encouraged a high degree of vertical integration, which has persisted, in part, because of inertia. Moreover, vertical integration, like horizontal dominance, is increasing—again, usually through mergers and acquisitions rather than expansion. Importantly, excessive vertical integration superimposed on horizontally concentrated product markets can foreclose the entry of rival firms.

Third, significant political and economic power is wielded by regional authorities in Russia, a feature of other large transition economies, such as China. This is evident in the tight control of important economic activities within a region. Such control, in combination with vertical integration, helps freeze the high degree of structural autarky engendered under the Soviet system, when producing consumer goods was a local responsibility and enterprises served only local markets. Worse, it strengthens administrative—as opposed to economic—geographic market boundaries and fosters the regional segmentation of the Russian economy, hampering the establishment of a unified economic space, vigorous interregional competition, and natural economies of scale. Local authorities engage in a variety of practices to limit the interregional movement of goods and services, including charging duties on the "import" or "export" of certain alcoholic beverages; maintaining regional price controls on some agricultural products; imposing registration fees on workers from other oblasts; granting tax or credit preferences to support the building of local "business champions"; and supporting arbitrarily exclusive licensing. In this regard, it is telling that in recent years some of the most frequent violations dealt with by the Ministry of Antimonopoly Policy and Support for Entrepreneurship have been anticompetitive actions by local governments.

Barriers to new entrants

According to official estimates, in 2000 more than 70 percent of Russia's GDP came from the private sector, up from less than 10 percent just eight years earlier, at the start of reform. This is a remarkable achievement. But the expansion of Russia's private sector is due mainly to privatization of state-owned enterprises, not creation of new enterprises.

Most new entrants in Russia are owner-manager firms—mainly small and medium-sized enterprises. There are about one million registered small and medium-sized enterprises (generally defined as business establishments with fewer than 250 employees); they employ about 13 percent of the Russian labor force and produce about 12 percent of GDP. These figures, however, are likely to be inaccurate, because much small business activity is still in the informal economy and thus goes largely unreported. Nonetheless, in comparison with other transition countries, the growth of small and medium-sized enterprises in Russia has been exceptionally slow: the percentage of national employment accounted for by small and medium-sized enterprises is 37 percent in the Czech Republic, 58 percent in Georgia, and 37 percent in the former Yugoslav Republic of Macedonia. Importantly, the geographic distribution of small and medium-sized enterprises in Russia is highly skewed. Whereas Moscow and St. Petersburg account for 22 percent and 10 percent, respectively, of all small and medium-sized enterprises, 28 other regions account for only about 0.5 percent of the total each.

Evidence suggests that in many sectors, the principal constraints on entry by new private firms in Russia are the anticompetitive market structure and the anticompetitive conduct of existing dominant firms, which is often sanctioned or supported by local governments. In effect, incumbents do not leave enough structural economic space for new entrants to make a go of it.

Moreover, impediments to entry include the lack of competition in and poor quality of (state-owned or controlled) infrastructure services, as well as blocked access to warehousing and distribution channels; weak mechanisms for resolving commercial disputes; the lack of access to seed capital and competitively priced credit; the difficulty of obtaining suitable business premises and real estate; the absence of rules-based procedures for, and the complexity of, business licensing, registration, and inspections; and corruption and organized crime.

In the key infrastructure services—electricity, heating, natural gas supply and transmission, and rail transport—state-dominated monopolies still play a major role. In purchasing infrastructure inputs—if service hookups can even be arranged—manufacturing firms (particularly new, smaller ones) have little choice: there is usually only one supplier; pricing is not cost-based; and the quality of service is often poor. On the output side, manufacturing firms must deal with underdeveloped distribution or warehousing facilities outside the major Russian cities. The lack of refrigeration facilities is a particularly serious problem, making shipment of perishable products across regions extremely expensive. Many intercity roads are in poor condition, making long-haul trucking hazardous.

In Russia (as in most other transition economies), contracts are hard to verify and enforce. Private property rights are not secure and lack credibility. The lack of efficient methods for resolving commercial disputes substantially increases the cost of entry. Most businesspeople in Russia attempt to resolve differences among themselves rather than take cases to the overburdened courts. And if a company does go to court, enforcement of compensation for successful plaintiffs collecting debts is notoriously weak.

Persuading financial institutions to back start-up businesses can be challenging even in industrial countries; in transition economies, where capital market imperfections are pronounced and institutions that intermediate savings into investment capital are typically not yet fully developed, the problem is particularly acute. In Russia, bank loans for new businesses—if they are available at all—are short term (typically six months) and expensive. As a result, most start-ups of small and medium-sized enterprises are funded out of personal savings. According to the State Committee on Small Businesses, only 15 percent of small businesses in Russia have received bank credits in recent years.

Access to commercial real estate in Russia is often limited because of municipal administrations' monopoly ownership and control of urban land. In theory, enterprises have the right to privatize associated land plots; in practice, property rights and procedures are unclear. Less than 10 percent of the land under privatized enterprises has been privatized.

The average new business applicant in Russia must deal with a multitude of agencies at both the federal and the local levels and obtain approval of myriad registration and licensing forms. But new firms rarely consider these administrative barriers, however time consuming, to be the most problematic aspects of registering and licensing, conventional wisdom to the contrary. Indeed, firms that specialize in helping new businesses navigate the process have become a new growth industry. Far more onerous—although it has received much less attention—is the lack of uniformity in procedures and fees across regions, and the scope for discretionary conduct by licensing, registration, and inspection officials. In business surveys, it is typical to find that about one-third of questioned firms indicate they are forced to obtain a license that, in their opinion, was not legally required, and more than 10 percent indicate that they pay licensing and registration fees over the legal limit. It is therefore not surprising that the licensing and registration process is fertile ground for corruption. A not atypical anecdote has an entrepreneur paying the equivalent of $7,000 for a license, of which only $800 goes to the government.

Corruption as a barrier to business entry in Russia—as in many other transition economies—is pervasive: virtually all firms pay bribes to tax inspectors, customs officers, and a host of local bureaucrats who visit firms several times a year. The result is that, often, firms must increase staffing simply to deal with inspectors—a nonproductive activity. In addition, most enterprises have to pay organized criminal groups to survive; these groups' levies commonly start at 5 percent of profits but are often higher and are usually collected as flat monthly fees.

Agenda for reform of competition policy

As Russia's fiscal stance improves (in part because of higher oil prices) and budget constraints harden economy-wide—that is, as firms and government agencies engage in cash transactions, bills are paid on time, and subsidies (including direct budgetary support and indirect subsidies such as tax arrears that are not penalized) are eliminated—inefficient large enterprises will likely continue to decline in importance. But proactive structural reforms are needed to foster enduring competition.

One set of competition policies should focus on reforming anticompetitive incumbent enterprises. The thrust of these policies should include more effective demonopolization and disintegration of anticompetitive dominant firms; prohibition of mergers and acquisitions that reduce the number of sellers and increase structural dominance; penalties for business practices—such as collusion, price fixing, and predatory pricing—designed to drive out competitors or deter entrants; and protection of consumers from unfair trade and false advertising practices. In the advanced countries, implementation of such policies is challenging and the track record is mixed. In transition economies as complex as Russia, their implementation is even more difficult because of protests from vested interests, and the significant political economy costs entailed by large restructurings mean they will take time. That does not make them any less necessary, however.

The other main prong of competition-enhancing reforms—measures to reduce barriers to entry—can be undertaken in the shorter run and should be implemented in parallel with policies dealing with incumbent firms. Even when existing firms have attained structural dominance, entry (indeed, just allowing for the credible threat of entry) can instill contestability and competitive performance, especially in markets where sunk costs are relatively small, thereby making exit easier should demand soften. Job creation by new firms will make it easier to restructure inefficient incumbent firms and lay off redundant workers. Greater openness to imports and foreign direct investment are also critical ingredients in engendering competition through the entry of new firms.

Russia's competition statutes are based on those in the industrial countries, including the European Union countries and the United States, and they are, for the most part, sound. The problem is implementation. The Ministry of Antimonopoly Policy and Support for Entrepreneurship is headed by a reformer, but the agency's budget has been drastically cut over the years, forcing it to retrench its regional branches, and skilled employees have been difficult to attract and retain. Competition policies in Russia, as in other transition economies, have focused on deterring anticompetitive conduct by incumbents rather than on correcting underlying imperfections in market structure, and steps to encourage entry have concentrated on providing financial support for small and medium-sized enterprises rather than on removing regulatory and institutional barriers and improving the overall business environment.

Competition policy toward incumbents. A more robust enforcement regime is needed in Russia to redress the substantial market imperfections that give incumbents a competitive advantage and to make their markets contestable. Countries that have made progress in this area emphasize dismantling excessive horizontal and vertical dominance; preventing anticompetitive mergers by implementing clearly defined and widely publicized merger guidelines that set parameters for distinguishing between procompetitive and anticompetitive mergers; establishing credible and sizable penalties for collusion and price fixing (cartels in the United States are subject to criminal sanctions); and ensuring that there is a strong, rules-based competition policy agency with political teeth and effective implementation capacity.

Competition policy toward entrants. In reducing barriers to entry, the priority is to deal first with markets where there is already significant structural dominance; other markets can be dealt with subsequently. Proactive policies to facilitate entry should concentrate on reforming infrastructure and distribution services; strengthening the judiciary and associated institutions for more efficient adjudication and enforcement of commercial disputes; enacting broad-based land reform; instituting uniform, rules-based procedures for licensing, registration, and inspections; and fighting corruption and organized crime.

Providing targeted support to small and medium-sized enterprises through government-subsidized lines of credit is likely to be counterproductive. Such support would undermine market-based reforms of the banking sector and nascent commercial intermediation by Russian banks. Worse, particularly in the context of weak property rights, it breeds corruption. Policies that could be helpful in this regard include strengthening the legal framework for venture capital and investment funds, supporting local banks that provide credit to small and medium-sized enterprises on commercial terms, and facilitating private cofinancing of projects by small and medium-sized enterprises and local banks.

Lowering entry barriers must focus not only on creating favorable conditions for potential rivals within a local market but also on enabling competitors based in other oblasts to sell or invest in the local market. This is critical to redressing Russia's regional market segmentation. It means that the federal government must have stronger enforcement authority to deal with the anticompetitive practices of local governments.

This article draws on Harry Broadman (ed.), 1999, Russian Enterprise Reform: Policies to Further the Transition *(Washington: World Bank).*

Suggested readings:

1. *J. David Brown and John S. Earle, 2000, "Competition, Geography, and Firm Performance: Lessons from Russia,"* Transition *(World Bank)*; http://www.worldbank.org/html/prddr/trans/augsepoct00/pages27-30.htm.
2. *Paul L. Joskow, Richard Schmalensee, and Natalia Tsukanova, 1994, "Competition Policy In Russia During and After Privatization,"* Brookings Papers on Economic Activity: Microeconomics, *Brookings Institution.*
3. *Ben Slay, 1998, "Russian Competition Policy: Medium Term Overview" (unpublished; Middlebury, Vermont: Middlebury College).*

Harry G. Broadman is Lead Economist in Europe & Central Asia Regional Operations at the World Bank.

China Joins the WTO: How, Why, and What Now?

THE OVERALL, LONG-TERM, EFFECTS SHOULD BE POSITIVE, BUT DON'T EXPECT TOO MUCH, TOO SOON.

By Penelope B. Prime

This article analyzes the process and probable effects of China's entry into the WTO from several different angles. The prospect of China's membership has been controversial, both within China and in the international community, slowing the process considerably. A key factor pushing China's application forward has been China's significant move toward a market-oriented economy in the 1990s. However, adapting to the negotiated WTO package will be only part of the major changes China is likely to experience in the coming decade.

The story of how China joined the World Trade Organization (WTO) is, on one level, a simple one: the advanced nations, led by the United States, let China in once they felt its economy had reformed sufficiently to meet WTO requirements. On another level, the technicalities of the bilateral and multilateral negotiations were by no means simple. China was too advanced in some sectors for WTO member countries to be comfortable giving it developing country status, which brings with it loose timetables and "differential and more favorable treatment" for meeting WTO obligations.[1] But China was also not a developed economy by most measures, as its delegation insisted. Hence every aspect of China's entry has been carefully negotiated, adding to the time it has taken for its application to be completed. In the end, the full protocol incorporated thousands of lines of tariffs and specific agreements, covering approximately 1,500 pages (O'Neil, 2001).[2]

Another piece of the story is that certain leaders in China championed this cause unflaggingly. In particular, key members of the Ministry of Foreign Trade and Economic Cooperation (MOFTEC) believed strongly in China formally re-joining the international economy. Premier Zhu Rongji, who has a reputation as a reformer, was a key supporter and probably the main reason the issue was kept alive. The Republic of China (Taiwan hereafter) had been an initial member of GATT when it was formed in 1948 but then resigned in 1950 in the aftermath of the civil war and the move to Taiwan (Tucker, 2000). The People's Republic of China (China hereafter) applied to regain its seat in 1986. The final chapter was not written until November 11, 2001, when the WTO trade ministers gave formal approval for China's membership at their annual meeting, with Taiwan's approval following a day later.

Somewhat unexpectedly, the terrorist attacks on the U.S. in September 2001 led to a flurry of negotiations and compromises that cleared the final hurdles for China's membership. President Jiang Zeming, in his call to President Bush immediately after September 11, reportedly asked that this issue among others not be lost in the events that would follow the attacks. The tenacity of China's leaders' push to join WTO over a decade and a half is remarkable in the light of difficult transition challenges and serious opposition at home.

Why China Wanted to Join

Faced with the complexities of joining WTO, and the fact that joining meant China's laws, trade policies, and domestic business regulation would have to change dramatically, why would China's leaders place such importance on this step? Part of the answer can be found in the dynamics between reforms in China, world events, and policy decisions made by WTO member countries, in particular the United States.

While China is not a democratic or particularly open society, people have competing interests that shape what happens there. Although it is not always apparent from the outside, Beijing does not represent all of China; MOFTEC does not represent all central ministries; and Zhu Rongji does not represent all of the central leadership. Debates, uncertainty, and foot-dragging within China about the benefits of changing to fit the norms of international capitalism are additional reasons why the process of joining took so long. Once a consensus was reached at the highest levels of leadership in early 1999, however, formal debate over the wisdom of joining was forbidden. Prohibiting debate angered academics, journalists, and others who understand the importance of airing different views; and the prohibition of debate did not end the opposition.

The roots of opposition are tied to the very beginnings of reform. In 1978, China had no foreign investment and very little trade. Contrast that with the present, where China has been the largest recipient of direct foreign investment in the developing world since 1992 and is among the top ten trading countries in the world.[3] Although the reforms that opened China to international markets were gradual, by the mid-1990s foreign invested enterprises began to gain serious market share. Coca Cola and Pepsi had basically taken over the entire soft drink market in China, and the presence of others like Procter & Gamble and Volkswagen was ubiquitous with products and advertising. In addition, multinationals looked invincible and overpowering. Some popular examples were that Microsoft's capitalization was one and a half times the size of both the Shanghai and Shenzhen stock exchange put together, and Wal-Mart's annual sales represented forty percent of China's total sales revenue (Wang, 2000, pp. 60, 62).

Two sides of the debate emerged at this time.[4] One side argued that China was relying too much on foreign investment and that development of the domestic, national economy should be the priority. The other side argued that in fact China still had too little foreign investment, and that more liberalization was required to insure progress. The Asia crisis in 1997 gave the national economy advocates the upper hand. By 1998 it looked as if China would stop pushing so hard for WTO membership and focus on the Asia-Pacific Economic Cooperation (APEC) forum and other regional organizations instead (Hai, 1998).

A year later everything changed. Zhu Rongji arrived in Washington in April, 1999, with a surprisingly concessionary package designed to pave the way for a U.S. blessing on China's membership. We still do not have a full understanding of the internal bargaining that allowed for such a serious renewed push to join WTO. However, there are a number of factors, both economic and political, that probably played a role in tipping the scales back toward membership.[5]

China's supporters of liberalization saw the WTO as a way to continue the reform process.

The most widely cited reason for China's push to join is that supporters of liberalization saw it as a way to continue the reform process. For example, numerous plans have been initiated to restructure and revitalize state-owned enterprises since the mid-1980s, but only minor progress has been made. With the opening of many sectors to foreign competition, it is expected that numerous state companies will either have to rise to the occasion and compete successfully or close. The state sector is supported by the banking system, which carries a high burden of non-performing loans. Serious banking reform is therefore necessary to avoid a major crisis. The experience of the Asian crisis brought this point home for many in China and created a sense of urgency. With WTO membership, foreign companies and banks would increase their presence in the Chinese market, setting examples and creating competition for the domestic system.

A second factor may have been a result of watching the high-tech revolution of the 1990s. Chinese leaders want China to be part of these developments, and there may be increasing awareness that this would be much easier if China was seen as a credible partner in the international economic system, which would include protection of intellectual property. WTO membership is also expected to attract more foreign investment, some of which would bring desired new technology or help enhance China's own capabilities for technological development. The fact that China joined the Information Technology Agreement, which phases out all tariffs on information technology products by 2005, gives credence to this as one factor supporting membership.

A third factor concerns exports. China's exports have increased substantially throughout the reform period, helping China earn foreign exchange for needed imports and spurring growth via demand. Continued increases, however, are problematic. The willingness of countries to open their markets even further to Chinese goods is being tested by political resistance to what is seen as unfair trade in terms of China's willingness to reciprocate. This problem would be greatly reduced within the WTO framework, because China will then be seen as part of the fair trade system. In addition, quotas blocking more Chinese imports will be phased out as part of the terms of China's membership. Both of these changes will help increase China's exports.

The fourth factor is political. Once China joined WTO it would no longer be hostage to annual Congressional reviews in the U.S., where all kinds of grievances were raised as possible reasons to deny China Normal Trade Relations (formerly "Most Favored Nation") status. Further, once a member of WTO, Chinese negotiators would have some influence in making the rules of international trade and therefore be able to weigh in on the issues that concern them. They also would have more credibility and clout to deal with their own grievances on dumping and other trading issues. Finally, China wanted to make sure that Taiwan did not join first so that China would have a say in that economy's status in the organization.

The Final Steps

Despite the combination of factors that caused China to make its offer to the U.S. in April 1999, the process continued to be less than smooth. President Clinton, for domestic political reasons, rejected Zhu Rongji's offer. In May, the U.S. bombed the Chinese Embassy in Belgrade, upsetting relations and all negotiations. Once negotiations resumed, after many meetings and seemingly little progress, the U.S. and China finally completed their bilateral agreement on November 15, 1999.[6] After much debate within the U.S. Congress, the House voted 237 to 27 in favor of granting China Permanent Normal Trading Rights (PNTR) May 24, 2000, followed by the Senate's favorable vote of 83 to 15 on September 19. Although the PNTR vote was not required for China's WTO membership, it meant that the U.S. would be in compliance with WTO rules when China joined, and therefore the U.S. economy would enjoy the benefits of the negotiated package.

The U.S. bilateral agreement opened the way for the European Union to complete its agreement, which virtually assured that China would join. However, numerous issues continued to stall the process. At the end of 2000, even the bilateral negotiations were not yet finished, with Mexico being one of the last. Then, in April 2001, a U.S. spy plane collided with a Chinese plane, causing renewed tensions and delaying progress. By then, as well, there was speculation that even some in China were having second thoughts. At the National People's Congress in March, Premier Zhu was quoted as acknowledging frankly that adjusting to WTO would be difficult, implying that having more time would be desirable (Kazer, 2001).

Over the summer the process continued to stall over several issues. The American insurance company, AIG, had been allowed to operate in China with wholly owned subsidiaries since 1994. The new WTO rules, however, stated that foreign invested insurance companies must have at least fifty percent Chinese ownership. European companies, along with Chinese negotiators, did not want to make an exception for AIG, but AIG was already operating under the original agreement and would have to seek out partners retroactively. Further, China wanted to use price controls in agriculture to help cushion the transition, after they had agreed they would phase them out.

The final stages of the process were pushed forward by the terrorist attack on the U.S. on September 11. Most likely due to a high-level decision in the U.S., all sides agreed to disagree on the AIG issue and to let it be resolved within the WTO framework once China was a member; and the agricultural price control issue ended in a compromise (Kahn, 2001).[7] On September 17, China was cleared to join, with formal approval conferred on November 11 at the annual meeting of trade ministers in Doha, Qatar. China became the 143rd member on December 11, 2001, with Taiwan becoming the 144th member on January 1, 2002. A fifteen-year quest had been completed. The milestones of this quest are summarized in Table 1.

The Impact on China

The possible impact on China of joining WTO has been the subject of much speculation. Given all of the changes China is facing with or without WTO, it may well be difficult to sort out the effect of WTO *per se*. Some of China's own analysts have estimated that about ten million jobs will be lost in farming, autos, aluminum, petrochemicals, and steel; and about ten million jobs will be gained in services, textiles, garments, and non-farm rural activities in the first five years. International trade is expected to nearly double, and there is great hope for a surge in foreign investment. Increases in efficiency are expected to increase average gross domestic product one percent per year or less, largely from resource reallocation more compatible with comparative advantage, combined with increased exports and technological investment.[8] These estimates seem to be reasonable and they do not indicate major upheaval or fantastic paybacks.

The bigger story lies in how joining could change the nature of the debate and policy choices within China. WTO establishes a structure where a rules-based trade policy is required, backed by a legally binding contract between governments and a government-to-government dispute settlement process. Being part of this structure will make a significant and lasting difference in at least two ways: it will challenge China's past economic policy principles, and it will alter the distribution of fortunes of particular interest groups within China.

In the past, economic planning supported a national development strategy in China. The importance of planning has declined since reforms began in the early 1980s, but much of the planning mentality and some of the tools continue today. For example, policies of targeted import control, low-cost loan access, trading rights, and even pricing have been used to promote production in selected sectors. Each new five-year plan targeted technologies and industries within an overall logic of the development process. To speed up the acquisition of desired technologies in the 1990s, domestic market access was allowed to

TABLE 1

CHINA AND TAIWAN JOIN THE WTO: MAJOR MILESTONES

1947	Republic of China is one of the original members of the General Agreement on Trade & Tariffs (GATT)
1949	People's Republic of China is established on the mainland and Republic of China moves to Taiwan
1950	Republic of China resigns from GATT; People's Republic of China denounces GATT for ideological reasons
1986	People's Republic of China applies to renew membership in GATT; Hong Kong joins as a customs territory
1990	Taiwan applies to join as a customs territory
1992	Taiwan gains observer status and informal agreement is reached that Taiwan would join after China
1995	GATT is replaced by the World Trade Organization (WTO)
15 November 1999	U.S. & China announce bilateral agreement
19 May 2000	European Union & China finish agreement
24 May 2000	U.S. House of Representatives vote 237 to 27 in favor of granting China Permanent Normal Trading Rights (PNTR)
19 September 2000	U.S. Senate vote 83 to 15 in favor of PNTR
10 September 2001	Required by U.S. law, President Bush certifies the U.S.-China bilateral WTO agreement
14 September 2001	WTO members finish agreement for China to join
11 November 2001	WTO ministers formally accept China as a member, followed by Taiwan the next day
11 December 2001	The People's Republic of China officially becomes the 143rd member of WTO
1 January 200	Taiwan as "Separate Customs Territory of Taiwan, Penghu, Kinmen and Matsu (TPKM)" officially becomes the 144th member of WTO

sweeten many bargains with foreign firms. To support industry, and for self-defense reasons, the principle of self-sufficiency in grain has been a foundation of China's agricultural strategy for decades. Also underlying China's opening to global markets was the principle of maintaining balanced trade, backed up with a fixed exchange rate and the ability to limit imports when necessary.

None of these principles are valid under China's negotiated WTO agreement. Thus, the policy debate and tools will have to move from planning for favored industries to maintaining macroeconomic stability by indirect market means. The expected result is a move towards more global and regional specialization and an output mix driven by consumer demand. Markets, not planners, will determine whether China will have a trade deficit or a trade surplus, and there will be pressures to eventually let the exchange rate float as well.

Change in China since reforms began in the late 1970s has been consistent with more marketization and fewer government directives. In this sense joining WTO is just the next step in China's transition. But there is a difference. China bas made an agreement with most countries of the world to give up an important set of policy tools in order to be a full member of the international community. Member countries will be watching for compliance, and China will be using the international agreement to achieve domestic change.

Overall the long-term benefits should be positive for China, but in the transition stage there will be serious costs, especially in terms of short-run employment. Further, those who will gain from the agreement are completely different from those who benefited from the old strategy. The winners and losers are summarized in Table 2. The legitimacy of the Chinese government will depend on how China's leaders handle this transition while staying within the boundaries of WTO compliance.

TABLE 2

WTO REDISTRIBUTES BENEFITS

Winners	Losers
The private sector	Many state-owned companies
Consumers	Banking
Exporters	Insurance
Transport: containers	Telecommunications
Services: household and professional	Automobiles
Textiles and apparel	Heavy industry, e.g. steel, aluminum
Light manufactures, e.g. electronics, toys	Farmers; e.g., grain, soybeans & cotton
Non-farm activities in rural areas	State trading companies

Reasonable Expectations

China's participation in WTO is a major milestone for both China and the international community. It is not a panacea, however; and its benefits have been exaggerated, perhaps dangerously so. Some commentaries in the U.S. have suggested, for example, that China's participation in WTO will bring about liberal political change. WTO is an economic agreement about trade. It does not address, nor should we expect it to affect, political constraints or human rights conditions. To make too much of this important agreement is to invite a backlash against it if things do not go as well as people hope. Even in the economic realm, expectations are unrealistic. Some in the U.S. are counting on WTO to reduce the large U.S. trade deficit with China by expanding U.S. exports to China. This bilateral deficit, shown in Figure 1, has grown from $13 billion in 1991 to $84 billion in 2000.[9]

Growth in U.S. exports to China, however, may not depend primarily on WTO. The most important determinant of U.S. exports to China will be how fast China's economy grows. An analysis by Mark Frazier (1999) shows that U.S. exports to China have grown approximately fifteen percent per year between 1990 and 1998—a period with very high overall growth in China averaging nearly ten percent. More recently, China's growth has slowed and is expected to be about seven percent per year, if all goes well. It is likely growth will be even slower than seven percent as the country makes difficult adjustments and deals with a global slowdown. Hence, the growth of U.S. exports to China would also slow, even as WTO agreements kick in. This would no doubt catch the attention of business and political leaders here.

While the future overall effect on U.S. exports is uncertain, the U.S. economy will gain due to increased transparency and predictability about the rules of doing business with China. Furthermore, certain sectors such as agriculture, industrial products, insurance, and financial services will be especially helped by the agreement. In agriculture, the average tariff rate on key U.S. products will fall from thirty-one percent to fourteen percent, which could generate an additional $2 billion a year in agricultural exports. Items in this category include beef, poultry, cheese, oranges, apples, wine, and grapes. Cotton exports should also be helped by a large reduction in tariff-rate quotas. In the industrial sector, autos, auto parts, wood and paper products, and high tech products such as telecommunications equipment and semiconductors will benefit from a variety of lower import barriers. In insurance, reinsurance is now completely open, non-life insurance can be wholly foreign owned within two years, and life insurance allows fifty percent foreign ownership. All geographic limitations will be phased out within three years. In banking, there will be full market access within five years. Partial foreign ownership in telecommunication companies will also be permitted, with geographical restrictions phased out over time.[10]

Although China should also benefit from joining, a backlash in China is possible. China's challenges are immense. The road forward is going to be very difficult under the best of circumstances, which would be the case with or without WTO membership. Many state-owned enterprises must lay off large portions of their work force, and some will close. The banking system has far too many branches and employees. Agriculture is so inefficient in terms of labor-land ratios that farmers are having trouble making a living. Estimates vary, but perhaps as many as 140 million people are underemployed, and 16-18 million are outright unemployed in urban areas. While the macroeconomic effect of joining WTO is expected to be a wash in terms of employment, the resulting restructuring will add to many people's existing worries in a very visible way.

FIGURE 1

U.S. TRADE DEFICIT WITH CHINA (CHINA'S SURPLUS WITH THE U.S.)

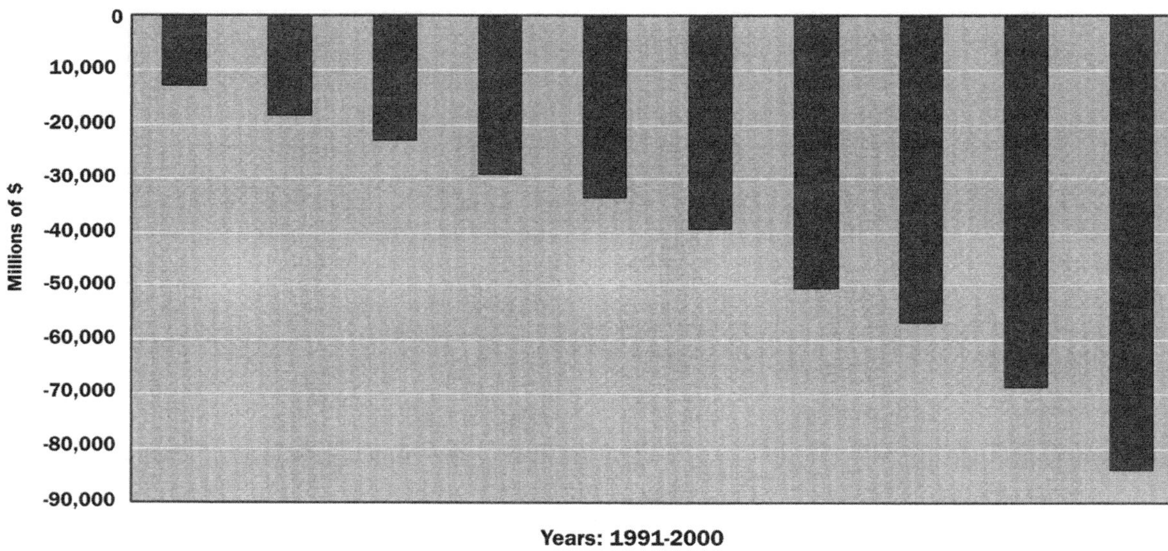

Note that these figures are based on the U.S. methodology, which show a larger bilateral deficit than the Chinese figures largely due to the treatment of trade flows through Hong Kong.

China's economic nationalists opposed to China's entry into WTO could seize on these problems to bolster their argument that joining puts China at risk of exploitation and vulnerability to international markets. Adding economic pressure at a difficult time, China's exports have been hurt in the current global recession. WTO could be construed as a tangible reason for China's troubles. If WTO is blamed, inevitably this blame will be transferred onto the U.S., hurting U.S.-China relations.

Another focal point in U.S.-China relations is Taiwan. There is no doubt that the economies of China and Taiwan will become much more integrated as a result of both becoming WTO members. Taiwan is in the midst of major restructuring to lower manufacturing costs, which is largely being achieved by moving offshore. The destination of choice has been the mainland, even before the WTO agreements. The question is how this increasing interdependency will affect China's treatment of Taiwan, and whether it will strengthen or weaken the political support in Taiwan for accepting a status subordinate to China's central government in Beijing as required by Beijing's "one country, two systems" formula. China could try to resolve trade issues through internal negotiations as it does with Hong Kong. This would lessen the benefits of joining for Taiwan, as it would not be treated as a separate entity. Or, China could use the structure of WTO to further relations with Taiwan, including the possibility of establishing direct trade links. It is in the U.S. interest for China and Taiwan to work together peacefully towards resolving their differences. The WTO provides an important international framework, agreed to by both sides, for that to happen.

Going Forward: Implementation

Now that the treaties have been signed, the next step is to implement the agreements. In China, both the central and local governments are addressing this enormous task. Fundamental aspects of implementation are already in place, such as meeting transparency requirements and lowering tariff rates. Day-to-day implementation, however, will require making sure local laws are in compliance and enforced, training custom officials, and the like. Shanghai, for example, has set up a WTO Affairs Consultation Center to provide information and training, and to demonstrate that Shanghai will be in compliance. Universities, think tanks, and government agencies in China have published a variety of books on WTO and distributed them widely across China. These books address the hopes and concerns of the general population as well as the tasks of the officials that will have to implement the changes. Despite these efforts, this phase of increasing awareness and carrying out implementation will not be easy or quick.

Outside of China, surveillance of the progress of implementation is also taking shape. As part of the WTO agreement, a Transitional Review Mechanism was set up as a forum for members to bring concerns to China's attention. In the U.S. government, the Department of Agriculture has set up a China Task Force to monitor progress, and the International Trade Administration has a five point Compliance Plan to be monitored via the Trade Compliance Center under the Market Access and Compliance Division of the U.S. Commerce Department.[11] In addition, there are monthly meetings of the Trade Policy Staff Committee, chaired by the U.S. Trade Representative Office, for U.S. Government agencies who want to follow China's progress.[12]

Nonetheless, despite compliance oversight and a wholehearted effort on China's part to play by the rules, more—rather than less—conflict between foreign businesses and the Chinese bureaucracy is likely. In addition to hundreds of laws that need to be re-written, the rules of doing business are in flux. While most of these changes are for the good, confusion will increase in the short-term. Patience and realistic expectations will help. The important point is that China has joined the international global economy in a major, and probably irreversible, way.

REFERENCES

Frazier, Mark W. 1999. "Coming to Terms with the "WTO Effect" on U.S.-China Trade and China's Economic Growth." The National Bureau of Asian Research. September. *http://www.nbr.org/publications/briefing/frazier99/index.html* (September 21, 2000).

Hai, Wen. 1998. "The WTO and China's Objectives as a World Trading Power." *In China in the New Millennium: Market Reforms and Social Development*. James A. Dorn, Ed. Washington, D.C.: Cato Institute. Pp. 175–190.

Kahn, Joseph. 2001. "China Clears Last Hurdle on Path to Trade Group." *New York Times*. September 15. P.B1.

Kazer, William. 2001. "Zhu warns of WTO Pitfalls." South China Morning Post. March 6, 2001. *http://special.scmp.com/ChinaWTOBid/Article/FullText_asp_ArticleID-20010306064134704.asp* (March 23, 2001).

Li, Shantong; Zhi Wang, Fan Zhai, and Lin Xu. 2000. *WTO: Zhongguo yu Shiyue* (WTO: China and the World). Beijing: Zhongguo Fazhan Chubanshe.

Ma, Jun. 2001. "Quantifying the Impact of China's WTO Entry." Global Markets Research, Emerging Markets, Deutsche Bank. December 14.

O'Neill, Mark. 2001. "Ministry Moves to Publicise Pledges," South China Morning Post, November 27, *http://special.scmp.com/reports/chinajoinswto/news/ZZZCR4E81UC.html* (February 7, 2002). Tucker, Nancy Bernkopf. 2000. "The Taiwan Factor in the Vote on PNTR for China and Its WTO Accession." NBR Publications: NBR Analysis: Vol. 11, No. 2, Essay 1. *http://www.nbr.org/publications/analysis/vol11no2/essay1.html* (September 21, 2000).

Wang, Yong. 1999. "Why China Went for WTO." *The China Business Review*. July-Aug. Pp. 42–45.

Wang, Yong. 2000 "China's Domestic WTO Debate." The China Business Review. Jan.-Feb. Pp. 54–62.

Notes

1. The Enabling Clause, Part IV of the GATT agreement.
2. The full WTO protocol provided by the Chinese government can be found in English and Chinese at *www.moftec.gov.cn/moftec.cn/wto/wtolaw.html.*
3. World Bank, *www.worldbank.org/data/datequery.html* (February 22, 2002), and World Development Indicators CD-ROM 1998.
4. A version of this debate is presented in Wang (2000).
5. For one Chinese scholar's perspective, see Wang (1999).
6. A summary of the U.S.-China Bilateral WTO Agreement, as well as a link to specific agreements by industry, can be found at the U.S.-China Business Council website at *http://www.uschina.org/public/wto.*
7. Annex 4 of the Protocol lists all of the products that will retain "state pricing" or "government guidance pricing" for some time. The agricultural products listed include tobacco, certain grains, vegetable oil, and cotton.
8. The Development Research Center of the State Council has done a series of estimates. See references to this work in The China Business Review, "The Impact of WTO Accession on China," Jan.-Feb. 2000, pp. 40, 42. The Development Research Center has also published a book of its results (Li, et al, 2000). See also, Jun Ma (2001) for another set of estimates.
9. U.S. Department of Commerce, International Trade Administration, *http://www.ita.doc.gov/td/industry/otea/usfth/tabcon.html* (March 23, 2001 and October 12, 2001), Table 8.
10. *www.uschina.org/public/wto/ustr/generalfacts.html* (March 2, 2001).
11. As part of this effort the Department of Commerce has set up a website to inform U.S. businesses on China's obligations and compliance at *www.export.gov/china.*
12. *http://usinfo.state.gov/regional/ca/ushchina* (February 7, 2002).

Penelope B. Prime is Professor of Economics in the Department of Economics & Finance at Kennesaw State University in the University of Georgia System, where she directs its China Research Center. She has also taught at Emory University, Georgia State University, and Carleton College. Dr. Prime has also worked with the World Bank and the U.S. Census Bureau and has consulted with companies doing business with China. She earned her Ph.D. in economics at the University of Michigan.

CHINA'S ECONOMIC POWER: Enter the dragon

BEIJING

ASK what has been the most stunning economic event of the past century, and many people might cite the case of China in the two decades since it opened up. In that time the economy has grown more than fivefold, incomes have quadrupled, and 270m Chinese have been lifted out of absolute poverty. Yet with a couple more decades' hindsight, that achievement might be superseded—by what may now be about to happen in the world's most populous country.

Much of China's growth up to now has been merely of a catch-up kind, as animal spirits were unleashed after agricultural communes were disbanded and restrictions on travel and informal enterprise were lifted. The government, in other words, did not have to do much except stand back. And for all the growth in the country's exports as China became a manufacturing colossus, only in 1993 did China's share of world trade reach its pre-1939 peak. Today, average income is a mere $950 a head, and the disparities in wealth are huge. China is still a poor country, in places abjectly so.

The coming two decades, on the other hand, offer the possibility of an even more extraordinary pace of economic change. These could be the decades when China truly joins the world, and when the crushing legacy of a socialist economy is swept away. China certainly has the potential, over this period, to become the second-largest economy in the world. Of course, that would not mean that all Chinese would grow rich. But China no doubt has the means to attain "middle income" status—putting the prosperity of its people, currently 1.3 billion souls, not far from South Korea or Portugal today. That would be an extraordinary feat for so large a population in so short a time. The geopolitical effects would also be immense.

A new taste for reform

This is the moment to contemplate such a future, because over the past year or so (and after seven years of falling growth) China's rulers have shown a determination to tackle the thorniest issues in the economy that they have never shown before. The most obvious symbols of that determination are the promises that were made, and the steps now being taken, to ensure that China is brought into the world trading system. Nearly all the agreements are in place for China to join the World Trade Organisation (WTO) this year, after 15 years of trying. Over the next five years the country will slash tariff and non-tariff barriers, as well as open up sectors of the economy that have long been off-limits to foreigners, such as banking, telecoms and distribution. China promises to protect foreign intellectual property, and get rid of a raft of local-content requirements that have hobbled foreign manufacturers.

But WTO membership is just the first of the reform initiatives. The central government has declared war on most parts of the socialist economy, all the time insisting it is sticking to "the socialist road". It is bent on separating business from government, by getting rid of many smaller state enterprises and corporatising others. It wants to develop financial markets that bypass a decrepit state banking system and award capital to the deserving. It is building a national infrastructure of roads, railways and fibre-optic lines that promise for the first time in history to tie up the disparate parts of the Chinese empire, creating something like a unified economy.

The government is also encouraging new sources of domestic demand by privatising socialist housing (in the biggest cities, two-fifths of residents now own their own homes). It is trying to develop a clear and effective tax system, using information technology, it hopes, to monitor and crack down on local-government corruption. And it is attempting to patch together a set of social-welfare initiatives to catch the 5m-odd people being thrown out of work each year by state enterprises, as well as to provide pensions for an ageing population. Most of these ventures are politically fraught, and not for the faint-hearted. In his annual report to the National People's Congress this week, the prime minister, Zhu Rongji, promised more, not less, pain as reforms are redoubled: shutting down more loss-making enterprises, for instance, and selling others.

If the government makes good on all its promises, what assumptions can one make about future growth? First, note that assumptions are rosier if the government's own figures are used. Official growth statistics have long been exaggerated, for a number of reasons. For one, local officials cook the books to make their region look good. For another, China still produces goods that pile up as inventories and are never sold. Yet their production gets added to GDP, when it should be subtracted. The problem is that no one knows by quite how much official GDP is overstated. Last year's announced growth of 8% was perhaps one or two percentage points too high. At least the trend in GDP is fairly reliable, and at least the government is trying hard to improve the quality of its data.

Over time, the figures should get more believable, not less.

Andy Xie, an economist at Morgan Stanley in Hong Kong, reckons that if China sticks to its WTO commitments and, in effect, moves to a market-based economy by 2005, it will grow at 7% a year till 2005, then at 9% during 2006–15, as it reaps the benefits of restructuring, before slowing a bit thereafter. If so, by 2020, China's economy would have grown to $10 trillion in 2000 dollars, making it the size of America's economy today. Income per head will be $6,700. If China were to conform to global norms more quickly than the WTO framework demands—perhaps as a result of foreign pressure and trade tensions, or of domestic pressure to speed change along—then it would grow by 10% a year between 2006 and 2015, passing the $10 trillion mark by 2015. And if China's reforms run into the sand? More of that later.

A giant sucking sound

One of the immediate consequences of impending WTO membership is a swift increase in commitments of foreign direct investment (FDI): last year, committed FDI rose by over a third. Already, though, China's stock of FDI, at $350 billion, and growing by over $40 billion a year, is massive. It is the world's third-largest, behind America ($1.1 trillion) and Britain ($394 billion), and way ahead of countries like Brazil and Mexico that opened their markets much earlier than China. The mainland now accounts for about one-third of emerging markets' total stock of FDI, according to Nicholas Lardy of the Brookings Institution in Washington. Nearly four-fifths of all FDI going to South-East and East Asia, not counting Japan, is sucked up by China—and to its neighbours' growing alarm.

Traditionally, the bulk of FDI to China has gone into its export industries. Foreign trade has grown from almost nothing in the late 1970s to $475 billion last year, far faster than the growth in world trade as a whole (see chart). And foreign-invested firms have grown to account for half of all exports from China. Foreign investment has helped make China a formidable export machine. The country will no doubt continue to be one, thanks to a near-limitless pool of extraordinarily cheap labour, including a large and growing supply of educated graduates. Mainland computer engineers earn about one-tenth as much as their Taiwanese counterparts, and they are almost as good.

China's manufacturing is getting more sophisticated and employing more capital. Mr Xie argues that even as it moves up the manufacturing chain (eg, to semiconductors and to information-technology hardware, of which it is the world's third-biggest producer), China will not lose its advantages in cheap, labour-intensive areas such as toys, textiles and shoes. Without China's cost structures—that is, its economies of scale and its low standard of living—other exporters in the region, from Indonesia to South Korea, will have trouble staying in business: China can just about out-export them all.

Stellar
Trade growth, 1977=100

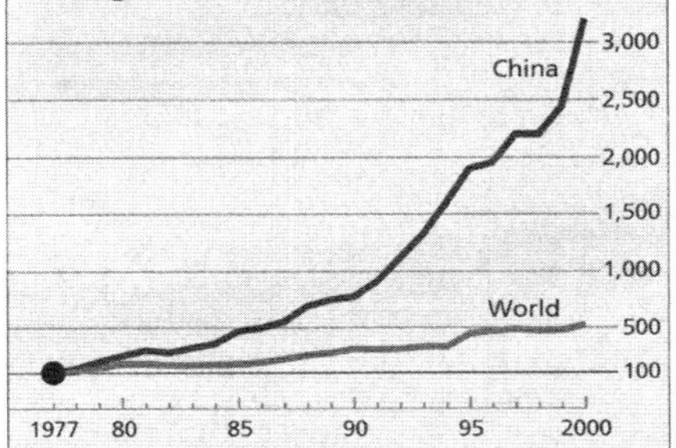

Source: Nicholas Lardy, Brookings Institution

This realisation comes as a profound shock to China's neighbours, most of whom have built a development strategy over the past few decades around export-led growth. It will soon come as a shock outside the region: to exporters in India, for instance, and Mexico, who thought themselves far removed from the Chinese threat. Indeed, Mexico has been very reluctant to sign up to China's entry to the WTO, and has been the final country to do so.

On the face of it, China's seems to be an export-driven economy, too. After all, annual exports are equivalent to at least 23% of GDP, making China the world's ninth-largest exporter. Even so, the brute figures conceal how imperfectly China's export sector is tied to its hinterland. Firms wholly or partly owned by foreigners account for about one-half of China's imports as well as its exports. Much export manufacturing, in other words, consists of processing industries that ship in components, bolt them together and ship them out again, often through Hong Kong. The foreign-dominated export sector, especially in China's handful of "special economic zones", should be thought of as an enclave, a giant version of the *maquiladoras* on the Mexican border with the United States. China, says Mr Lardy, is only shallowly integrated with the world economy.

Segregration carries costs. The technology and the management skills that foreign investment typically brings with it are not easily adopted by domestic firms. Meanwhile, economic growth is stifled within China by the dominance, in many sectors, of the state, by barriers to trade and local protectionism, and by the absence of proper capital markets. For Zhu Rongji and other reformers, WTO entry is important for its domestic consequences. Certainly, with its ability to export, China is a clear net beneficiary of the globalisation of trade. More important, though, is the fact that WTO membership will spur competition at home, acting as a rod to beat back the baneful influence of the state.

Goodbye, hermit China

The "price" that China pays for this is to allow foreigners in. It is the potential scale of China's domestic market, after its entry to the WTO, that most appeals to foreign multinationals. After decades, or rather centuries, of foreigners' dashed dreams about the money to be made from adding an inch to every Chinaman's shirt-tail, the promise that China has long held out may be about to be matched by reality.

Already, in unprotected sectors of the mainland economy, multinationals are a dominant force. Between them, McDonald's and Kentucky Fried Chicken have almost 700 branches. Kodak has half of the market for film and photographic paper, with Fuji holding most of the rest. Procter & Gamble is the biggest seller of shampoo, while foreign manufacturers, led by Motorola, Ericsson and Nokia, have 95% of the market for mobile phones, the world's biggest market in terms of handset sales. Coca-Cola says that China is about to become its biggest Asian market. Some estimates put foreign involvement at about one-tenth of the whole economy. With WTO membership, the proportion could easily double.

Yet China is not yet integrated into the world trading system, and it is no better integrated domestically. Think of China's potential not so much as an international trading economy, but as a vast "continental" one: a proto-America, as it were. Just as America's growth in the 19th century took off with the building of the railways and of a national financial system, so China hopes to unify its hitherto fragmented, disjointed economy. Until recently, it took less time to ship a container from Shanghai to Seattle than from Shanghai to the inland city of Chongqing, 1,000 or so miles up the Yangzi river.

Just a dozen years ago, China had no highway system linking its provinces; now it has over 12,000km (7,500 miles) of such highways. The number of passenger flights has trebled in the past decade. There were 36m new subscribers for fixed-line telephones in 2000 alone, and 42m new mobile subscribers: fixed-line penetration, at 17% of households, grew 30-fold during the 1990s. Internet use, though still tiny, is more than doubling every year. China is integrating fast, and information technology is helping.

Financial integration also holds great promise. Until recently, the big four banks were captive lenders to state-owned enterprises. The state's share of the economy has fallen—to below half, according to some calculations—yet state-owned industries still control more than 70% of all fixed assets and 80% of all working capital in manufacturing, according to Mr Lardy of the Brookings Institution. The corollary is that private enterprise is stifled.

The government has bold plans to develop equity markets and to clean up the state banks. Already, debt-equity swaps have taken some 1.4 trillion yuan ($150 billion) of dud loans off the books of the banks, which have been ordered to lend in future only on merit. Equity markets have assumed a growing role in providing finance: 620 billion yuan last year, compared with 440 billion in 1999. The foreign portion of that grew nearly sevenfold, to 180 billion yuan. Shareholder discipline, at least in theory, should shape up management. Certainly, the flotations of some of the biggest Chinese companies that have recently come to market—Petrochina, China Mobile—were preceded by giant restructurings to make the companies look more like western ones.

Is the regime serious?

This raft of bold reforms has still to reach the other shore. Hopes in China have foundered before. This time, there will be proper ways to measure progress. China must successfully join the WTO, and stand by its commitments within it. It must continue to separate business from government, which eventually means getting the Communist Party out of both. The next step in this process is developing capital markets which reward good management and punish bad. A great deal more privatisation will be needed. Some analysts are sceptical about the chances of success. Stockmarket regulators, for instance, have announced sweeping initiatives, such as delisting money-losing companies, demanding more financial disclosure and setting up a second stockmarket for entrepreneurial companies. "But the rhetoric," says Mr Lardy, "is far in excess of the action."

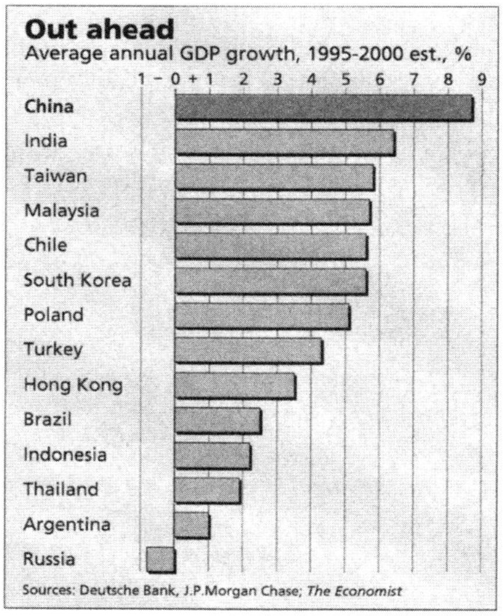

Yet the regime is deadly serious about reform. It rests its legitimacy upon the goal of getting reform-driven growth, banishing Communist Party corruption along the way, and providing a safety net to catch the victims of wrenching change. Conservative ideologues have largely been beaten. When the current batch of Communist leaders steps down late next year, the new generation that will take its place should be much more cosmopolitan and reform-minded. If it is not, there is cause for worry. For the final measure of progress will be whether the leaders consider reform to the Communist Party's monopoly on power.

What are the economic implications abroad of a China resurgent? In the near term, China's growth promises to be a comfort for the region during a difficult time. Asia's exporters are concerned that America may be on the edge of a recession from which they would suffer grievously: after the Asian crisis of 1997–98, Asian economies counted upon strong American demand for their exports to pull them back from trouble.

China, on the other hand, will scarcely be affected. Jun Ma, an economist at Deutsche Bank in Hong Kong, estimates that even if China's net exports declined by a quarter this year (after growth of the same last year), a mere half-percentage point would be knocked off the country's growth. This reinforces the point that China's is a continental economy, driven by domestic demand.

It is possibly reassuring for China's neighbours to know that the giant would scarcely stir if the world economy turned down. Chinese imports grew by a staggering $55 billion last year, suggesting that the country is even becoming a regional engine of growth. But China's export threat to neighbouring economies underscores their predicament: in order to compete, they need to undertake much-postponed structural reforms themselves.

Longer-term, some groups in America will also see a resurgent Chinese economy as a threat. China's $60 billion trade surplus with the United States is already a bone of contention, while labour interests, among others, resent China joining the world. Many of the resentful ignore the fact that ties between the American and Chinese economies are already close, and multifaceted. Sales by American companies in China are now almost as large as American exports to China, while investment flows are every bit as important as trade flows. Shutting China out of the world would harm a lot of American interests. Moreover, as Mr Xie of Morgan Stanley emphasises, there is the prospect of some $40 trillion of new wealth over the next 15–20 years to be created by Chinese reforms, and foreigners are being offered a big share—perhaps one-fifth—of it.

These are the economic ties that increasingly bind China to its reforms and to the rest of the world. There are other, less formal ones. Some 50,000 Chinese study in American universities each year, for instance, and there are now even more American-educated Chinese than Soviet-educated ones. The ties are certainly more complex than they have ever been. They require a great deal more effort to manage. But they are surely safer for all that than few ties at all.

OVERVIEW

Changing today's consumption patterns—for tomorrow's human development

World consumption has expanded at an unprecedented pace over the 20th century, with private and public consumption expenditures reaching $24 trillion in 1998, twice the level of 1975 and six times that of 1950. In 1900 real consumption expenditure was barely $1.5 trillion.

The benefits of this consumption have spread far and wide. More people are better fed and housed than ever before. Living standards have risen to enable hundreds of millions to enjoy housing with hot water and cold, warmth and electricity, transport to and from work—with time for leisure and sports, vacations and other activities beyond anything imagined at the start of this century.

How do these achievements relate to human development? Consumption is clearly an essential means, but the links are not automatic. Consumption clearly contributes to human development when it enlarges the capabilities and enriches the lives of people without adversely affecting the well-being of others. It clearly contributes when it is as fair to future generations as it is to the present ones. And it clearly contributes when it encourages lively, creative individuals and communities.

But the links are often broken, and when they are, consumption patterns and trends are inimical to human development. Today's consumption is undermining the environmental resource base. It is exacerbating inequalities. And the dynamics of the consumption-poverty-inequality-environment nexus are accelerating. If the trends continue without change—not redistributing from high-income to low-income consumers, not shifting from polluting to cleaner goods and production technologies, not promoting goods that empower poor producers, not shifting priority from consumption for conspicuous display to meeting basic needs—today's problems of consumption and human development will worsen.

But trend is not destiny, and none of these outcomes is inevitable. Change is needed and change is possible.

In short, consumption must be shared, strengthening, socially responsible and sustainable.

- *Shared*. Ensuring basic needs for all.
- *Strengthening*. Building human capabilities.
- *Socially responsible*. So the consumption of some does not compromise the well-being of others.
- *Sustainable*. Without mortgaging the choices of future generations.

Trend is not destiny—change is possible

Human life is ultimately nourished and sustained by consumption. Abundance of consumption is no crime. It has, in fact, been the life blood of much human advance. The real issue is not consumption itself but its patterns and effects. Consumption patterns today must be changed to advance human development tomorrow. Consumer choices must be turned into a reality for all. Human development paradigms, which aim at enlarging all human choices, must aim at extending and improving consumer choices too, but in ways that promote human life. This is the theme of this report.

The 20th century's growth in consumption, unprecedented in its scale and diversity, has been badly distributed, leaving a backlog of shortfalls and gaping inequalities.

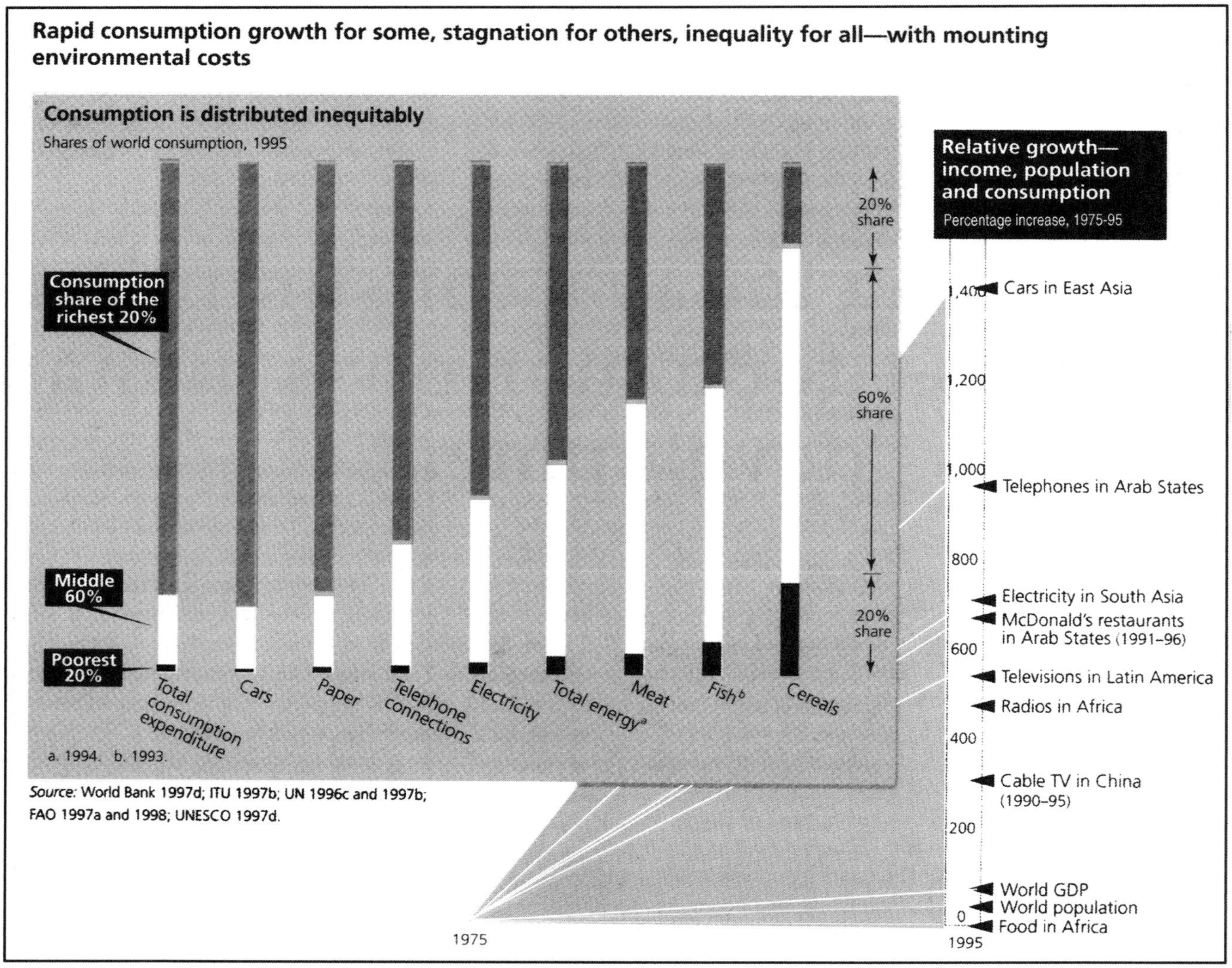

Rapid consumption growth for some, stagnation for others, inequality for all—with mounting environmental costs
Consumption is distributed inequitably
Shares of world consumption, 1995
Consumption share of the richest 20%
Middle 60%
Poorest 20%
Total consumption expenditure
Cars
Paper
Telephone connections
Electricity
Total energy[a]
Meat
Fish[b]
Cereals
20% share
60% share
20% share
a. 1994. b. 1993.
Source: World Bank 1997d; ITU 1997b; UN 1996c and 1997b; FAO 1997a and 1998; UNESCO 1997d.
Relative growth—income, population and consumption
Percentage increase, 1975-95
1,400
1,200
1,000
800
600
400
200
0
Cars in East Asia
Telephones in Arab States
Electricity in South Asia
McDonald's restaurants in Arab States (1991–96)
Televisions in Latin America
Radios in Africa
Cable TV in China (1990–95)
World GDP
World population
Food in Africa
1975
1995

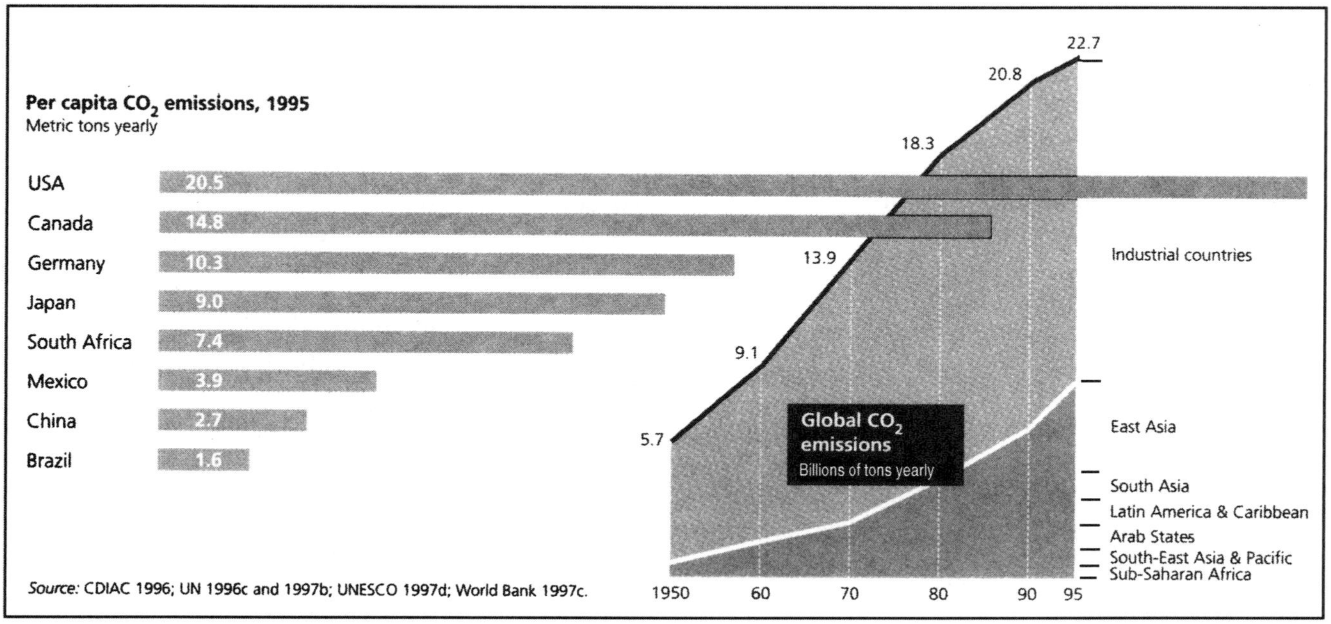

Per capita CO_2 emissions, 1995
Metric tons yearly
USA 20.5
Canada 14.8
Germany 10.3
Japan 9.0
South Africa 7.4
Mexico 3.9
China 2.7
Brazil 1.6
Source: CDIAC 1996; UN 1996c and 1997b; UNESCO 1997d; World Bank 1997c.
Global CO_2 emissions
Billions of tons yearly
5.7
9.1
13.9
18.3
20.8
22.7
Industrial countries
East Asia
South Asia
Latin America & Caribbean
Arab States
South-East Asia & Pacific
Sub-Saharan Africa
1950
60
70
80
90
95

Consumption per capita has increased steadily in industrial countries (about 2.3% annually) over the past 25 years, spectacularly in East Asia (6.1%) and at a rising rate in South Asia (2.0%). Yet these developing regions are far from catching up to levels of industrial countries, and consumption growth has been slow or stagnant in others. The average African household today consumes 20% less than it did 25 years ago.

The poorest 20% of the world's people and more have been left out of the consumption explosion. Well over a billion people are deprived of basic consumption needs. Of the 4.4 billion people in developing countries, nearly three-fifths lack basic sanitation. Almost a third have no access to clean water. A quarter do not have adequate housing. A fifth have no access to modern health services. A fifth of children do not attend school to grade 5. About a fifth do not have enough dietary energy and protein. Micronutrient deficiencies are even more widespread. Worldwide, 2 billion people are anaemic, including 55 million in industrial countries. In developing countries only a privileged minority has motorized transport, telecommunications and modern energy.

The new human poverty index (HPI-2) shows that some 7-17% of the population in industrial countries is poor

Inequalities in consumption are stark. Globally, the 20% of the world's people in the highest-income countries account for 86% of total private consumption expenditures—the poorest 20% a minuscule 1.3%.
More specifically, the richest fifth:

- Consume 45% of all meat and fish, the poorest fifth 5%.
- Consume 58% of total energy, the poorest fifth less than 4%.
- Have 74% of all telephone lines, the poorest fifth 1.5%.
- Consume 84% of all paper, the poorest fifth 1.1%.
- Own 87% of the world's vehicle fleet, the poorest fifth less than 1%.

How rewarding is today's pattern of consumption in terms of human satisfaction? The percentage of Americans calling themselves happy peaked in 1957—even though consumption has more than doubled in the meantime.

Despite high consumption, poverty and deprivation are found in all industrial countries and in some they are growing. This year's Report presents a new index of poverty in industrial countries—multidimensional measure of human deprivation, on the same lines as the human poverty index presented in *Human Development Report 1997* for developing countries but more appropriate to the social and economic conditions of the industrial countries.

The new human poverty index (HPI-2) shows that some 7–17% of the population in industrial countries is poor. These levels of deprivation have little to do with the average income of the country. Sweden has the least poverty (7%), though ranked only thirteenth in average income. The United States, with the highest average income of the countries ranked, has the highest population share experiencing human poverty. And countries with similar per capita incomes have very different levels of human poverty. The Netherlands and the United Kingdom, for example, have HPI-2 values of 8% and 15%, despite similar income levels.

HPI-2 shows conclusively that underconsumption and human deprivation are not just the lot of poor people in the developing world. More than 100 million people in rich nations suffer a similar fate. Nearly 200 million people are not expected to survive to age 60. More than 100 million are homeless. And at least 37 million are without jobs, often experiencing a state of social exclusion. Many conclusions about deprivation apply to them with equal force.

Ever-expanding consumption puts strains on the environment—emissions and wastes that pollute the earth and destroy ecosystems, and growing depletion and degradation of renewable resources that undermine livelihoods.

Runaway growth in consumption in the past 50 years is putting strains on the environment never before seen.

- The burning of fossil fuels has almost quintupled since 1950.
- The consumption of fresh water has almost doubled since 1960.
- The marine catch has increased fourfold.
- Wood consumption, both for industry and for household fuel, is now 40% higher than it was 25 years ago.

Yet growth in the use of material resources has slowed considerably in recent years, and much-publicized fears that the world would run out of such non-renewable resources as oil and minerals have proved false. New reserves have been discovered. The growth of demand has slowed. Consumption has shifted in favour of less material-intensive products and services. Energy efficiency has improved. And technological advance and recycling of raw materials have boosted efficiency in material use, now growing more slowly than economies. Call this dematerialization. The per capita use of basic materials such as steel, timber and copper has stabilized in most OECD countries—and even declined in some countries for some products.

So, non-renewables are not the urgent problem. It is two other crises that are nudging humanity towards the "outer limits" of what earth can stand.

First are the pollution and waste that exceed the planet's sink capacities to absorb and convert them. Reserves of fossil fuels are not running out, but use of these fuels is emitting gases that change the ecosystem—annual carbon dioxide (CO_2) emissions quadrupled over the past 50 years. Global warming is a serious problem, threatening to play havoc with harvests, permanently flood large areas, increase the frequency of storms and droughts, accelerate the extinction of some species, spread infectious diseases—and possibly cause sudden and savage flips in the world's climates. And although material resources may not be running out, waste is mounting, both toxic and non-toxic. In industrial countries per capita waste generation has increased almost threefold in the past 20 years.

Second is the growing deterioration of renewables—water, soil, forests, fish, biodiversity.

- Twenty countries already suffer from water stress, having less than 1,000 cubic metres per capita a year, and water's global availability has dropped from 17,000 cubic metres per capita in 1950 to 7,000 today.
- A sixth of the world's land area—nearly 2 billion hectares—is now degraded as a result of overgrazing and poor farming practices.
- The world's forests—which bind soil and prevent erosion, regulate water supplies and help govern the climate—are shrinking. Since 1970 the wooded area per 1,000 inhabitants has fallen from 11.4 square kilometres to 7.3.
- Fish stocks are declining, with about a quarter currently depleted or in danger of depletion and another 44% being fished at their biological limit.
- Wild species are becoming extinct 50–100 times faster than they would naturally, threatening to tear great holes in the web of life.

The world's dominant consumers are overwhelmingly concentrated among the well-off—but the environmental damage from the world's consumption falls most severely on the poor.

The better-off benefit from the cornucopia of consumption. But poor people and poor countries bear many of its costs. The severest human deprivations arising from environmental damage are concentrated in the poorest regions and affect the poorest people, unable to protect themselves.

- A child born in the industrial world adds more to consumption and pollution over his or her lifetime than do 30–50 children born in developing countries.
- Since 1950 industrial countries, because of their high incomes and consumption levels, have accounted for well over half the increase in resource use.
- The fifth of the world's people in the highest-income countries account for 53% of carbon dioxide emissions, the poorest fifth for 3%. Brazil, China, India, Indonesia and Mexico are among the developing countries with the highest emissions. But with huge populations, their per capita emissions are still tiny—3.9 metric tons a year in Mexico and 2.7 in China, compared with 20.5 metric tons in the United States and 10.2 in Germany. The human consequences of the global warming from carbon dioxide will be devastating for many poor countries—with a rise in sea levels, Bangladesh could see its land area shrink by 17%.
- Almost a billion people in 40 developing countries risk losing access to their primary source of protein, as overfishing driven by export demand for animal feed and oils puts pressure on fish stocks.
- The 132 million people in water-stressed areas are predominantly in Africa and parts of the Arab states—and if present trends continue, their numbers could rise to 1–2.5 billion by 2050.
- Deforestation is concentrated in developing countries. Over the last two decades, Latin America and the Caribbean lost 7 million hectares of tropical forest, Asia and Sub-Saharan Africa 4 million hectares each. Most of it has taken place to meet the demand for wood and paper, which has doubled and quintupled respectively since 1950. But over half the wood and nearly three-quarters of the paper is used in industrial countries.

Poor people and poor countries bear many costs of unequal consumption

The poor are most exposed to fumes and polluted rivers and least able to protect themselves. Of the estimated 2.7 million deaths each year from air pollution, 2.2 million are from indoor pollution, and 80% of the victims are rural poor in developing countries. Smoke from fuelwood and dung is more dangerous to health than tobacco smoke, but every day women have to spend hours cooking over smoky fires.

Leaded petrol, used more in developing and transition economies than in industrial countries, is crippling human health, permanently impairing the development of children's brains. In Bangkok up to 70,000 children are reported to be at risk of losing four or more IQ points because of high lead emissions. In Latin America around 15 million children under two years of age are at similar risk.

These environmental challenges stem not only from affluence but also from growing poverty. As a result of increasing impoverishment and the absence of other alternatives, a swelling number of poor and landless people are putting unprecedented pressures on the natural resource base as they struggle to survive.

Poverty and the environment are caught in a downward spiral. Past resource degradation deepens today's poverty, while today's poverty makes it very hard to care for or restore the agricultural resource base, to find alternatives to deforestation, to prevent desertification, to control erosion and to replenish soil nutrients. Poor people are forced to deplete resources to survive; this degradation of the environment further impoverishes them.

When this reinforcing downward spiral becomes extreme, poor people are forced to move in increasing numbers to ecologically fragile lands. Almost half the world's poorest people—more than 500 million—live on marginal lands.

The poverty–environmental damage nexus in developing countries must be seen in the context of population growth. In the developing world pressures on the environment intensify every day as the population grows. The global population is projected to be 9.5 billion in 2050, with more than 8 billion in developing countries. To feed this population adequately will require three times the basic calories consumed today, the equivalent of about 10 billion tons of grain a year. Population growth will also contribute to overgrazing, overcutting and overfarming.

How people interact with their environment is complex. It is by no means simply a matter of whether they are poor or rich. Ownership of natural resources, access to common properties, the strength of communities and local institutions, the issue of entitlements and rights, risk and uncertainty are important determinants of people's environmental behaviour. Gender inequalities, government policies and incentive systems are also crucial factors.

In recent times environmental awareness has been increasing in both rich and poor countries. The rich countries, with greater resources, have been spending more on environmental protection and clean-up. The developing countries, though they have fewer resources, have also been adopting cleaner technologies and reducing pollution, as in China.

The world community has also been active on environmental problems that directly affect poor people. Such areas include desertification, biodiversity loss and exports of hazardous waste. For example, the Convention on Biological Diversity has near-universal signature, with over 170 parties. The Convention to Combat Desertification has been ratified by more than 100 countries. But the deterioration of arid lands, a major threat to the livelihoods of poor people, continues unabated.

And there are other immediate environmental concerns for poor people, such as water contamination and indoor pollution, that have yet to receive serious international attention. Global forums discuss global warming. But the 2.2 million deaths yearly from indoor air pollution are scarcely mentioned.

Competitive spending and conspicuous consumption turn the affluence of some into the social exclusion of many

Rising pressures for conspicuous consumption can turn destructive, reinforcing exclusion, poverty and inequality.

Pressures of competitive spending and conspicuous consumption turn the affluence of some into the social exclusion of many. When there is heavy social pressure to maintain high consumption standards and society encourages competitive spending for conspicuous displays of wealth, inequalities in consumption deepen poverty and social exclusion.

Some disturbing trends:

- Studies of US households found that the income needed to fulfil consumption aspirations doubled between 1986 and 1994.
- The definition of what constitutes a "necessity" is changing, and the distinctions between luxuries and necessities are blurring. In the 1980s Brazil, Chile, Malaysia, Mexico and South Africa had two to three times as many cars as Austria, France and Germany did when they were at the same income level 30 years earlier.
- Household debt, especially consumer credit, is growing and household savings are falling in many industrial and developing countries. In the United States households save only 3.5% of their incomes, half as much as 15 years ago. In Brazil consumer debt, concentrated among lower-income households, now exceeds $6 billion.

Many voice concerns about the impact of these trends on society's values—and on human lives. Do they further deepen poverty as households compete to meet rising consumption standards—crowding out spending on food, education and health? Do these patterns motivate people to spend more hours working—leaving less time for family, friends and community?

Globalization is creating new inequalities and new challenges for protecting consumer rights

And is globalization accelerating these trends in competitive spending and rising standards?

Globalization is integrating consumer markets around the world and opening opportunities. But it is also creating new inequalities and new challenges for protecting consumer rights.

Globalization is integrating not just trade, investment and financial markets. It is also integrating consumer markets. This has two effects—economic and social. Economic integration has accelerated the opening of consumer markets with a constant flow of new products. There is fierce competition to sell to consumers worldwide, with increasingly aggressive advertising.

On the social side local and national boundaries are breaking down in the setting of social standards and aspirations in consumption. Market research identifies "global elites" and "global middle classes" who follow the same consumption styles, showing preferences for "global brands". There are the "global teens"—some 270 million 15- to 18-year-olds in 40 countries—inhabiting a "global space", a single pop-culture world, soaking up the same videos and music and providing a huge market for designer running shoes, t-shirts and jeans.

What are the consequences? First, a host of consumption options have been opened for many consumers—but many are left out in the cold through lack of income. And pressures for competitive spending mount. Keeping up with the Joneses has shifted from striving to match the consumption of a next-door neighbour to pursuing the life styles of the rich and famous depicted in movies and television shows.

Second, protecting consumer rights to product safety and product information has become complex. Increasingly, new products with higher chemical content, such as foods and medicines, are coming on the market. When information is not adequate, or safety standards are not strictly enforced, consumers can suffer—from pesticides that are poisonous, from milk powder that is contaminated.

At the same time the consumer receives a flood of information through commercial advertising. An average American, it is estimated, sees 150,000 advertisements on television in his or her lifetime. And advertising is increasing worldwide, faster than population or incomes. Global advertising spending, by the most conservative reckoning, is now $435 billion. Its growth has been particularly rapid in developing countries—in the Republic of Korea it increased nearly threefold in 1986–96, in the Philippines by 39% a year in 1987–92. In 1986 there were only three developing countries among the 20 biggest spenders in advertising. A decade later there were nine. And in spending relative to income, Colombia ranks first with $1.4 billion, 2.6% of its GDP.

Poor countries need to accelerate their consumption growth—but they need not follow the path taken by the rich and high-growth economies over the past half century.

Not only have consumption levels been too low to meet basic needs for more than a billion people, their growth has often been slow and interrupted by setbacks. In 70 countries with nearly a billion people consumption today is lower than it was 25 years ago. It cannot be raised without accelerating economic growth—but growth has been failing many poor people and poor countries. Despite the spectacular growth of incomes for many people in Asia, only 21 developing countries worldwide achieved growth in GDP per capita of at least 3% each year between 1995 and 1997—the rate needed to set a frame for reducing poverty.

Some suggest that developing countries should restrain their consumption in order to limit environmental damage. But this would mean prolonging the already scandalously deep and extensive deprivation for future generations.

Developing countries today can leapfrog to growth patterns that are pro-environment and pro-poor

Developing countries today face a strategic choice. They can repeat the industrialization and growth processes of the past half century, and go through a development phase that is inequitable, and creates an enormous legacy of environmental pollution. Or they can leapfrog to growth patterns that are:

- Pro-environment, preserving natural resources and creating less pollution and waste.
- Pro-poor, creating jobs for poor people and households and expanding their access to basic social services.

If poor countries can leapfrog in both consumption patterns and production technologies, they can accelerate consumption growth and human development without the huge costs of environmental damage. They can incorporate many of the available technologies that are not only less environmentally damaging but clean—solar energy, less energy-intensive crop production, cleaner paper production technologies.

Leapfrogging technologies will enhance the prospects for development by saving the huge costs of environmental clean-up that many countries are now incurring. The cost savings will go beyond the direct costs of cleaning up old toxic sites, scrubbing coal power plants and so on. Health care costs linked to environmental damage can also be saved. And leapfrogging will bypass the lock-in that can result from inappropriate infrastructure development.

Some argue that the scope for cheap, effective and politically less contentious antipollution policies is very limited in poor countries. This is a myth. Many actions have already been taken. And further options exist:

- Higher yields can be achieved through more intensive agricultural methods rather than more fertilizers and pesticides.
- Phasing out lead in petrol costs only 1–2 cents per litre for the refinery, as Mexico and Thailand have shown.
- Solar power and compact fluorescent lightbulbs can increase efficiency fourfold and reduce the need for rural electricity grids.
- Clean four-stroke engines can be made compulsory for motorcycles and three-wheelers, as Thailand has done.

These show what is possible. But to realize the potential, more needs to be done to develop and apply innovations.

Affluent societies in industrial countries also face strategic choices. They can continue the trends in consumption of the past decade. Or they can shift to consumption that is pro-people and pro-environment.

Continuing past trends would increase industrial countries' consumption by four- to fivefold over the next half century. Some argue that growth must be slowed and consumption downsized. But the real issue is not growth of consumption but its impacts on people, the environment and society. If societies adopt technologies that diminish the environmental impact of consumption, if patterns shift from consuming material goods to consuming services, growth can help, not hinder, moves to sustainability. The strategic choices of rich countries as the world's dominant consumers, will be critical in determining the future.

AGENDA FOR ACTION

Five goals are central:

- Raise the consumption levels of more than a billion poor people—more than a quarter of humanity—who have been left out of the global expansion of consumption and are unable to meet their basic needs.
- Move to more sustainable consumption patterns that reduce environmental damage, improve efficiency in resource use and regenerate renewable resources—such as water, wood, soils and fish.
- Protect and promote the rights of consumers to information, product safety and access to products that they need.
- Discourage patterns of consumption that have a negative impact on society and that reinforce inequalities and poverty.
- Achieve more equitable international burden-sharing in reducing and preventing global environmental damage and in reducing global poverty.

The key is to create an enabling environment for sustainable consumption—where both consumers and producers have the incentives and options to move towards consumption patterns that are less environmentally damaging and less socially harmful. People care about the impact of consumption on their own health and safety—and the broader impact on the environment and society. But they are caught up in a system of limited choices and opportunities and perverse incentives. Here's a seven-point agenda for action.

1. Ensure minimum consumption requirements for all—as an explicit policy objective in all countries.

"Everyone has the right to a standard of living adequate for the health and well-being of himself and his family, including food, clothing, housing and medical care and necessary social services.... Everyone has the right to education" (Universal Declaration of Human Rights). These principles of universalism and human rights acknowledge the equal rights of everyone—women, men and children—without discrimination. They demand governance that ensures that all have enough to eat, that no child goes without education, that no human being is denied access to health care, safe water and basic sanitation and that all people can develop their potential capabilities to the full extent.

Strong public action is needed to meet these goals. This means a mix of public provisioning in basic social services and an enabling environment and incentive system for private and voluntary action. It means:

- Strong public policies to promote food security—ranging from conducive monetary, fiscal, commercial and pricing policies to institutions and incentives to promote local production and distribution.
- Priority public expenditures for basic social services—education, health, safe water, basic sanitation. Not only should services be expanded, but access should be made more equitable. Studies in many countries show that

access favours the better-off rather than the poor, and urban rather than rural populations.

- Infrastructure for transport and energy to provide affordable and efficient services for people, not just economic growth. This means, for example, public transport, paths for bicycles and pedestrians and energy from renewable sources in rural areas.
- Incentives to develop "poor people's goods"—low-cost housing materials, energy-saving equipment and food storage systems.
- Institutions and legal frameworks that secure people's rights to housing, to common property, to credit.

John Kenneth Galbraith wrote 40 years ago about private affluence amid public squalor. Far from narrowing, the contrasts have grown, and to them are added private and environmental squalor.

2. Develop and apply technologies and methods that are environmentally sustainable for both poor and affluent consumers.

Human development can be sustained with purposeful action. The challenge is not to stop growth. It is to change the patterns of consumption and production, using new technologies to achieve greater efficiency and to reduce waste and pollution. Many such technologies are already in production or on the drawing board.

Sustainable growth of consumption and production depends on major advances in cleaner, material-saving, resource-saving and low-cost technologies. Also needed are consumption options that are environmentally friendly and low cost and affordable for the poor. But many do not yet exist—these need to be invented. And those that exist need to be better marketed—goods that use less energy and fewer renewables (water and wood), that create less waste and pollution and that are low in cost. Such options may be available in some countries—the zero-emission car, for example—but not worldwide, or they may be only at the experimental stage. Public expenditure on research and development in energy has declined by a third in real terms since the early 1980s. Moreover, less than 10% goes to energy efficiency improvements. The rest goes largely to fossil fuel and nuclear energy development. The case is strong for firms and governments to support more technological development and application.

Rather than attempting to pick and promote winning technologies, governments can help create a dynamic marketplace to perform that task more effectively. The state can require all energy providers—public and private—to supply a fixed minimum share of energy from renewable sources—either by generating it themselves or by purchasing it from other providers. This approach both ensures the introduction of renewable energy sources in the market and stimulates innovation of more efficient and lower-cost technologies.

The benefits of cleaner technologies have been well demonstrated, as with the reduction of material use in OECD countries. Many technological solutions already exist for environmentally friendly goods, but current pricing structures undervalue environmental costs and benefits—and thus reduce market incentives. Increased public support for further research and development could accelerate the pace of technological progress.

There is a particular need for technologies to meet the requirements of the poor. About 2 billion people in developing countries lack access to electricity. Meeting this need through clean, renewable sources of energy can reduce poverty and indoor air pollution. The sun and wind are available at no cost to villages that have little hope of being connected to electricity grids. Windpower, now the world's fastest-growing source of energy, meets only 1% of global demand. India aims by 2012 to provide 10% of its electricity from renewables, which could provide half the world's energy by the middle of the next century.

Perhaps most important among technologies for the poor are those for agricultural production in ecologically marginal environments. Improvements in food production in much of Asia and Latin America would not have been possible without the green revolution—the scientific breakthroughs that provided high-yielding varieties of rice, wheat and maize. The world average yield of these crops has more than doubled over the past 20 years. But this did not happen in areas of lower rainfall and in the more fragile ecological zones, where people subsist on millet and sorghum—and on cattle, sheep and goats. The world average yield of millet and sorghum increased by only 15% over the past two decades.

A second green revolution is needed for these people, among the world's poorest. But this should not just repeat the first revolution—it needs to aim both at increasing yields and incomes and at preserving and developing the environmental base.

The private sector has a critical role too—not just to meet the challenges of social responsibility but to produce environmentally friendly, poverty-reducing goods. The market for environmental goods alone is estimated at $500 billion. But for the private sector to act, it needs the right signals from prices and incentives in the market.

3. Remove perverse subsidies and restructure taxes to shift incentives from consumption that damages the environment to consumption that promotes human development.

Many developing countries use subsidies—on staple foods and basic energy supplies, for example—to help poor people survive and reduce poverty. Yet at the same time, most countries tax employment and subsidize pollution and environmental damage directly and indirectly. Such "perverse" subsidies are particularly common in the sectors of energy, water, road transport and agriculture. Total subsidies worldwide in these four sectors are estimated at $700–900 billion a year. They are also often distributionally regressive, benefiting mostly the wealthy—often political interest groups—while draining the public budget.

The absolute amount of subsidies is about twice as large in the OECD countries as in the rest of the world. In the OECD countries agriculture is most heavily subsidized (more than $330 billion), followed by road transport ($85–200 billion). In developing and transition economies the largest subsidies go to energy ($150–200 billion) and water ($42–47 billion). In the words of the Earth Council, "the world is spending hundreds of billions of dollars annually to subsidize its own destruction."

Environmental taxes—charging for pollution, congestion and depletion—have proved highly effective in both industrial and developing countries. They have been widely used in Western Europe and are the well-accepted core of green tax reforms—the Swedish air pollution tax and the Dutch water pollution tax, for example. But not just in Europe. Malaysia's effluent charges and Singapore's automobile taxes are well established and effective.

In Europe the social costs of environmental damage, unaccounted and unpaid, are estimated to average more than 4% of GDP. Estimates for the United States range from 2% to 12%. Users are encouraged to make excessive and wasteful use of road transport, with private cars most underpriced and most environmentally damaging.

Removing perverse subsidies that encourage environmental damage, lower economic efficiency and benefit the wealthy—and imposing environmental taxes instead—can be a catalyst for reducing inequalities and poverty and improving the prospects for equitable growth. Environmental taxes raise revenues that can be used to spend on environmental protection, to reduce taxes on labour, capital and savings or to improve access to social services for poor people.

The policy instruments described above present a win-win opportunity for changing consumption patterns to reverse environmental damage and increase the consumption of the poor. Removing water subsidies, for example, would reduce water use by 20–30%—and in parts of Asia by as much as 50%. That would make it possible, without large, environmentally destructive water development projects, to supply safe drinking water to most of the 1.3 billion people now lacking it.

Another example: congestion charges can finance improvements in public transport and expand transport options. They can ease congestion, save time, lower the costs of public transport and, usually, improve the distribution of income. Road transport subsidies in developing countries amount to $15 billion. The increased involvement of the private sector in financing, building and operating public transport systems in the 1990s is creating pressure to reduce road subsidies and increase user fees. Argentina cut subsidies to suburban rail systems by $25 million between 1993 and 1995 when it privatized the operation of urban transport.

The benefits of a shift from taxing employment to taxing pollution and other environmental damage could be considerable. An OECD study on Norway suggests that a revenue-neutral shift would reduce unemployment while encouraging recycling and reducing environmental damage.

More and more countries are realizing that old policies and subsidies have adverse consequences. Thus energy subsidies in developing countries have fallen from more than $300 billion in the early 1990s to about $150–200 billion today. Environmental taxes are multiplying. But perverse subsidies are still huge, and environmental taxes have reached nowhere near their potential. Even in the Nordic countries, where some of the most interesting experiments are being carried out, pollution taxes and congestion charges raise only about 7% of government revenues.

4. Strengthen public action for consumer education and information and environmental protection.

The expansion of consumer choice has little significance if choices are based on wrong or misleading information. Strong public action to protect consumer rights is needed to offset vastly unbalanced information flows dominated by commercial advertisements.

Consumer rights must be defended through:

- Strict standards for consumer health and safety.
- Product labelling about the content and proper use of products and their environmental and social impact.
- Information and awareness campaigns about potential health hazards, such as smoking tobacco and the improper use of feeding formula for infants.

Advertising can serve positive purposes, but controls are needed, especially on television advertising targeting young children. Sweden bans television advertising directed at children under 12.

Where price incentives are inadequate, environmental laws and regulations are needed. Skilfully devised, controls can be enabling for the consumer, not restricting. But implementation is as important as legislation. Strong institutions, free from corruption, are needed to enforce regulations in such areas as rights to land, security of tenure in housing and accurate information on consumer goods to protect the interests of poor people.

Regulation and market interventions can be mutually reinforcing. Sometimes regulation is needed to initiate action that can later be taken further with price incentives. At other times price incentives can be used to make a start—with regulation later to ensure wider compliance, especially after fostering social acceptance.

A new approach that has gained considerable interest and momentum in recent years is self-regulation through publicizing information on industrial polluters. This encourages the production of information about pollution generation, both as a source of incentive for behavioural change and as a benchmark for subsequent regulation. A well-known example is the US Toxic Release Inventory, which requires businesses to report the amounts of toxic materials that they put into the environment. Many companies respond by reducing pollution to preserve their reputations.

5. Strengthen international mechanisms to manage consumption's global impacts.

Environmental damage crosses borders. So do shifts in consumption patterns and habits. Poverty and inequality are issues of global magnitude and thus cannot be tackled by nations singly. They require international action.

International responsibilities for ensuring the sustainability of natural resource use have been debated in numerous forums. The Kuala Lumpur Meeting of the Parties to the Basel Convention on the Ban on Hazardous Waste agreed to ban the export of such waste to poor countries. Both the Convention on Biological Diversity and the Convention on International Trade in Endangered Species of Wild Flora and Fauna have been quite successful.

Although some of these agreements sometimes fall short of expectations and ideals, they are steps in the right direction. The recent Kyoto Meeting on the United Nations Framework Convention on Climate Change has set industrial country targets for emissions of carbon dioxide and proposed a Clean Development Mechanism to assist developing countries. Both the financing and the institutional arrangement for this mechanism must be dealt with by the global community. Another problem that needs to be addressed: the continuing decline of official development assistance and the mounting unsustainable debt of poor countries.

Many global instruments to tackle environmental and poverty issues are under-developed—such as environmental trading permits, debt swaps and fair trade schemes. These instruments tend to be double-edged swords, however, and need to be carefully negotiated so that they do not penalize poor nations and make them even poorer. Trading environmental permits should not mean permanently giving away the rights of developing countries. A coordinating global institution in the form of the proposed international bank for environmental settlements is needed to develop and manage these instruments equitably.

6. Build stronger alliances among the movements for consumer rights, environmental protection, poverty eradication, gender equality and children's rights.

Consumer groups have been a powerful force for protecting consumer rights worldwide. They have helped remove unsafe products from the market and promote proper labelling and the supply of safe and low-cost goods.

Now consumers increasingly are using the power of their purses to push the interests of communities even halfway around the globe. Studies in Europe show that consumers are willing to pay price premiums of 5–10% for products that are more environmentally sound (in production, operation and disposal).

Businesses are responding to consumer demand for cleaner, safer products. Evidence from Eastern Europe shows that firms exporting to the European Union tend to have cleaner production processes than firms that produce for the domestic markets, which are less environmentally demanding.

Conventional wisdom assumes that environmental damage is a necessary consequence of economic growth. This is wrong. Environmental damage is a drain on economic growth, and it is possible to pursue a path to growth that does not damage the environment.

Poverty eradication, environmental sustainability, consumer rights protection—all these build on one another. Eradicating poverty does not require growth that ignores consumer rights or destroys the environment. Quite the opposite. Protecting consumer rights and protecting the environment are necessary for eradicating poverty and reducing inequalities.

There is great potential for building closer alliances among the environmental movement, the women's movement, the movement for children, consumer groups and pressure groups against poverty. Already their central concerns show great convergence. Stronger alliances are needed—and possible—if each movement emphasizes the common need for human development. United and mobilized together, these groups can achieve much more.

7. Think globally, act locally. Build on the burgeoning initiatives of people in communities everywhere and foster synergies in the actions of civil society, the private sector and government.

The growing number and strength of consumer and environmental movements around the world—including the 2,000 town and city Agenda 21s that have been prepared—reflect the commitment of people to taking collective action. Many opinion surveys show that people place a higher value on community and family life than on acquiring material possessions. And many people are asking how they can give more emphasis to human concerns.

Some 100 countries have prepared national human development reports, assessing their present situations and drawing conclusions on actions to achieve more human patterns of development. Most of these plans have analysed needs in the critical areas of education, health and employment, often linking them with opportunities for generating resources from reduced military spending.

These initiatives in many cases are the outcomes of successful alliances of the government, institutions of civil society and international organizations.

Progress has also been made in the area of sustainable consumption and a cleaner environment as a result of civil pressure, public action and private sector responses. The instruments: eco-taxes and subsidy removal, stiff environmental regulations backed by penalties, community efforts for better management of common resources (erosion control, reforestation) and more equitable provisioning of public infrastructure and services.

This shows what is possible. It also shows that support exists for a cleaner environment, a more equitable society and the eradication of poverty. Individuals, households, civil society groups, governments and private businesses—all have a role, and together their complementary efforts can build even more energy and synergy for action.

In the poorer countries many priorities in consumption still need to be addressed. Increases in consumption should be planned and encouraged—but with attention to nurturing the links, to making sure that the increases contribute to human development and to avoiding extremes of inequality. Forward-looking perspectives are also needed—to avoid infrastructure and institutions that may lock a country into unsustainable or socially dysfunctional consumption.

In the better-off countries—most of the industrial countries and some of the richer developing countries—the challenge is different. The priority to eradicate poverty and ensure the basic needs of all remains. Indeed, the failure of the richest countries to do that is a scandal. But as general living standards rise and the proportion in poverty falls, the balance of attention in economic and social policy needs to shift. Increasingly, the policy focus needs to move towards enlarging the options for patterns of consumption in which human creativity can be lived out and carried forward with diversity and fulfilment, with most of the population at comfortable levels of consumption, well above the margins of subsistence. These policies need to be combined with those of the environment and human development.

Recent experiences give considerable hope, with more evidence showing that changes in consumption patterns towards sustainable poverty reduction are possible.

Hope brings challenge. The high levels of consumption and production in the world today, the power and potential of technology and information, present great opportunities. After a century of vast material expansion, will leaders and people have the vision to seek and achieve more equitable and more human advance in the 21st century?

Test Your Knowledge Form

We encourage you to photocopy and use this page as a tool to assess how the articles in *Annual Editions* expand on the information in your textbook. By reflecting on the articles you will gain enhanced text information. You can also access this useful form on a product's book support Web site at *http://www.dushkin.com/online/*.

NAME: DATE:

TITLE AND NUMBER OF ARTICLE:

BRIEFLY STATE THE MAIN IDEA OF THIS ARTICLE:

LIST THREE IMPORTANT FACTS THAT THE AUTHOR USES TO SUPPORT THE MAIN IDEA:

WHAT INFORMATION OR IDEAS DISCUSSED IN THIS ARTICLE ARE ALSO DISCUSSED IN YOUR TEXTBOOK OR OTHER READINGS THAT YOU HAVE DONE? LIST THE TEXTBOOK CHAPTERS AND PAGE NUMBERS:

LIST ANY EXAMPLES OF BIAS OR FAULTY REASONING THAT YOU FOUND IN THE ARTICLE:

LIST ANY NEW TERMS/CONCEPTS THAT WERE DISCUSSED IN THE ARTICLE, AND WRITE A SHORT DEFINITION:

We Want Your Advice

ANNUAL EDITIONS revisions depend on two major opinion sources: one is our Advisory Board, listed in the front of this volume, which works with us in scanning the thousands of articles published in the public press each year; the other is you—the person actually using the book. Please help us and the users of the next edition by completing the prepaid article rating form on this page and returning it to us. Thank you for your help!

ANNUAL EDITIONS: Economics 05/06

ARTICLE RATING FORM

Here is an opportunity for you to have direct input into the next revision of this volume. We would like you to rate each of the articles listed below, using the following scale:

1. **Excellent: should definitely be retained**
2. **Above average: should probably be retained**
3. **Below average: should probably be deleted**
4. **Poor: should definitely be deleted**

Your ratings will play a vital part in the next revision. Please mail this prepaid form to us as soon as possible. Thanks for your help!

RATING	ARTICLE
________	1. How Much for a Life? Try $3 Million to $5 Million
________	2. Things That Every Economist Takes for Granted Could Help a Lot of Other People Avoid Some Costly Mistakes
________	3. U.S. Is Far More Efficient Than in '70s—But Also More Determined to Consume
________	4. Counter-Terrorism: The Private Cost of More Security
________	5. Smoke Signals
________	6. The Core of the Problem: Three Hard Years Push West Michigan Apple Growers Out of the Business
________	7. Sour Times for Cranberry Growers
________	8. Is Wal-Mart Too Powerful?
________	9. Deregulation Harms Public, Group Claims
________	10. The Slippery Scope of Antitrust Law
________	11. The Real Price of Gas
________	12. Patent Medicine
________	13. The Eco-Economic Revolution: Getting the Market in Sync With Nature
________	14. Congested Parks—A Pricing Dilemma
________	15. Looking Ahead To Our Place In The Next Economy
________	16. The Earning Power of Women Has Really Increased, Right? Take a Closer Look
________	17. After 40 Years, What are Some Results and Lessons of America's War on Poverty?
________	18. Election-Year Shuffle on the Minimum Wage
________	19. Debating the Minimum Wage
________	20. Some New Studies Look at What to Do About the Troubled American Health Care System
________	21. Social Security: Note to Congress—Compromise
________	22. Beyond a President's Control
________	23. Greed Is Not Good
________	24. The Deficit: America's Credibility Gap
________	25. Bush: Grow Slowly and Carry a Big Debt
________	26. The Deficit That Didn't Just Happen: A Sober Perspective on the Budget
________	27. Notes From Underground: Money That People Earn and Spend Outside the Realm of Official Economic Calculations Is Nonetheless Real

RATING	ARTICLE
________	28. Why Are Taxes So Complicated, and What Can We Do About It?
________	29. Tax Reform R.I.P.
________	30. Link Between Taxation, Unemployment Is Absent
________	31. Go Figure
________	32. What Should Central Banks Do?
________	33. The Science (and Art) of Monetary Policy
________	34. How Does Monetary Policy Affect the U.S. Economy?
________	35. The Maestro Slips Out of Tune
________	36. The Cycles of Financial Scandal
________	37. Bank Mergers Don't All Win Raves
________	38. Managing a Globalizing World: An Overview
________	39. Foreign Economic Policy for the Next President
________	40. No Stepping Back: America's International Economic Agenda for 2003-05
________	41. Asymmetric Globalization: Global Markets Require Good Global Politics
________	42. Variety, the Spice of Life, Has Measurable Value. But It's not Easy to Determine
________	43. As Job Exports Rise, Some Economists Rethink the Mathematics of Free Trade
________	44. Master of Disaster
________	45. Workers' Rights: Labor Standards and Global Trade
________	46. The Fall and Rise of the Global Economy
________	47. America's Record Trade Deficit: A Reflection of Economic Strength
________	48. Free Trade Area of the Americas: NAFTA Marches South
________	49. Eliminating Child Labor
________	50. Trade in the Americas: All in the Familia
________	51. Ready for a Rebound?
________	52. A Stronger Euro for Europe?
________	53. Competition and Business Entry in Russia
________	54. China Joins the WTO: How, Why; and What Now?
________	55. China's Economic Power: Enter the Dragon
________	56. Changing Today's Consumption Patterns—for Tomorrow's Human Development

(Continued on next page)

NO POSTAGE NECESSARY IF MAILED IN THE UNITED STATES

BUSINESS REPLY MAIL
FIRST CLASS MAIL PERMIT NO. 551 DUBUQUE IA

POSTAGE WILL BE PAID BY ADDRESEE

McGraw-Hill/Dushkin
2460 KERPER BLVD
DUBUQUE, IA 52001-9902

ABOUT YOU

Name Date

Are you a teacher? ❒ A student? ❒
Your school's name

Department

Address City State Zip

School telephone #

YOUR COMMENTS ARE IMPORTANT TO US!

Please fill in the following information:
For which course did you use this book?

Did you use a text with this ANNUAL EDITION? ❒ yes ❒ no
What was the title of the text?

What are your general reactions to the *Annual Editions* concept?

Have you read any pertinent articles recently that you think should be included in the next edition? Explain.

Are there any articles that you feel should be replaced in the next edition? Why?

Are there any World Wide Web sites that you feel should be included in the next edition? Please annotate.

May we contact you for editorial input? ❒ yes ❒ no
May we quote your comments? ❒ yes ❒ no